THE OFFICIAL PRICE GUIDE TO

QUILTS

Second Edition

Liz Aleshire and Kathleen Barach

House of Collectibles
New York

Published by House of Collectibles, 1745 Broadway, New York, New York 10019. Distributed by the Random House Information Group, a division of Random House Inc., New York, and simultaneously in Canada by Random House of Canada Limited, Toronto.

 House of Collectibles is a registered trademark and the colophon is a trademark of Random House, Inc.

www.houseofcollectibles.com

Printed in the United States of America

Cover Quilts from the Collections of the Authors, Marty Child and Dottie Whitner.

Unless otherwise specified, all photographs are courtesy of the authors.

ISBN 1-4000-4797-8

10 9 8 7 6 5 4 3 2 1

First Edition

*To my Mother who, along with my Father, raised me to believe I
can do anything.*
To my Family, including Liz, who still believe I can do anything.
*And to Donald, my heart, my soul, my rock, who helps me do every-
thing most importantly conquering cancer.*

Kathleen Barach

To my Family:
To Nancy, Mark and Colleen
*To Mother Baigert who 'adopted' me; and to her and Father
Baigert who raised nice children who married nice spouses and who
also raised nice children; all of whom took me in when I needed
another home:*
Kathy and Donald
Kevin, Laura and Marie
Lynn, Buz, Brian, Jeffrey and Katie

*But mostly to Kathy who puts up with all my crazy ideas and who,
even though battling cancer, did this book with me and for me.*

*Finally, to Bennett Cerf for founding Random House just so I could
be one of its authors!*

Liz Aleshire

ACKNOWLEDGEMENTS

Many people helped with the information provided in this book, we are especially grateful for the time and effort of these special people, who are some of the most knowledgeable, gracious and helpful people in quiltdom:

Frank Geeslin of American Quilts, Gloria Hall of Grandma's Quilts, Marie Miller of Marie Miller Antique Quilts, Sharon Stark of Sharon's Antiques/Vintage Fabrics, and Stella Rubin of Stella Rubin Antique Quilts.

Marty Child of Calico, Etc. in Cheshire, CT, who, like many of her contemporary quilt fabric shop owners, sponsors antique quilt programs, as well as supports the creation of the next generation of spectacular quilts.

Dottie Whitner, who came through in a pinch by providing wonderful assistance and some great quilts.

Special thanks to Dorothy Harris, our kind and supportive editor, who remembered us; to Roger Generazzo who was tolerant, helpful and who found us, and Lindsey Glass.

Also, to everyone else at Random House who added their expertise to the production of this book.

Thanks to you all!

CONTENTS

THE QUILT LISTINGS

Pieced Quilts

Appliqué Quilts

Other Quilts

INTRODUCTION

There are as many reasons to collect quilts as there are quilts in existence. Like fine art, each quilt is unique. Quilts may vary in workmanship, color balance, degree of difficulty and design execution, but each quilt is an art unto its own. For the vast majority of quilts, the maker, or makers, are unknown. Instead of a deterrent, this lack of knowledge can lead the collector on a fascinating trail of discovery to find a quilt's origins. Or, more likely, the mystery of the quilt will stimulate the imagination. The truth about the origins of a quilt could be less fascinating than the stories we conjure ourselves, while touching, using, or displaying it.

Again, like fine art, each quilt that survives today was once someone's treasure. The fact that they did survive for 50, 100 or 200 years is proof that they were carefully stored, preserved and cared for, that someone valued them beyond their functional value. That quilts were made for function is a fact. That functional quilts did not survive their use is a fact. Also a fact is that the quilts that survived the centuries were made for their visual charm and not their functional value. The great care taken in design, fabric choice, execution, and preservation proves that quilts were created as more than just bed covers. They were created as art.

These art treasures of the past are also today's treasures. Because the majority of antique quilts are unsigned and undated, today's collector needs to be knowledgeable about dating characteristics. *The Official Price Guide to Quilts* gives novice and advanced collectors a handy, user-friendly guide for dating quilts. This book covers the history of quilting, including technological advances in making and designing fabric, the improvement of color-fast dyes, and the invention of the sewing machine. It also includes trends in quilt block patterns and when a pattern came into popular use.

And quilts present our history. They've been made to commemorate national anniversaries, political campaigns, presidential assassinations; as help and comfort to the soldiers of the Civil War; to promote awareness for the Women's Suffrage Movement and AIDS research; to raise money for churches, schools and institutions; even to guide slaves searching for freedom along the Underground Railroad.

The Official Price Guide to Quilts gives you the tools you need to recognize an authentic antique quilt and avoid buying a fake. We researched over 40 books, at least that many articles, and surfed the web extensively as well as interviewed collectors, dealers and quiltmakers from all over the country to write this book. While no single book can give you all the information you need to find your way in the world of quilt collecting and history, this one is guaranteed to get you started. Browse through the price listings, read the chapters and use the bibliography and source listings in the back to start your own quilt collecting journey.

Prepare to be awed, fascinated and informed! Most of all: Enjoy!

1 Why Collect Quilts?

You'll probably buy your first quilt for decorative or emotional reasons. There, hanging in an antiques store, at a flea market, or in a quilt shop, is *the* quilt in just the right colors to match your bedroom, living room, or den. Using quilts for decoration is as old as quilting itself and as new as the most recent issue of *Better Homes and Gardens* or *Architectural Digest*. Quilts, with their bold or soft colors, geometric or curved patchwork, complement any decor from Colonial to Victorian to modern, from farmhouse to mansion to corporate office.

Even if it isn't the right color scheme, something about a quilt may speak to your heart. Whether it's the pattern or pattern name, the exquisite workmanship, the history of the quilt, or the story of the woman who made it, something makes it impossible for you not to buy it. The first quilts in most collections were purchased simply because the buyer fell in love with them, which, according to some collectors, is still the only reason to buy a quilt.

Falling in love may explain the first quilt purchased, but what compels collectors to keep buying? Quilt collecting, like most collecting, can be termed a disease. The first acquisition leads to many others, and the search for the best and the brightest demands delving into history, technology, technique, and art so that the collector gains an extensive knowledge of quilt lore that is as valuable as the quilts themselves. The first quilt might match your living room, but the second, third, fourth, hundredth is bought for other reasons. Two collectors told us they bought quilts because they love everything about textiles: the history of cloth, clothing, and decorative textiles; the history of dyes and dyeing; how textiles were, and are, used. Another collector narrowed down her selections by buying only quilts, tops, or blocks signed or dated by the maker.

Quilts tell us stories of our country, our families, and the women who made them. Quilts, as we know them today, are uniquely American. Quilting is far older than our country; the women who crossed the Atlantic brought quilting skills and techniques with them. But it was the American quiltmaker who improved quilt design, creating intricate and deceptively simple designs of geometric piecing or appliqué. It was here that quilts were raised to art. In cre-

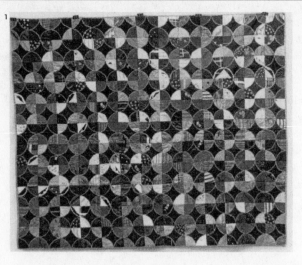

1 This Snowball Quilt is done in the Victorian style, with silk and satins, and yellow feather topstitching. Done around the turn of the century it has, as one would expect, quite a bit of fabric deterioration. Quilt courtesy of the Wilson Family.

ating and elevating quilts, American quiltmakers documented much of our history. There were quilts made to commemorate the centennial of our nation's birth, to re-create in fabric the Lincoln-Douglas debates, and to honor First Ladies. There is even one created for the Nixon resignation. The New England Quilt Museum curated a show consisting solely of quilts focusing on presidents, presidential candidates and campaign issues with one quilt dating from the late 1700s. There is a quilt block pattern designed to represent the Women's Christian Temperance Union and a quilt using the initials and symbol of the National Recovery Act. The California Heritage Quilt Project found a quilt that had been pieced in a wagon train bound for California.

Historic quilts are not confined to the telling of our nation's past. There are many quilts, unsigned, undated, that commemorate family events. Weddings, births, and even deaths were occasions to make quilts created from the fabrics used in the bridal gowns, christening outfits and baby clothes, and the clothes of the deceased.

Quilts were always prized possessions. At least those known as best quilts. Few, if any, functional quilts survive today because their very functionality wore them out. The quilts that survive are those that were special then as well as now. Friendship quilts, given to families moving westward, were highly prized by the recipients. They knew they'd never see their friends and family in the old hometown again. To reminisce, to return home if only for a few moments through memory, the recipient had only to unpack the lovingly made souvenir, read the blocks, and caress the cloth—she was home again. To the pioneer, making quilts was a special challenge. Given the lack of materials, time, light, and energy, these quilts must have been of great importance to the people who made them. During the Civil War, quilts were looted from homes. The soldier with a quilt had a blanket, a cushion, a raincoat, and a knapsack for other, more breakable loot. Soldiers knew to slit the fabrics and search for money sometimes stuffed inside a quilt, supposedly safe from marauders. Families of the westward migration also stuffed their money safely inside a quilt. *See illustration #1.*

"Quilts are, in sum, incomparable documentary artifacts that reflect the time during which they were made as well as revealing much about the makers themselves," wrote Jean Ray Laury in *Ho for California!* Quilts as historical documents, revealing both our history and the inner sense of beauty of the makers, may be the oldest form of American memorabilia. Older even than Paul Revere's silver and pewter, older than the Hitchcock chair.

Unraveling the history of a quilt is another reason to collect. At a quilt show held at Center Congregational Church in Meriden, Connecticut, several old, hexagonal blocks pieced of triangles were brought to the show for identification. Even some of the individual triangles in the blocks, from fabric of warm brown prints indicative of the late 1800s, were carefully pieced; the prints matched so well that the seams were almost invisible. The owner didn't know the pattern. Neither did anyone else. But as we continued the research for this book, we discovered that those elongated hexagons were the basic block pattern for an Ocean Waves quilt. It was a thrill to solve that puzzle!

Historical documentation isn't the only reason to collect quilts. Sheer admiration for the textiles, workmanship, pattern and color balance are also strong draws toward quilts. We can only marvel at the time, care, and sacrifice that went into each and every antique quilt on the market today. What better way to collect samples of the history of textile design and quality than to do it with quilts? Some workmanship is excellent, whether done by women with no formal training in design, drafting, or geometry who nevertheless produced geometrically precise piecing for such complicated designs as stars or compass rose quilts, or done by women who used pre-designed, even precut quilt kits to make their creations. Patterns and assembly styles have a history of their own, from the simple one-patch designs such as the hexagon to the ornately decorated stitching of a Crazy Quilt to the complex appliqué of a Baltimore Album quilt. The use of available color over the four centuries quilts have been made is astounding. With no art training and using an eye developed only by instinct, emotional response, and sometimes little choice as to color because of the unavailability of manufactured dyes or materials for homemade dyes, quiltmakers startle, amuse, awe and amaze us with their color sense. *See illustration #2.*

"Handicrafts represent a particularly rewarding area of investigation, for the needle became the most common means of creating the ornamentation that reconciled utility and art," noted Jean Ray Laury in *Ho for California!* "No craft achieved this union more successfully than the uniquely indigenous American art form, the quilt."

Some quilts were made by men, but most were made by women, which is another reason to collect quilts. Quilts are one of the few, if not the only, antique collectibles made predominantly by women. The "soul" of every quilt is the woman who made it, whether she signed it, dated it, or left its origin a mystery by doing neither. In fact, most women didn't sign or date their quilts, leaving us to marvel at what we can see: her innate design sense, use of color, selection and assembly of pattern, and workmanship. These ancestors put into their quilts what they were too shy or reserved to speak aloud: memories, aspirations, ambitions, love. Included in every quilt, if we look for it, are clues to the maker's past. Those clues can be as obvious as the lambs, pansies, shooting stars, or feather and blanket stitching of a silk or velvet crazy quilt. Those are clues that tell us what was important in the quiltmaker's life and that she had more leisure, and probably more money, than other women. A two-color quilt can be a clue to

2

2 These blocks were a mystery until research showed they were the basic block of the Ocean Waves pattern. Made in the 1880s, they are true scrap bag blocks incorporating numerous colors and printed fabrics. Quilt courtesy of the Zimmer Family.

a more prosperous family or it can mean that only those two fabrics were available to a pioneer woman. Also likely is that only one basic fabric was available to her and she dyed a portion of it to make an exceptional example of the two-color quilt.

Workmanship, both good and bad, provides clues to a quiltmaker. Was she trying out a fad and therefore inexperienced with the technique? Is the inferior workmanship because it was her first quilt? We can only imagine the hours that went into an elaborately pieced or appliquéd quilt with its thousands of tiny, closely placed stitches. Was that superior workmanship accomplished because she had more time to devote to it than other quiltmakers? Or was it simply perseverance and the pursuit of perfection? To our modern eyes a quilt is either well done or inferior, pretty or ugly. But to the now anonymous makers, each quilt represented their best attempt to create something beautiful out of something useful. Their sense of pride is evident in the few photos that survive of pioneer women sitting proudly in their small rooms or on the porch of a rough-hewn cabin accompanied by their quilts either finished or in progress. That the pioneer woman chose a quilt to be the single prized possession to be photographed with her tells us a great deal about her.

There's a warming of the soul that occurs when we view the work of a woman and know that the quilt, whatever its quality by today's standards, was designed and made for a special purpose in her life, even if that purpose was known only to her and is now buried with her. Though she may be gone, her quilt remains. There, in our hands, on our bed, on our wall, is a connection to that unknown woman that affirms and confirms our existence perhaps more than all the biographies, awards, and commendations associated with the history of women. And, how much more proud are we of these works of art if we are fortunate enough to have had them handed down to us from the creator, a family ancestor! Quilts are not only documents of history, they were first documents of love: love of country, love of family, and even love of self. No stronger link with feminine past can be made than to own the anonymous outpouring of love a quilt represents. Thus with a quilt, we warm ourselves twice. Once with the physical radiance, touch, and feel of the quilt around us, and then again when we are caught in the romance of the maker's mysteries.

Quilts, unlike other art, are tactile. They invite and allow us to touch them. In fact, they demand it. We can wrap ourselves up in them, sleep under them, hang them on a wall, and touch to our heart's content. Who would carefully caress a Rembrandt between their fingers or snuggle with a marble statue? Quilts were made by women to be touched, caressed, viewed, each a tactile work of art both beautiful and functional.

We collect quilts because they are art. The event that did the most to define quilts as art occurred in 1971. The event was the exhibit *Abstract Design in American Quilts*, presented by the Whitney Museum of American Art in New York. One of the criteria for the show was that the quilts be viewed solely as works of visual art and not in the context of their historical significance or the fame of their makers. The show successfully shifted the thinking of the general public as well as art critics in viewing quilts, both antique and contemporary, as works of art. Suddenly the color and design choices and uniqueness of pattern were recognized as art. The show was organized by Jonathan Holstein and Gail van der Hoof and the quilts chosen from their collections. But the controversy over defining quilts as art was hardly over. Next there came a separation of art quiltmakers from antique and contemporary quiltmakers.

In *The Pieced Quilt: An American Design Tradition,* Jonathan Holstein, author and organizer of the Whitney Museum exhibit, wrote: "The women who made pieced quilts were not 'artists,' that is, they did not intend to make art . . ." Jean Ray Laury, now considered the Mother of the Art Quilt, was quoted in the *Crossing Boundaries* exhibit catalog (presented by the Art Quilt Network) as saying: "The traditional quiltmaker intended her quilts to function as a decorative bedcover, . . ." *See illustration #3.*

We take exception to the belief that all quilts before 1960 were made solely as functional, decorative items for the home. We don't believe, and history does not support, the myth that quilts were made for function only as if all our ancestral quiltmakers had no idea they were creating an art object. There have always been cheaper, easier, less labor-intensive ways to make blankets. If warmth were the only reason women made quilts, there wouldn't be any quilts today. After all, what bright, intelligent woman, whether she resided in Baltimore or on the deserted Plains, would spend the time making those beautiful quilts just to have a blanket on a bed? Yes, frugality may have dictated the use of scraps to construct a quilt, and many a scrap of leftover fabric and used clothing was incorporated into quilts. But many, even in the most remote, desolate, and deserted sections of the country were made from new material. We maintain that any antique quilt that survives to this day is art because it was knowingly made to commemorate, to add beauty, and to last. Why else would the generations after the quiltmaker have saved them so carefully? The quilts that survive today are art because that was the intent when they were made. Otherwise, they would have been worn out, or used for a saddle blanket, as a door for a chicken coop, in a dog's bed, for privacy across the outhouse door, or to replace a shutter in a barn like the myriad of functional quilts made over the centuries. The quilts that survive today are art because they were made intentionally to be handed down from generation to generation, family to family. They were made with painstaking care to be

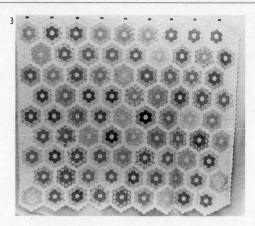

3   A Grandmother's Flower Garden
without the traditional green
diamond 'path', this quilt from
the 1930s uses uniform yellow
centers and a variety of scrap bag
fabrics. Quilt courtesy of the
Warner Family.

treasured. Whatever we think of their design and color choices today, quiltmakers made best quilts their art. The antique quilts we collect today were consciously made to be beautiful, not just functional.

The final reason we collect quilts is the same as the first. Putting all historical, intellectual, and artistic implications aside, ultimately you will collect your quilts because of their unique emotional impact, because something in them touches your eye, heart, and mind.

Whatever your reason for collecting quilts, you'll need to go armed with the knowledge of how to date, authenticate, and determine quality of workmanship. The next chapters begin your journey.

2 How to Start a Collection

Quilts are so closely connected to family life and lore that your relatives are your best contacts to start a quilt collection. There is probably at least one quilt already in your family even if it's the one owned by your aged second cousin twice removed and was made two or three generations ago. Even if no one has quilted since, or if your childhood memories include images of Grandmother, Great-Aunt, even Grandfather stitching one square to another or appliquéing scraps on a ground fabric to form a flower or animal, you know there's a quilt somewhere in the family. Tell everyone in the family that you're interested in owning that quilt.

The obstacle in this approach is that other members of your family may also want Great-great Aunt Agatha's quilts. Work out an equitable division if you can—one that doesn't include ripping the quilt down the middle! One nightmare story we heard involved two sisters who couldn't agree on who should own their grandmother's sampler quilt made in the early 1800s. In desperation, and one assumes sheer frustration, one sister finally cut the quilt, kept half and sent the other half to her sister. Quilt collectors all over the world still shudder over that loss. Relinquish your claim to the family quilt before you allow it to be cut into pieces.

All too often, as the scores of quilts in the hands of dealers testify, no one in the family really wants that antique quilt. Quilt collecting lore abounds with stories about quilts found in old trunks in attics, barns, and garages, the owners unaware of their value, history, or even their existence. As tastes changed, walls were repainted or repapered or, as opinions of grandmother's workmanship and design choices changed, quilts were relegated to storage chests. No one wanted them, but no one was willing to throw them out either. This cavalier treatment of family history has created the supply of quilts available to us today. Don't let that happen in your family. Ask if anyone has a quilt they don't want. Ask your relatives to search through those unopened-for-decades trunks, boxes, and barrels. Great-great Aunt Agatha's orange quilt may not be to your tastes or fit the décor of your living room, but it's a part of your family history and shouldn't be lost. With the relatively cheap investment of a quilt rack, that quilt can once again see the light of day and be admired for its history, if not its color scheme.

The California Quilt Heritage Project documented 3,300 antique quilts in California alone all in the hands of descendants of the makers or private collectors. In 2002 the Connecticut Quilt Search Project published the results of its search in *Quilts and Quiltmakers Covering Connecticut*. The book tells the tale of the project and how it documented a total of 3,058 items. More than half of our states have completed their own quilt projects and the numbers of quilts retained as family heirlooms is astounding.

But as the number of generations increases between the original maker and the current owner, these quilts become candidates for sale. The history of the quilt may be lost or the details distorted as it was handed down so that the owner is no longer sure of the accuracy of its provenance. Or, the current generation may have no interest in keeping a quilt its members don't view as particularly pretty or well-done. A family line may simply die out because there are no heirs, and the quilt then goes to the highest bidder at an estate auction. By telling everyone in your family that you're interested, you can reap the benefits of their disinterest and become the proud owner of an antique quilt with real meaning—a blood tie. Despite its orange and purple color combination, despite its mismatched points or long quilting stitches, the family quilt will be the most prized of your collection.

Don't confine yourself to completed family quilts. Works in progress for you to finish or to commission a professional quilter to finish are also gratifying because of the familial tie. If your relatives are relieved to empty that trunk of its old quilts, imagine how happy they'll be to get rid of that box filled with miscellaneous odds and ends of fabric they also couldn't bring themselves to throw away. Unfinished tops and squares, made by an ancestor, are a glorious find because you become part of a multi generational quilt project. Liz Aleshire, one of the authors of this book, has already completed and quilted three tops found in two different attics and two more purchased while researching this book. One, a basket quilt, was probably started by her grandmother-in-law. The sashings were added by her mother-in-law and Liz completed the borders and quilting. The other two were both tumbler quilt tops owned by cousins-in-law, made by their grandmother, and found during renovations of the ancestral farmhouse. All three are now prized possessions of the makers' daughters and granddaughters.

Don't pass up that box of old clothes or fabrics either! You may need it to authentically complete the top you found in a trunk or purchased from a dealer. Aleshire's scrap bag includes family fabrics that date from the late 1940s. She uses them to repair and complete quilts to make new family heirlooms. *See illustration #4.*

Once you own that family quilt, you'll want to document it as best you can. Ask the current owners to tell you anything they know about the quilt, including the maker's full name, when the quilt was made, the pattern name, and any stories connected with it. If it's a quilt you remember, write down your memories. If there are any family Bibles, histories, or letters, check through them to get more information about the maker or her ancestors and descendants. If all you have is a name, try to find the cemetery where the maker is buried and copy the information from the tombstone. Or check with the church the maker belonged to. They may be able to supply you with dates of birth and death or even anecdotes.

With the dates in hand, you can check newspaper morgues to find the maker's obituary and maybe the birth announcement. From those articles, you'll find either names of descendants

4

QUILT INFORMATION FORM

DATE:_____   Quilt Code/Number: _____

TECHNIQUE: Patchwork____   Appliqué____ Trapunto____   Reverse Appliqué____

PATTERN:_____ PRICE:$_____ Size:_____

PREDOMINENT COLOR(s):_____ Photo Available:___

STYLE: Scrapbag____   Coordinated____   # of Fabrics:_____

STYLE FEATURES:(Borders, flowers in basket, set, sashing, backing, etc.

_____

AGE: _____   HISTORY/MAKER: _____

QUILTED: (Tied_____) Hand____ Stitches per inch_____   Machine_____

    Even stitches____ Uniform length_____ Amount of Quilting_____

WORKMANSHIP: Excellent____   Very Good _____ Good____ Fair____ Poor_____

    "Invisible" applique stitches____ Points/junctions/corners match_____

    Good color balance/arrangement_____ Other _____

CONDITION: Excellent____   Very Good _____ Good_____ Fair____ Poor_____

    Torn/worn top____ Torn/worn back____   Torn/worn binding _____

    Repairs____ Faded ____ Stains_____ Soiled _____ Other _____

_____

GENERAL COMMENTS: _____

SELLER'S NAME:_____ Website/E-mail:_____

LOCATION: _____

NOTES/COMMENTS:

4 This is a good example of the information you'll need to gather when studying a quilt whether the information is just to keep for future reference or you'll use it to decide to add to your collection. It is the form we used for collecting and documenting the listings in this book.

or parent's names and have more information to track the maker down through family Bibles and histories. Researching a family quilt also starts you on your family's genealogy!

Next, carefully check the quilt and note the colors, print patterns, and type of fabric, the pattern, style of assembly, and workmanship. These are clues to the age of the quilt. Also note the condition of the quilt. Are there any worn spots? Is the binding frayed? Are there any stains or color loss? Has it been washed or do the quilting lines still show on the fabric? Keep a careful record of this information. You'll need it to document the age of the quilt, to properly repair and clean it, and to satisfy your own curiosity. Each quilt you add to your collection, whether it's a family heirloom or purchased, should be documented the same way. Keep a notebook, file, or scrapbook solely for your quilts. On page 9 is a modified version of the form we used to find over 800 quilts and prices listed in this book. It lists all the important information you need, or want, about each quilt in your collection.

Even while you're notifying family that you'd like to own now, or inherit, the family quilts, you're probably attending quilt shows, going to shops and dealers, and watching for quilts at fairs, flea markets, and tag sales. As you do this, notice if your eye gravitates to a certain type of quilt. Once you've exhausted the quilt sources in your family, you'll buy to add to your collection and at some point that means you'll specialize. You'll find that you prefer piecework over appliqué, or Victorian-era crazy quilts over the simpler, less elaborate crazy quilts of the early 1900s. Maybe you prefer to collect only log cabin quilts, or only Sunbonnet Sues. You might even pick a certain time period, say the miniatures period of the late 1800s through the 1940s during which some quilts were made with tens of thousands of tiny pieces. Maybe you'll specialize in exquisite workmanship preferring only those quilts with stitches 10 or more to the inch or without a single point mismatched. You might even specialize by collecting quilts of predominantly one color. One collection, owned by collectors Paul Pilgrim and Gerald Roy, shown at the Museum of the American Quilter's Society in Paducah, Kentucky, featured 40 antique quilts made using orange fabric. You might decide to collect only signed and dated quilts or quilts where the maker and history are known. Or, you might specialize in commemorative, political, or social statement quilts. The possibilities for specialization are endless. Only by seeing what's available in the marketplace can you decide what quilts you want. Specializing may take years, but the hunt is so enjoyable that you shouldn't mind waiting to decide.

One way to enjoy the hunt is to attend as many quilt shows and fairs as you can. Even shows of contemporary quilts can help you decide what you want to collect while increasing your store of knowledge about quilts and quilt history. Quilt shows abound with experts eager to talk about their specialty. Show quilts are usually better documented because they're loaned by the owners. Because many of these loaned quilts are family heirlooms, the owners know when they were made. Take notes on these quilts. We'll talk later about using those notes to do your own dating.

So far we've described the collection process of being a quilt "picker." Pickers are the folks who scour the countryside looking for quilts to sell to dealers who, in turn, sell to you. The only other step a picker takes to find quilts that we haven't discussed is by knocking on doors to ask families if they have quilts they want to sell. Pickers make the rounds of flea markets, antique shows, and door-to-door appointments with families to find quilts.

You can be your own picker if you have the nerve and the time. Many pickers started as collectors. Picking means a lot of traveling. If the thought of 30 phone calls or visits to find one quilt doesn't bother you, try it. But, pickers are professionals at what they do. They know patterns, workmanship, quality, condition, and price. Until you're well educated on those aspects of quilt collecting, don't rush into the job. It is one way to educate yourself about quilts, but the education could be costly if you don't acquire the quilts the dealers and collectors want. Most quilt pickers work part-time. Relatively few do it full-time, year-round.

After finding quilts from family and friends, or by scouring the countryside being your own picker, your next step toward building a collection is to establish a relationship with a reputable quilt dealer. Quilt dealers should not be confused with quilt shops. Shops usually offer supplies and fabrics for contemporary quilt makers or new quilts either commissioned by the shop or taken in to sell on consignment. Quilt dealers specialize in antique quilts, tops, blocks, and fabrics and sometimes quilting ephemera: tools, sewing cases, machines, books. You should find a quilt dealer with a good reputation who is knowledgeable about quilts and has been involved as either a dealer or collector for more than five years. We've listed dozens of these dealers in Sources.

You need to develop trust with your quilt dealer, and that requires asking questions. You should ask how the dealer acquires quilts. You want a dealer with a wide network of pickers or other dealers, so you know there is possible contact with a large supply of quilts. Does this dealer do quilt repair, or have contact with someone who does? What's the dealer's policy on letting the customer know that a quilt has been repaired? While you can do anything you want to a quilt, it's imperative that the dealer let the buyer know what's been done. Remember that quilts are dated by the last work done to them. Without documentation that it was repaired, even a new binding can take a quilt out of antique status and make it contemporary and therefore less valuable. A reputable dealer will point out repairs and improvements made to a quilt while noting that the original work is from an earlier period. Some repairs will not affect the value of an antique quilt if done correctly by acceptable restoration techniques that are noted in the provenance. For instance, on most quilts, the binding is the first spot to wear, because, when in use on a bed, may drag or rest on the floor. Ideally, quilts should be in original condition, but a badly worn binding may devalue a quilt more than putting on a new binding would. The important point to remember is that your dealer should admit to repairing a quilt. A dealer who passes off a repaired quilt as an original would be, in our opinion, untrustworthy.

A relationship with a dealer becomes more important as you start to specialize your collection, and is essential if you are not confident of your own ability to recognize and date an antique quilt. Because they have a greater number of contacts across the country, quilt dealers are more likely to find you the quilt you want faster and cheaper than you could yourself. Along with their knowledge of quilts, quilting and quilt history, dealers know the marketplace for price and availability of quilts better than the nonspecialized antiques dealer who might have just a few quilts in stock along with a myriad of other Americana memorabilia. As a specialist focused on quilts, the quilt dealer can be your best source for additions to your collection.

For the price guide portion of this book, {see page 111} we assembled a list of quilts with descriptions and prices. Many of these were beautiful, excellently made, and in great condition.

But the quilts in the quilt dealers inventories were not the best quilts they found for sale. Just stopping in a quilt dealer's store isn't enough. Not every quilt on the market ends up in a showroom. In fact, the really good ones are scooped up before they get to the store. Many quilts go directly from the dealer to a buyer because dealers constantly look for quilts for their best customers. When found, the quilt goes to the collector. Remember that trust between collector and dealer works both ways. If your dealer doesn't trust you, then he or she is less likely to invest in a quilt before offering it to you. Dealers get to know their customers' likes and dislikes and are more apt to buy a quilt on speculation if you've dealt honestly and fairly with them in the past. The moral of this tale is that building a trusting relationship with a quilt dealer means that a greater supply than just what's in the showroom is available to you, and you'll be the collector getting first pick on the type of quilts you want.

Once you've established a relationship with a quilt dealer, you'll want to arrange a method of viewing the quilts. It isn't necessary to have a quilt dealer close by because most dealers are happy to send you a photograph of the quilt along with its story. Of course, seeing and holding the quilt in your hands is a much better way to evaluate the quilt than looking at a photograph. But photos are a good way to weed out prospective additions to your collection. If you've established with the dealer that you are very serious about quilts, and have good credit (which you'll probably have to establish by paying before delivery several times), dealers will send you quilts to view in your home or office. Usually they're mailed, sometimes shipped, and always insured; not a single dealer we spoke to complained of losing one because of the shipping company's ineptitude.

Be specific with your quilt dealer. List your preferences for size, condition, workmanship, and pattern name. Also list your exceptions. A truly magnificent crazy quilt not in the best condition might be acceptable to you. If you don't tell the dealer that, you might miss the one quilt you really want because the dealer stuck to your list of ideal specifications.

It might appear that a quilt dealer is the last place you should contact for quilts. Wouldn't flea markets, antiques shows, and auctions be better? They might be if, and it's a big if, *you* know everything you need to know about quilts to spot a fake or confirm the date of a quilt. Dating a quilt, as we'll see, is tricky. The history of textiles, dyes and dyeing, styles of quilting, and patterns is complex. When did cotton quilts become the norm? When was a lavender dye perfected? Which is older: the Victorian crazy quilt or the miniaturized postage stamp quilt? Can you tell the difference between silk and satin? Is the batting cotton, wool, or polyester? Is that really old fabric or has it been tea-dyed to look old? Can you tell if that funny brown fabric was originally brown or was it a green that faded to that color with age?

"Determining the age of a quilt is a matter of finding enough reliable clues in the quilt to build a case for a date," wrote Barbara Brackman in her book *Clues in the Calico* "Even knowing something as specific as the date a pattern was published or a scrap of fabric printed cannot tell you exactly when the quilt was made." In the past, just as today, many quilts were made from scrap bag fabrics. Bits and pieces of cloth left after making clothing, still-good pieces of fabric cut from old clothing, fabric from the last quilt made all went into the quiltmaker's scrap bag. A scrap bag, like Liz's, dating from the 1940s, can contain fabric from many generations accumulated over many decades. One piece of 1960s fabric in a quilt dates it to that time period unless you know that the piece was used only to repair the quilt and isn't part of the original work.

You have to be a combination of detective and scholar to learn how to date quilts. Before you can go off completely on your own to the nonspecialized antique quilt sources, you need to know as much as you can about the history of quilts and textiles. To start your education, read Chapters 3 and 4. {See pages 20 and 35.} We've included a brief history of quilting and the strongest dating clues we found in our research. At the back of the book {see page 279} is a Bibliography which can get you well on your way to being quilt-literate.

We suggest that as you attend shows and fairs you jot down notes on quilts that have been dated. Of course, the only dates we can be absolutely certain of are those quilts that were signed and dated by the maker. Take down all the information and clues on those quilts. These notes should include colors used in the quilt, types of fabric, pattern names, quilting patterns, the backing fabric, and the batting material if known.

Carry graph paper to jot down a block pattern you never saw before. Quilt block names number in the thousands, and the same block can have many different names. When you come across one you don't recognize, graph it out and add it to your files.

Start a fabric file by collecting fabrics that are dyed in certain colors but of different ages, as you see them offered at quilt dealers. Eventually you'll have samples that graphically show how the color red or green or brown has changed over the years. These samples will also show how fabric ages. As we'll see in Chapter 4 {see page 35}, some dyes made fabric deteriorate faster than other fabrics in the same quilt. Some dyes faded quickly and some lasted, as vibrant as new, for decades.

Don't limit yourself to quilt shows and fairs. Go to museums, too. Museums go to great lengths to date their acquisitions as closely as possible. Take the same notes, paying special attention to any exceptional features of the quilt noted in program books or on signs. These notes, from shows and museums, along with your reading, form a reference file you can refer to when dating quilts you want to purchase or checking the accuracy of a quilt already assigned a date.

Complete your quilt education by attending more shows and going to more museums. This time, however, appraise the date, workmanship, and condition of the quilt before you read any signs and program books, or ask the owner. Once you've settled on a date, check your results with the program book or owner. If your date agrees with the assigned date, all your work and study has paid off! Your education isn't complete, it never will be, but at least you know you're on the right track.

If it all seems like a lot of work, it's only because you've just begun. The quilt quest is fascinating, and as you journey along you won't notice that you're working—it'll all seem like fun! Educating yourself also ensures that you won't get stuck with a quilt that's been misrepresented, which is why we suggested that in your search for quilts to add to your collection you go first to a dealer—until you know what to look for to evaluate a quilt yourself. Now you're ready to be a quilt picker and to scour the nonspecialized antiques shops, flea markets, and auctions on your own. Because these suppliers are antiques generalists, not quilt specialists, they're more easily misled about the real age and condition of a quilt. You have to be the expert, the picker, to find the bargain.

Find flea markets, tag sales, and antique shows by reading your local papers or by reading a regional newsletter, newspaper, or magazine that lists them. Get familiar with the antiques magazines available. Many list upcoming shows and events. Find quilt dealers by checking the yellow pages in phone books. Most libraries have phone books for at least the capital cities of each state. When checking the yellow pages, be careful. Names listed under "quilts" may often be general antique stores that happen to carry a few quilts. Call first so you don't waste a trip.

Go to these sources with some idea of what you want or just to add to your store of knowledge. When you find a quilt that you want, always ask the dealer if there's any story behind it or anything else known about the quilt. It's up to you and the dealer, whether you'll haggle over the price. Some dealers simply won't negotiate on price while others enjoy dickering so much you're almost cheating them out of half their fun if you simply hand over the money. In either case, it never hurts to ask if the price is firm or if you can negotiate.

There are a slew of stories about quilts found at tag sales and garage sales for paltry sums like five dollars. It probably doesn't happen as much as the folklore implies, but it does happen. Liz Aleshire, on a tag sale foray, found a 20" × 20" square made of silk hat bindings using the puff square method. Liz finished the three-dimensional piece with satin borders and antique buttons. The cost of the piece found ignominiously tossed in a box? Liz paid only five dollars for what now elicits many compliments.

One tip on attending tag sales is to read the ads closely. Those that say they're emptying a house or an estate should probably be first on your list to visit. You're more likely to find a quilt no one wants at a sale of that type than you are at one where a family merely cleaned out its closets and is taking a chance on getting some money for the detritus. Here you can dicker on the price if you want. People expect to negotiate prices at these owner-run clearing-house sales.

The place where you'll really need quilt dating, condition, and workmanship education is at an auction or estate sale. An auction can be exciting and stimulating, also overwhelming and intimidating. Unless you're an expert and can set a realistic price for a particular quilt and stick to it, you're better off saving auctions for entertainment only and buying your quilts elsewhere. Should you decide to venture into this arena, however, there are some things you should know.

Quilts are sold at various types of auctions, from those exclusively for quilts to auctions that include a variety of related and unrelated items to estate auctions where a quilt just happens to be part of the household merchandise. There are many large and small auction houses around the country that present auctions that may offer a few, or dozens, of quilts at one time. These are often called "Americana" auctions and may include textiles, furniture, tools, home or cooking implements, and antique decorative pieces with the quilts.

Christie's and Sotheby's are two of the biggest and best known national auction houses. Regional or local auction houses can be found in the yellow pages or listed in local newspapers.

You can find out what's offered and when by calling the auction house directly. Request to be added to the mailing list to receive notice of future auctions. Many auction houses charge for this. Catalogs from the bigger auction houses cost five dollars and up; they may be thick glossy volumes complete with pictures and extensive descriptions. Smaller auction houses may have glossy brochures or simple typewritten listings.

The prime rule, if you decide to chance a purchase at auction, is to look over the merchandise extremely carefully. There's always preview time before any auction, sometimes even days before, to see the offered merchandise. Previewing doesn't mean standing a few feet away and admiring the pattern or colors. It means taking the quilt out of its box, down from its rack, or off the table and really looking at it. Unfold the quilt and look at the back as carefully as the front. It's wise to never bid on a quilt that you haven't previewed. Everything looks good from a distance or in a photograph. It's in the preview that you get the close look, an inspection that reveals any flaws.

At the preview, spread the quilt out and look at everything: squares, borders, and other features. Do the colors balance? Does the quilt look like something you want to own or give as a gift? There may be one square badly torn or of completely different colors that changes the whole look of the quilt. If you hadn't unfolded it you would have missed the flaw. Check every inch of the quilt for the quality of workmanship and its condition. At auctions, it's always buyer beware, for items are sold exactly as you see them. If you get your treasure home and discover flaws, you have no one but yourself to blame for not inspecting the quilt carefully. There are no returns at auctions.

The final decision before you attempt to bid is to determine how much you think the quilt is worth and how much you're willing to pay for it. Many of the larger auction houses will note an "expected price" in the catalog can be helpful. This price, however, is often higher than the item finally sells for, as price depends on who is at the auction and willing to buy.

When you've made the decision to bid on a quilt, there are a few other steps to take before the bidding starts.

All auctions have a standard procedure they expect you to follow should you be the successful bidder. You must make arrangements for payment before you even start bidding. If you're not familiar with the requirements of the particular auction to which you're going, *ask*. A few auction houses may take a credit card, but most will not. Unless you're prepared to pay cash, all auction houses require that you establish credit before they accept your check. This is not really credit, per se, but verification that your check will be good. This step may be as easy as showing a major credit card and photo I.D. or as complicated as direct contact with your financial institution. Be sure you arrive at the auction early enough to establish your credit. Ask if the auction will take a personal check or requires a bank check. Find out if they will hold items for you until you can get the proper check. Most will not, or will hold for only a very short time.

If you plan to pay cash, the auction house may require that they see a certain amount before they allow you to bid. This may seem paranoid, but if you are the successful bidder, and then can't pay for the item, the auction house has lost the sale and may not be able to recoup.

After being approved as a buyer, you'll usually be given a bidder number. At the bigger houses, this may be a plastic number that you hold up for the auctioneer to see. It may also be a number scratched on a piece of cardboard or slip of paper. At some auctions, you may not get a number at all. You might be asked for a refundable deposit on the number to be sure you return it at the end of the auction. In any case, once you have done the preliminaries, you may then find a place, either standing or seated, from which you make your bids. Sit down, relax and wait for the auction to begin.

If you are not familiar with the bidding procedure, ask. You may feel foolish, and the auction staff may look at you like you have two heads, but this will be nothing compared to what you'll feel when someone else walks out with your treasure because you didn't know how to make your bid. It's wise to go to a few auctions before you become involved in active bidding, just to see how it goes and to determine if you can stand the pressure and the pace.

The bidding process is just as hectic and confusing as those you've watched parodied on TV sitcoms. The auction house needs to sell the maximum amount of merchandise in the shortest possible time and usually the bidding process goes fairly quickly, if not at a lightning pace. The auctioneer will announce the item to be bid on, usually with the catalog number, if there is one. He may or may not describe the item, giving you time to recognize it as the quilt you want. He will then offer a price at which he wants the bidding to start.

If the starting price seems too high to you, don't bid. If no one starts the bidding, the auctioneer may drop the beginning price. Don't let this fool you into thinking that the quilt is necessarily going to sell lower than the price the auctioneer first mentions. The auction house hopes that once people start bidding on an item, desire and excitement will override sensibility and thoughtfulness, pushing the price higher and higher.

If others start bidding at the first price the auctioneer mentions, and the price is higher than you are willing to pay, you may have to rethink your top price, or, more wisely, let the quilt go. Unless you have unlimited funds, you should set a reasonable price for the quilt you want and not go over it. Unless, of course, this is the quilt you cannot live without and you want to break the bank for it.

During the bidding, pay close and careful attention. Raise your hand or your number when the next price is offered, if you are willing to pay it. If the auctioneer goes from $200 to $300 and no one takes the $300, and you are willing to go to $225, say so. The auction house would prefer you to go up in the increments it offers, but it will take other bids.

If the auctioneer doesn't acknowledge that you waved your number on the offered bid, be more aggressive next time. Auctioneers are very good at reading the most subtle signs, but if you sit like a bump on a log, barely moving, they will think you are asleep and not bidding. Usually, once you have joined in the active bidding, the auctioneer will keep an eye on you in order to offer you other opportunities to bid. Just remember that if someone else is willing to go higher, he is not going to look to you for long.

Remember, too, that the decision of the auctioneer is final. If you feel that he didn't see you wave your hand or hear you shout your bid and he gave the sale to someone else, your whining about his lack of awareness won't change his mind. Next time, pay closer attention or make yourself heard.

When the auctioneer says "Sold!" and you are the highest bidder, hold up your hand or your number so that the auction staff can make note of you. If you have no other items on which you wish to bid, you may now leave the floor and pay for your quilt. Be aware that most auctions will add what is called a buyer's premium onto the price of your quilt. This can be a flat fee or a percentage, and it is almost the standard in the auction industry. It pays the auction house's bills, leaving the actual price of the item sold to give the seller. You should figure this premium into your pre-auction calculations of what the quilt is worth and how much you're willing to spend.

If reading about an auction has your heart pounding in anticipation, then you are an adventurous soul and ready to take wallet in hand and head for the nearest auction house. If it has your heart pounding in fear, then scurry back to your ever faithful quilt dealer and find your treasures there. Auctions can be great places to find and buy quilts. They can also be great places to spend too much and get stuck with overpriced merchandise.

Finally, with the explosive growth of the Internet, online shopping is added to our list of quilt sources. Although referred to as auctions, sales offered through sites such as eBay and UBid differ greatly from the sales offered by auction houses like Sotheby's and Christie's. The most obvious difference is that the preview is not at a location where you can pick up, unfold, and closely inspect your prospective quilt purchase. In online auctions your preview will be only from a picture. A photograph might be worth a thousand words, but it doesn't give the whole picture. Reduced in size to fit the computer screen and sometimes of poor quality itself, a photograph probably won't show accurate colors, workmanship flaws, fading, stains you can't live with, or large, inept quilt stitches. So, when purchasing online, it's imperative that you deal with an Internet auction house that offers some guarantee, return policy, or fraud protection. For instance, eBay offers both fraud protection and an escrow option for buyers to ensure that they're happy with their purchase. But some of these options, like eBay's escrow option, are contingent upon the seller agreeing to participate. Beware of a seller who refuses to give you a trial period during which you can return the quilt for a refund if it doesn't pass muster upon close inspection. We'd suggest opting not to buy a quilt online unless such a guarantee policy is offered. *See illustration #5.*

There are also numerous retail antique quilt sources on the Internet. Try entering the search words "antique quilts" like we did and you'll get a list of 43,000 sites that offer information on the history of quilts and quilting as well as quilts for sale. Searching on "antique quilts resale" brought us to a list of 5,231 antique quilt sale sources! Online dealers operate much the same way as the antique quilt shop dealers you use now. You can build a relationship with them that will produce additions to your collection you didn't think possible. These dealers have a wider range of quilt sources than those folks who operate only as pickers traveling the country to find quilts for resale. Again, you should never buy from an online dealer who doesn't offer a guarantee and return and refund options.

So here's how it works. If you want to cruise the options at online auctions, make sure you read or participate in any online help offered. Sites like eBay and UBid offer interactive help op-

5 Racks of quilts stand waiting for buyers in the Quilt Barn at the Kutztown Folk Festival, an annual event held in Pennsylvania. Regional fairs are often good sources for traditional contemporary quilts. And, many antique shops use similar display methods for antique quilts. Photo from the authors' collection.

tions that explain everything you have to do or know to buy or sell online. Again, make sure your online auction house offers some kind of reference or critique feedback on buyers that you can view and that it offers some kind of fraud protection.

Once you're reviewed how to buy online, start looking at the listings to see if anything appeals to you. Here's where your education on the history of quilting, fabric, dyes, and patterns will be invaluable in judging the accuracy of the dating information given in each quilt's listing. We'd recommend, as we did in becoming your own quilt picker, that purchases online be attempted only once you're confident in your abilities to recognize the real thing from a fake.

If you find a quilt that interests you, you're ready to buy. Since the rules and road map for buying on line vary with the site, follow the examples and information given in the site's help options to continue with your purchase. Don't be daunted by the process of buying online. The reputable sites have made it simple as long as you've read their help information. The sites we checked for help on using that site had detailed, clear instructions on the buying and selling process. Do a little reading first and your purchase will be easy. Like traditional auction sites, you'll be competing with other buyers to purchase the quilt. Check the site often to see if you've been outbid and decide if you want to increase your bid. Set yourself a limit that you can afford and stick to it.

When buying from antique quilt dealers online (as opposed to online auctions), the routine search is the same. Searching for a list of "antique quilts retail" will give you a substantial list of opportunities. Check each site first for a return and refund policy. We strongly suggest not even looking at what's offered on a site that doesn't offer a return guarantee. We stick to our statement that the only way to judge the quality of a quilt is to hold it in your hands and inspect it. In our opinion, any retailer who doesn't offer a guarantee is less than reputable.

Search through the listings on the site, paying careful attention to the size, condition, and date offered in the listing to be sure that quilt falls into your collection criteria. Enlarge and view the photograph and take as close a look as you can. If you decide you want the quilt, follow the site's instructions for placing an order. Don't be surprised if the dealer wants a check or credit card up front. Like your relationship with a traditional dealer, you'll need to establish a credit history before you can expect to have quilts sent to you on consignment.

Buying online is safe, easy, and comfortable. But it requires that you know even more about the history and dating of quilts. You'll need to be sharp, confident in your knowledge, and willing to take a risk to buy antique quilts online. Misrepresentations abound in the dating of quilts, more of it based on inaccurate folklore and incomplete education than on fraud. If you're more knowledgeable than the dealer, you stand a better chance of acquiring a "find:" that lovely quilt, at an affordable price, that's actually older and in better condition than the dealer's appraisal.

If acquiring all this knowledge seems a little intimidating, remember that all quilts start with a single stitch, and your collection starts with a single quilt. Take it slow and use your current collection of quilts, however small, to look for the signs included in the chapters on history and dating. {See pages 20 and 35.}

Welcome to the exciting world of quilt collecting. Your journey has begun!

3 The History of Quilts and Quilting

Americans didn't invent quilting. They didn't even invent the art of quilting. There is evidence that quilting was done in Ancient Greece, India, and China before the birth of Christ. Persians used quilting to make prayer rugs, carpets, and draperies from linen, silk, and satin. Portuguese traders brought quilting to Europe as did the returning survivors of the Crusades. The Crusaders used appliqué and piecework to make their banners and flags. Middle Ages folk of all means quilted coats and hoods, and soldiers wore quilted items to cushion their heavy armor. By the 11th century, quilting had spread throughout Europe and was used especially for bed clothing.

One quilt historian mentioned a great freeze that took place across Europe in the 14th century that led to even more quilting. It is during this period that the first quilt frame was used and that the Italian style trapunto, or stuffed, quilting began. By the 1600s, quilting was used to add warmth, weight, and beauty to all kinds of outer and underclothing as well as to bedspreads and bed furnishings. When the settlers arrived in the New World, they brought along not only quilts but also quilting techniques.

"It is quite certain that quilts were among the household furnishings given precious space on the first small ships to the New World," wrote Jonathan Holstein in *The Pieced Quilt: An American Design Tradition*. "And it is likely there were some fine quilts carefully tucked into chests with other treasured household items."

That these quilts were brought with the Colonial settlers out of necessity there is no doubt. We'd also argue that they were brought for their family heirloom and sentimental value as well, just like the pioneer families carried their quilts with them to the West. Quilting was well known in the Old World, as evidenced by the fact that the oldest whole quilt in existence dates from 1708; it is an appliqué in the Broderie-Perse style using India chintz. Although completed in the 18th century, this oldest surviving quilt contains fabric from the 1600s.

Broderie-Perse is the method of cutting large printed designs from imported chintz or calico. The cut pieces were placed on a ground fabric of white cotton or linen, their edges turned under and sewed down. This method of cutting out pre-printed forms is the earliest known appliqué design. The fabric used for Broderie-Perse came primarily from India imported to Europe as early as the mid-1600s. This 17th century quilt, now in Levens Hall in England, is typical of the English-style quilt with its large central motif. It is this central medallion style that Colonial needleworkers revised and adapted to create a uniquely American style of quilting.

The first quilts made in America were probably simple designs made of whole cloth created more out of necessity than for beauty. Whole cloth quilts were simply that: two pieces of cloth stitched together with a batting in the middle. There are at least 15 date-inscribed quilts that exist today from the 18th century made by American needleworkers, and 4 of these are whole-cloth quilts, according to Barbara Brackman in *Clues in the Calico*. The balance of these 15 18th-century quilts are pieced and appliqué dated after 1770. The oldest quilt in America is a McCord quilt dated 1726.

No form of needlework achieved hobby status until the mid to late 18th century. Even then, needlework was never just a creative outlet, it was a woman's occupation.

"To create with brain and fingers, with needle and thread, goods of admittedly economic value, was perforce a part of a woman's job," wrote Ruth E. Finley in her 1929 book *Old Patch-work Quilts*. Quilts were considered so economically valuable, in fact, that they were listed along with other assets in personal and wedding inventories. Their disposition was noted in wills. Purchases of quilting materials were listed in account books. Advertisements for quilt materials were placed in Colonial newspapers as early as 1721.

Quilting, and attendant services such as printing homespun cloth, were a cottage industries in Colonial days. Homes had looms to make their own cloth, which was then taken to professional dyers who decorated the homespun cloth by hand painting or hand printing using woodblocks or copperplate. Once a quilt was pieced, the Colonial housewife who could afford it could hire someone else to quilt it. To learn the finer techniques of needlework, schools were formed. Bridget Suckling ran a needlework school in Boston in 1751, but only the wealthy could afford it.

Even with the opportunity to hire the work out, all women were expected to do needlework. For the wealthy woman, quilting was a way of keeping herself busy, but for the poor it was a necessity. Quilting was within the means, often the necessity, of everyone in Colonial America.

Girls started their needlework training at an early age. Most learned by doing, guided by their mothers. The wealthy attended special schools such as the one run by Bridget Suckling. Often, needlework education began at the age of four or five. Anywhere between six and eight, a Colonial girl started her first quilt, laboriously working, matching, ripping out clumsy stitches, and replacing them with small, even ones. Tradition dictated that each bride take with her when she married, as part of her dowry, a baker's dozen of quilts. The thirteenth quilt was her bridal quilt and made after she was betrothed. If a bridal quilt was started before a girl was betrothed, it was said she'd never marry. Another superstition about bride's quilts stipulated that these were the only quilts to include hearts in the pattern or quilting design. To place a heart in one of the other dozen of her quilts was to invite spinsterhood.

It was only in needlework that a woman held full control. Her dowry, income and home were controlled by her husband. Finley states, emphatically, that women didn't even have control over their own clothing. She notes that the man ordered the material for his wife's and daughters' gowns when he ordered his own clothing. Although Finley implies that women had no choice in the matter, it seems improbable that the Colonial husband came home with fabric for his wife's gowns that she had never seen or approved. While technically the husband did control important aspects of her life, it would take a rare man, totally devoid of common sense, not to let his wife pick out her own dress fabric from whatever small choice was available.

Whether she chose it or not, women certainly held full sway in how fabric was used in the home. As life became easier in Colonial America, with the increased availability of quality imported goods, Colonial women stamped their mark on the art of quilting and created works of beauty as well as utility. Women who could afford it cut cloth and experimented with appliqué technique. The poor turned to piecing patterns using up the leftovers from other needlework.

Politics also entered into the creation of quilts. From the very beginning, England attempted to discourage the development of manufactured textiles in the American colony. Massachusetts and Connecticut had laws that every family must plant and raise flax to turn into homespun. If they made their own, there was no need to demand manufactured fabric or to rely on England for imports. Imported cloth was one of the highly taxed items that led to one of the most familiar of our country's slogans: "No taxation without representation." The importation of cotton into the Colonies cut into England's wool and linen business, so purchasing these fabrics was pronounced illegal. When the Colonists bought the banned cotton anyway, England imposed a double tax on the goods. So easily accessible today, it seems ludicrous that the scarcity and high cost of fabric would have helped foment a revolution. But cloth, and what can be made from it, is so essential to daily life that that is exactly what happened. Although not as dramatically remembered as the Boston Tea Party, the taxation of calico and the discouragement of a textile industry in America also fueled the American Revolution. Even after the Revolution, England outlawed the exportation of cloth-making technology, going so far as to search passengers traveling to America for machine blueprints. It wasn't until the 1790s that America's first cotton mill opened. Samuel Slater, an engineer, memorized the plans and specifications of mass-producing cotton cloth machines, took his knowledge to the Colonies and opened Slater's Cotton Mill in Pawtucket, Rhode Island. Alexander Hamilton started the Society of Useful Manufacturers in 1791 to produce cotton cloth, but England flooded the new country with cheap imports and the venture failed. By 1810, however, 87 cotton and printing mills thrived.

The oldest quilting pieced pattern is the crazy quilt style. It was out of necessity that American quiltmakers first started experimenting with new patterns. Leftover scraps of fabric were sewn together, haphazardly, to fit them with each other to create an assembled whole cloth that could be quilted into a bed covering. Until the Colonial time, quilts were primarily made of whole cloth. Even the expensive Broderie-Perse style quilt required a piece of whole cloth as a ground for the appliqué . The high price of imported fabric coupled with the English-

6 This large crazy square made with cotton, satin and silk was once part of a whole quilt. The seam allowance folds and some of the stitching is visible along the edges. It's unusual because of the choice of predominantly lighter fabrics. Quilt from the authors' collection.

imposed tax on calicoes turned cloth into an expensive commodity. Scraps were saved to be used, somehow, later. Even worn clothing was cut of its good spots, salvaging fabric that could be used elsewhere. Every inch of cloth was saved. It had to be. *See illustration #6.*

". . .The family quilt was like the turkey soup made from the left-overs of the Christmas feast," wrote Finley. "A positively last appearance." This last appearance of the household fabric resulted in what we regard as the single most significant American contribution to quilting: blocks.

Blocks were already an element of quilts. Adelaide Hechtinger wrote in *American Quilts, Quilting, and Patchwork,* that early-18th-century quilts were made of four blocks, each 36" square. When these were assembled, an 18" border was added, making the completed quilt 108" square. Beds were large in those days, states Hechtinger, and high off the ground to accommodate a trundle bed beneath. Quilts were made large enough to cover the bed, as well as to cover several, sometimes many occupants sleeping together.

Block-style quilting as we know it today is the result of a gradually increasing quality of life as much as it was from economics or necessity. Imports arrived more frequently in America and goods were cheaper, at least for those living along the eastern seaboard. Yankee peddlers went inland carrying printed textiles in specially designed wagons with flaps on the sides to protect and display the bolts of cloth. More of the necessities of life were provided for, and quiltmakers tired of the functional whole-cloth or four-square quilts. They decided to make their bed coverings beautiful as well. Quiltmakers experimented with smaller blocks, cutting fabric pieces into precise geometric forms and assembling those together. Once enough blocks were pieced, they were assembled into a quilt top.

"Precious as the material might have been, quiltmakers preferred to trim them into geometric shapes rather than piece them as they came as in the crazy quilt. . .," wrote Holstein. These cut geometric forms were more pleasing, more challenging. An improved lifestyle and less expensive goods made block-style quilting affordable and creative expression possible.

". . .The block-style furnished a work method and a geometrically based aesthetic which was endlessly variable and could be manipulated for the most diverse results," continued Holstein. "No two quilts are ever alike."

With the advent of the block style, quiltmakers were able to plan a quilt rather than letting the fabric dictate its design. Even Broderie-Perse dictated the form of the central medallion style quilt because of its use of pre-printed designs on chintz fabric. Simply rotating a pieced block a quarter turn could result in a very different, very dramatic change in the overall pattern of a quilt top. Variety was indeed endless with the pieced block when quiltmakers added their own color and fabric choice to the basic block design. Reversing placement of light and dark fabrics within a pieced block was enough to create what looked like a completely different pattern.

Block-style quilting made the whole job easier. Instead of working with a bulky piece of cloth the same size as the finished quilt, blocks were small and portable. They could be worked on in short periods of time whenever that time was available. They could be carried with the quiltmaker so that her hands were never idle, even when visiting. Suddenly, piecing could be done anywhere. And just as suddenly, geometric quilts of great beauty were produced, and a woman could express, through her quilts, her innate creativity. And, blessing of all blessings, it was still economical! Thrifty, even, because now the quiltmaker could use up all the scraps of fabric left over from her other needlework and still produce something of value. Block-style patchwork flourished from its beginnings in the mid-1700s.

The most important aspect of the advent of block-style quilting is that it spawned hundreds of geometric patterns still used today and also led to the creation of album, autograph, signature, friendship, bride, presentation and sampler quilts. These quilts are among the most collectible today. *See illustration #7.*

Quilting bees date from Colonial days and are another purely American addition to the art of quilting that continues to the present. Today's quilt guilds and clubs are the natural evolution of the Colonial quilting bee. And they're held for the same reasons: furthering the education of the individual on quilting technique; sharing patterns and fabrics; talking, laughing, and yes, gossiping; and gathering together in a social context. Today's quilt groups work in a different format. Rarely does the group meet to finish another member's quilt unless it's a fund-raising project.

Bees were different in Colonial and pioneer days. Then, quilting bees were family and community events involving women, men, boys and girls. Guests arrived early, admired the quilt top and set to work attaching it to the quilt frame. They spent the rest of the day talking and quilting. Husbands and sweethearts were invited to supper and arrived wearing their Sunday best clothes. After supper, all stayed for talk, games, and dancing. One of our sources noted that in 1752, a quilting bee was held in Narragansett, Rhode Island, that lasted 10 days!

Bees were also part of courtship. One superstition practiced at bees was for the young men and women to hold the completed quilt while a cat was placed in the center. Whomever the cat

7 The tradition of the quilting bee is alive and well at the Kutztown Folk Festival. Modern quiltmakers gather around the frame, just as their ancestors did, and discuss quilting techniques with attendees at the annual fair. Photo from the authors' collection.

jumped over to get off the quilt was the next of the group to get married. Sometimes a betrothed man might design a quilt for his bride-to-be to make for their new home.

Usually a quilting bee consisted of eight women, seven guests and the hostess. To work comfortably and efficiently, this meant two women on each side of the quilt, their heads bent over the job, talking and sharing details of their lives. In rural areas, where a neighbor traveled a long distance to attend, the quiltmaker might wait until she had two tops to quilt and invite 15 women. They would work in shifts, alternating between quilting and preparing the evening meal until the stitching was completed.

Although the tradition of a bride bringing 13 quilts to her marriage meant that girls started piecing and appliquéing their tops early in life, they rarely finished the quilts until they were betrothed. The expensive part of finishing a quilt is adding the batting and backing. Since this wasn't necessary until the girl needed to furnish a new home, the tops were stored. Any girl who invited her friends over for a quilting party to work on her tops was actually announcing her approaching marriage. In some areas it was considered bad luck for the bride to make her own bridal, or 13th, quilt. At the bee to complete this quilt she could help mark the quilting lines, but she wasn't allowed to stitch on it.

Girls not old enough to be married held friendship bees. Each girl brought enough scraps from her own clothing to make a block. When the blocks were finished, they were set, and the completed top was given to one of the guests. The girl who received the quilt then gave a friendship bee of her own at which another girl was given a quilt. The round continued until each of the guests received a completed quilt top.

Around the 1840s, bees became exclusively female gatherings. The men weren't invited, and the dinner, dancing and games ended. Gone too was the courtship aspect of the quilting bee. But for the pioneer women who joined their husbands and families in the westward migration, bees continued to be eagerly sought social events. Alone they pieced, but together they quilted. Often there was only one quilt frame in the area, another reason for continuing the tradition of quilting bees. Alone on the frontier, there was often a rifle propped up against the quilt frame. A startling contrast to the simple thread, needle, and scissors the quilters used but, when needed, as much a necessity in the face of attack from wild animals as the quilt was to ward off the cold.

In urban areas, Album parties were held to make quilts for revered members of the community or a soon-to-be-moving-away, much-beloved minister's wife. Bees were also held to raise money for the church by either raffling off the finished quilt or by working for hire to quilt someone else's patchwork top.

Bees became quite exclusive and political, too. The inexpert or disliked women of the community weren't invited to join in the work. Any woman who wanted to get ahead or fit in, was wise to sharpen her needlework skills. And bees could have been the starting point for the feminist movement. We found two references that stated that Susan B. Anthony, to further her cause of giving women the vote, gave her speeches where the women were—in church basements at quilting bees!

The first half of the 19th century saw quiltmaking flourish. Advances in technology and a lifestyle with more leisure time had their affect on the art of quilts. In 1814 the Lowell Cotton Factory opened in Waltham, Massachusetts. It was the first factory in the world to combine, under one roof, all the operations of producing cloth from ginning raw cotton to producing finished yardage. Imported materials were available in great variety and at a cheap price. In fact, even after the War of 1812, England did its best to discourage the growth of textile manufacturing in America by flooding the United States with cheap cotton fabric. So strongly did the British want to preserve their import position that they actually sold the fabric at a loss to cut into domestic sales. Because of this importation of reasonably, even cheaply priced goods, American quiltmakers incorporated much English-made cloth into their quilts well past the 1850s. It's possible to find quilts with English fabrics in the tops and homespun for the back.

The period from 1775 to approximately 1840, was a boom period for quiltmaking.

"The decline in fabric prices and increasingly available fabric, plus a rising middle class with money to spend on fabric, made the quilt a more universal bed covering. . .," wrote Barbara Brackman in *Clues in the Calico*. In the early 1800s, quilting patterns were available that could be traced on fabric using a wheel. In 1810, the first agricultural fair was held in Pittsfield, Massachusetts, and soon regional fairs were being held all over the United States, a trend that continues today. Prize categories for needlework, quilts in particular, were part of the fairs. The competition among quiltmakers was friendly, but intense. Quilts were judged by the quality of the work, beauty, or originality in the use of a regional pattern. These show quilts exhibited the woman's thrift and work and reflected her expertise as a homemaker. Winning first prize at a country fair made a quiltmaker famous throughout her county. Gaining a reputation for expert needlework was sometimes more valued than the dictionaries, encyclopedias, newspaper subscriptions, and cash given as prizes. It was at these fairs that regional patterns were disseminated. Quiltmakers copied the winning designs to re-create and adapt them on their own. Like bees, fairs added to a woman's quilt knowledge and pattern pool because they exposed her to a greater number of quiltmakers. Women's fairs started in 1833 with the Philadelphia and Boston branches of the Female Anti-Slavery Society selling the needle-work of its members to raise money for their cause.

Also during this period, 1775–1840, quilting remained a source of income for women who needed to work. In Philadelphia, women with no means of support were hired by the Female Society for the Relief and Employment of the Poor to do knitting, spinning, and quilting. In 1831, the average daily pay for these professional quilters, if they were expert, was 15 cents. Stitching of less quality earned the women 12.5 cents per day.

In 1830, the first edition of *Godey's Lady's Book* appeared and, starting in 1835, the magazine often included quilt block patterns. Magazines would not become a major source of quilt patterns until 1875; except for Godey's, which was aimed at urban, middle-class women. For pattern sources, most quiltmakers continued to trade patterns among themselves and copy them from quilts entered in fairs.

Economic changes in the 1840s caused further changes in the making of quilts. From this time on, except for the pioneers, the popularity of quiltmaking alternately waned and peaked, influenced by depressions, economic booms and wars. As a general rule, during periods of prosperity, quiltmaking declined. During recessions and depressions, quiltmaking increased. It also appears that quiltmaking increased during periods of national unity such as the Civil War, the Centennial held in Philadelphia in 1876, both World Wars and the Bicentennial period.

Starting in the 1840s it was more common to see urban women working outside the home. Domestic textile production increased and cloth was still inexpensive and plentiful. Quilting was one of the forms of needlework included in the category of "fancy" handwork, skills even the working urban woman retained. Although she no longer had to make quilts out of necessity, she had both the money and the materials to create quilts of beauty. It is during this period, from the 1840s through the Civil War, that geometric pieced quilts saw the most development and innovation. "The most extraordinary examples of optical illusion quilts began to develop from the mid-nineteenth century onward, as block-work quilts became the preferred American system for construction," wrote Laura Fisher in her book *Quilts of Illusion*.

Not everyone in the country was enjoying the fruits of a growing economy. While eastern seaboard quiltmakers reaped the benefits of a plentiful supply of cheap fabric by returning to the more fabric-intensive appliqué-style quilts, pioneer families began their treks west in search of more land to farm or lured by the prospect of gold. For the pioneer quiltmaker, cloth was scarce and, when she could get it, expensive. During the westward expansion, many quilts were taken along. Quilts were used for more than warmth while sleeping. Wagon train travel was dirty, gritty, and exposed to the elements. Quilts were used to warm and comfort the ill, injured, and newly born. They were even used to wrap the dead before burial. All this took its toll on the family quilt. Given these circumstances, it's amazing that any survived at all. Yet, the California Heritage Quilt Project located 3,300 antique quilts that settled in California originating from 46 states, five other countries and three territories. Some of these quilts arrived in California via ship while others survived the tortuous Panama route carried by donkey across the isthmus.

Pioneer quiltmakers, by necessity, returned to old methods. They grew their own flax, and raised sheep. They carded, spun, and wove their own wool on spinning wheels and looms. They saved every scrap of fabric left over from other projects, including the last remnants of the calico dresses brought with them from the east. They collected natural dye recipes from neighbors and the folks back home to create their own colored fabrics. When fabric was available, they bought it and then shared scraps with their equally isolated neighbors. It's not unusual to find antique quilts from the same area made by different quiltmakers but containing the same swatches of fabric. Not all pioneer women made quilts. Settling the wilderness was a time-consuming and back-breaking job. Many didn't have the time, money or materials. But those who did, created beautiful geometric quilts of bright shades of red, green, purple, blue, pink, and yellow. Even for these isolated pioneer women, civilization arrived, and it wasn't long, relatively, before they too were creating quilts as much for their own enjoyment as out of necessity.

It was in the mid-1840s that the sewing machine was invented. Original models cost $500, a sum well out of reach of even the middle class. It took Isaac Singer to bring the sewing machine to the masses. Singer invented the installment plan and enabled quiltmakers to take to the new technology in droves. By 1860, the company was selling 111,000 sewing machines a year, each with a price tag of $75. By 1871, the price had dropped to $25. Quiltmakers grasped the new technology quickly, and Holstein estimates that fully half of all the quilts made after 1860 were machine pieced, a time-saving technique still used by most quiltmakers.

In the middle of this important period in the evolution of quilt design, the country went to war—with itself. Old traditions of thrift and economy returned as cloth manufacturers turned their machines to the production of uniforms and blankets. Women's groups of both the North and South turned their quiltmaking talents to providing quilts for soldiers. In *Quilts: A Window to the Past*, Victoria Hoffman notes that an astounding 250,000 quilts were made for Civil War soldiers! Most of these were used in hospitals. Since sterilizing a quilt was impossible, when a soldier died, the quilt was burned. In a 1987 article for *Quilting* magazine, Joseph Harriss told about a quilt made by the women of Westport, New York, for the town's militia Company A. Westport's Company A fought at Antietam, Gettysburg, and Richmond. The quilt was returned to Westport by Company A's survivors—the last three men. Many quilts were lost in the burning of the South and many were stolen and used so thoroughly that their remnants were thrown away. Fabric was again scarce, especially in the South. Northern embargoes on both domestic and imported cloth to the South increased prices to a high of $100 per yard. Once again, every scrap of fabric was saved to be used again, including militia uniforms, flannel sheets, old coats, cloak linings, and even petticoats.

Many commemorative quilts were made during this period depicting heroes, generals and leaders of both sides. Northern appliqué quilts included eagle designs and flags with all 34 stars, an obvious statement of their Union sentiments.

After the Civil War, cloth was once again plentiful and inexpensive. In fact, as the country converted from wartime to consumer production, manufactured goods of all kinds were readily available. Although it was in this time period that the first mass-produced, ready-made blankets appeared, quiltmakers stuck to their needles to produce bed coverings. It was still the most economical method of providing night warmth. In the late 1860s, six yards of cotton for a quilt top cost only 36 cents. Three yards of backing fabric sold for 75 cents, and batting prices ranged, according to quality, from 28 to 77 cents. A manufactured blanket cost anywhere from $2.25 to $8.00. When an entire quilt could be made with materials costing less than $1.50, why buy blankets? To save time and labor, of course, and eventually mass-produced blankets ate into hand made quilt production. Increased technology produced copies of previously high-priced curtains, hangings and Oriental rugs. Women turned to other forms of fancy-work, like needlepoint, to satisfy their creativity.

The last quarter of the 19th century saw quiltmaking reach an epiphany. The Centennial Celebration held in Philadelphia in 1876 revived interest in all forms of needlework including quilting. The fad for Colonial-style furnishings produced a quilting frenzy.

"Women whose families had left them quiltless were forced either to collect or make quilts in order to be in fashion," wrote Penny McMorris and Michael Kile in *The Art Quilt*. What we know as typical of Amish quilting began in the last quarter of the 19th century. This same period brought a revival of the Crazy Quilt style. Once the lowliest of quilt designs, a purely functional use of leftover fabrics, the crazy quilt reached its high point in the late 1800s and became the quilt of choice. The Crazies were exquisite, elaborate, and expensive. Silk, satin, brocade, and velvet were bought expressly to make these quilts—no leftovers for these family status symbols! The Album quilt also developed during this period. In its short, two-decade-long appearance, the Baltimore Album Quilt, the most elaborate, most exquisitely worked of all album quilts, made an indelible mark on quiltmaking history. They were highly valued as gifts then and are equally valued by collectors today.

But eventually the frenzy died out. "Eighteen-eighty is an important date in the progress of American womankind; for it was only after 1880 that woman's economic and political status really began to change," wrote Ruth Finley in *Old Patchwork Quilts*. "Freed in the end from psychological as well as material restraints, woman closed the gate at the end of many a road. Her journey of more than two and a half centuries along the trail of her patchwork was finished. The story of her heart, as written in this particular work of her hands, was done."

Unfortunately, Finley was correct. The late 1800s and early 1900s saw the advent of quilts made from printed cloth premiums—usually flags—included in coffee, tobacco, flour, sugar and tea purchases. The first brochure of pieced and appliquéd quilt designs was published in 1898 and included 420 patterns. But it wasn't enough. By the late 1800s, quilting was a rare pastime. There were still some clubs, the occasional article in a women's magazine and prize categories at regional fairs, but quiltmaking took a back seat to the technology of mass production. In the 1890s, ready-made comforters were available in dry-goods stores. Although available since before the Civil War, factory-made blankets were not in general use until the late 1800s and early 1900s.

Finally, the fashion trend toward manufactured bedspreads further reduced the amount of quiltmaking. In 1903, *Cutter's Red Book of Ready Reference* was published. In it, the use of quilts on beds was discouraged as out of fashion. To replace them, the book recommended all-white, manufactured spreads. The convincing argument was that once a quiltmaker's labor was added in, a manufactured spread was actually cheaper than a quilt. Many quilt owners turned their pieced and appliqué masterpieces over, showing the plain white side, decorated with quilting instead of the patchwork top. *See illustration #8.*

8

8 This Pine Tree variation is done in a lovely green and gold paisley fabric on a white ground. Made in North Carolina in the early 1900s, its simple border and classic block arrangement create an elegant look. Quilt courtesy of Cindie Freeman.

But quilting never disappeared. In 1915 the first full-length work on quilting, *Quilts: Their Story and How to Make Them*, by Marie D. Webster appeared just in time to be used by a new wave of quiltmakers. Not only advice was available. In the quilting revival that occurred "between the wars" as Carter Houck described it in an article for *Quilt Craft* magazine, new dyes and new print technology produced inexpensive cottons in many colors and prints. Manufacturers produced what are now called "the pastels." These fabrics, farthest from the soft colors we'd call pastels, were bright prints dotted, sprigged, lined and detailed with flowers, art deco geometric designs, zigzags, plaids, stripes, or figures of animals, people, or cars and airplanes. Some of these prints were so gaudy that it's a wonder they found their way into clothing at all. In fact, many of them didn't. They were bought expressly by quiltmakers to include in their art because they were affordable. A yard of these whimsical prints could be purchased for a pittance by today's standards, between 9 and 18 cents a yard.

Even through the Great Depression, quilts were made from these fabrics. Depression-era quilts are among the most endearing of all quilts ever made. This was the era of Sunbonnet Sue, Scottie Dogs, airplanes, scrap bag Trip Around the World, the Double Wedding Ring, Grandmother's Flower Garden, and Dresden Plate. In the late 1920s, fabric stores carried not only reproductions of old glazed chintz and upholstery fabrics, but also cloth printed with old quilt designs. Called cheater cloth, the pre-printed design eliminated the need to piece a block—the fabric came printed with it! Cheater fabrics are still available today. The Great Depression saw many a quilt made from the printed cloth of feed bags. Sometimes, Depression-era quilts were used to pay debts in lieu of cash, and some were even used to meet tithing pledges at church.

To meet the demand of the quilting revival, the years 1927 through 1939 saw the most quilting brochures ever published. Patterns were developed by specialized businesses such as the Home Art Studios, Colonial Pattern Company, McKim Studios, and Ladies Art. Quiltmaking supply houses, such as Mountain Mist, also created patterns and supplied them free inside their packaging. Newspapers ran their own quiltmaking and pattern columns or bought syndicated columns. In 1934, over 400 newspapers ran regular quilting columns.

In 1933, Sears, Roebuck, and Company sponsored a quilt contest in conjunction with the Chicago World's Fair named the Century of Progress Exposition. Many of the 24,878 quilts entered in the contest for a $1,000 first prize were pictorial; all were beautiful, and fueled the raging interest in quiltmaking.

Also contributing to the quilt revival of the 1920s and 1930s was Eleanor Roosevelt's active promotion of American arts and crafts, which gave all women's arts new status. The WPA even funded some quilt projects. The social, political, economic and patriotic events of those decades revived the practice of using a quilt to make a statement. Political and commemorative quilts were made again and many quilts were made with the Scottie dog pattern, which originated with Roosevelt's little dog, Fala. Following a tradition almost as old as our country itself, quilts as fund-raisers helped to buy at least one bomber for use in World War II.

It was toward the end of the war that quilt kits abounded. Entire quilts, with color, size, and design already chosen and, in some cases, the fabric already cut into pattern pieces, were readily available. According to authors Penny McMorris and Michael Kile (*The Art Quilt*), the proliferation of these kits, which eliminated color and design decisions, led to the decline in quiltmaking that followed World War II. Opportunities for creativity and individuality were starkly reduced using the kit method.

It's more likely that the post-World War II decline in quiltmaking should be attributed to rapid changes in the lives of women. Many kept their war-production jobs and started careers, leaving little time to devote to needlework of any kind. The 1950s were a prosperous and optimistic period. Quilts were a reminder of the Depression. In the fifties, scrimping was over. Machine-made quilts were available in department stores, the result of the quilting revival of the previous three decades, which spurred manufacturers to produce cheap reproductions of antique quilts. The forties, fifties, and early sixties passed with many fewer quilts made and little added to quilt design or innovation. The Baby Boom sent women back to their sewing machines but it was to produce needed clothing, not quilts.

Then, the beginning of a new revival occurred when Vogue Magazine included photographs of interior home design that included patchwork quilts. Soon, all the magazines followed suit, using quilts in their photo spreads depicting the perfectly decorated home. The late 1960s also saw a renewed interest in the arts and crafts of the late 1800s. According to McMorris and Kile, both the use of quilts for interior decoration and the crafts revival were reactions against the increased technology of the time. People were turning away from what they perceived to be the evils of industrialization and surrounding themselves with examples of a simpler time and lifestyle and prime among these examples were quilts.

Inflation, unemployment, and the gas crisis all contributed to a return to quiltmaking. Making and using a quilt as a wall hanging was cheaper than throwing out what you had and buying new furniture. Quilts were also viewed as valuable gifts. The same amount of money one would spend for a much smaller gift could produce a stunning quilt. By the end of the 1960s, quiltmaking was once again established as the darling of all needlework.

From 1965 to 1974, sales of all hobby supplies doubled. For the first time in many years, companies selling how-to books and quilting supplies saw profits rise. Magazines and newspapers were once again carrying, on a regular basis, columns and articles about quilting. The seventies, with the Bicentennial looming ever closer, began a nostalgia craze that increased the value and status of antique quilts and quiltmaking in general.

"...For it is only recently that quilts have been acknowledged as the visual precursors of many of the design innovations and color systems that were later employed in practitioners of Op Art and other contemporary painting," wrote Laura Fisher in her book *Quilts of Illusion*. Museums exhibited collections of antique quilts, showing them hung on walls rather than spread on beds, and the quilt began its slow yet unswerving journey toward achieving art status.

The Bicentennial fueled this latest quiltmaking revival. *Good Housekeeping* sponsored a national quilt contest. The magazine estimated 3,500 entries and received over 10,000. Quilts from kits were not eligible. The quilts had to be traditional or innovative designs. The 1970s produced the next evolution in quilt design, the art quilt. Quilt shows were held in halls, schools, and churches all over the country in tribute to the 200th anniversary of our country's birth. Quiltmakers went back to work or entered the hobby for the first time.

Art quilts aside, the Bicentennial quilt revival will be remembered for its plethora of sampler quilts and the use of coordinated fabrics. The sampler quilt, with each block a different pattern, was still the best way to learn quiltmaking quickly. By completing 20, 24, or 30 different blocks, the beginning quiltmaker learned most of the piecing and appliquéing techniques she needed to "graduate" to more difficult designs or to create her own. These sampler quilts, which we think will be the collectible quilt of the Bicentennial period, were made with coordinating fabrics. The 1970s were not a scrimping time any more than the 1950s were. Fabric was bought expressly, exclusively, and sometimes expensively, for quilts. The scrap bag quilt, though some were made, was mostly ignored. This trend toward complementary fabrics in a quilt continues today. Personally, we hope that contemporary quiltmakers will eventually return to their scrap bags and innovate with them.

There are also those historians who believe that, along with the nostalgia craze started by the Bicentennial, the feminist movement also fueled the current quilt revival. The interest of contemporary women in their female ancestors necessitated the study of quilts. As women became more and more aware of the contributions of their grandmothers and great-grandmothers, quilts were recognized as valuable records of their ancestors lives. With this recognition came the realization that quiltmaking was one way to preserve their own history as well.

One outgrowth of the renewed interest in quilts from the Bicentennial period is the many quilt discovery projects that occurred across the country. Usually organized by state, these committees of knowledgeable quiltmakers and historians advertise special days and locations where residents can bring their prized family heirloom quilts, or collections, to be photographed, dated and appraised. In this way, thousands and thousands of quilts are now recorded, with pictures including the details of their pattern, maker and history. Estimates are that the hundreds of hours of work by these groups have uncovered only about 10 percent of the antique quilts that exist today.

Another vital contribution from the documentation of existing antique quilts is the increased information available to quilt historians. Because the quilts were closely studied and their histories recorded, several myths about quiltmaking history are being challenged. Perhaps quilts were not quite as common in Colonial days as was previously thought. Certainly, quilts were not only made when fabric was in short supply. In several periods of our history, quiltmaking flourished when fabric was plentiful.

Finally, the myth that all quilts were created solely from necessity is being refuted. It seems that if we could let go of legend and let our common sense prevail, we'd be able to see in our antique quilts that they were always works of art. Quilting was, and is, time consuming, and homemakers have always been thrifty and efficient. To spend the countless hours it takes to make a quilt of striking beauty when it was necessary only to tie three layers together, would have been ridiculous—an endeavor scorned by any practical, frugal homemaker. Logic dictates that the creation of quilts had to be a work of love and art. If for nothing else, we owe a debt of thanks to the quilt-recording projects for dispelling the myth that quilts were made only out of necessity. The women who made these treasures from the past knew they were creating beauty, not solely function.

At the height of the 1970s quilt revival, quilts from the previous century were considered the most valuable to collect. Because they were "of our own time," 20th century quilts were overlooked as collectibles.

". . . The '20s and '30s were still too close to have great appeal," wrote Carter Houck in *Quilt Craft* magazine. "Collectors looked to the 19th century for pieces 'worth having' and the owners of 'Depression Quilts' that had come down in their families used them at best in the kids' rooms and at worst in the driveway when they had to get down to inspect the nether regions of a car."

Fortunately, that attitude no longer prevails in the new millennium. Starting in the 1980s, with the advent of the quilt documentation projects, many people realized the importance of quilts from the first half of the 20th century. As we became more interested in the history and significance of quilts, we realized that we had a pool of quiltmakers from those years who were not anonymous. Here were quiltmakers we could actually talk to, with their own quilts that we could see and feel. From these 20th-century quiltmakers we gained a firsthand knowledge of the period and the quilts they produced, complete with memories, anecdotes, and experiences we could share. Our longing to know the intimate details of a quilt could be satisfied. Written records are readily available. It's possible, and sometimes relatively easy, to trace a family's path of migration, locate descendants and verify clues, suggestions, sentiments, and opinions included in a quilt. We realized that we should preserve our own books, papers, letters, and memories so that future generations would know the reasons for our choices rather than be left answerless, wondering and imagining.

Quiltmaking survives today because it is as beautiful and versatile an art as it ever was and because it continues to make and reflect history. Though interest in it may wane and peak over long periods of time, we're sure this art will continue for many more centuries. Certainly the collection and preservation of quilts will continue. Very soon, those coordinated-fabric sampler quilts made during the Bicentennial will join their precursors as valuable collectibles.

Now, in the year 2003, quiltmaking and collecting is going strong. As mentioned in Chapter 2, a cursory search on the Internet provides over 43,000 listings for quilts and quilt history. Fabric stores set aside space solely for quilting fabric and supplies, and classes are as popular, if not more so, than they were during the Bicentennial. Quilt guilds and national organizations abound and membership grows. Quilt appraisal certification courses are offered by these national organizations and professional appraisers are choosing to specialize in quilts. Methods and patterns are used by today's quiltmakers, including a resurgence of paper piecing, that were popular as long as two centuries ago.

No, Americans didn't invent quilting and they didn't invent using quilting technique or its result as decoration. But they did challenge their creativity and expand quiltmaking beyond what it was, discovering what it could be: art.

4 Dating a Quilt

Approximating the date a quilt was completed is important in determining its value. Age isn't the only standard for value. A truly stunning but newer quilt is sometimes far more valuable than a dull, older one. But the age of a quilt is important. Unless the maker dated it, determining the age of a quilt is an exacting, sometimes instinctive, job.

The easiest way to date a quilt, of course, is if the maker thought to include the day and year she completed her quilt. One collector found a crazy quilt with two dates: 1894 and 1896. This quiltmaker started her crazy quilt in 1894 and took two years to complete it, finishing in 1896. We're very grateful to this quiltmaker because she has added immeasurably to our study of antique quilts simply by adding those two dates. She left us a record of what fabrics were available during those years, of what style of quilt was popular, and the quality and diversity of stitching patterns used by quilters in the last years of the 19th century.

There were fads and fashions in the way a quilt was signed, just as different patterns were popular at different times. Easily located dates on quilts are those that were written in pen or indelible marker or those that were appliquéd. Dates and signatures quilted on are the most difficult to find because they tend to blend in with the rest of the quilting stitches. Check both the back and front of a quilt, especially the borders if the quilt has them, inch by inch, looking for a date or signature worked in quilting stitches.

Most quiltmakers didn't sign or date their quilts, so if you don't find one, don't despair. Dating without notation on a quilt is tricky but not impossible. All aspects of the quilt must be taken into consideration: the fabric, colors, patterns, quilting style, batting, thread and techniques used can all point to a quilt's age. The specifics of dating follow in this chapter, but we'll give you one example now:

A quilt's age is determined by the date it was finished, not started. Many quilts are multigenerational, sometimes skipping a generation between the original maker and the finisher. For

9

10

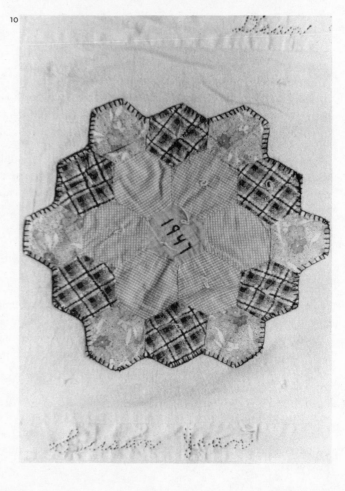

9 Knowing the maker and date of a quilt is important to a collector. This close up of red embroidery on a white ground shows the initials of the maker and the year it was finished. Quilt courtesy of the Atwater Family.

10 In an unusual assembly, this Grandmother's Flower Garden block is appliquéd to yellow fabric. Color balance is excellent in this scrap bag block. The yellow sashing has embroidered names of the maker's descendants. It's also dated. Quilt courtesy of the Belden Family.

whatever reasons, (death, illness, lack of time, or boredom) someone started a quilt, never finished it, and stored it away. Along comes a descendant, daughter or granddaughter, who discovers the uncompleted quilt in a drawer or trunk. Delighted over her find, she finishes the quilt using fabrics from her own time period. Although the original fabrics may be much older, the addition of new fabric and the completion process dates the quilt to the time it was finished. The older fabrics can, and should be, noted in the documentation of the quilt, but it is still dated to the time period when it was finished. If the finisher knew when the quilt was started and included that date along with the finish date, this would add to the value of a quilt. Most multigenerational quilts are neither signed nor dated. The moral of this tale is that quilts should be dated by finding the newest, youngest fabric, binding, or thread used in it. *See illustrations #9 and #10.*

Even when a quilt was completed by only one quiltmaker, the newest fabric is still the most accurate judge of when it was made. Scrap bag quilts are still in style and have been for centuries. A woman's scrap bag can include some very old fabrics. Just because they're used in a new quilt doesn't make that quilt an antique.

"My own scrap bag contains fabric 50 years old," notes author Liz Aleshire. "It's full of remnants from my grandmother, my mother and myself. I'm still making quilts from these scraps."

Other considerations for dating a quilt include checking the batting and thread, noting a popular color or fabric print style specific to a period in textile history, and studying the waning and peaking of quilting techniques and styles. And that's when dating gets tricky.

If you're going to pursue this hobby or invest your money in quilts, you'll have to educate yourself on the fads and fashions of four centuries of quiltmaking. Although that sounds like a daunting task, don't despair. It's fun! We'll get you started in this chapter to increase your knowledge and hone your instincts. We certainly can't cover the dating of quilts in the detail you'll require in a book of this size. But we hope we'll pique your interest, sending you to the Bibliography at the back to begin your journey to quilt historian status.

Your education should include, along with the books listed in our Bibliography, any you can find on your own. Ours certainly isn't a complete list. You'll want to visit museums, both quilt and textile, and add their papers, exhibit catalogs and specially published books to your collection. You'll want to scour through old textile manufacturers' catalogs, examine advertisements in old newspapers for dry goods, and read and study the tips for home decoration found in old magazines. Make notes and compile your own date-specific list of quilt attributes. Cruising the Internet provides a wealth of information and detail to add to your knowledge.

Most important, you'll need to look at quilts. Go to as many quilt shows as you can. Find all the dealers in your area and visit them. Watch for quilt dealers and shops everywhere you go. Make notes of these visits, too, recording the exceptions you find, always adding to your growing pile of quilt lore and fact. At some point you'll find yourself questioning the date a museum or dealer has on a quilt and you'll know then that you're well on your way to being an expert.

We're extremely grateful to one author on quilt dating and we strongly recommend you start your own historical quest with Barbara Brackman's *Clues in the Calico* and *Encyclopedia of*

Pieced Quilt Patterns. Ruth Finley's book, *Old Patchwork Quilts,* is also valuable for placing certain block and quilting patterns to their place in history.

To accurately date a quilt, you should know something about the material it's made from.

Fabric

Until the 1900s, there were only four sources from which to make fabric and these were all natural. Animal sources were silk and wool; plant sources were linen and cotton. Quilts were often made incorporating different types of fabric as well as different weaves and textures. It wasn't too long, however, before quiltmakers realized that using the same type of fabric throughout was both easier and more pleasing when finished.

You'll need to know about these four types of natural fabrics. Silk is cloth woven from cocoon wrappings, primarily those of the silkworm. Silk was always a high cost, luxury fabric. A wide variety of imported raw silks and silk goods were available. Bombazine (or bombazeen) was introduced after the 16th century. It had two distinctive features. First, it was woven with a silk warp and a worsted weft. Second, it was dyed after it was woven instead of before. The sheen of silk was imitated in other fabrics, most notably in chintz by using a glaze and in worsteds by pressing.

Wool is cloth made of carded, short-staple wool fibers. It was the English wool broadcloth industry that the British tried to protect by discouraging a textile industry in the American colonies. Once the wool was woven, it was shrunk to tighten the weave. The finished fabric was dense, heavy, and warm. When a wool was calendered, it was pressed between two heated rollers that produced a sheen to the fabric. Calendered wool was finely woven and shiny. It was a popular fabric from 1750 to the 1840s, so a quilt with this fabric strongly points to those dates.

Linen is made from fibers from the flax plant. It was an arduous process, even given that everything done in Colonial days was arduous, to make linen from flax. It took over a year to grow the flax, remove the seeds, rot the plant, separate the fiber from the chaff, separate the fine, weavable fibers from the tow, spin it, and weave it. That any linen was made at all seems a super-human feat to us. In an effort to find work for the poor and to encourage the manufacture of linen in America, the Massachusetts General Court, in 1753, put a tax on coaches and similar vehicles to raise money to promote a textile industry. This law was the response to England's increasing stranglehold on the colonies. The law circumvented English authority and pushed the colonists closer to independence.

Before we go on to cotton, let's discuss linsey-woolsey. Linsey-woolsey is a fabric with a linen warp and a woolen weft. It's a coarse fabric used more for utility than for best quilts. There is still some confusion over linsey-woolsey quilts. We found references to quilts made of linsey-woolsey, quilts made with a linen top and a wool back called linsey-woolsey, and quilts made of whole-cloth wool that were intricately quilted also called linsey-woolsey quilts. As near as we can come to clearing up the confusion is that a linsey-woolsey quilt must be made of linsey-woolsey fabric. What is commonly referred to today as a linsey-woolsey is a top layer of woolen or glazed worsted dyed a single color, usually dark but sometimes in a light blue, raspberry or pink. The backs of these quilts were made from a coarser woolen fabric in its natural color or dyed yellow or gold. This was layered with carded wool and intricately quilted with floral, feather, heart, cornucopia, interlocking circle, or crossed diagonal designs. They are also noted for their notched-out corners so that the quilt would lay flat on the bed with its edges hanging around the bedposts. These quilts are huge and heavy. Some of these style of linsey-woolsey quilts were probably imported. Even those made in the United States used imported fabric for the tops and either homespun or old fabric for the backing. There is also a linsey-woolsey made from a top layer of linen and a backing of wool.

The weaving of woolens and linens and the combination linsey-woolsey was common in Colonial households. The weaving of cotton was not. After the Revolution, a cotton industry had to be developed but England owned all the patents for the necessary machinery: spinning jenny, fly shuttle, spinning frame, and power loom. No one was allowed to bring the technology to the new country.

From ancient times, cotton fibers have been spun into cloth. Five thousand years ago, the peoples of India, Pakistan, Peru and Mexico grew cotton. There is some evidence that Native Americans used cotton in the Southwest as many as 1300 years ago. Cotton arrived in Europe in the 3rd century, B.C., with Alexander the Great. India chintzes, either hand painted or dyed using a wax-resist method, were cheaper in Europe in 1630 than silks and velvets. These India chintzes were highly valued because of their color fastness. Some of these were glazed, giving them a wonderful surface sheen.

In 1754, chintz patterns with vegetable dyes were printed in London. The spinning jenny, capable of spinning 8 to 11 threads at a time, was invented by James Hargraves in 1765. In 1769, Richard Arkwright used a roller spinning method that pulled and twisted yarn, then wound it on spools in one application. *See illustration #11.*

From the time of the Revolutionary War until the present day, quiltmakers preferred cotton, especially calico. Today we know calico as a cotton printed with small figures, but in the past it meant any cotton, plain, printed, or white, and included chintz and muslin. Even the spelling of the word has changed over the centuries from *callicoe* in 1700–1775, to *calicoe* in 1775–1825 and finally to *calico* as we know it today. Calico was the most popular fabric for gowns, hence it was also popular for quilts. Half of the textiles made in the world today are cotton!

It's important to know something about the various weaves of cloth. There are three main weaving patterns: plain, satin, and twill. From these all other variations are derived. In the plain weave, warp and weft threads are equal. The filling yarns, or wefts, pass under and over the warps in alternating rows. This is also called the taffeta or tabbyweave. Plain weave is so common among all fibers that it's not reliable for dating.

In the satin weave, the weft threads, those that run side to side on the fabric, don't go over and under each of the warp threads, those that run the length of the fabric, as they do on the plain weave. These "loose" thread lengths on the surface of the cloth produce the high sheen. Although the same process of weaving is used, there's a difference between satin and sateen. Satin is usually made from silk or silky threads while sateen is made from cotton.

11 This close up of a Trip Around the World assembly using the hexagon of Grandmother's Flower Garden shows the traditional 'bands' of tones of color. Quilt courtesy of the Belden Family

The twill pattern is similar to the satin in that the weft doesn't go over and under each warp thread but may go under one and over two. Unlike the satin weave, however, the pattern is alternated so that it produces diagonal lines over the fabric instead of the smooth, surface sheen of satin weave. A short trip to a fabric store will get you enough samples of each weave so you'll be able to recognize them when you see them.

The compactness of the weaving is measured by the number of warp and weft threads to the square inch. The more compact a weave, the more durable the fabric. Tightly woven fabric is of higher quality. To give you some idea of the numbers, tobacco cloth is a very loose weave with a count of 20 threads. Fine percale sheeting, on the other hand, is a tight weave averaging 200 threads to the square inch. The cotton most typical in quilts is a standard weave of 50 to 75 threads per square inch. To determine the quality of a weave, use a magnifying glass or loupe to count the threads. The style of weaving is rarely used to date a quilt, but it does help to distinguish quality fabrics from cheap ones.

Glazes are used on fabrics to make them stiffer and give them sheen. As noted before, glazes were used to make cotton competitive with silk. Glazes, made from wax, egg whites or resins, were applied to plain and twill weaves. Another style of glazing was to calender. In this process the fabric is forced between two heated cylinders. The combination of heat and pressure creates a surface glaze on the fabric.

No discussion of quilting fabric is complete without mentioning homespun. Homespun fabric is one way to date a quilt. By the second quarter of the 19th century, homespun was a thing of the past in all but the most remote areas of the country. Settled communities had ready access to cotton. Any quilt containing homespun should be dated before the 1830s. But, it's not as easy to identify homespun fabric as you might think.

Homespun fabric is defined by irregular-sized threads. The thickness of the thread varies randomly throughout the fabric and the weave is loose, supposedly the result of the inferior expertise of the colonial spinner and weaver. However, some home spinners created homespun of very high quality with even threads and a tight weave. Some textile manufacturers produced a cheap backing cloth that could be described the same way as the traditional definition of homespun. In fact, fabric that looks like homespun is still available in stores today. So just looking at the fabric and noting thread irregularities and loose weaving isn't sufficient to call a cloth homespun.

There are ways to tell, however. Most homespun is from wool or linen. The quilts called linsey-woolseys, that we discussed earlier, could have homespun backing fabric. The first thing to check on homespun wool is the number of plies in the thread. If the cloth was woven from single ply thread, chances are it's homespun. If a double ply of threads was used, then the piece was probably manufactured.

A fabric claimed to be cotton homespun should be tested by determining if the quilt was made in a cotton-producing region, and if the quiltmaker was so isolated from civilization that she simply had to invest her time in hand spinning. Even if the answer is yes to both these tests, it still doesn't guarantee that the cloth is homespun. Home-produced wool and linen were used in quilts, and pioneer families, isolated from dry goods stores, did make their own fabrics, but finding homespun in a quilt is much rarer than once believed.

There are other difficulties in dating a quilt by determining its fabric content. Fabric names and styles have changed over the four centuries of quilting. A fabric we recognize today may have had a different name a hundred years ago. Some fabrics have disappeared and new ones been created. Even the names that did exist 200 years ago have come to mean something else. For instance, at one time cotton was a term used for certain woolen cloths that date from the 15th century. The process of raising the nap on wool was once called cottoning. Chintz once meant any printed cloth, usually with a glaze but not always. Today chintz can be plain or printed but is always glazed. Florence M. Montgomery in her book *Textiles in America 1650–1870* lists 60 fabrics made from wool! Ruth Finley lists over 20 fabrics that no longer exist.

As we move closer to our own time, there were some fabric styles that are good indicators of the date of a quilt. For most of the 19th century, ending approximately in 1875, a fabric called sarcenet cambric was popular. This was an opaque cotton of fine weave with a smoothness that approached silk. From 1875 to 1925, cotton flannel in plaids and stripes was used to back wool quilts. You can safely place such a quilt within those years. In that same period, pile weaves became popular for quilting. Pile weaves, velvets and corduroy, add an extra yarn, loosely woven, into the fabric. These "loose" yarns actually stick up from the fabric and are evenly cut to produce the soft, fuzzy texture of their surface. These fabrics were combined with the brocades, taffetas, and satins in crazy quilts.

Another distinctive fabric popular approximately from 1880 to 1920 was cretonne. It was used for curtains and upholstery and found its way into scrap bags and then into quilts. It was a twill weave with large prints and unglazed. In the 1890s, feed sack prints were introduced, and many of these found their way into quilts and were used until the 1940s. These were loosely woven cotton printed in bright patterns. They were especially popular during the Depression. Quilts of Sunbonnet Sues, Dresden Plate and Double Wedding Ring patterns made from feed sack cloth can still be found.

The first quarter of the 20th century saw the quality of fabrics deteriorate. Weaves were less compact, the result of trying to keep prices down, and dyes weren't colorfast. There was a chintz produced that was so cheap it lost its sizing in the first wash. *Chintzy* became a popular word for anything cheap, and what was once the highest quality cotton used in quilts became the most ignored. Inexpensive but quality cottons were available in limited, plain colors such as blue, gray, black, and maroon.

Cotton sateens were popular in the second quarter of the 20th century, making them a good indicator of the age of the quilt. Synthetic satin was also popular for whole-cloth quilts and tied comforters. Coverlets of satin, in the puff style, were popular during the 1925–50 period, so popular, in fact, that manufacturers mass produced them.

Polyester was invented in 1953 and was soon used in quilting. Its durability, colorfastness, and resistance to creasing made it seem the fabric of the future to quilters. Polyester and polyester/cotton blends are used in quilts intended for utilitarian purposes. Quilters today may choose polyester/cotton blends to complete baby and high-use bed and lap quilts to ensure they'll stand up to hard use and repeated washings. But tradition prevails, and today's dedicated quilters have returned to the use of 100 percent cotton in their prized quilts.

We've included some specific fabric names, descriptions and definitions in the Glossary.

Color

Throughout history people have searched for better, brighter, colorfast dyes. They turned to plants, the soil, rocks, even animals. As technology and science advanced, they turned to synthetic compounds as well. The Phoenicians, Greeks, Romans, and ancient Peruvians searched for better dyestuffs. Early textile fragments uncovered in archaeological digs show that dyeing fabric was well known in Mesopotamia, India, and Egypt by 3000 B.C.

Rarely does a single color give us many clues as to the date of a quilt. Luckily, quiltmakers have chosen print fabrics for their quilts from the very beginning. These printed fabrics and their use at different periods over the history of quilting, combined with what we know were fashionable combinations of colors, do provide us with evidence of a quilt's date.

Different fabric fibers need different methods of dyeing. Some natural dyes don't fix to animal fibers and a mordant must be added to the dye mix to make the fabric absorb the dye. *Mordant* comes from the Latin word *mordere*, which means to bite. That's basically what a mordant does. It allows the dye to "bite" the fabric, or become fast. Mordants are metallic oxides or minerals such as alum, cream of tartar, ammonia, chrome, tin, iron, copper sulfate, tannin, vinegar, baking soda, or oxalic acid. Some metallic salts that worked on both animal and vegetable-based fabrics were used as mordants because they improved colorfastness. To place several colors on the same fabric, a mordant is used so that the dye used with it "bites" or bonds only where the mordant lies on the fabric.

The resist method of dyeing is the opposite of mordanting. In this method the portions of cloth that are not to be printed are treated with a resisting chemical. When the fabric is dyed, the dye will not take to the fabric treated with the resist and in these areas, the background color shows through. In half resist, the areas where dye is not wanted are only partially pro-

12 This kit quilt, completed in the early 1900s, shows considerable color fading. The quilting stitches, at ten per inch, are well done. Quilt from the authors' collection.

tected from the dye. This produces a blend of colors, or, in the case of white, a lighter shade of the background color.

Until 1856 the only dyes available for either manufacturers or individuals were derived from vegetable, mineral, or animal sources. Among these were blue, from indigo; browns and Turkey red from the roots of the madder plant; black from logwood; and yellow from the wood of the fustic tree in the West Indies. Madder was grown in the American colonies in small amounts. Most was imported. Indigo was the only commercial dye crop grown in America, and southern ports exported tons of it to the world. *See illustration #12.*

Quiltmakers joined in the quest for colorfast dyes. It just didn't make sense to put all that work into a best quilt, one that you wanted to give as a gift or hand down to your children, only to find that the colors bled, faded, or crocked and then ruined it. Over the centuries they tried the new dyes brought on the market, rejected those that were inferior, and returned to those that were colorfast.

Dye recipes, like quilt patterns, were handed down over generations. *Godey's Lady's Book* regularly printed dye recipes. Fabric was dyed at home commonly up to 1860, and women knew their recipes so well that they manipulated them, as they did their favorite family food recipes, to produce shades and tones of color they wanted. Often they dyed entire bolts of cloth—as much as 20 yards at a time. Piece dyeing continued in the home through the 1950s, and actually continues to today. In 1863, the first packaged dyes of natural sources were marketed. In 1880, the first synthetic dyes were available for homemakers to purchase and use. Up until World War I, Germany was the best source for good synthetic dyes. Now, the United States is the number one exporter of dyestuffs.

Just as it's hard to determine if a fabric is homespun or manufactured, it's also difficult to recognize a home dye job from a manufactured one. Homemakers and manufacturers used the same commercial dyes and both did good and bad jobs using them. Don't assume a low-quality dye job was done in the home.

"Most of the blotchy, fading fabrics we see in old quilts were probably factory fabric," wrote Barbara Brackman in *Clues in the Calico*.

Gingham fabrics are weak indicators for dating fabric. In these fabrics, the yarns were dyed with a color and then woven together to produce the checks and stripes. Ginghams derive their color scheme from weaving, not printing, and were so widely used over the centuries that they are not a good indicator for dating the quilts that incorporate them.

Color loss on a quilt contributes more to a loss in value than stains. Sometimes, as we'll see when we get to specific colors, loss is indicative of a time period. In this case it can increase the value of a quilt simply because we know more about that quilt's history. It shows how the dye affected fabric over time.

We'd like to point out some general trends in the use of color before we get down to specifics. For reasons we'll soon cover, the colors most preferred in Colonial days, if the ads from the period are read, were blue, crimson, and green. It's not too surprising, actually, since these dyes resulted in the most colorfast fabrics of the time. Red and white, and blue and white, were, and continue to be, traditional color choices for such patterns as drunkard's path and Irish chain.

New dyes for brown, based on manganese, were introduced in 1825. These browns were brighter, less dull than the browns achieved from vegetable sources. They worked particularly well as backgrounds, as they didn't overpower other colors printed on them. The Civil War with its attendant low cloth supply and high prices brought the cheaper browns back into use. Even these new browns took a back seat, for a time, to the lavender and gray colors popular in the 1850s. Madder-brown dyes were still used as dyes until the end of the 1800s. Some of the "new" brown dyes didn't stand the test of time. They corroded the cotton where the dye had fixed. You'll find quilts with holes in the tops that correspond to the figure or print on the fabric. Those holes were probably created by the corrosive effect of the dyes.

Aniline dyes were introduced after the middle of the 19th century. The discovery of aniline for use with dyes added colorfast mauves, alizarin red, greens, and other browns to a quilt-maker's range of colors.

More quiltmakers purchased fabric specifically for quilts starting about 1840. From then until the turn of the century, there was a fashion for quilts of only one color combined with white. Turkey red or green with a white background fabric were the most often chosen. Navy, red, or green were chosen to go with white in two-color quilts. One quilt historian surmised that so many of these quilts survived to our time because their basic colors made them difficult to decorate with. One-color and two-color quilts are valued by collectors.

There was a tan period in quiltmaking history dating from the 1860s through the 1880s. There's an odd blue, described as a dark blue with green-turquoise overtones that can date a quilt to the 1870s and 1880s. Rusts were popular in quilts from 1885 to 1910. A cotton print with a black background was a popular fabric for quilts starting in 1890 and continuing through the first quarter of the 20th century.

The early 1900s saw a revival in the use of tan in quilts. Popular color schemes were blues and green in the 1920s with lavender making a brief comeback in the 1930s. This was also the period of the pastels, those brightly colored, often thought gaudy calicoes so popular in Dresden Plate and Double Wedding Ring quilts. The 1920s and 1930s were also the time of the feed sack cottons with their bright prints.

Let's get specific.

White

White, as an indicator, isn't very date-specific. It's been used in quilts during all periods. To get them white, natural fibers had to be bleached. Sun bleaching fabrics was common until 1774 and the discovery of chlorine. Chlorine shortened and simplified the bleaching process, but it also damaged the fibers and made the cloth wear out sooner. Grass bleaching became popular again in the 1930s and 1940s to remove the lettering from flour and sugar sacks so they could be used in quilts. The only white that can point to a date for a quilt is actually a print on white. From 1870 to 1925, quilters used white background shirting fabrics distinctive for their small figured prints. After 1925, use of these shirting fabrics died out, and quilters returned to plain white fabric.

Blue

This is another color that has had so much use over the centuries that it isn't a good indicator for dating. Indigo was the only blue dyestuff available until 1856. It was still used as late as 1880. Indigo grew in India and Egypt, and the dye was introduced to Europe in the 16th century. Although it was highly valued for its color fastness, indigo was difficult to work with. It required an alkaline agent because it was insoluble in water—the very feature that made it colorfast. Once the fabric was dyed and dried, the dye stayed through many, many washings. When aniline dyes were invented in the middle 1850s, they gradually took indigo's place as the favored blue dyestuff because, also colorfast, they were easier to work with.

Prussian blue was a dye used in Colonial America, but it's a dating clue to the period from 1830 to 1860. Prussiate of potash combined with iron salt produces a white solution that turns blue as it dries and oxidizes. Prussian blue was first used in a broadcloth made in Philadelphia in 1832 named "Lafayette" blue. This vibrant blue was used in plain cottons and prints. It was common in florals and chintz-scale pillar prints and as a background for rainbow prints. It was often used with a dull tan. Fabrics containing Lafayette blue indicate a middle 1800s date.

Light blues have also been heavily used by quiltmakers over the centuries and don't generally indicate a date. But one light blue, with a violet tone, was popular with checks, florals, and geometrics in shirting fabrics from approximately the 1870s through the 1890s. Watch for this violet-tinged light blue as an indicator of the late 1800s.

A grayish blue, called cadet blue appeared as a background color around 1890. It was usually printed with a small figure, a stripe, or a dot. Used for everyday clothes and aprons, this colored fabric found its way into the quiltmaker's scrap bag.

The pastel period of the 1920s and 1930s is also noted for its use of navy and cadet blue. In the midst of the Depression, the 1932 Sears catalog included both bright, cheery pastels and the solid navy and cadet blues.

Red

Madder, a red dye derived from the plant *Rubia tinctorum* originally from Asia Minor, is one of the oldest of dyestuffs. There is evidence that the Egyptians, Hebrews, Greeks, Lybians, and Romans grew and used madder. It was a major trade item between the Orient and Europe. By the Middle Ages, madder was used in Italy, France, and Holland. It produced a red that became known as Turkey red from the mistaken European assumption that any Mediterranean country was part of Turkey. Madder produced a very fast color and some very old antique quilts still sport the vibrant red with little color loss. It took from 13 to 20 different steps to produce a fabric colored Turkey red. In the 1750s the secret of producing this vibrant color was brought to Europe. The process was never attempted on a commercial level in the United States but it was the most important of red dyes used through the 1800s. The synthetic alizarin, which offered a much faster, easier process to achieve the vibrant red, was introduced in 1868.

You need to be very familiar with Turkey red to distinguish it from later red dyes. Usually a red that has stayed vibrant in a quilt that has other date indicators can be classified as true Turkey red and dated sometime after the 1830s or 1840s. Since Turkey red was used for over 100 years, printed fabric with the red as the background is a more reliable indicator of date. Calicoes with Turkey red as the background for tiny cones, flowers, or geometric prints are good indicators of the early 1800s.

You can also determine a Turkey red from its distinctive wear pattern. As Turkey red wears, the color comes off of individual yarns rather than changing color or fading in patches. When this happens, the fabric appears to have white streaks running through it. The process needed to achieve Turkey red was quite hard on fabrics. If only the red patchwork on a quilt seems lighter in the loft parts of the quilt, that's an indication of Turkey red fabric. At one point, home dyers could get a synthetic dye labeled Turkey red. Since Turkey red is a process, not really a dye, these dyes didn't live up to their name. They turned color, fading to either brown or pink. The presence of faded red fabric in a quilt is a good indicator of a date between 1875 and 1925.

There were other red dyes available. Cochineal was brought back to Europe by the Spaniards when they found it used in Mexico. Taken from the bodies of insects, cochineal dyes were used more for fine cloth than were the cheaper madder dyes. The cochineal, along with red, produced pink, crimson, and scarlet. It was a prominent dyestuff after 1793. Annatto dye, derived from the seeds of a tropical plant, produced pink, reddish-orange, and blues for cotton and silk. Brazilwood was used in Colonial America in the early 1800s, but its use declined as Turkey red became more popular.

During the last quarter of the 19th century and the first quarter of the 20th century, American textile manufacturers produced a very popular, very cheap red background fabric with various black figures printed on it. Called robe prints or Garibaldi prints, the most common figures were anchors, horseshoes, tennis rackets, paisley cone-shaped feathers and florals. A dull burgundy, actually a purplish-red that didn't fade was manufactured from about 1890 through 1925. There was also a red tinged with cinnamon used in the last half of the 19th century that is referred to as "madder-style." It was used on all cloth from cotton to silk. It's distinctive for its orange tinge and was used to produce colors ranging from red to red-brown. Prints with this background used light purple and light blue as accent colors.

Most pinks are not good date indicators because they, too, had a long period of popularity both in early quilts and in those as late as between 1925 and 1950. Double pinks, a dark pink print on a light pink background were very popular from 1875 to 1900, so these bright pinks are an indicator of that period. A plain pink, sometimes found in sateen weave, was very popular as a dominant color theme in quilts made in the second quarter of the 20th century.

Brown

Brown is a difficult color to use to verify the date of a quilt. Brown was the easiest color to produce from natural dyes. Clay-pot browns were made in the south using distinctive red dirt. Mud dyeing was simple. Cloth was literally buried in mud, thereby producing a terra-cotta shade. Butternut and black walnut shells were used as brown dyes. There were, of course, many recipes and synthetic dyes developed as well. Shades of brown can narrow down a date, but it takes time to train yourself to distinguish them.

A light tan, with a green tinge, is the tan used with the Lafayette or Prussian blue dyed fabric we discussed earlier. Popular from 1830 to 1860, a tan with this blue is a valid date indicator. There was also a manganese bronze-style tan, almost khaki, that was printed with red and white figures from 1850 through 1910 and was especially popular toward the end of that time frame. *See illustration #13.*

Another reason browns are difficult to identify and date is that they may not have been browns originally. Many fabrics faded to brown with use, washing, and age. Appliquéd fabrics that are obviously stems and leaves but done in tans or browns were probably the correct green when they were made. Brown grapes and roses were not the result of a weird color scheme chosen by the quiltmaker. They are the result of inferior dyes. Fabrics used from the end of the 19th century at the start of synthetic dyes just didn't hold their original colors. Green, purple, blue, and red all faded to shades of brown. Some reds faded to a salmon-tinged tan while blues and purples faded to khaki. Don't assume the browns and tans you see in a quilt are as they were intended. Clues that a fabric has faded to brown can be found by inspecting the pattern. Roses are not brown and most stems and leaves aren't either. Since quiltmakers copied nature, there's no reason to assume that any of them decided to appliqué a brown rose by choice.

Quilts with a predominantly brown color theme, not that way because of fading, can be assumed to be from before the 20th century. In the early 1900s, quiltmakers turned to blacks, grays, and blues as dominant color themes. The brown color scheme made a short revival in the 1970s and 1980s.

Browns are among the first fabrics to deteriorate because of the iron mordant used to fix the dye. The mordant weakens, or tenders, the fabric. You'll often see fabric with rotted holes in the shapes of the prints that originally adorned it.

Green

There was no single vegetable dye to create green. A method to dye fabrics green in one application wasn't discovered until 1778. Until that time, a combination of yellow and blue was used, one color placed on top of the other, to create green. This process worked fine for plain fabrics, but green in a printed calico was difficult. The overlay color, whether it was yellow or

13 From the 1830s, this nine patch has its blocks set on point and uses a zigzag, instead of frame, sashing arrangement. The scrap bag colors include pinks, grays, browns and others and shows a nice color balance in the set of the squares. Quilt courtesy of the Warner Family.

blue, had to be overprinted. If the hand or stencil printing didn't line up perfectly with the first color, the printed figure had an edge of yellow on one side while the other side of the print showed a strip of blue. The process always delivered a green that was tinged with either yellow or blue, depending on which dye was stronger. Greens could also fade differently. If the blue faded from a quilt's flower stems, it left them yellow. Blue stems and leaves is an indication that the yellow faded out of an overdyed fabric. How else can we explain blue leaves and stems? Surely no quiltmaker would depict flowers with blue stems when they don't exist in nature. Over dying to obtain green continued until the last quarter of the 19th century.

Mineral green dyes were not as bright or true as the vegetable dye combinations. They still used overprinting and some were colorfast, but they lacked the vibrancy of their vegetable dye counterparts. If you find a lifeless green, it's a good indication of a date in the first half of the 19th century.

Charles William, a Swedish chemist, experimented with a dye that used two chemical salts that did not require overprinting to produce green. But the first solid green using a roller and a single step application is attributed to the Oberkampf factory in Jouy, France, in 1810. Single-step application of green dyes didn't become common until 1875, after synthetic dyes were developed. Overprinting blue on yellow or yellow on blue was still being done during this time. If the overprinting was done expertly and the prints lined up perfectly, it's difficult to tell if a green is a single application or an overprint.

The synthetic green dyes didn't hold up well either. They have faded to a tan, slightly khaki, slightly mustard color that indicates the period from 1875 to 1900. If your quilt has some tan in it, try lifting or pulling it up slightly so that you can see the seam allowance. More protected from the effects of use and washing, the seam fabric may be the original shade of green. A tan or brown fabric quilted with green thread is also an indication that it was originally green, since quiltmakers tended to match their thread color to the fabric color. Some historians believe that those red, white, and tan quilts dated from the end of the 19th century originally were red, white, and green. As quiltmakers noticed their greens fading to tan, they stopped using green fabrics in their quilts. From 1890 to 1925, green was not a common color in quilts. If you've bought a quilt with an attributed date between 1875 and 1900 with green in it, determine how the green was achieved. If you don't, and you hang or wash the quilt, you may find your lovely green quilt turning tan. The inferior synthetic dyes of the late 1800s and early 1900s could even fade completely to white.

There is a colorfast, dark green that appears in quilts from the last half of the 19th century. This was an indigo or Prussian blue overdyed with chrome yellow that has kept its color very well. A Nile green was manufactured in the 1920s and 1930s. It is one of the colors reproduced in contemporary fabrics, making repairs to the Depression-era quilts that contained it a little easier.

As you look at quilts, you'll notice that there's a lot of green background fabric printed with tiny figures. These fabrics were common in three periods of quiltmaking: the 1870s, 1930s, and 1970s. You'll probably have to see a lot of these fabrics to tell the difference in their ages. Watch for quilts that have valid dates, from other dating clues, to learn which is which.

Yellow

There were many yellow dyes, both domestic and imported, that American quiltmakers used. These plants included turmeric, sassafras, white oak, barberry tree, dock, golden rod, hickory, and peach. But the three most popular dyes were fustic, quercitron, and chrome yellow.

Fustic was an economical dye used in the colonies. There are records of its use dated 1661. The fustic yellow was colorfast but dull. Fustic was also used to produce other colors.

Quercitron was derived from oak tree bark and made in America. Beginning in 1785, it was an export commodity to England. Quercitron produced a bright, colorfast yellow. It was used mostly to dye woolen fabrics but was used on cottons and silks as well. Combined with other dyes, quercitron was an important ingredient to make olive, oranges, red-yellows, and, cinnamons.

Chrome yellow was a mineral dye that, although fast on cottons, didn't fix well on wool. It first appeared in the United States in the 1830s.

Yellows are good clues to dating a quilt to the mid- to late-1800s. There's a burnt orange, popularly used in charm quilts and log cabins, that you can rely on as an indication of a date in the last half of the 19th century. Butterscotch-colored cloth is also an indicator of that period. Cottons of plain yellow and calicoes with yellow background color date a quilt to the late 1800s, as does a plain cotton with a true orange color.

For all of the 1800s and into the first 10 years of the 20th century, there was a long-standing popular fabric with a navy background printed with bright yellow figures. Tangerine, melon and peach are indicative of the period from 1925 until about 1950.

Two yellows, both popular, tend to crock over time. Crocking is the loss of surface color on a piece of fabric. These two are the plain, chrome orange and a loud, gaudy yellow-orange that one historian called safety yellow because it reminded her of the lines painted down the middle of our streets and highways. The safety yellow is a good clue to the mid-1800s or after. If you have a quilt with one of these chrome orange or safety yellow colors, always store it layered and wrapped with acid-free tissue paper (see Chapter 8). If you don't, the color will crock off the orange or yellow and onto other fabrics in the quilt, creating permanent, unsightly spots and blotches.

How a yellow feels on the quilt can be an indication of the print method used for it. A yellow that feels raised, or textured as you touch it was probably achieved by direct or overprinting with chrome yellow while a yellow that feels smooth was probably dyed. The textured, raised yellow is an indication that the fabric dates from between 1830 and 1860.

Black

Early black dyes came from logwood. Black was a hard dye to use, but it was in use in England from about 1580. The logwood black was combined with other dyes to produce navy and green and was in use until the beginning of World War II. Black dyeing was mordant style, and silks and cottons were especially affected by the harsh dyeing process. Black is another color that tended to eat away the cloth where it was applied, leaving distinctive, pattern-shaped holes behind. It wasn't until the 1890s, just in time for the crazy quilt period with its high use of black fabric, that a reliable dye was created. Then, black colorfast cottons became readily available.

Black provides us with several clues helpful to dating quilts. In cotton quilts, black was used from approximately 1890 until 1925, when the new dye became available. For silk, black was a predominant color from 1860 to 1910. Wool quilts incorporate black from about 1880 to 1925. With the advent of the pastel period starting in the 1920s, black went out of favor except among Amish quiltmakers, who still use it as a design element today.

Prior to the Civil War, black was used primarily to print designs and figures on Turkey red cloth. It wasn't used as a color on its own until after the 1860s. In the last half of the 18th century, black was a required fabric for the fashionable quilts of the day: log cabins, crazies, and fan quilts.

Black background prints indicate the 1890s through 1925. These multicolored, bright prints used magenta, purple, yellow-green, pink, and gold as their accent colors. The designs look modern.

Black figures were closely printed on white backgrounds to produce the shirting fabrics so popular from 1890 to 1925. The designs were so small and so closely packed that, from a distance, the fabric appears gray.

Fabric with a gray background, or plain gray fabric, was used after the 1940s. The prints are easy to spot because they are especially whimsical. While visiting dealers and shops, we saw several examples of this fabric showing gypsy dancers in brightly colored clothes, figures busily at work, and farm animals.

Purple

We include this color because there are at least two specific periods in quiltmaking history when it was popular. Purple provides valuable, reliable clues to dating a quilt.

There was an orchid, or purple dye available in ancient times derived from lichen. It was used in America for wools and silks throughout the 18th century. Cotton didn't take this dye well. It was almost impossible to get a true purple on it.

In 1856 a man named Perkins (we couldn't find his first name in any of our sources) discovered a lavender dye using coal-tar aniline. It was referred to as mauve, sometimes mauvine. Queen Victoria wore the color in 1862. It was several years before the dye reached the United States, but even then natural dyes continued in use. By the end of the 19th century, all dyers were using the imported aniline dyes. Because Germany supplied most of these synthetics, World War I created a shortage of dyes, which spurred domestic production.

There were two purple periods in quiltmaking history. The first was around the time of the Civil War. Before synthetic dyes, purples were a lifeless lavender that tended to fade to brown or pink. Be careful dating a purple or lavender fabric in a quilt. This color was available, in varying qualities of tone, all of the 19th century. Don't assume that a fairly bright, unfaded purple is necessarily a synthetic. Perhaps the quilt was properly stored and unaffected by light.

The second purple period came during the 1920s to the 1950s, when dyes that produced a stronger purple and a true lavender became available. Plain and print purples as well as lilac, raspberry, orchid, and lavender are strong indicators of the second quarter of the 20th century.

Dating a quilt by color is tricky. Use, washing, and exposure to light may have caused bleeding, fading, and migrating of the colors. Improper storage could cause crocking fabrics to stain the fabrics placed on top of them. Harsh dyes, mordants, and resists also took their toll on quilts and quilt colors. Investigate thoroughly, look at lots of quilts and hone your instincts for recognizing colors as they are and interpreting what they were. We recommend that you continue your quilt color education with *Dating Fabrics: A Color Guide 1800–1960* by Eileen Jahnke Trestain.

Printed Fabric

The prints on fabric have their own tale to tell about the age of a quilt. Creating fabric decorated with figures, geometric shapes, or designs is accomplished by one of four methods: direct, discharge, mordant, or resist.

In direct printing, a color or colors, is applied to a solid-colored fabric or a plain white fabric, or a white design can be applied to a colored background fabric.

The discharge method used a previously dyed background fabric and then bleached out the design, turning the figured area to white. After the discovery of chlorine as a bleaching agent in 1807, fabrics that incorporated the discharge method will show wear in the bleached areas before the background sections do.

Use of the mordant method meant that up to four colors could be applied to the same background cloth. Since different dyes required different mordants to make them fix to the cloth and stay there, the use of four mordants meant that when the cloth was dyed, only those areas treated with a mordant that attracted a specific dye would result in that color. The area not treated with the right mordant remained either the background color or the color attracted by a different mordant.

In the resist method, wax or a chemical paste is applied to the fabric in the shape of the design wanted. When the dye is applied, it won't fix to the treated areas so that they stay the same color as the background. After dyeing, the resist substance is removed and the fabric shows the design intended.

Printers can combine these methods, using the mordant and discharge operations together or the resist and mordant methods to produce multicolored printed fabrics.

The most frequently used methods of applying dye were hand painting, wooden block, copperplate and roller printing. Woodblock and copperplate printing are clues to dates before 1850. Roller prints were not used before 1800. Ikat prints, like ginghams and plaids, are actually a weaving method, not a result of printing. In this method, the yarns are dyed before weaving and the pattern results from the way the yarns were woven. Tie-dying was also used.

Woodblock printing used the mordant method. A different mordant, or strengths of the same mordant, and a separate woodblock were used for each design element in a print. India chintz was so popular and so expensive, that cotton prints imitating it were produced in both France and England using the wood-block method.

By the end of the 1700s, a factory in France printed the imitation chintzes using the copperplate method. They were called "toiles de Jouy" after the town where the factory was located and were usually one color printed on white for use in upholstery and curtains. Copper sheets, with the design cut into them, were pressed onto the cloth to print fabric up to a yard square. This vastly reduced the time it took to print fabric. *See illustration #14.*

The next labor-saving and cost-reducing advance in printing technique was the advent of cylinder printing. Similar to copperplate, the designs were engraved on copper cylinders. Each cylinder inked a different color, but the advantage was that the process was continuous. Unlike copperplate, cylinders didn't require stopping to move a new piece of fabric under the plate. Cylinder printing was invented by a Scotsman, Thomas Beel, in 1783. It was first used for upholstery and curtain fabrics and usually printed only one color. Other colors were added later by plate methods. By 1835, multiple cylinders were used, each controlled to add a different color. Cylinder printing was improved when pantograph methods etched several series of a design to the same cylinder, further reducing production costs.

There are ways to recognize the different printing methods. Copperplate printing is highly detailed, usually depicting a scene such as a landscape, fair, or cityscape. Intricate florals and trees were popular patterns. These prints were usually one color. The fabric ranged anywhere from 33 to 45 inches square. In some copperplate prints you might find a fine white line running through it. This is probably not a design element but the result of poor registration caused by inexpert application. Registration is the matching of the design elements so that it's impossible to tell where the plate ends. If the registration is off, the design doesn't match and the fine white line appears. Some of the prints from copperplate soak through the fabric to the back in a fainter shade than the original. Unless you have an unfinished quilt, you won't be able to see this, but you can look for it if you find uncut fabric you think was printed with copperplate.

Early cylinder printing used a roller only 16 inches in circumference. Look for where the design repeats on a piece of fabric. If you measure from repeat to repeat, you'll get the length of

14

14 The Tumbler pattern is popular for charm quilts where no two pieces of the same fabric are used in the quilt. There are some fabric repeats in this quilt but it's an excellent example of the variety of prints, geometrics and representational fabric available in the 1930s. Quilt courtesy of Kathryn Robinson.

the original design. If this length is greater than 16 inches, and you have other clues to an early date for the quilt, then it was probably pressed with a plate rather than rolled.

Different styles of printed fabrics were used differently over the course of quiltmaking history. Chintz, over the centuries, has consistently meant a cotton with a large-scale design that was glazed. We still recognize a chintz today by its large print. But the size of the print today and the size of the print in the late 18th century are drastically different. Today a chintz print is a larger design than our calicoes. But in the past, a chintz pattern was the size of a bed top. It was these chintzes that quiltmakers prized for Broderie-Perse. This type of appliqué requires cutting out that large-scale design and stitching it down on a whole-cloth background. It was difficult work because of the size of the piece. The large tree of life pattern, done in this medallion style, is indicative of a date before 1850. Eventually, quiltmakers made work easier for themselves and began cutting smaller design elements out of fabric to appliqué in a design of their own choice. Palm trees and game birds were popular in the first half of the 1800s while floral wreaths and baskets were made from approximately 1790 until the late 1840s. You will also find references to palampores from this period also made from chintz.

So popular was the fashion for cutting out design elements from printed fabric that, in the early 1800s, chintz fabric was designed in Europe in patterns sized to be cut and used specifically for the corners and centers of quilts.

There is one other fabric print that dates from the 18th century. Paisley originated in Kashmir, India, but by the end of the 18th century, Scotland was producing a quality copy. Paisley fell so out of fashion in the 1870s that the mills in Paisley, Scotland, stopped producing it in 1886.

By the 1820s and 1830s, the American textile industry had found its footing. Calicoes were produced with a small floral print for the design. In the 1830s and 1840s, American factories designed geometric chintzes based on quilt patterns. Beautiful printed cottons were made.

The most popular were red and green backgrounds with small yellow or black figures. Geometric designs on cloth were popular from 1840 through 1900.

In the 1850s the first "cheater" cloth came on the market. These fabrics simulated patchwork patterns and provided a shortcut to assembling a quilt top. Since the fabric was already printed in blocks resembling pieced work, all the quiltmaker had to do was cut out the squares and sew them together. In the 1850s these were imitation chintz patches. Log Cabin and Charm quilt cheaters, colored with madder dyes, appeared in the early 1900s. In 1933, Sears offered grandmother's flower garden, Dresden Plate, and Double Wedding Ring patterns in cheater cloth style.

Plaids are poor age indicators because they were used often in quilts. They fell out of fashion after the Civil War but were revived briefly in the late 1800s and early 1900s.

The 1880s were a boom period for print fabrics. During this time there were many notable and beautiful prints produced: small floral sprigs on dark backgrounds, checks, stars, small bouquets and black and white designs. This was the period of the shirting fabrics, those white backgrounds covered with tiny black dots, swirls, leaves, tennis racquets, oars, horseshoes, anchors, sailboats, and baseballs as well as geometrics. Startling geometric designs were produced in the 1880s through the 1890s. Many of these designs stayed in production for many years. The Ely Manufacturing Company, Chicago, Illinois, still produces eighteen designs dating from 1878.

The invention of copperplate printing created the commemorative print. These were available as early as the end of the 1700s. Europe imported a commemorative depicting George Washington in 1785. The last half of the 19th century produced many commemorative fabrics, which appeared as both yardage for quilts and as handkerchiefs that could be incorporated into a quilt. There was a "The Union Forever" commemorative with a star and clasped hands, several depicting Ulysses S. Grant, at least one for Horace Greeley, many for the Centennial and for Queen Victoria's Jubilee. Presidential campaigns produced many pieces of commemorative cloth.

There are two other date indicators for printed fabric. As a general rule, the greater the number of colors in a single fabric piece, the better it indicates a date either before 1875 or after 1925. In between those dates, it was much cheaper to print a single color on a ground fabric.

The second date indicator deals with registration, or design matching. Printing several colors on a cloth makes it difficult for each color to line up in the proper place on the design. To counteract this, and to cover up any mistakes, a solid black outline was added to character prints in some fabrics before 1850. White halos around figures also indicate a pre-1850 or 1925–1950 date. Multi-colored, perfectly registered printed fabric was at its peak from 1840 to 1890.

Technique

How a quiltmaker worked, the type of quilt made, how stems and leaves are represented, and the quality of the work all give us general dating clues.

"Although exceptions occurred, especially in the category of silk Show Quilts, late nineteenth century cotton quilts generally show lower levels of hand workmanship," wrote Brackman in

Clues in the Calico. Brackman attributes this decline in work quality to the increase in popularity of the sewing machine. The new machine, and the availability of ready-made clothing and furnishings, freed women from the yoke of needlework. It was no longer necessary to teach young girls the uses of the needle. Without all that practice, needlework skills declined.

Stems, animal eyes, and faces were commonly hand painted on quilts made before the 1850s. Hand painting returned during the Crazy Quilt period when flowers and animals were added to the heavily embroidered blocks. The 1920s brought a minor fashion, revived in the 1960s, of drawing on cloth with crayon. When the wax was washed out, the dye stayed. Liquid embroidery pens and markers were used to create some quilts in the 1950s.

Embroidery was used extensively in quilting for several periods. Embroidered quilts of the 1880s and after depict designs in outline embroidery only and usually in a single color. These were sentimental, simple designs of flowers, children, pets, fans, cattails and crosses. Embroidery was essential to the Crazy Quilt of the Victorian era. Herringbone, feather, and buttonhole stitches, as well as other fancy embroidery covered the seam lines of the crazy quilt patches. Embroidery decorated the blocks, too, showing the quiltmaker's favorite things. After World War I, floral baskets, state birds, nursery rhymes, and the alphabet were popular designs for outline embroidery quilts. Signature quilts were often single-color embroidery designs.

One trend that might explain the number of unfinished early-20th-century quilt tops available today was the custom of quilting "on shares." A client purchased enough fabric for two quilts. The quilter made one quilt for the client and kept the remaining fabric to make a quilt for herself or to sell.

There are two appliqué formats. The medallion style was popular before 1840 and used the very large-scale chintz patterns that were cut out of the cloth and appliquéd to a whole-cloth ground fabric. The block style became popular after 1840 because it was easier to work with the smaller piece of cloth.

There are three types of appliqué. Broderie-Perse dates back to the 17th century and was the most common in the 18th and early 19th centuries for medallion-style quilts.

The conventional style is the evolution of Broderie-Perse. To make the work simpler, smaller pieces of fabric were used. A piece of cloth is cut in the desired shape, its edges folded under and then stitched to a ground fabric. Conventional appliqué was used in both the body of the quilt and in the borders. The album quilts of the later 1800s are all done in appliqué. Conventional appliqué fell out of favor for a while at the turn of the century, but reappeared in the 1920s and 1930s.

Reverse appliqué is also an old technique with examples appearing from the last three centuries. In reverse appliqué, the top layer of fabric is cut away to reveal the backing fabric. The inside edges of the cut design are folded under and stitched down. This is a tricky, time-consuming method of quiltmaking and finding them is rare.

There are appliqué patterns such as Sunbonnet Sue, Whig Rose, and Rose of Sharon that many quiltmakers copied and used. But appliqué quickly became an individually designed form. Designs were sketched on paper and then cut out of fabric. Some pieces were cut free-hand, and many an appliqué has been designed around the shape of a cookie cutter, teacup, or other household item.

Appliqué stitches should be invisible with only a few exceptions. The most popular stitches were the blind and the overcast. Embroidery stitches were sometimes used to represent flower stems and leaves. One strong date clue is the use of the sewing machine to appliqué. These stitches were not invisible and they weren't meant to be. Machine owners purposely stitched their appliqué by machine to show off the new technology. There are examples of this from the 1860s. A black buttonhole stitch used around the outside edge of appliquéd designs in the years between 1925 and 1950 is another appliqué stitching date indicator.

There are several methods of assembling pieced blocks. One is called the English style. A paper pattern is cut out, the fabric wrapped around it, pressed, and then whipstitched to another piece formed the same way. The last step is to remove the paper backing. This method was used primarily in the 19th century. If you can find a top with the paper inserts still intact, check for a date on the paper used. It's an excellent way to accurately place a quilt in its proper period.

The foundation method, or pressed piecing, was popular in the last quarter of the 19th century, particularly to make log cabin quilts, crazy quilts and string quilts. In this method, the quiltmaker started by cutting enough large squares to get the dimensions she wanted. To these foundation squares, she stitched the pieces of her pattern until she covered the original square. Sometimes newspapers were used as foundation squares. We saw one log cabin quilt top that still had the newspaper on the back. If cloth is used, you can sometimes see a foundation fabric in a finished quilt by looking through pieces of the top cloth that have rotted or torn.

Assembling pieced blocks by seaming them together with a running stitch is called the American method. Today, quiltmakers add a quarter-inch seam allowance to their pieces, but there is some evidence that past quiltmakers used only a $3/16$" seam. Starting at the beginning of the 20th century, log cabin quilts were assembled using the American method. Crazy quilts and string quilts still use foundation squares.

Trapunto, or stuffed quilts are a very old style. These were popular before the Civil War.

Finishing edgings had fashions and fads as well. A quilt with cutout corners indicates that it was made before 1860. Scalloped borders were popular after the 1840s, hitting a peak in the period from 1925 to 1950, and used with the Double Wedding Ring pattern. Fancy borders with cords, braids, tassels, and lace were used on show quilts in the last half of the 19th century. Fringed quilts are generally dated before the Civil War. Folded triangles, called prairie points, were used starting in the mid-1800s but were most common after 1925.

Finishing strips made of bias binding point to the 20th century. Twill tape was used before the Civil War.

You must be careful dating a quilt by its border or finishing. So many quilt tops were completed years after they were made that the border might be made from a much newer fabric or with a newer technique or style. If you find a quilt with a new border or edging, it's customary to date the top and the border separately and document when each was made.

There were other special techniques of quilt construction popular for brief periods. Victorian Puff quilts were made from satins and velvets at the end of the 19th century. Squares were cut and the corners folded to achieve a cup shape. These were stuffed and then whipstitched together.

The Yo-Yo quilt was popular from 1925 to 1950. This was not a three-layered quilt. Circles of scrap bag fabrics were cut, the outside edge of the circle was gathered together, and the result pressed flat. The circles were sewed together with the small gathered opening to the back. These were novelty quilts and used primarily for decoration. The many spaces between the yo-yos wouldn't keep anyone warm. Some of these quilts were backed with a plain colored cotton.

The Cathedral Window quilt is another nonquilted decorative top. Squares of cloth are folded and refolded with other cloth stitched in the middle. Usually muslin, or a plain colored fabric was used for the window frame part and scrap bag fabrics were used for the centers. Although the pattern dates to 1910, it was most popular in the 1960s and 1970s.

Quilting

Quilts that are tied aren't technically quilts. They should be called comforters. Tying was a shortcut. It took much less time to tie a top than to quilt it. Comforters were made for utility. Another reason a top was tied rather than quilted was because of the weight of the fabrics used. Heavy velvets and wools were difficult to quilt through, so they were tied instead.

Earlier quilts had more stitching than those made after the introduction of polyester batting. Wool and cotton batts tended to shift in washing and lump in unquilted areas. Quilt designs were stitched no farther apart than half an inch to prevent the batting from shifting.

Quiltmakers were, and still are, very picky about the designs they choose for stitching their quilt tops. There was plain quilting using diamonds; single, double, or triple rows of diagonal lines referred to as crossbars; and clamshells. Fancy designs included floral bouquets, pineapples, spider webs, oak leaves, cornucopias, princess feathers, wreaths, and stars. There were quilting sampler quilts created before the Civil War that, like appliqué samplers, used a variety of quilting patterns.

Stipple quilting dates to the first half of the 19th century. Hundreds of stitches and stitching lines were used to dramatically puff unquilted areas. Fan quilting, with its groups of concentric half circles is a clue to the latter part of the 19th century and the early years of the 20th. Self-quilting, also known as shadow quilting or outlining is the method of quilting one-quarter inch away from the seam line around each patch in a pattern; this is a 20th century technique, as is machine quilting.

Colored thread to match the color of the fabric has always been used for quilting. White is a favorite color, while the Amish use black thread. Patterns were penciled on the quilt top but quiltmakers also used stencils and paper patterns they traced with a wheel. Two of our sources mentioned the use of a chalk-covered string that was snapped down on the quilt top once it was in the frame to mark the straight diagonal lines of crossbar quilting. But it does seem, to us, that this is a highly inaccurate method of marking quilting lines, not to mention messy.

The way some quiltmakers signed their quilts gives us some idea of the quilt's age. Fast inks that didn't corrode fabric were available in the late 1830s. The advent of these new inks may have contributed to the craze for autograph quilts in the 1840s and 1850s. Signatures during this later period were elaborate and included verses and small drawings. Cross-stitch was used until the 1850s. Embroidered signatures are more commonly found on quilts after 1875. Appliquéd signatures were used in all quilting periods but were most common from 1840 through 1900. There was a short period, from 1840 through 1850, in which stamped and stenciled initials and dates were used. Signatures were also worked into quilting patterns. These are difficult to find and require close inspection of the quilt top and borders. Quilted signatures and dates are uncommon in 20th-century quilts.

Thread

There is some discrepancy in the earliest date that cotton thread was manufactured. One source said it was first produced in a factory in Paisley, Scotland, in 1812. Another source noted a story about Hannah Wilkinson Slater, whose husband, Samuel Slater, memorized the equipment blueprints for cotton-producing machines, and then opened the first mill in the United States in Rhode Island. The story goes that Mrs. Slater recognized that the cotton yarn spun for the cloth in her husband's factory was also suitable for sewing. Her husband started marketing his thread near the end of the 18th century. For most of the 1700s, thread was made from silk, wool, or linen, rather than from cotton.

A better way to pin down a quilt's age is to count the ply of the quilting thread. Inspect the quilt for a loose piece of stitching thread. Note the twist to the thread and twist the end in the opposite direction. Count the number of individual strands that unwind and you have the ply count. The invention of the sewing machine created problems with the thread then available. Three-ply cotton thread was available after 1800, but it wasn't strong enough to withstand the rigors of use in a sewing machine. A simple, six-ply thread was produced after 1840 that was stronger and solved the problem. Around 1860, a complex six-ply thread was introduced. Instead of just twisting six strands of yarn together as in the simple six-ply, the complex took three strands of two-ply thread and twisted them together. When you unravel the thread end you find in your quilt, note if it's simple or complex six-ply.

There's a fairly easy way of finding out if repairs have been made to an antique quilt, or if new borders or bindings have been added. Thread made after 1963 will glow under a black light because of the synthetic dyes and methods used.

Batting

Cotton and wool battings were used in quilts since their very beginnings, and up to the 1950s. Whether a cotton or wool batt was used is not a date identifier, because both were used equally as often. Some wool batts inside cotton quilts shrank so badly that they actually pulled the quilt in and made it smaller. Puckers cover the top and back. These quilts are sometimes described as gathered. But you can't assume that a quilt you find in this condition has a wool batting. The gathered effect can also be due to improper washing in hot water.

There is a raging controversy, however, over whether cotton batting can be used as a dating tool. Adelaide Hechtinger in her book *American Quilts, Quilting, and Patchwork*, states that if there are cottonseeds in a quilt batting, it could be dated as early as 1793. Hechtinger's rule of thumb is if there are seeds every few inches, this dates the batt to around 1850. A batting with two or three seeds to the square inch is probably from before 1830. She also advises knowing where the quilt was made. A quilt made in the north would have more seeds remaining than one made in the south because southern quilters had greater access to the cotton gin than did northerners. Hechtinger also notes that it's not easy to date cotton batting after the 1830s because all cotton was ginned and therefore free of seeds. You can test to see if your quilt has cottonseeds in it by squeezing it between your fingers or by holding it up to the light.

Well, in our opinion, the seeds-left-in-the-batting theory just doesn't make sense. Early quilts were closely quilted. The stitches were small and even and the patterns close—not more than a half inch apart—to prevent the batting from shifting and lumping in the wash. Cottonseeds, at least the ones we saw and felt, are about the size of orange seeds. They're big, thick, and round and would be impossible to quilt around in those close patterns. Quilts were too important to the maker's sense of artistry and creativity to allow even one cottonseed to remain and foul up her quilting!

We don't agree there were so many seeds left in cotton batting that you can safely use them to date a quilt. But, there was plant debris. These were seed husks, small pieces of stems, and leaves—all the pieces too difficult to remove by hand or by ginning. Cotton cleaned by machine was not refuse free. At times, it wasn't even seed free! In 1897 there were various qualities of cotton batting available to the quiltmaker, ranging in cleanliness and whiteness. A cheap batt, presumably the least free of debris and not a pure white, sold for eight cents a role. The best batting sold for a quarter a roll. When you hold a quilt up to the light and see small dark spots in the batting, they are probably a clue to a cheap batting rather than to a date. We're not alone in our opinion, either. Barbara Brackman's book, *Clues in the Calico,* confirmed our opinion. Those dark spots you see when you hold an antique quilt up to the light are plant debris, not seeds.

The first commercial cotton batting appeared on the market in 1846, produced by Stearns & Foster. The company is still in business today, producing both cotton and polyester battings under the name Mountain Mist. Polyester batting was introduced in the 1950s but didn't gain popularity until the quilting revival of the late 1960s. Quilts filled with a polyester batting have a different look to them. They're puffier, with more loft in the unquilted areas than a cotton batting gives. Polyester batting will spring back after compression, and the whole quilt feels smoother and slippery when rubbed. Polyester batting doesn't shrink, shred, or shift in washings so it doesn't require the amount of close quilting that cotton and wool demand. The presence of polyester batting means that your antique quilt was very recently an unfinished top.

It was also mentioned that some earlier, cheap quilts were filled with newspaper. We agree with Brackman that the paper felt and heard inside an antique quilt is probably there because it wasn't removed from a foundation-style assembly before it was quilted. Both conclusions go counter to the care and attention an expert quiltmaker gives her art, but paper inside quilts does exit. We just prefer the second explanation to the first.

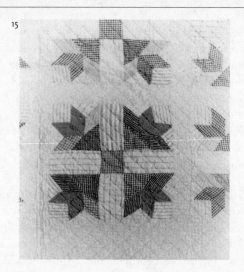

15 This Lily variation has blocks set in the traditional style. The workmanship is excellent with all points matching. The ginghams are black and white which have faded to soft shades. Other fabrics are pinks, light blues, and reds. Finely stitched grid quilting completes the quilt. Quilt courtesy of the Zimmer Family.

Borders

Borders are the picture frames of quilts. Not all quilts have borders, but those that do are more valuable to a collector. Generally, borders were applied only to best quilts which is why so many of the quilts that have survived to today have them. It's probably also why we prefer our quilts with borders.

A border of chintz was typical on early quilts. An unpieced border of chintz is a good indication that the quilt was made before the Civil War.

Conventional appliqué on borders became popular after the 1840s. Appliquéd borders of chintz using the Broderie-Perse method were common before 1860. The chintz bouquets, baskets and bows used were sometimes connected with swags of matching fabric. The swag-style border was also popular in the 1930s.

Zigzag borders framed quilts in the 1880s but were also used before 1850 and after 1930.

Pieced borders in the Sawtooth and Flying Geese patterns were used in all periods of quilt-making. Sawtooth borders in the quilt top, usually forming the Feathered Star patterns, began in the Victorian period. Triangle and cone borders were popular pieced patterns in the second quarter of the 20th century. Strip borders were composed of two or more long pieces of different fabrics which were then quilted in a cable or feather design. Their use is connected to the invention of the sewing machine. They were always popular in Amish designs.

In 20th-century quilts you'll often find a pieced border framing an appliqué top, or an appliqué border around a pieced top.

Backing

The preferred backing fabric for a quilt has always been white cotton or muslin. Dating a quilt from the backing isn't accurate because many tops were finished long before they were

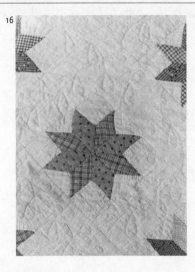

16 The assembly of this Eight-point Star shows less than skillful assembly. Note that the center of the star does not meet with the knife-point seams that reveal expert workmanship. The quilting, straight line around the points of the star, and leaf and vine in the sashing show experience. Quilt courtesy of the Dean Family.

assembled into the fabric and batting sandwich and quilted. A clue to an early-19th-century date is the presence of two lengths of a loose weave cotton sewed down the middle to make one large piece.

When feed, flour, and sugar sacks came printed with designs and labels, they were saved and stitched together for the backing fabric. A quilt with many squares of fabric stitched together to form the back might be made of feed sack bags. If you look at them closely, you might even be able to see the brand names that were originally printed on them. When a quiltmaker saved these bags, she generally bleached them to remove the brand-name labels. Another way to tell if your quilt has feed sack fabric is to look for the line of holes that marks the original stitching that formed the bag. Feed sack fabric was available in the latter part of the 19th century and well into the 20th. Cotton feed sacks with prints on them or with quilt patterns, date from the 1930s and 1940s.

Overall Design

One design trait of the late 1700s was the use of the medallion style, a central motif cut from chintz, appliquéd, and surrounded by strip borders. There was also simple patchwork using mixed fabrics with different weights and textures together. Four-block quilts were made from four pieces of cloth, each block one yard square. To these were stitched large appliqué designs. One source stated that this design was a regional variation exclusive to Pennsylvania quilters, but another noted that it was the precursor to block-style quilts.

The set of a quilt is the way block-style quilt tops are put together to form an overall design. We've already noted that the framed medallion set was popular before the 1840s but it's still used today by contemporary and Amish quiltmakers. When block-style quilts caught on because of their ease of assembly, the blocks were first placed, or set, right next to each other. This style is still used in geometric and puzzle patterns where the blocks must be adjacent to get the full effect of the optical illusion. When appliqué quilters turned to block-style, they added inner frames to their blocks, called sashings. These strips of fabric were generally narrower than the outside border strips. Blocks could be set straight which resulted in horizontal and vertical sashings, or on point, which created diagonal sashing lines. "Strip sets" refer to Wild Geese, Roman Coins, or bar patterns where scrap bag pieces are joined together in long strips and then sashing strips of contrasting colors are added between. The whole is then framed with a border. Strip sets are a clue to early-19th-century quilts up to the Civil War, but they were also used by the Amish through the middle of the 20th century. *See illustration #16.*

We covered what must appear to be a lot of material in this chapter to help you date the quilts you see and want to buy. We left as much, probably more, out! Your study of quilts will continue over a long period of time, as it did for us in the time it took to research this book. After a while, you'll be dating with the best of them, arguing with collectors and dealers over the fine points. It becomes instinctive after time, and we were proud when we noticed that we were capable of doing it ourselves. Developing instincts for recognizing and dating a valuable quilt takes time, but it's well worth it.

5 Condition

Finding quilts in pristine condition is difficult now, and it's only going to get harder. As the supply of antique quilts diminishes, more and more quilts that have seen moderate to heavy wear will show up on the market. As we'll see, these quilts, because of special qualities, may be more valuable than an ordinary quilt that's never been used or washed.

All things being equal, a beautiful, well-executed quilt that has never been washed is of greater value than one that has. A quilt that still shows the marks the maker made to guide her quilting stitch is more valuable than one that doesn't because it proves the quilt was never washed (this is not the case with the judging rules of contemporary quilts). Marked, unwashed quilts are extremely rare, which explains their increased value.

The condition of fabrics in the quilt gives clues to the amount, if any, of use and washing. Unwashed fabrics appear crisper and stiffer than washed ones. Their colors look truer, fresher, and brighter. Some color fading occurs every time a quilt is cleaned, and fabrics that look softer, feel smoother, and have colors slightly duller than new fabrics are the result of washing. When all the colors in a quilt look faded, it is probably due to many washes.

The look of a washed quilt is different from that of a new one. First, look at the seams and unquilted sections of the quilt. If these appear slightly puckery, or more puffy, this is a clue that the quilt has been washed. Unwashed quilts, if assembled correctly, should be fairly flat and smooth overall; seams should be straight and not have a gathered look. The batting should be evenly spread with no bunches or lumps. In a never-washed or hardly-washed quilt, you can feel compressed batting in place under the quilt stitches. In one that has been washed many times, the quilting thread may have shrunk slightly, pushing the batting to either side of the stitching line and forcing more batting into the unquilted areas. The thread in seams can also shrink, giving the unquilted area of the quilt more loft, or height. The whole effect of washing on a quilt makes it appear and feel softer and look as though it needs a pressing. These small wrinkles, crinkles, and puckers are the best indication that the quilt has been washed many times.

Washing can, conversely, add to the appeal of a quilt. Those very same wrinkles, crinkles, and puckers add more texture to the quilt top and may actually increase its visual impact. Certainly the fact that this was a much beloved quilt to someone adds to its nostalgia appeal. In some cases, particularly with the bold colors of the Amish quilts, washing may soften colors rather than fade them and this can also increase the visual appeal of the quilt.

Another clue to washing is to check the batting. Before the arrival of today's polyester battings, quilts were filled with cotton or wool. As we saw in Chapter 3, cotton and wool batts required substantial quilting to prevent finding all the batting in a lump in one corner after the first wash. Polyester batting stays in place, even after washing, and this is one reason why newer quilts have less quilting stitches across the top. Cotton and wool battings needed many tiny stitches close together to hold the filling firmly in place. The new polyester battings require less quilting to keep them from separating and lumping. Make a sandwich of your hands on the top and bottom of a quilt. With fingers and palms facing each other, move your hands along the quilt and feel for batting lumps. Some will be obvious, others less so, feeling more like an extra thickness was included rather than being an obvious lump. Sometimes the bunched batting is visible to the eye. Check the bottoms and edges of any large, unquilted areas of the quilt, and you may find lumps of batting resting there comfortably after giving up the battle with the wash. You can even spot batting lumps by holding the quilt up to the light and noting the dark spots in the quilt. Shifted batting decreases the value of a quilt simply because the collected lumps may be so noticeable that the quilt won't hang well on a wall. Its evenness of warmth on a bed is also diminished. A quilt with lumps of loose batting means there are spots with no batting at all. Some of the quilt will keep you warmer than other parts. Don't despair if you fall in love with a quilt with bunched batting. These quilts should also be preserved, but the price should reflect the condition. And, the quilt can be repaired. How to fix it, and whether you should, is the subject of Chapter 7.

Another clue to an unwashed quilt is the presence of sizing or glazing on the fabric. Fabrics were sized and glazed to add stiffness. Chintzes were usually glazed but held their sheen longer than other glazed fabrics. After repeated washings, the glaze wears off, leaving the fabric softer and more pliable than when it was new. Look for the surface sheen that indicates that a fabric was glazed or sized. If it's still there, then the quilt has not been washed, or at least, has not been washed too often.

Don't reject a quilt simply because it has stains. Many stains can be removed by washing with little or no damage to the quilt. If a quilt has been washed before, and you have that confirmed by the dealer you bought it from or determine it yourself from the above indications, then you can follow the directions in Chapter 8 to wash out the stains and surface dirt. If you've purchased a never-washed quilt with stains, ask your dealer to recommend an expert quilt cleaner. There's no greater disaster than to wash a quilt for the first time only to find that the colors ran and ruined it. Not all quiltmakers, either antique or contemporary, washed their fabrics before making the quilt. Don't take the chance of washing an unwashed quilt yourself. There are cleaners who specialize in quilts who can safely clean the quilt for you. Your dealer should be able to make a recommendation. If not, check with your local historical society or a museum for a recommendation. *See illustration #17.*

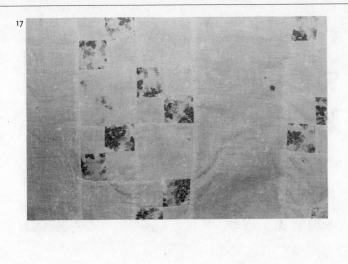

17 The stains on this four-patch baby quilt detract from its value because other factors make the quilt common: the workmanship in the seaming is not expert; the pattern is not rare, and there's nothing spectacular or unusual in the fabric choices. If the quilt pattern or fabrics were unique, or, the workmanship better, the stain would not detract as much from the value of the top. Quilt from the authors' collection.

Often, the dealer has already cleaned a quilt before it's offered for sale simply because it will sell better with the stains and dirt removed. It's fine to say that stains should not sway your decision to buy an otherwise exceptional quilt, but many people, especially first-time buyers, are turned off by a stained quilt. Make sure you ask the dealer if a quilt with stains has already been cleaned. It might be that the stains are permanent, in which case the price should be lower than the same quality quilt without stains. A reputable dealer should tell you up front if a cleaning has been attempted and failed. Mildew, for instance, is one stain that is almost impossible to remove. If you can live with the stains, consider yourself lucky for getting a great quilt at a wonderful price.

Fabric deterioration is another factor to carefully consider in the quilt you select. Tears, rips, and puncture holes are obvious indications of heavy use. As we'll see in Chapter 7, these can be repaired, but they really should decrease the value of a quilt. Here again, many times a dealer will go ahead and repair a quilt before it's offered for sale. If this was done, the dealer should point it out to you. The rule of thumb is that a dealer can do anything he or she wants to a quilt as long as the buyer knows repairs or cleanings have been done. Repairs already made to a quilt should be noted before the sale and the price should reflect it. A repaired quilt is not as valuable as one in original condition, no matter how well the repairs have been done. *See illustrations #18 and #18A.*

Badly damaged quilts offered for sale as is, with their rips, tears, and wear left alone, are best known as cutters. Most dealers will go ahead and repair a quilt that shows promise. The less unique quilt that needs work will be offered at a reduced price as a cutter. Or, the dealer will go ahead and cut the quilt using the good sections to make smaller wall hangings, crib quilts, or other items. Cutting up antique quilts to produce smaller products is not as prevalent a practice today as it was in the early 1990s. A greater resepect for even excessively worn quilts has led dealers to offer these quilts as is, at reduced prices. The buyer can then use such a quilt

18 This Strip, or Ribbon, Quilt was made in the 1860s and shows much fabric deterioration, splitting and loss. Silks, satins, and velvets of that era did not stand up well to the passage of time. Quilt courtesy of the Atwater Family.

18A A close look at this Snowball Quilt shows fabric pieces literally shattered and shredding apart. It's still valuable because of its distinctive design and exceptional embroidery. Quilt courtesy of the Wilson Family.

as a research tool, studying its workmanship and technique. A worn quilt, with tears and holes, offers greater opportunities to learn about quilting than one you wouldn't dream of taking apart to study.

There are quilt sellers who repair quilts and pass them off as original work and fabric. It's frowned upon in the industry and these dealers are few and far between, but they do exist. Which is all the more reason to buy only from a dealer you trust who was highly recommended to you.

Worn spots on the top of a quilt can also be repaired or left as is. After all, one of the reasons we buy quilts is for their nostalgia and sentimental value. The fact that a quilt is worn thin proves it was well loved by its previous owners. Worn fabric pieces within the quilt top should be carefully inspected. If the worn spots affect all the different fabrics within the quilt top, the wear is probably from use. Some frayed, thin, and weakened fabrics are the result of inferior dyeing. This shows up particularly with the acid reds of the late 1800s. If the worn spots on your quilt top show up only in one of the fabrics and all the pieces of this same fabric show wear, it is probably the result of these acid dyes. This fabric deterioration marks a specific time period so well that the wear has little effect on the price.

Silk crazy quilts, even when the fabric starts turning brittle and the pieces are frayed, may be of greater value than another quilt in perfect condition. The silks and satins used in these quilts during the Victorian period just haven't held up as well as other fabrics. But, once again, they are such excellent examples of a specific period of quilt history that they retain their value even in fair to poor condition where a cotton quilt would not. Because the silk crazies will continue to deteriorate to the point where they can't be used at all even to hang, wool crazy quilts will supplant them and continue to increase in value because the wool crazies can be hung and used to illustrate the same period of quiltmaking.

Bindings are generally the first part of a quilt to show the effects of wear, washing, and use. As the outside edge of the quilt, the binding is the part that rubs along the floor most often. It is also the part most often grabbed when we snuggle into a quilt. The binding is the most frequently repaired and replaced part of a quilt. *See illustration #19.*

The Dresden plate quilt pictured here was made by Liz Aleshire's great-grandmother in the early 1900s. It was most likely made from a precut kit popular at the time. The indication that this is a kit quilt is the low number of different fabrics in the plates. There are too many of the same fabrics for it to have been made from a typical scrap bag. It has mildew stains, some of the plate sections are rotted away so that only the seams are left, the sashings have worn through on the outside blocks, and the binding has already been repaired once.

Originally this quilt was self-bound. That means that the backing fabric was turned over to the front and stitched down as the binding. When this frayed and wore out, a less expert seamstress repaired it by simply folding an inch or two of the quilt to the back and stitching it down. The uneven, highly visible stitches in blue thread show that this repair was done by an inexpert seamstress. Whoever repaired it wanted simply to keep using the quilt, because she ignored the design elements of the quilt by folding over parts of the Dresden Plate patterns of the blocks and the chain quilting in the borders to make her new binding. Because of the way she fixed it, when viewed whole, this quilt looks like it never had left or right borders, and the

19 Showing much use and wear, this predominantly blue Dresden Plate kit quilt has a torn binding, tears on the back, many tears and splits on the front. It does have nice cable, grid and outline quilting but it presents serious problems for a quilt restorer. Stabilization may be the only recourse for keeping the original work of the maker and the period fabrics. Quilt from the authors' collection.

top and bottom plate blocks look like parts were lopped off. Inspecting the back shows the extra fold in the edges of the quilt and reveals the original self-binding.

Unfortunately, great-grandmother's beautiful Dresden Plate quilt, so indicative of the pastel period, wouldn't be regarded as worth much more than a cutter to a dealer. Kit quilts, regardless of age, are not equal in value to an original design This one has large patches of mildew stains that won't come out; it's been much used and shows it; the fabric deterioration in the plate patches is extensive and the result of wear, not inferior dyeing; and the repairs did little more than accelerate the wear along the edges of the quilt so that now the sashings as well as the bindings and borders need extensive repair. But it will never become a cutter because of its sentimental value. This quilt still has many possibilities, and we'll refer to it extensively in Chapter 7.

As with other repairs, a dealer should tell you if the binding has been replaced or if it is original. A quilt with its original binding in good condition should be valued higher than a quilt with a poor binding or no binding at all. A quilt with an original, but poor binding should be valued higher than a quilt with a new, replaced binding, even if period fabrics were used for the repair. Remember, if it's not original, it's worth comparatively less than a quilt that has all its original parts. Some dealers don't point out a replaced binding. Customers want quilts in excellent condition, and the temptation to replace a binding and pass it off as original is a great one. Dealers we talked with and visited all noted on their price tags any repairs or replacements they had made to a quilt, and their prices always reflected those changes. Remember to ask questions. If repairs aren't noted but you're pretty sure they've been made, question that dealer thoroughly on all aspects of the quilts for sale. *See illustration #20.*

Color loss, or fading, can be caused by washing or overexposure to bright lights or direct sunlight. If the fading shows all over the different fabrics in the quilt, in other words evenly over the top, the fading is probably from use and cleaning. If there are streaks of fading over the

20

20 The center of this Pinwheel block shows fabric fading. The virtual straight line of the color loss in the triangle on the center left, indicates the quilt was displayed, while folded, in bright sunlight. Quilt courtesy of the Wilson Family.

quilt top they are probably the result of exposure to strong light. Remember this when you display, hang, or drape the quilts you've bought. Any bright light, and certainly direct sunlight, will fade the parts of the quilt it plays on the most. Color loss devalues a quilt. A faded, streaked quilt is less valuable than one that has faded evenly overall, and the unfaded quilt is more valuable than the one that has faded from use and washing.

There are exceptions. As already mentioned, Amish quilts with their bold colors and combinations tend to soften and mellow with use and washing. Streaks of fading caused by sunlight or bright display lights will devalue these quilts, too, but washing sometimes adds to their visual effect rather than detracting from it. An unwashed Amish quilt has its own appeal of sharp, crisp color, while the washed one may make the colors glow in a way the unwashed cannot.

There is also a green used in the late 1800s that has had a tendency to fade to a mustardy-tan color that is so indicative of the period that the design has to be pretty awful to devalue the quilt that incorporates it. It's seen mostly in appliqué and can be readily recognized as the stems and leaves of the flower designs. It does sometimes show up in pieced geometric quilts, too. The color faded so uniformly that it was once thought that it was the color of choice. But, so many Rose of Sharon and Whig Rose quilts showed up with the same tan fabric, and it seemed illogical that so many quiltmakers would choose tan for stems and leaves, that investigations revealed that it had been green and then faded to the tan color. In some cases, you can see the original green by slightly lifting the piece to see the seam allowance underneath. This may be a shade of the original green that hasn't faded to the tan because of less exposure to light and washing solutions. This faded-to-tan green is another exception that proves the rule. Although color loss normally devalues a quilt, this faded green is so indicative of a quiltmaking period and style that it shouldn't devalue the quilt. Sometimes the faded pieces enhance the design and these quilts become more valuable. When these formerly green pieces detract from the design, then the quilt might be less valuable even though it strongly indicates a period of quiltmaking history. Your emotional reaction to the quilt will tell you which is which. If you still like the impact of the quilt even with the odd-colored stems and leaves, then the faded color "works" for you. If the quilt doesn't hit you, then the fading detracts from its appeal.

A quilt with permanent crease lines was improperly stored. As we'll see in Chapter 8, quilts should be stored in cloth and refolded at least twice a year to avoid making permanent creases in the fabric. These creases devalue a quilt. Again, it isn't reason enough not to buy and preserve a good quilt, but all things being equal, creases should mean a lower price for the quilt than it would fetch without them.

Remember that condition counts less than you think. The truly unique quilt will overcome stains, rips, frays, poor repair, and fades. But as you become more and more knowledgeable about quilts and quilt collecting, you'll be able to judge the condition of a quilt, know when one has been repaired, and, therefore know how it affects the price. If nothing else, it helps you find a reputable dealer. The dealer who notes repairs and replacements, cleanings, and permanency of stains on the quilts for sale is dealing honestly and is one you can trust.

6 Workmanship

Workmanship means the quality of work within a quilt, including stitching, assembly, quilting, fabric choice, color balance, and design, and how these factors affect the value of a quilt.

The most easily recognized and evaluated aspect of workmanship in a quilt is the quality of the quilting stitch. A quilt is three layers: top, batting, and backing. It is the thickness of the batting and the weight of the fabrics used for the top and backing that determine the degree of difficulty in sewing the quilting stitch. Obviously a heavy wool quilt with a thick batt is extremely difficult to stitch through and can result in relatively large stitches. This is the reason why wool and velvet Crazy Quilts and Log Cabins are tied rather than quilted. Their thickness prohibits the fineness of stitching that the expert quilter demanded of herself. In fact, many Crazy Quilts and Log Cabins are not quilted because they have no batting.

In cotton quilts, with medium to light batting, quilt stitches should be small and even. Except for the miniaturization period where, for a short time, the number of tiny pieces in a quilt rather than expert stitching determined a quilt's worth, quiltmakers have always competed to make their quilting stitch the smallest of their peers. One of our sources stated seeing a quilt with 20 stitches to the inch! We saw several quilts with 10 stitches to the inch, fewer with 12, and most were in the 6 to 8 stitches per inch range. A quilt with 10 or more quilt stitches to the inch should be priced slightly higher. *See illustration #21.*

As important as the number of quilt stitches per inch is the uniform length of each stitch. All else being equal, a quilt with stitches of varying length throughout should be valued less than one where the stitches are all approximately the same length. These are the hallmark of the expert quilter.

Even if the stitches are relatively large or uneven, sometimes the amount of quilting can compensate for the lack of expert stitching. A Lone Star with its plain set squares covered with princess feather stitching, wreaths, cornucopias, or floral quilting designs is of greater value

21 This Star of Bethlehem quilt shows more workmanship problems with mismatched seams in the center where four blocks meet. The seam lines should have intersected perfectly. The quilting is excellent. Quilt courtesy of the Zimmer Family.

22 The blocks on this Nine Patch are not aligned. Each block should have been set squarely in line with the one above and below it. Although the top is made of vibrant fabrics, the poor workmanship makes it a very affordable top. Quilt from the authors' collection.

than one with mere outline stitching. An overall quilt pattern such as the single, double, or triple parallel rows of stitches that run diagonally across the top makes a quilt more valuable than if the quiltmaker merely stitched quarter-inch outlines around the block patterns. A white-work quilt (also called whole-cloth and sometimes miscalled trapunto) is one of the most valuable because its pattern is derived from the quilting and not from any pieced or appliqué pattern sewed on the top. *White-work* is a term held over from the past when these quilts were done only with white thread on white cloth. There has been a trend in recent years, and always among Amish quiltmakers, to use a ground fabric and thread of a color instead of white.

A good quilting design should add to the surface texture of the quilt, either highlighting or contrasting the patchwork pattern chosen for the top. While, technically, quilting is only to hold the three layers of the quilt sandwich together and keep the batting from shifting and lumping, this is another area where quiltmakers rapidly added beauty and expertise. Hundreds, perhaps thousands, of hours go into exceptionally worked quilts, and it's likely that at least half of that time was spent solely on the quilting. Expert quilting adds greatly to the value of a quilt, even if other elements are not exceptional.

Appliqué stitches should be virtually invisible. Again, these stitches should be small and even. To check appliqué stitches, pull (lightly, please!) on the appliquéd patch to lift it slightly from the ground fabric. Note the placement of the stitches. Tight, small stitches that can be seen only while lifting the appliquéd patch are the most desirable. Curves and corners on appliqué should be smooth and unfrayed. Fraying on the inside curve of an appliqué patch indicates an inexpert maker who left too little seam allowance or didn't correctly slit the seam to make an even, flat curve.

There is one exception to the invisible appliqué stitch. In the approximately 20-year period after the Civil War when the sewing machine was invented and became popular, some quiltmakers showed off the fascinating new technology by appliquéing with a topstitch done by machine. If you can accurately date a quilt with machine appliqué to this time period, the topstitching should add to the value instead of detract from it. However, this is a matter of opinion that may differ among quilt dealers and collectors. Although machine assembly does not detract from the value of a quilt, some collectors still devalue a quilt with machine appliqué. We choose to honor history and the advent of the new technology by according these quilts a higher value. Quilts with machine quilting, no matter when they were made, are less valuable than those with hand quilting because the machine stitch simply isn't as well done as hand stitching or as time consuming. Even now, when less and less free time is available to anyone for any hobby, machine quilting and appliqué is popular but should decrease the value when compared with a hand-stitched quilt. *See illustration #22.*

The next most obvious example of good workmanship is the alignment of the sashing strips. These strips of cloth used to separate individual quilt blocks from each other should match perfectly on the horizontal and the vertical. Sashings strips that are offset from each other represent poor piecing of the block. Inaccurate cutting or piecing of the patches in a design might make each block a different size and force the sashing out of line. Puckers in the corners of individual blocks or along the outer seam line can be the result of forcing a too-big block to fit the sashing. Conversely, puckers or gathers in the sashing might have been necessary to fit a too small block into the quilt top. Generally, sashings are the same color throughout the quilt, and a piece of a different fabric within a sash might mean the maker ran out of the right fabric. Unaligned sashings usually indicate poor workmanship and would make a quilt less valuable than one with perfectly aligned, uniform sashing strips. When quilt blocks are "forced" to fit a sashing, or vice versa, bulges appear in the quilt. Unless tucks and gathers are used, even quilting won't flatten the quilt and quilts should be flat. Also look for sashings that are slightly wavy and block designs that may be distorted because of the quiltmaker's attempt to force them to fit the sashings. Photographs in this chapter illustrate these workmanship points.

There is an exception, however, to the rule of perfectly aligned sashings. Some antique African-American-made quilts, (discussed in Chapter 34) use unaligned sashings as incorporated design elements. Using different fabrics within the sashings, instead of the coordinated fabric in traditional quilts, is also a design selection in these quilts. Quilts that show these design elements should not be devalued because of them. We must, instead, be aware, as is made clear in Chapter 34, that they are part and parcel of the maker's art and not a reflection on the workmanship. Even in these quilts, however, puckers and gathers should not exist. Seams should be flat and even. *See illustrations #23 and #23A.*

For your next clue to good or excellent workmanship, inspect the individual blocks in a pieced top. The points of each pattern piece that make up the square should match with the others. Probably the most notable example of poor workmanship can be seen in a Lone Star, either bedsize or blocksize, where the diamond points don't match. If the middle diamonds of a Lone Star (or star of Bethlehem as it's called in the Northeast) don't match, each succeeding strip of diamonds will be successively off point. The quiltmaker who didn't rip out those patches and start over is guilty of inferior workmanship, and that quilt is not as valuable as one where all the points match and align perfectly. *See illustration #24.*

23

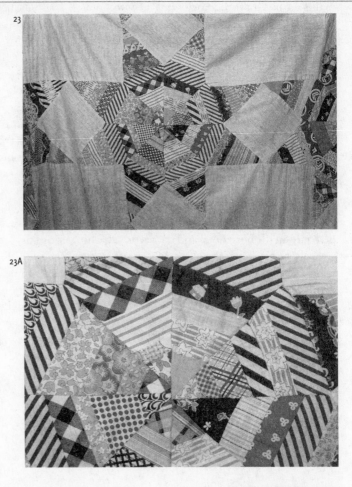

23A

23 The triangles of this Eight-Point Star are strip pieced and when viewed from a distance this top looks spectacular. While the colors are vibrant, the assembly is poor. Each inner point of the diamonds should meet precisely in one point.

23A The close-up shows that the seams of the eight diamonds are way off. There's also a pucker where the yellow inset square was 'forced' to fit the star. Quilt from the authors' collection.

24 This star top shows better matching where the points meet in the center but it does show some rippling in individual diamond patches due to 'forcing' the pieces to fit. The folds and bulges shown here will make this top difficult to display and even harder to quilt. It's probably the reason the top wasn't finished. Quilt from the authors' collection.

24

The more complex the pieced block, and the better the workmanship, the greater the value of the quilt. This is particularly true in Compass Rose Quilts or Dahlia quilts that are difficult to piece and keep points matched. Many pieced blocks use curved pattern pieces, and these are even more difficult to match perfectly because some of the edges are cut on the bias. As a rule of thumb, if the points match, the quilt is more valuable and the more pattern pieces there are in a pieced block, the more valuable the quilt.

The choice of fabrics is the next item to inspect while you're deciding to buy a quilt. Quilts of cheap cottons or the chintz of the late 1800s that was so bad it gave rise to the term *chintzy* (applied to anything, or anybody, cheap) will be of less value than quilts made with quality cloth. We've already mentioned that a basket quilt is a multigenerational quilt assembled with sashing strips made of truly inferior cloth. Already wearing thin, the sashings preclude use of the quilt and even make it foolhardy to hang it for any length of time. We're assuming the woman who added the strips was not an expert quiltmaker or seamstress, for if she was, she would have picked better fabric for this important part of the quilt. The blocks are made of strong, high-quality shirting fabrics assembled with small, expert hand stitching, leading us to conclude they were made by another woman who knew the feel and desirability of good, strong cloth and who was much more experienced. The quilt was left as is and then quilted to preserve the added work in this multi-generational quilt. Sentimental value is sometimes more important than correcting flaws.

Cloth that is rotted or fraying may or may not be the result of poor fabric selection. Rot and deterioration overall is probably a strong indication that the quilt was not properly stored, washed, or cared for. But, as we saw in the section on dyes and dyeing in Chapter 4, some fabric deterioration can be the result of the old acid dyes used to print the fabric. For some periods of history, quiltmakers used the best fabric available but because of inferior technology, it just didn't last. Quilts with overall fabric deterioration, or poor fabric selection, are less valuable and should be priced accordingly.

Some aspects of design are considered part of workmanship: block arrangement, color balance, and borders.

How a quiltmaker arranged the blocks in a quilt attests to her artistic eye. Most basket blocks are arranged with the handles or flowers pointing in the same direction, but some quilters place them in sets of four with the handles pointing to the inside of the resulting square. If the entire quilt top is assembled in multiples of these groups of four, this is also a pleasing design. That odd sensation you feel but can't name when you view a quilt means that there's something not quite right about it and the reason may be that the pattern balance is off even in a small way. *See illustrations #25 and 25A; #26 and 26A.*

Many quiltmakers obviously arranged, rearranged and rearranged again their finished blocks to find just the right order to piece them together into a top. Many quilt patterns create totally different visual effects by simply turning them inward or outward in relation to each other. Few quilters assembled the pine tree in any way other than upright—looking like a tree. There are a couple, however, who assembled the block in groups of four, like the basket quilt, and created a stunning optical illusion. Generally, when a quiltmaker assembled a pattern nontraditionally and the result is a startling re-creation of a traditional pattern, these quilts are

25

25A

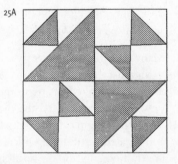

25 & 25A Old Maid's Puzzle
Complex Assembly. The way a
group of blocks is assembled to
made the final quilt can
camouflage the basic block. The
Old Maid's Puzzle can be very
confusing when the blocks are
turned and set without sashings.

26

26A

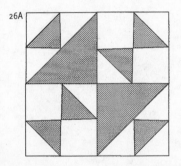

26 & 26A Old Maid's Puzzle: Simple
Assembly. Take the same blocks
and set them in the same
direction, add sashings, and the
block is easily identified.

27

27A

27 The abundance of different fabrics in this Hourglass quilt is a feast for the eyes. Created in the early 1900s it has nearly every color imaginable but from a distance appears predominantly brown. Quilt courtesy of the Dean Family.

27A A close-up of the quilt shows less than perfect assembly. With all those small pieces, we can probably forgive the quiltmaker. She did keep an interesting scrap bag!

more valuable. They are yet another testament to the fact that quilts were *created* not just made.

Color balance is another design aspect that greatly affects the visual and emotional impact of a quilt. Working from scraps and leftover fabrics, most quiltmakers didn't have the luxury of working with large lengths of coordinated fabrics such as we use today or that were available to the wealthy. Scrap bag quilts are by far the biggest percentage of quilts available. Antique quilts of coordinated fabrics are rarer but not impossible to find. Because their color balance was built in right from the beginning of the work, coordinated fabric quilts may have greater visual impact and therefore more value. *See illustrations #27 and #27A.*

But, just as they did with their patterns, quiltmakers worked with their scrap bag blocks, shifting them around the top of the quilt, offsetting a light block with a dark, constantly rearranging them so that the colors blended, contrasted, and moved the eye across the top of the quilt. This is not something they did unconsciously. Blocks were not merely pieced, thrown in a pile, and then picked up in turn and sewed together. The expert quiltmaker would have spent considerable time arranging the blocks to get the best possible, most pleasing use of color, even if it was done by instinct alone.

Another aspect of color balance is contrast. In a quilt like the Log Cabin, contrast is the strongest design element. Each Log Cabin block is divided in half on the diagonal with darks on one side and lights on the other. If fabric colors are chosen that are too close in tone and don't offer enough contrast, the prime effect, the interplay of light and dark of the Log Cabin is lost. Assembly of the Log Cabin blocks in the jagged Streak o' Lightning, the squares of Barn Raising, or the rows of straight furrows should highlight the contrast between light and dark fabrics. If the dark and light rows are not obvious and easily distinguished, then the quiltmaker didn't arrange her colors with enough contrast within the blocks. A Log Cabin with obvious light and dark contrast, pleasing to the eye, is more valuable than one without that contrast.

Other quilt patterns rely on contrast for their optical effect. The Tumbler pattern is one. This is a one-patch design, like the hexagon. Tumblers look like a profile of a glass, hence their name. It's a rectangle that's wider at the top than at the bottom. Half the pieces are cut from light-colored fabrics or prints and the other half from dark. A light tumbler piece is sewed to a dark, upside-down tumbler piece, the alternating pattern is continued until there is a row long enough to fit the dimensions of the quilt. The second row starts with a dark so that its pattern of light and dark is the opposite of the first row. Tumblers were often made as charm quilts, no two fabrics repeating anywhere in the top. If the fabrics contrast well, the effect is a kaleidoscope of light and dark colors and print textures. If they're too close in shade, the kaleidoscope effect is lost in the jumble of similar color tones. *See illustration #28.*

The hexagon is another one-patch design sometimes used for a Charm quilt but more often seen in Grandmother's Flower Garden quilts. In these, the hexagons are arranged in circles to form the flower. Each circle is usually the same fabric or at least the same basic color, even if in different tones. In this pattern there are three or four circles of color to make the flower, and the circles can be arranged with alternating light and dark rings, can go from light in the center to dark on the outside, or can be the reverse. The flowers are then set off with another row

28

28 This close-up of an 1880s Ocean Waves patch shows the lengths to which an expert quiltmaker will go in order to have a polished look. One tiny corner was pieced together, not only to get a whole triangle, but a whole triangle with the printed pattern matched! Block courtesy of the Zimmer Family.

of white hexagons between the flowers. Traditionally, small green diamonds joined the flowers together, but more often the white row that sets off the flower is also used to join the blocks together.

We saw one spectacular scrap bag nine-patch variation that was so well planned that each block was assembled with a light and dark side, divided on the diagonal like the Log Cabin block. When assembled in the Straight Furrows style, these nine-patch blocks produced dark and light bands that were highly contrasted and visually pleasing. Yet the entire top was the usual mix of scrap bag solids, prints, and dark and light fabrics and done in the simplest quilt block.

Remember that the use of color is controlled by the quiltmaker. Sometimes what seems to our eye unbalanced may just be the planned effect of the artist. If a color or piece of fabric leaps out at you, determine why. Perhaps that odd bit of orange or that dark grouping of fabric pieces was intended to draw your eye to that portion of the quilt. Maybe that's the signature or date patch; maybe the pieces are from the clothing of someone special to the quiltmaker and so, to the maker, deserved noticeable placement. Perhaps the artist's eye saw something else in the pattern that she wanted to point out. Sometimes oddly placed color creates a whimsical quality in a quilt that makes it all the more valuable. Of course, sometimes, a quilt is just out of color balance. It doesn't mean it shouldn't be bought and preserved. It just means it will fetch a lower price.

Borders enhance a quilt's value just as a frame enhances a painting. A properly designed border, in the right color scheme, once again draws our eye to the important part of the quilt, its pattern. Prairie points and saw tooth borders are rare because of their degree of difficulty and therefore increase the value of the quilt to the collector. A good border, like a good frame, adds to the overall beauty of a quilt. It shouldn't be so noticeable that you see the border and not the quilt and it shouldn't be so weak that it fails to highlight the design of the quilt top.

These are the basics of workmanship. Look for your own examples of good and bad work-manship, quilting, design, color balance, and borders. Learn to analyze the quilts you see—both the ones you like and the ones you don't. Instead of trusting only your instinct, judging solely on immediately liking or not liking a quilt, soon you'll be able to distinguish why a quilt appeals to you and why it doesn't. But don't lose track of those instincts! Emotions play a large part in the appeal of a quilt and we don't want to get so educated that we pay attention only to technique. The overall impact of the quilt on your sensibilities is of far more importance in your decision to buy it than all its technical aspects combined.

7 Repair and Finishing

There are several levels of controversy concerning the repair and restoration of quilts. At the first level, there is discussion over the terminology. Some quilt historians feel it's impossible to restore a quilt, claiming that no one can truly return a quilt to its original state. They feel it's more accurate to say a quilt is "repaired" than to refer to it as "restored."

Despite this fine-tuning of terminology, there are still many people repairing quilts who call themselves quilt restorers. In fact, most professionals who repair quilts still use the term *restoration*. As a technical point, we agree that *repair* is the proper term, so this chapter will refer to repairing a quilt, not restoring it. Remember, though, that there are people who still refer to the repair process as restoration. When you're looking for an expert to repair your quilt, look for the title *restorer*. After reading and reviewing this chapter, you'll know what questions to ask a professional to make sure the repairs to your quilt are done the way you want them done. *See illustrations #29 and #29A.*

At the next level of controversy, some historians, dealers, and collectors are very particular about how repairs are made to a quilt. The preferred method of fixing frayed, rotted, or deteriorated fabrics is to either stabilize or appliqué appropriate fabrics over the damaged piece. It is considered tampering with the history of the quilt to remove a damaged piece of fabric and replace it. To quilt purists, only fabrics of the same period as the ones in the quilt should be used to repair it, and then they should be appliquéd over the original, damaged piece. This way, if at some point in the future your quilt needs to be closely examined for its historical or technical significance, then the original fabric is there, underneath the new, to be studied. As our knowledge of quiltmaking history grows, these pieces of fabric and the way the quilt was assembled could add a great deal to quiltmaking knowledge; thus, many experts believe that all the original work should be left in the quilt.

On the other hand, there are those who believe that an error in judgment on the part of the original quiltmaker should be corrected. Using this theory, the example we used in Chapter 6

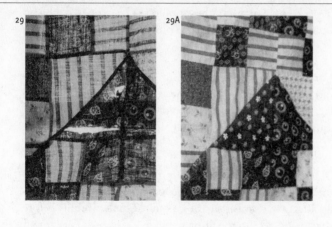

29 The strong brown and blue dyes in this quilt top have eaten away the fabric and caused splitting.

29A This close up of the same block shows repairs made by appliquéing fabric over the frayed and split piece shown in the previous picture. Even though an exact fabric match was impossible, care was taken to match the new fabric to the print style and tone of the original fabric. Quilt from the authors' collection.

would mean that the work of one generation of quilters would have been lost by replacing the sashings on the basket quilt. The one off-colored center hexagon on a grandmother's flower garden quilt should be replaced. That stark, one-time use of the ghastly orange fabric should be replaced with something more color-balanced to the rest of the quilt.

Why shouldn't we replace the ghastly orange with a piece of fabric more pleasing? A quilt historian could argue that a valuable piece of information would be lost. Why was it there? Did the quiltmaker simply run out of fabric? If she did, why didn't she just get more? Was she too far from town? Was she out of money? Was the orange a piece from a family fabric that had sentimental meaning? Or, was it actually a design element included on purpose? Perhaps this quiltmaker remembered and believed the superstition that a perfect quilt, or a perfect anything, meant attempting to imitate God. Rather than invite His wrath, perhaps she purposely included the one piece of orange as an imperfection? Even if the imperfection were left in, we may never know the real answer, but the absence of the single piece of orange means no one will ever ask the questions. And that's why some quilt historians object to the removal of original fabric no matter its damaged condition or jarring effect.

Yet, we're sure that quilt historians would agree that a quilt that smacks the artistic sensibilities so strongly as the one ghastly piece of orange among the balance of the fabric would mean that that quilt is headed for the garbage heap and will be lost to history. If a quilt doesn't appeal to us, its chances for preservation are severely limited. It wouldn't be cared for or displayed. It seems far better, in this case, to fix a quilt so that most of it will be used and preserved rather than throw it away. Quilts that are badly worn or with poor design elements can be purchased cheaply. They're worth less because of their poor condition. Since they're already devalued, what's the harm in repairing the quilt so that it can be used with pride?

We'd agree with both arguments. Certainly a quilt that is damaged but is of great historical, technical, or family significance should be preserved as is. It is a record of its time and maker.

If we are to learn anything from these exceptional quilts, they should not be tampered with no matter how noble the intention. Only when left alone can these quilts reveal to us the full extent of the maker's intent and art.

Museum-quality quilts, damaged or not, should be left as is. But we also believe that badly damaged but beautiful quilts should not be discarded. If this means a new binding, new borders, new fabric pieces, then so be it. Ultimately it is the decision of you, the owner, that is the final determination on whether a quilt should be repaired or left alone. In Chapter 8, we'll see how to care for a quilt so that any further damage is avoided.

Some quilt damage is permanent. Discoloration, color loss, color migration, and dye deterioration is permanent, as are mold and mildew stains. These types of damage can only be covered up. Permanent damage should affect your decision to buy a quilt. Think carefully before you buy a damaged quilt about what it will take to repair or stabilize it. Once you've bought it, you can follow the advice in this chapter on how to cover over the damage or learn to live with it as is.

If you decide to repair a quilt, make sure you know how or find a professional who does. Most experts agree that you should use period fabrics to repair a quilt. Once you know the approximate time period during which your quilt was made, you can begin hunting for replacement fabric from that same era. Most quilt dealers have a selection of period fabrics they use for their own repairs and make available for sale. At the very least, if you've established a relationship with a dealer, you can tell them what you need, and they'll keep an eye out for it as they search for more quilts. We'll talk about cutter quilts later but they are also a source for period fabrics. A cutter with usable fabric from the same time period as your quilt can be cut to provide you with period material. While you're looking for period fabrics, keep an eye out for thread, too. To be strictly accurate, you should use 100 percent cotton thread of the same weight and color that was used originally.

The Basket quilt discussed in the last chapter was finished using new material for the borders. Although author Liz Aleshire didn't change the sashings or the baskets, leaving them as the original work of the previous two quiltmakers, if she were to finish that quilt today, after researching this book, she'd finish it with period fabrics rather than new. The quilt isn't ruined. It's a beautiful example of a multi-generational quilt. It just isn't accurate. If you can be accurate, do so. There are sources for period fabrics and thread, and these should be used if possible. There are also sources for new fabrics in period colors and designs. If all else fails, you can use some of these reproduction fabrics. Your common sense should prevail. The important thing is to preserve the quilt as closely as possible to its original design, fabric content, and artistic intent. *See illustrations #30.*

Before you begin your repairs, you should document the quilt thoroughly. Make a graph of the quilt, noting the blocks and fabric pieces that need repair. It's also a good idea to photograph the pieces you'll cover with fresh fabric. Get high-speed film for use in low light to take these pictures. A camera flash will contribute to the deterioration of your quilt because it is a high burst of intense light. Also photograph the bindings or borders that need repair. When you finish the repairs, take pictures again of the same spots with the fresh fabric. Photographs in this chapter show the before and after of damaged sections of a Jacob's Ladder quilt. Au-

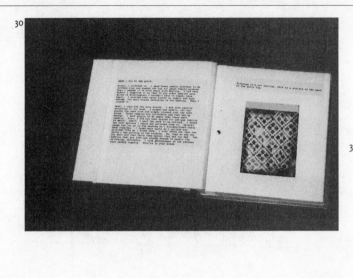

30

30 A good way to document your quilt is by creating an album like the one pictured here. Take photos of the quilt right after purchasing it and before any repair or stabilization is completed. This album was made detailing a Jacob's Ladder top that was repaired and then quilted. Quilt from the authors' collection.

thor Liz Aleshire made the repairs and documented them in a photo album to give to the quilt's recipient, in this case, co-author Kathy Barach.

If you do the work yourself, keep notes on how it was done and on any special problems you encountered. Note, also, where you found the replacement fabrics. The after pictures noted earlier show the replacement fabric. While it is period, it doesn't match any of the fabrics originally included in the quilt. Liz noted that fact in the quilt history album she gave to Kathy with the quilt as an example of special problems encountered while finishing the top. At the end of your repair project, you'll have detailed records of the process. Keep these together with any documentation you have of the quilt and its maker. This should include any personal stories about the quiltmaker, where and when the quilt was made, where and when you bought it, and how much it cost. You can keep all this documentation in a separate folder or you can stitch a muslin pocket to the back of the quilt and keep it there. With this last method, remember to wrap the documentation in acid-free paper so the oils from the paper and the chemicals from the photographs won't seep through to damage the quilt further. Or, you can be very formal and give a quilt history album to the recipient.

To begin your repairs, you should never remove the damaged piece of fabric in a quilt top. The Tumbler Quilt, pictured on page 86, was repaired using period fabrics, already cut by the original quiltmaker and found with the quilt top. Here again, the repairs are inaccurate. Although period fabric was used for the repair—and finding the pieces precut with the top meant that these were the same pool of fabrics used originally, a rare find—the old, frayed, and stained pieces were removed. Our determination of this quiltmaker's decisions while making her quilt is diminished because these fabrics were removed. In justice to the quilt, period fabric was used and replacement selections were made based on the other pieces in the quilt. On the other hand, the Jacob's Ladder mentioned above was repaired accurately. The damaged pieces were left in the quilt and the new pieces were appliquéd over them. *See illustration #31.*

31

31 This classic example of a one-patch Tumbler Quilt was a top found by a family in 1989 accompanied with enough extra pieces to finish the quilt. After forty years in storage the quilt began a new life. The dark blue border is new, but the blocks are all 1930s fabric. Quilt courtesy of Nancy Groves.

So, don't remove those torn, worn pieces from your newly acquired quilt. Instead, measure carefully and prepare a cutting template for the exact size and shape of the piece that needs replacing. After washing the fresh fabric, cut out a piece using the template and adding a half inch seam allowance around all sides. Lay the new piece over the old one, turn under the seam allowance, and pin it down. Make sure all of the damaged piece is covered and that the new piece doesn't overlap on any of the adjoining pieces. Leave the replacement fabric piece slightly loose, with a small bubble to it, to accommodate quilting stitches if needed. Blindstitch the new piece down. Continue covering the worn spots on your quilt, exactly matching the pattern pieces of the original until all the damaged areas are covered. *See illustrations #32–#32B.*

We saw two whimsical exceptions to covering damaged pieces exactly as they were originally cut. One was a cotton crazy quilt with the squares separated with solid sashings inexpertly pieced and unaligned. Both the sashings and the appliquéd replacement fabrics used to cover holes in them actually add to the light and frivolous nature of the quilt. Instead of detracting from the beauty of the quilt, the irregular-sized squares and rectangles of the unaligned repair pieces add a further touch of humor and movement in the quilt.

The second nontraditionally repaired quilt is a double nine patch that obviously needed a new binding. Most of the top in the quilt was in good shape, but a few blocks needed replacing. In the close-up, we can see that one of these blocks was repaired the right way, by appliqué, but the repairer didn't shape the replacement block to the exact size of the original. The few places this occurs does jar the symmetry of the quilt. It is the repair of the border that gives this quilt a whimsical look. The owner repaired it following accepted technique. She appliquéd the replacement pieces and even quilted through them after they were applied. But she replaced the binding in small strips rather than using ones the same length as a side. And, she pieced each strip on individually so that, as you can see in the close-up photo, some of the pieces are wider and extend further over the top of the quilt than others. These repairs give this quilt a decid-

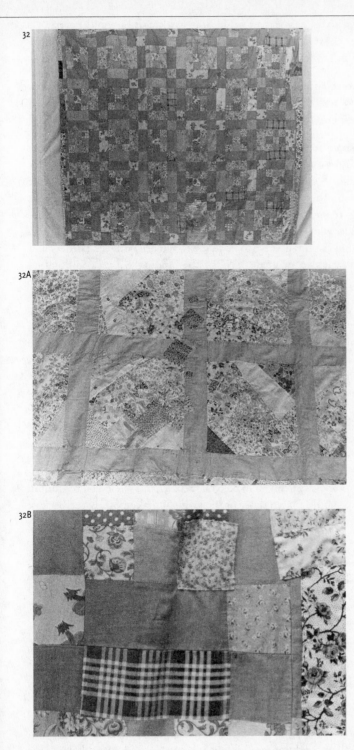

32 This tied comforter has a heavy blanket inside and shows signs of heavy use. Probably made in the 1920s, this piece holds some very interesting but non-professional repairs. Quilt courtesy of Laura Caro.

32A This close-up of the comforter shows patches appliquéd over tears in both the squares and the sashing. Rather than detracting from the appearance of the comforter, the patches add an abstract look. These type of repairs, although expedient at the time they were made, shouldn't be used to repair an older, more valuable quilt.

32B A look at the binding of this quilt also shows an interesting, although not recommended, repair. New fabric was stitched over the old binding, and in this case, extends into the original block to cover up the original frayed binding.

edly whimsical look that should make any viewer smile. The workmanship on the repairs is good. The replacement fabric is not from the same period, but the repairer did select new fabrics that matched the intensity and tone of the original scrap bag fabrics.

Neither of these quilts has been repaired according to the "rules" but in these two examples, the results made us happy they weren't. They're offbeat and irregular but the workmanship is good and the end result is pleasing to the eye.

Bindings are usually the first spots on a quilt to wear. The Dresden Plate quilt, discussed in Chapter 4, needs to have its binding replaced. One attempt at repairing the binding has already been made by simply folding the quilt around on all four sides and slip stitching the edge down. This repair will be removed. Since the border is also badly worn in spots, and is the same fabric as the binding, repairs will have to wait until suitable replacement fabric is found. Ideally, the owner should wait until she finds the exact fabric to match the original. This is probably impossible. A decision will have to be made to replace both the borders and the bindings with similar period fabric, or to just replace the binding with a coordinating piece.

Dealers regularly replace the worn bindings on quilts. It improves their salability if not their accuracy or originality. Replacing a binding is not as serious, except to purists, as replacing other parts of a quilt. As with all repairs made to a quilt before it's sold, the dealer should note it in the documentation of the quilt so you know when you buy it that repairs have been made, what fabrics were used, and whether the repairs were made by hand or machine. The price should reflect the repairs because the quilt is no longer completely original. But, as we've discussed before, a repaired quilt is much preferred to throwing one away, and as long as the dealer notes the repairs, you can feel confident purchasing it.

As you make the initial inspection of your quilt, documenting the damaged parts that need to be covered or replaced, you should also note the way it was made. Check the length of the assembly, appliqué and quilting stitches. When you make your repairs and when you re-quilt it, your stitches and workmanship should match those of the original maker. Study the back of the quilt to determine this quiltmaker's stitching style. Once you've documented the workmanship of the original quiltmaker, your repairs should reflect that same level. You'll destroy the integrity of the quilt if you replace long, uneven quilt stitches with your usual tiny, even ones. Quilt experts agree that repairs should be made duplicating the stitch length, quilting pattern, and workmanship of the original maker. If not done the same, the repairs will stand out, jarring the overall unity of the quilt.

While we agree that every attempt possible should be made to preserve a quilt as is, it's not always feasible. Some quilts are just too badly worn, overused, or uncared for to save whole. These are called cutter quilts. It's an apt title because a cutter quilt is taken apart and its good pieces used elsewhere. These salvaged pieces can be used as period replacement fabrics for less worn quilts. Or, if large enough, they can be cut down to crib or wall hanging size, rebound, and sold in their new form. There's no doubt that the basket quilt discussed in Chapter 5 would have had its inferior sashings removed by a dealer. The basket blocks themselves, with good workmanship and in excellent condition, could then be sewed into a new quilt or sold as a set. Because this quilt remained in the same family, and the sashings represent the work of the second generation that worked on the quilt, they were preserved as is. A dealer, sentiment aside, would not have left those inferior fabric sashings in.

Cutter quilts have been cut to make pillows, pocketbooks, totebags, and stuffed animals. Salvaged sections of worn quilts have been incorporated into clothing. Even designers, such as Ralph Lauren, have bought quilts to cut down for their clothing lines. The problem is that many people cut down quilts that should not be considered cutter quilts. Many quilts that should have been preserved whole are now gone forever. There is strong feeling among quilt historians that there is no such thing as a cutter quilt. A quilt too far gone for sale should be used for study purposes. A collector can use a cutter to determine assembly and stitching techniques or to get a rare view of the wrong side of a top to determine fabric dating.

A quilt placed in the cutter category should have a lower price than even most unquilted tops. Because they're so cheap, they're the perfect investment for study, salvage, or repair. Don't overlook the cutter quilt while you're searching for additions to your antique collection. If you have any knowledge of quilting, or some sewing background, a cutter can be the perfect place to learn about quilts and to teach yourself accurate repair techniques. And you'll be preserving a quilt, even if only in parts, that otherwise would be discarded. Be sure to let your dealer know that you're interested in cutter quilts. Usually a dealer won't invest in them because they don't appeal to most buyers. If you let your dealer know you want them, you can both save some history.

What do you do with an antique quilt that you don't want to repair or that repairs to would destroy the historical significance or design elements? For instance, a silk crazy quilt, considered the primary representative sample of quilting from the Victorian era, with frayed, cracking, or shredded fabric shouldn't be repaired. Because the silks in these quilts deteriorated so badly, period fabric is extremely difficult to find in good condition. Crazies are also particularly design sensitive. Only the original quiltmaker would be able to explain her choices of shapes, colors, and textures in such a quilt. But the very nature of the fabric deterioration makes these quilts almost impossible to preserve by any of the methods we've discussed. You can't vacuum them. The shredded fabric would be sucked into the cleaner, and surrounding fabrics, which appeared undamaged, could ravel and shred under the stress of vacuuming, thus extending the deterioration of the quilt top. Silks, velvets, and wools from this period, or any period for that matter, should never be washed. It's doubtful that you'll find a professional cleaner, even one with experience in chemically cleaning quilts, who will agree to clean one. The unique design elements of these quilts shouldn't be covered up with replacement cloth, period or not. But something must be done. *See illustrations #33 and #33A.*

It's called stabilizing. There's an excellent discussion of how to stabilize a quilt in Nancy O'Bryant Puentes's booklet, *First Aid for Family Quilts*. Puentes advises using either Crepeline, a special single-filament silk fabric, or nylon tulle also known as bridal illusion. You may want to dye these fabrics to match the colors you need to cover, but you don't have to. The very presence of the repair alerts the viewer to an interesting aspect of the quilt. A stabilization repair can be as much a conversation starter as the quilt itself.

The process is much the same as covering a damaged piece with a replacement piece. A piece of the tulle or Crepeline is cut to the size of the damaged piece and sewed through the seam

33

33A

33 The center of this Puff Quilt is made with men's silk hat bands and was found in a box of junk at a flea market. Purchased for $5, satin borders and buttons were added to complete the find. In the lower right corner is an example of stabilization. Quilt from the authors' collection.

33A This close-up of the corner block of the Puff Quilt shows an example of stabilization using nylon netting appliquéd over the frayed and split puff.

line, over the top of it. Unlike covering with fresh fabric, no seam allowance is added. The effect of this method is to hold the damaged piece in place. This thin layer will protect it from further shredding from handling and keep the shredded pieces in place. It won't stop the deterioration process, but it will slow it down because the original fabric will have a protective layer, a buffer, over it. Using tulle or Crepeline over damaged pieces gives them a slightly frosted look but should be almost invisible until inspected closely. The photograph in this chapter that shows stabilization repair is of a puff quilt made from silk inner bands from men's hats. The small piece was picked up at a tag sale, one of those ubiquitous stories of the fantastic find—it cost only $5. In this case, instead of removing the shredded, rotting piece, the square was covered with tulle.

Stabilizing is one instance where tiny stitches shouldn't be made. As Puentes points out, the smaller the stitch, the more tiny holes are made in the fragile fabric. These holes will eventually accelerate the deterioration. Use larger stitches to prevent adding to the damage. We strongly recommend Puentes's booklet for anyone with a quilt contemplating stabilizing, repair, or cleaning.

Don't assume that an expert quiltmaker is also an expert quilt repairer. Although the same basic techniques are used, repairing a quilt takes different expertise and knowledge than making one from scratch. There are questions you should ask anyone you hire to repair your quilt. Will period fabrics be used? Who determines what will be repaired and what will be replaced? Insist that original fabrics remain and that pieces be covered, not replaced. Ask that the original workmanship be duplicated even if it isn't up to perfect quiltmaking standards. If you just want your quilt stabilized, make sure the repairer knows what that means and has the right materials for the job.

If you're having your quilt professionally cleaned, make sure the cleaner has experience with your type of antique quilt. Establish who does the stabilizing before your quilt is cleaned, you or the cleaner. Most often, you'll be responsible for stabilizing a quilt before cleaning. A cleaner with experience should be able to tell you what parts need stabilizing before cleaning to prevent damage. Any fabric stiff and dried with age should be softened, stabilized, or left completely alone. These fabrics are prime targets for rips and frays when cleaned.

Repairing your quilt can be expensive when you hire the work out. Learning how to do it yourself, starting with new sample fabrics to practice the techniques, isn't difficult and just may spur you on to a new hobby or business.

There are many excellent quilt tops available for sale. The same rules of workmanship apply to a top as to a finished quilt. Appliqué stitches should be small, even, and invisible. The design should be pleasing and color balanced, or so unique that its whimsical quality compensates for any other flaws in design.

The fact that a top is machine pieced should not detract from its appeal or value. Sewing machines have been popular for over 150 years. Many quiltmakers today machine assemble tops because it saves a great deal of time compared to hand assembly. Quiltmakers of the past knew this too. As long as the seams are flat and even and the points match, a machine assembled top is valuable, too. Not only are you preserving a quilt, you're contributing to its historical value by finishing it and adding a multi-generational quilt to the current stock of antique quilts.

34 These Odd Fellows Cross blocks were also salvaged from a bigger quilt. The seam lines still show on the edges. Antique blocks are extremely affordable for a beginner collector or a quilter who can't stand to see a quilt unfinished! Blocks from the authors' collection.

Quilting an unfinished top makes it more valuable than if it had been left as a top, but less valuable than a completed quilt from the same period. This is because, as noted earlier, the date of a quilt is determined by the newest work included in it. Documentation of the original work should be included in the history of the quilt, along with any work done to finish it. We believe tops should be finished.

Check fabrics for colorfastness in your quilt top. (Chapter 8 tells you how.) A top that is stiff or dried with age may be saved by soaking in a mild fabric softener and warm water several times. Be sure to rinse the top completely clear of the fabric softener before you dry it. Dry a top the same way you dry a quilt: Spread it on a sheet outside on the ground in the shade and place another sheet over the top. (See Chapter 8 for care, cleaning, display and storage.)

Inspect your quilt top closely. Check for any damaged pieces of cloth and repair them first, following the covering methods discussed earlier. Then, note the design, colors, and prints in the top. You'll be hunting for period fabrics in like colors and prints to add a border and bind the completed top. You'll also want to research the pattern. By studying other quilts made from the same pattern, you can decide on an appropriate quilting design. Perhaps you can find a top with the quilting lines already marked on it. If you do, you've got a real treasure. Not only do you have the original piecing but also how the quiltmaker intended to quilt it! Marked tops are rare. To be historically accurate, your research should reveal a quilting pattern appropriate to the period of the quilt. Since you're actually finishing a multi-generational quilt, you might want to exercise your own artistic sense by designing the quilting pattern yourself. There are many good books on quilting techniques. *See illustration #34.*

Completed squares are also available for sale. These may be the salvaged remnants of a cutter quilt or may have been found intact. Apparently many quiltmakers of the past started projects they couldn't, or wouldn't, finish. It's interesting to contemplate why these unset squares were left forgotten just as it's interesting to speculate on why a woman would complete a top and not quilt it. Did she not like the squares once they were done? Did she run out of fabric to finish it? Maybe she couldn't find the right color or print fabric for the sashings, border, or binding and placed the squares aside until she did. Were they sentimental reasons—such as bad memories—that made her turn away from finishing the top? It is just this speculation that makes the search for quilts, their repair, and finishing so intriguing.

Squares are probably the cheapest way you'll find to own an antique quilt. As the most basic part of the quilt, they're certainly the best way to learn how to quilt and still retain a piece of history. There's something very appealing to adding your own work and artistic sense to a quilt started decades earlier. If quilts have their maker's soul sewed into them, then by acquiring completed squares and finishing them into a whole quilt, we can add our own piece of ourselves to the original work. We think a greater joy is rarely found.

One note about adding fabrics to tops and squares: You'll inevitably have to add fresh fabric for borders, bindings, and, in the case of squares, sashings. Fresh fabrics will look, well, fresh. They may be brighter, cleaner, and stiffer than the original fabrics even if from the same period. After all, they haven't been washed, used, caressed, or folded as much as the fabrics in the top or squares. They'll look newer. Resist aging the fabrics with tea dying, cafe au lait, or microwaving. These are methods used to make new fabrics look old. Tea dying was used frequently around the Bicentennial to give new fabrics an old look but the tannic acid in tea causes the very deterioration of fabrics that we want to arrest in antique quilts. By tea dyeing, your brand new fabrics will look as old as the original quilt fabrics but will also probably deteriorate faster. Be careful in your selection of colors for replacement fabric so that they more closely match the original and stay away from tea dying or other artificial means of aging fabrics.

Whether you're preserving, stabilizing, repairing, or finishing your antique or family heirloom quilt, remember there are professionals willing to help. Of course they charge a fee, but at least you'll know you're not alone as you do your part to preserve a piece of your past. Quilt repairers and restorers have the same love of quilts as you do, and they treat every quilt they meet with the respect it's due. As with all other aspects of quilt collecting, get credentials and recommendations for the professionals you choose to work with.

And don't be afraid to study, research, and practice quilt repair so that you can preserve your prized quilts yourself!

8 Care, Cleaning, Storage and Display

Cleaning an antique quilt is so hazardous to its health that it should be attempted only when absolutely necessary and even then only after you've investigated all the methods available to you. Keeping any quilt clean, antique or new, actually starts much earlier than the first wet or dry wash. Much of the advice in this chapter is geared toward preserving quilts and reflects a purist attitude toward that end. Caring for any quilt is not easy. What follows is the ideal and if it seems like hard work, it is. How much of this advice you follow depends on your resources, common sense, and emotional attachment to your quilts. You can cut corners if you like, but you must realize that in doing so you may also shorten the life of your quilt by taking a shortcut in its care, cleaning, storage, or display.

Determine, first, how and where you're going to use your newly acquired piece of American history. Quilts are much more fragile than most other antiques, and use wears them out quicker than it will a Hitchcock chair, a Revere tankard, or Depression glass. Textiles wear, deteriorate, and rot much faster than their antique counterparts, so give careful thought to their use.

If you're going to use an antique quilt on your bed, never sleep under it. That's the advice of Larry Zingale in the video *How to Buy Antique Quilts*. At night, take the quilt off the bed, fold it, and place it on the foot of the bed or drape it on a quilt rack, but don't actually spend the night tossing and turning under it. If it's nighttime warmth you're after, buy a new quilt and use it with the understanding that you'll wear it out sooner than you would if you took it off the bed at night.

To enhance the life of a quilt you do sleep under, Laura Fisher advises turning the quilt frequently so that a different edge is at the top of the bed. As you sleep with a quilt, your body oils rub into the fabric along the top edge. By changing the direction of the quilt frequently, this wear will take place evenly on all edges of the quilt, thereby prolonging its looks and life.

Whether you display your quilt on a bed or a wall, check the light in the room. Ultraviolet light is the most damaging element of your home environment to a quilt. Keep your quilts away from fluorescent lights or invest in filtering sleeves or shields for these lights. If you want to be absolutely sure your quilt won't be damaged by the sun's ultraviolet rays, you can replace window glass with UV-filtering glass or Plexiglas. If that seems prohibitive, you can cover the windows and doors with a Mylar polyester film or treat the glass with a polyester film or liquid metallized coating. If you're contemplating adding storm doors and windows, install ones with rigid acrylic made for filtering ultraviolet rays.

Never display or hang a quilt on a bed or wall that gets direct sunlight or near hot, bright lights. The visual effect of the lighting from a skylight on a quilt beneath it may be stunning but it can cause overall fading, or worse, patches of fading that will leave the quilt looking streaked and blotchy. It doesn't take long for fading to occur.

As for the temperature and humidity in your house, if you're comfortable, your quilt is, too. Maintain a temperature that's comfortable for you. If you're sweating from an increase in humidity, your quilt is also at risk. Place a fan in the room with the quilt to increase air circulation and to avoid mold or mildew forming on the fabrics.

A quilt that's hung, or displayed on a bed but not slept under, will benefit from the regular vacuuming and dusting you do normally in the house. If dust and dirt don't accumulate anywhere else in your home, they won't collect on your quilt to damage it either.

How much use your quilt gets determines how long it will last, and only you can make that decision. Nancy O'Bryant Puentes writes in her booklet First Aid for Family Quilts, that you should decide which of your quilts will get heavy use and which will get light use. The decision should be based on the knowledge that those quilts used heavily will wear out quicker than those you use only for display. Sleeping with a quilt, using one as a rug on the floor for a toddler, or letting pets sleep on them, will mean a much shorter life for any quilt, antique or new. Make the decision early, for much of the responsibility of preserving a quilt lies in how you use it.

Expect to clean a display quilt only about once every five years. If you've cared for it and stored it properly during that time, you shouldn't have to clean it more often than that. Even a stored quilt with a musty smell can be improved simply with an airing rather than a wet wash. Place the quilt on a sheet outside, on the ground, in the shade. Place another sheet on top of the quilt. Leave it out several hours. If you can't air the quilt outside, spread it on a bed and place several fans in the room to provide good air circulation. Leave it until the smell goes away or you determine it really needs a washing. If you rotate your display quilts, they'll get the airing they need while on display.

If a quilt does need to be cleaned, there are several steps to take. First, try vacuuming the quilt rather than going directly to a wet wash. A good vacuuming may remove most or all of the surface dust and dirt apparent on the quilt and some that isn't apparent but that can still damage the quilt. Never vacuum directly on the quilt and never vacuum, or wash, a quilt that hasn't been stabilized. The suction from the vacuum will pull and damage the fragile fabrics. Instead, cover the rough edges of a square of Fiberglas screening with twill tape. Place this over a section of the quilt and vacuum it through the screening, using the upholstery, attachment on your vacuum cleaner. Dirt and dust will be lifted off the quilt, but the fabrics won't be damaged from the suction. Proceed, vacuuming all sections of the top and back of the quilt. Inspect the quilt again. In most cases, vacuuming a well-cared-for quilt is sufficient to clean it.

If vacuuming didn't do the trick and the quilt still needs cleaning, you must first consider the content of the fabric, the condition of the quilt, and whether the colors might run. Never wash a silk, wool, or velvet quilt or a quilt with a wool batting. These quilts need to be professionally cleaned by an expert. Check with your quilt dealer, a professional trade organization like the National Dry Cleaners Association, a museum, or other quilt collectors for a list of names of professional cleaners with experience cleaning these quilts.

It's a good idea to check for colorfastness even in a cotton quilt that's obviously been washed before. And don't check just one corner of a quilt. You must check all the different fabrics in a quilt to make sure none of them will run. Puentes advises placing a drop of tepid water on a piece of the fabric and blotting with a white paper towel. If there's color on the towel, the quilt shouldn't be washed unless you're ready to accept the consequences of color bleeding to other fabrics and ruining the quilt. If there's no color on the towel, then the quilt is probably colorfast, but Puentes points out that this does not guarantee that the colors won't run.

Another way to test for colorfastness was included in a Harriet Hargrave column printed in *Traditional Quiltworks* magazine. Hargrave advises a four step method of testing for colorfastness. First rub a dry, white cloth over the fabric to be tested. If no color appears on the cloth, moisten the white cloth with cool tap water and rub the fabric again. If there's no color on the white cloth, dampen it with warm water and gently rub again. If there's still no color, mix your washing agent (to be discussed soon!) according to package directions and moisten the white cloth with that. Gently rub the fabric again. If the white cloth is still white, the quilt is probably safe to wash. Even with this method, there are no absolute guarantees that color won't run.

We'll discuss washing a quilt soon, but this is a good time to discuss what to do if you tested for colorfastness and the fabrics in your quilt still ran together in a wet wash. You must, according to Hargrave, not let the quilt dry. Once dry, the bleeding can be permanent. Instead, Hargrave recommends a product called Easy Wash® and soaking the quilt for 15 minutes. If this doesn't work, she recommends Snowy Bleach®. Neither is guaranteed to remove the color that has bled, but she's had good results with both products. The important thing to remember when fabric colors bleed, is to do something immediately before the fabric dries and the color damage becomes permanent.

So far, you've vacuumed the quilt and decided it still needs washing. You've tested the colors and it looks like they won't bleed. You're ready to wash. Both Hargrave and Puentes recommend using Orvus Paste®, which is a natural product and rinses out more thoroughly. Whatever you use, make sure it's a nondetergent, mild washing solution. Hargrave cleans her quilts using the washing machine because it's already designed to hold a lot of water. Never use the agitation cycle, but gently move the quilt in the water after it has soaked for about 10 minutes. If the water seems particularly dirty, you may have to repeat the wash process. Hargrave advises using the gentle spin cycle to force excess water out of the quilt.

"Spinning will not harm the quilt—it is only centrifugal force which is not agitating—and it is much easier on the fibers than handling a heavy, dripping wet quilt," she notes. She does not advise using the gentle spin cycle on king-sized quilts but suggests using a front-load washer

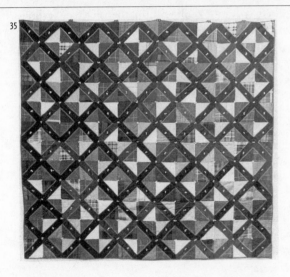

35 Triangles Make Diamonds on this visually pleasing quilt that is made of wools and wool twills. Made in the early 1800s, this quilt is in very good condition, and is tied. It has some lovely black feather topstitching in the block junctions. Quilt courtesy of the Wilson Family.

for anything bigger than queen size. Although we trusted her judgment on everything else, Hargrave was the only expert who recommended using the gentle spin cycle. Puentes's bathtub method, which we'll discuss soon, seems less stressful on the quilt even though it takes hours longer.

Laura Fisher recommends handwashing in a tub big enough to lay the quilt out flat. Since that's virtually impossible for anything larger than a small wall hanging, Puentes's method seems preferable. Puentes advises lining a filled bathtub with a clean, light colored sheet so that the edges hang to the outside of the tub. The water should be warm, not hot. Then, add the quilt, placing it in the tub by fanfolding it so that it's flat, not bunched up. She reccommends soaking the quilt for up to 12 hours, changing the water several times. If it still isn't clean, then she advises washing, using Orvus Paste® and following the directions on the package. Use the washing agent sparingly. It's better to wash the quilt a couple of times than to use too much of the cleaning agent. Never rub or wring the quilt but agitate the water and gently move the quilt to wash.

You may have to rinse the quilt up to 10 times to get all the cleaning agent out of it. An improperly rinsed quilt will attract dirt, and you'll be doing this difficult and arduous job again much sooner than is good for you or your quilt. Even if no suds appear after several rinsings, a couple more won't hurt as long as you're gentle with the quilt. *See illustration #35.*

Puentes advises leaving the quilt in the tub to drain out excess water. Its own weight will force a lot of the final rinse water out of the quilt. Only after it has drained this way for several hours should you lift the quilt out of the tub using the sheet to carry it rather than handling the wet quilt itself. Never hang a wet quilt on a clothes line! Its own weight can rip and tear the fabric, even in a new quilt. And, never dry a wet quilt in the automatic dryer—that's too much stress to place on wet fabrics. Instead, place the quilt on a sheet, or several sheets, spread on the ground in the shade. Puentes "blots" the quilt with heavy towels once it's down on the ground to remove more of the excess rinse water. Then, cover the quilt with another sheet, or several more, to protect it from debris, and leave it to dry making sure you check that it is never in direct sun. Drying a large, heavy quilt can take an entire day. In fact, Puentes states that washing a quilt takes an entire weekend.

Make sure the quilt is completely dry. If the top side feels dry to your touch, Hargrave advises carefully turning it over. Replace the top sheet and leave it to finish drying. Hargrave has dried quilts over bushes. Placing a sheet over the bush, she then placed the quilt on top of the sheet and covered the quilt with another sheet. The quilt dried faster because of the increased air circulation provided by keeping the quilt off the ground. Although this certainly saves time, we'd be a little concerned that the weight of the quilt might push bush branches through the fabric.

Drying outdoors may add brightness to your quilt. In *Collecting Quilts*, author Cathy Gaines Florence advises laying even a dry quilt that appears dull, outside on tall grass out of the sun. "The combination of ozone rays and chlorophyll-laden grass is a natural bleaching process that will further brighten the colors," she comments.

All of our experts noted that antique quilts deserve extra special attention. Before you attempt a cleaning, if you didn't do it when you bought the quilt, check with the dealer to document the fabric content, and the kind of batting used in the quilt and to consult on a cleaning method. As we've noted before, sometimes cleaning shouldn't be attempted even if the quilt is stained. But to attempt a cleaning without knowing what's in your quilt or checking for colorfastness is surely courting disaster. Ideally, you should have asked the dealer about cleaning methods and fabric content when you purchased the quilt, but if you didn't, call back and discuss it or hire another expert to evaluate the quilt for you. Quilt dealers and collectors we contacted also agreed that a museum-quality quilt should never be cleaned by anyone other than an expert.

Before we discuss how to hang a quilt, you should know how to store one. A quilt should never hang for more than six months and some experts recommend taking it down and letting it rest after three months. The rule of thumb is to let a wall quilt rest for as long as it was hung. Storage creates other problems that affect the life of a quilt. If improperly stored a quilt can suffer from rot, mildew, mold, rodents, and insects.

Never store a quilt in plastic, either tightly closed or loosely wrapped. There is always moisture in fabrics from the air, and even the most completely dried quilt will have moisture content. Storing a quilt in plastic traps that moisture inside and can lead to mildew, and eventually, rot. Quilts should be stored wrapped in cotton cloth, muslin, or in cotton pillowcases. Storing them in cloth allows the wrapping and the quilt to breathe and avoids mildew from trapped moisture.

There is plenty of debate on how quilts should be stored. Some experts feel quilts should be stored rolled, not folded, while others feel folding is less stressful in the long run than rolling. To store a quilt rolled, you'll need an acid-free tube, or a cardboard tube wrapped with acid-free tissue paper. Any good quilt shop should know a supplier of acid-free paper products. Roll the quilt with the top out. If any wrinkles or creases result from the rolling, they'll be on the backing and not on the top of the quilt. Roll loosely after placing a layer of acid-free tissue

36

36 In shades of gold and orange with lavender accents, this wonderful example of the traditional set and arrangement of the Star of Bethlehem was made in the 1920s. It is in pristine condition, having been handed down within the family. Quilt courtesy of the Zimmer Family.

on the quilt so that it separates the rolls of fabric from each other. Then wrap the outside of the roll with cotton cloth.

The problem with rolling a quilt to store it is that there's usually little room in a house to put it after it's rolled. Puentes advises placing the roll diagonally under the bed by supporting the ends of the cardboard roll with blocks so the quilt isn't sitting on the floor. She points out that this area must be carefully cleaned to remove dust, insects, and insect larvae from damaging the rolled quilt. *See illustration #36.*

In most homes, folding a quilt is the only realistic way to find a place to conveniently store it. When you store a quilt folded, several times a year you should take it out of its wrappings and refold it along different lines. A quilt stored for a long time in the same fold pattern will develop permanent creases along the fold lines and ruin the quilt.

Always store any quilt with acid-free tissue folded inside. Some of the dyes in antique quilts will migrate if they lay on top of other parts of the quilt. The tissue separating the fabric folds will stop this migration. Puentes advises placing wadded rolls of acid-free tissue along the fold lines to prevent a sharp crease from forming. Once folded, the quilt can be wrapped in cotton or placed in a pillowcase and then stored in a box. The multiple layers of box, cotton, and tissue paper will discourage rodent attacks as they forage for nesting material. Frequent checking and refolding of the stored quilt will discourage insect infestation and damage from their protein-eating habits.

Frequent changes in your display quilts will almost guarantee that they remain in good condition for many, many years. A quilt forgotten, even if carefully stored, is a target for damage. Use your quilts by rotating their display, giving them time to rest, naturally airing them, and keeping them clean.

How you display a quilt also affects its life span. A quilt left hanging for years, even one properly hung, will stretch, distort, even wear and rip along the stress lines of hanging. A quilt that's hung should be properly supported at least along the top. With larger, heavier quilts, a support along the bottom is also advised. Never hang a quilt by pushing pins through its top or by using clips. The quilt will sag and stretch in the spaces between the pins and clips and the quilt will be distorted. These stress points are the first to wear and tear.

Instead, follow the methods in any good quilt book to sew a casing or sleeve that is the same length as the quilt along the top, and sometimes the bottom, of the quilt. Slip a dowel or curtain rod through the sleeve and then hang it on the wall. Another interesting method is to sew Velcro strips to a wider strip of cotton twill tape. Then, sew the tape to the quilt. With both the casing and Velcro methods, Puentes advises that every third or fourth stitch go through all the layers of the quilt. This means there will be stitches showing on the front of the display quilt, but they will better distribute the hanging weight of the quilt. When the casing or tape is stitched only to the backing fabric, the weight of the quilt will wear the backing away and eventually it will rip. The other half of the Velcro strips are attached to lathing strips, sanded and finished to smooth them. Then the strips are nailed to the wall and the quilt is hung by pressing the Velcro strips on the back of the quilt to the strips on the wall. The advantage of this method is that all four edges of the quilt should have Velcro strips and the weight of the quilt is equally distributed on all four sides. Even then, Fisher suggests turning the quilt, if the design allows that, frequently so that a different edge is the top. This will prevent sagging and distortion of the quilt as it hangs.

In "Hanging Quilts" (*Traditional Quiltworks*, No.13), Linda Halpin advises placing a sleeve and dowel across the center back of a quilt that hangs on point. The top point of the quilt is hung on a nail in the wall with a loop sewed to the back. The center dowel is hung with nails or the curtain rod attachments that came with the rod.

One expert even advised attaching the quilt to a backing canvas and stretching that over a wooden frame much like an oil painting. For smaller pieces, say a single block or a small set of four blocks, framing is also an option. If the piece is framed under glass, however, make sure either the glass is not set tight to the piece or that the cardboard backing to the frame has small holes punched in it to allow for air circulation. An airtight frame will trap the natural moisture in the textiles and start mildew and mold.

We discussed in Chapter 7 the arguments about why a quilt should never be considered a cutter. If you have a badly worn quilt and don't want to cut it down to just the good parts or to make something else out of it, then be creative in how you display it. A nice quilt rack and some careful folding will display the good parts of a worn quilt quite effectively and you don't have to feel like you've destroyed a piece of history. Loft railings and bannisters are also effective display areas as long as you remember to check for dust and debris and rotate the quilts as you would the ones hung on your walls or displayed on your beds.

Just because they're valuable and you now know how to store your quilts, don't keep them in storage. Quilts were made to be used, and you should feel comfortable using yours in some way. Like everything else of beauty, quilts take some work to maintain their focus in our lives, but they're well worth the effort.

9 Appraisals: When and Why You Should Get One

By now you've figured out that acquiring expert status in dating and evaluating quilts is going to take time—perhaps years, depending on how much of your spare time you devote to it. The good news is you don't have to wait until you're an expert before you start a collection. Reading this book gives you an advantage over any other new collector who hasn't read it. Reading more books, like those listed in our Bibliography, will put you at an even greater advantage when you purchase your first antique quilt.

And speaking of that first purchase, you're not going to select it based on any store of knowledge you've acquired. You're going to buy your first quilt because you fall in love with it. Whether your taste is traditional, abstract, or eclectic, you should always buy a quilt because of its initial impact on your emotions. Did you immediately fall in love with it? Does it "speak" to you in ways you can't define? Have you discovered a surprising attraction to a quilt of electric blue and yellow Ohio Star blocks with orange sashings? If any of the above happens, your immediate response should be to *buy that quilt!* Always, always, always take a close second, even third, look at any quilt that evokes an emotional reaction from you. It means you've connected with the quilt. Buy it and do the research after to find its maker, age, type of fabric, quilting technique. Learning those things is a wonderful bonus that educates you, but the real joy is assembling a collection that evokes emotions. Even the electric blue, yellow, and orange Ohio Star quilt serves its purpose as your favorite and as a conversation starter!

Once you've educated yourself—which sometimes leads into a new career as a quilt appraiser or dealer—you'll be able to spot a good deal on a quilt that excites you. But, as you start collecting, while you're learning, you should consider using the services of an expert appraiser.

Appraisals are not just for determining the value of your quilt, although that is the primary result of the appraisal process. Appraisals are used to set the value of a quilt in the event of an estate appraisal either after a death or when preparing a will. There are firms and individual appraisers who specialize in just that—appraising estates. These firms are generalists, well-educated and very knowledgeable, and do their best to have a specialist in each private property area, but we recommend that you ask if they have an appraiser who has specialized in quilts. If they don't have a quilt expert, it makes sense to continue looking for a firm that does.

If you're donating the collection to a museum or historical society, tax laws mandate that a value be set on the quilt. How much you can deduct on your taxes for the donation will depend on the appraisal report.

You need a dollar value for your quilts so you can insure them. Antique quilts are scarce, important and valuable. If they aren't included on your insurance policy, their loss can be a devastating financial blow on top of the emotional distress. Those of you who are collecting quilts with an eye toward liquidating their value for retirement, college educations, or other investments, are strongly advised to obtain a professional appraisal and include them in your insurance policies.

An appraisal can also help if, or when, you decide to sell all or some of your collection. There can be a difference between the value placed on a quilt for insurance purposes (replacement value) and the value in anticipating a sale (resale value). While a quilt can be very valuable in terms of replacing it with something equal to its age and quality, that doesn't mean there's a buyer out there willing to pay that insurance value. Let's go back to our electric blue, yellow, and orange Ohio Star quilt. Yes, it's Amish. Yes, it's old. Yes, you know its maker, where it was made, and every owner over its lifetime. Yes, the quilt is indicative of its time. Yes, the workmanship is expert and the condition is fine. With those facts at hand, the quilt is quite valuable. But, the fact remains, it is electric blue, yellow, and orange! I'd buy it without even knowing its history, but I'll bet there aren't too many collectors out there like me who would appreciate it. Odds are, when you bought it, it had already sat in inventory for quite a while and unloading it to you surely precipitated a celebratory dinner for the dealer. So, just because you've decided to sell a quilt and its insurance value is high, doesn't mean you'll get that price. A resale appraisal will tell you what you can realistically expect as a selling price. You may learn that there is absolutely no market for that quilt at the time you want to sell it. Instead of embarking on a frustrating selling process that ends with disappointment, you might want to select a different quilt from your collection to sell.

There's also the question of insuring a quilt against loss or theft as well as natural disasters. If you decide to send your quilt off to a prestigious show, you'll need an appraisal to insure it for its art value. The U.S. Post Office won't insure a quilt for its art value unless there's a signed appraisal supporting the value. Without an appraisal, it will be insured for only the cost of materials.

While we're on the subject of lost quilts, we'd like to applaud the efforts of Maria Elkins and the new service she's offered on the Web. It's the Lost Quilts Come Home Page (See chapter 35, Sources for the Web address.) The site is dedicated to helping quilt owners recover lost or stolen quilts. Currently there are over a hundred quilts being shown that need to be found and returned to their owners. The site also gives statistics on how quilts are lost. One quilt, lost in a tornado, was recovered! The site also gives important information about care and protection of quilts. Check it out. It's a needed and welcomed service.

The final, and to us the most important, reason to get a quilt appraised is just sheer nosiness. You bought that quilt because it was beautiful to you. But, there's still that nagging curiosity about what it's really worth. Did you get a good deal? Has the quilt appreciated in value since you bought it? Is it really as old as the dealer told you? Is that small, fanciful print really feed sack fabric? How *does* that small stain on the quilt affect its value? A good appraiser can, and should, answer all those questions.

So how do you find a good appraiser? A recommendation from a friend who's dealt with one would be an excellent start. Consider the recommendation as a reference on the expertise, business sense, and results given by that appraiser to your friend. Word of mouth and networking are still the best ways to get information you need.

If you belong to a quilt guild, or if there is one in your area, you can ask it for a reference to an appraiser. Many guilds have antique collections and have probably used the services of an appraiser for their own insurance purposes. Many guilds will probably boast an appraiser or two on their membership rolls. If your area's quilt guild doesn't have its own listing in the phone book or a Web site, try asking at your local library or contacting the Chamber of Commerce. Both places maintain lists of nonprofit organizations in their market area and probably have a contact name, address, or phone number they can supply you with.

Historical societies, museums with quilt collections, and national quilting organizations would also have used the services of an appraiser. A call to any one of them would probably get you several recommendations. Our Sources chapter lists the current national appraisal organizations and their Web sites. They're also happy to make recommendations.

And then there's the Internet. A quick search using the key word "appraisers" brings you to the very organizations we list in Sources. Each site has their organization's code of ethics, mission, and a list of members categorized by the types of antiques they appraise. Some appraisal groups belong to the Appraisal Foundation. The foundation was empowered by Congress to create and establish standards for professional appraisers. The foundation created the Uniform Standards of Professional Appraisal Practice and works toward the adoption of USPAP by all appraisal trade organizations.

Be aware that a recommendation alone is not enough to go ahead and sign a contract with an appraiser. You need the answers to some simple questions.

Ask if he or she is a member of an appraisal trade society. These appraiser societies should certify their members, including a recertification process after three to five years to confirm that the appraiser has kept up with new information on the dating of quilts, fabrics, and techniques.

Your appraiser should also have signed and agreed to uphold an ethics policy that provides for a formal review of any claim to a deviation from that policy. The society should have in place a procedure for various forms of reprimand including the possibility of decertification. The ethics policy should include language prohibiting an appraiser from telling you that your quilt is valuable simply because he or she knows that's what you want to hear. Value must be documented from a close inspection of the quilt. A reputable appraiser does not bend to outside influence.

The ethics policy should also prohibit appraisers from benefiting off a quilt they've been asked to appraise. An offer to buy a quilt while under appraisal should cast doubts on the accuracy of the appraisal. If your appraiser makes an offer to buy be wary! Another good policy is that the appraiser should charge a flat fee or an hourly rate. Don't agree to an appraisal contract that specifies a percentage of the proceeds of a sale to go to the appraiser. If your quilt is up for sale, the appraisal should be just one step in the sales process. Conversely, don't expect the appraisal to clinch a sale. While the appraisal report should include a list of possible markets tested for your quilt while calculating its value, a reputable appraiser shouldn't make an offer on your quilt.

The association that certified your appraiser can supply you with its ethics policy. The International Society of Appraiser posts its Code of Ethics and Profession Conduct on its Web site. Ideally, prospective appraisers should include a copy of the association's ethics policy in the information they give you before you agree to use their services.

Ask prospective appraisers when they received certification or recertification. Also ask what they do for continuing education in the field of quilt appraising. New data on the history of quilting is constantly appearing. The research is extensive and active. Your appraiser should be up to date on the newest discoveries.

You'll find that many quilt appraisers are also dealers. As dealers, they're involved on a daily basis with all aspects of quilt history and current market information. Dealers can be excellent appraisers, because staying on top of their market gives them increased opportunity, and desire, to study quilts. There is no conflict of interest in an appraiser also being a dealer if he or she abides by the ethics code.

Only an appraisal will satisfy the requirements of a court of law or an insurance company. We'll bet one of the reasons you bought this book was because you already have at least one antique quilt at home, perhaps made by an ancestor. You found the book on the shelf and thought it would be interesting to know what Great Grandmother Glenda's tumbler quilt is really worth. A price guide like this one that includes history and dating tips gives you valuable information on evaluating the textiles, age, workmanship, and condition of your heirloom. But you must understand that the prices listed are only a guide. The listings we include represent the asking price of the quilts at the time we wrote the book. By the time you read this, a year after the book was written, the current market value of the quilts listed here, and your quilt, has probably changed. A price guide is not an alternative to an appraisal. It is a guide. We hope that this book spurs you on to other books, exhibits, and education.

You should receive a written report on the appraisal. The currently popular television show *Antiques Road Show* and appraisal fairs like it being held around the world do not result in a legally useful appraisal. Verbal appraisal will not help you to obtain the value of your quilt from an insurer in the event of its loss. Therefore, don't hire an appraiser who doesn't supply a typewritten report. Verbal details and handwritten, sketchy notes are not professional. A reputable quilt appraiser provides you with a formal document. This is a detail that should be settled before you sign a contract.

When you first approach an appraiser, discuss the purpose of your appraisal: fair market value, insurance value, resale value, or simple curiosity. Why you want the quilt appraised will affect the report for the reasons we've described earlier in this chapter. Discuss getting both a fair market value and an insurance appraisal if you're interested in seeing the difference.

The report should include how the quilt was inspected. For instance, if you requested a burn test to determine the fabric or thread content, the report should note that it was done and explain the results. The report should detail all the ways the appraiser came to the conclusions listed. It should include enough description of the quilt and its attributes so that nothing other than the report is needed to identify the quilt should the quilt be lost or stolen. You should always have photographs of your collection available for insurance purposes, but if the worst has happened and these are lost along with the quilt, the detailed description on the appraisal is an advantage.

A date is important on the appraisal report. As noted above, trends, availability, and condition of quilts can change, thereby changing the appraisal. If you haven't had your quilts appraised recently, say within the last five years, you should consider another appraisal to reflect an accurate current value.

The report should also include the qualifications, education, and measurable experience of the appraiser. A list of education completed, years in the business, and membership in organizations adds credence to the appraisal if you need to report a loss to your insurance company or insure the quilt against loss when it travels.

Someday you'll have the knowledge of a certified quilt appraiser. There are fewer than 100 appraisers certified in quilts in the entire country, and the more people educated about quilt history and value means that many more quilts will be preserved. In the meantime, appraising your quilt collection is practical and adds to your education. Every appraisal tells you something you didn't know about your quilt and quilting in general. There are quilts faked to look antique and fraudulent appraisers out there—even antique quilts are not immune to con artists.

Quilts are also not immune to misinformation. "There are many mistakes in print and more than a few exaggerations in family stories," wrote Barbara Brackman in *Clues in the Calico*.

The spot appraisers appearing on television often refute family folklore by proving an object isn't as old, as important, or as valuable as the stories handed down through the generations have indicated. Like the old game of telephone, in which the original message changes as it travels mouth to ear, family stories can get distorted over time.

We believe an appraisal of your antique quilt is essential. Luckily there are reliable, reputable people out there with the knowledge to supply them, and now you know how to find them and what to expect.

10 Trends in the Marketplace

Quilt collecting has its own history, starting in the early 1900s, when quilts made in the previous century suddenly became desirable for hanging on walls. The first quilt collections were, as stated by Penny McMorris and Michael Kile in their book, *The Art Quilt*, "an important change in status for quilts, which had, until now, been looked upon by art and antique collectors as objects unworthy of display and safekeeping." In fact, quilts were deemed so unimportant that even in the late 1960s you could pick up a pair of quilts for only $15. Antique dealers scooped up quilts, not for their own value, but to wrap their antique furniture in to avoid scratches, nicks, and gouges while in transit. Even in the early 1970s, at the very beginning of the nostalgia craze connected with the approaching national Bicentennial, quilts were commonly sold for as little as $25.

All that changed quickly. By the mid seventies, quilt prices had mushroomed, and the nostalgia craze, in full swing during the actual time of the Bicentennial celebration, greatly increased demand for quilts. Magazines touted quilts for decorating appeal, particularly with the country or colonial looks in interior decorating, which were also fostered by a desire to return to a simpler look and lifestyle. After the Whitney Museum exhibit of antique quilts, an important step in classifying quilts as art, galleries began hanging and selling antique quilts with their other art objects.

By the late 1970s and early 1980s, prices had skyrocketed and supply was dwindling. Quilt owners, who had previously been quite willing to part with grandmother's quilt, were now reluctant to sell. Finding quilts available for sale became more and more difficult as people realized the value and importance of their family quilts and as more people entered the market looking for quilts to resell. In a quilt-buying frenzy, pickers knocked on doors and begged people to sell what they had. Quilts became regular features in Americana auctions. This increased demand resulted in astronomical prices. At a January 1988 Sotheby's auction, one quilt with an estimated value of $6,000 to $8,000 sold for $13,200. Another quilt, estimated between $8,000 and $12,000, actually sold for $26,400. The record price paid for any quilt was

$176,000 for an 1840 Baltimore Album quilt in 1987 at a Sotheby's auction. One year later another Baltimore Album quilt dated 1848 sold for $110,000.

But the late 1980s reflected the downswing in the economy and the higher level of sophistication by quilt buyers. Some exceptional quilts, with high estimated values, didn't sell. More and more quilt collectors were specializing and therefore willing to wait for the exact type and style of quilt they wanted. The days when any quilt would sell, at an exceptional price, were gone. Buyers became choosy at each level of quilt collecting.

Interest in quilts has waxed and waned over the four centuries we've quilted, but the art never died out completely. Quilters subscribe to trade magazines in numbers over 100,000. The National Quilting Association, Inc. is the oldest organization in the country and annually offers grants and scholarships "to promote and encourage quilters to further their knowledge of techniques, craftmanship and development of ideas." NQA also encourages the study of quilt history.

Subscription and newsstand numbers for quilt magazines attest that interest in quilts is still growing. Quilt magazine sales number well over 100,000 monthly. In her book *Black Threads: An African-American Quilting Sourcebook,* author Kyra Hicks estimates that the number of quilters as a percentage of United States households is over 15 percent, representing approximately 15.5 million quilters! Hicks estimates dedicated quilters (among other factors those who spend over $15,500 per year on quilting) as 6 percent of all U.S. households.

The American Quilter's Society, founded by Bill and Meredith Schroeder now boasts a membership of over 50,000. AQS publishes its own magazine, and its book publishing and club divisions are booming as well. In 1991, the Schroeders opened the Museum of the American Quilter's Society, featuring the society's annual show, and drew over 11,000 quilt enthusiasts to Paducah, Kentucky, to view, take workshops, and learn about quilts. AQS also offers certification courses for those interested in becoming quilt appraisers.

Interest in antique quilts isn't confined to the United States. American quilts are sought by dealers in France, Switzerland, Japan, and Australia.

Current market information does not reveal a definite trend in sales volume. There are still many affordable antique quilts on the market for under $1,000 and many more of lesser age and quality for under $500. Most buyers are still looking for a unique wedding gift, and Double Wedding Ring quilts, followed closely by Grandmother's Flower Garden and Dresden Plate quilts, continue to outsell other patterns. Those three patterns are most frequently 20th-century quilts, hence the most affordable. Since most were made with soft pastel-colored fabrics, they appeal to the beginning collector or one-quilt buyer because of their decorative qualities. These quilts match almost any decor in any color scheme. But it also means these quilts are the most common. They don't particularly appeal to dealers or to the advanced collector because many were made from pre-cut, pre-designed kits that were popular in the 1920s and 1930s. With so much of the work already done for the quiltmaker, a lot of the mystique of a quilt is lost when it's made from a kit. A quiltmaker would have to have brought something truly of herself to the kit quilt to increase its value today. Kit quilts just aren't unique. Dealers find they must acquire them, however, because they stay in huge demand from the one-time quilt buyer.

As always, age is not the only factor determining the sales potential of an antique quilt. At one time, the older the quilt, the higher the price, hence a better investment. But the age of a quilt is no longer the sole determination of value. (Except, of course, if a hitherto undiscovered 16th or 17th century example suddenly shows up on the market!) Other factors, such as design, workmanship, condition, and pattern, always included in determining the value of a quilt, at times supersede age as the prime reason a quilt is collectible or valuable. The truly unique quilt, even if as new as 1930, may be as valuable as one from 1830. And rarity, no matter the age, adds to value.

Pictorial quilts, rarely done in anything except appliqué, continue in popularity and are usually priced higher than other quilts. Expert workmanship in an appliqué quilt is the primary determination of value. Pictorial quilts include commemorative family quilts, commemorative event quilts, political quilts, some friendship quilts, and album quilts. The most valued pictorial is the Baltimore Album quilt. With so few surviving to today, their value is always high.

Old pictorial quilts are rare. Appliqué was expensive and required the kind of leisure time available only to the wealthy. While pieced geometric designs are still plentiful, there are significantly fewer appliqué quilts than pieced, and fewer still pictorials.

Geometric designs with good color balance such as the ocean waves patterns of the 1890's appeal to collectors because of their optical illusion qualities. Indicative of the Victorian period, they are an alternative to the elaborate, sometimes overly fussy stitching of Crazy Quilts of the same date.

Silk and satin Crazy Quilts are rare. They'll always be popular, but the fabrics used haven't held up well and deterioration weakens their value to all but museums, which can afford to stabilize and preserve them. Crazies of the same period in velvet and wool are more available as the silk and satin crazy quilts continue to fray and wear away. Because wool and velvet holds up better over time, these quilts are still in excellent condition and will stay that way longer, increasing their value but making them good buys for today's collector.

Amish quilts, geometric and bold colored, will probably always be collectible. They have become so valuable, in fact, that there are fakes on the market. Worn Amish quilts are being cut and used together with artificially aged, new fabrics and passed off as antique. Some of the fakes are so good that only an expert checking the binding and backing can tell for sure. Make sure you have an Amish quilt appraised by an expert or buy them only from a dealer you trust.

Twelve years ago in a previous incarnation of this book, we predicted that African-American quilts would be the collectible category of the 1990s. Our prediction didn't materialize, but because of new events discussed in Chapter 34, we think there are more African-American-made quilts in existence than currently known. As the research continues, we're hoping these quilts will come on the market in greater numbers. Certainly their close ties to the development of the United States should make them collectible.

Our search for antique quilts revealed that the supply of antique crib quilts on the market has increased. At one time, larger quilts, cutters, were being cut down to crib size and passed off as original designs. (One tip-off to a fake crib size is to measure the size of the pattern blocks.

A crib quilt, smaller than a bed quilt, would have a scaled down version of a quilt block pattern. A 12" block, suitable size for a bed quilt, is too large in scale for a crib quilt.) The quilts we saw advertised seemed authentic, and we hope the fakes are gone. But, the possibility they exist is another good reason to remind you to establish a good relationship with a reputable dealer so you can avoid the pitfall of buying a fake passed off as authentic.

Another big trend in quilt collecting is the importance of provenance. Provenance is the history of a quilt as you know it. A retelling of the family lore surrounding your quilt is an example of provenance. Write down everything your family has ever told you about the quilt handed down to you. Include everything, even the funny, bizarre, or wild anecdotes connected to the quilt. Folklore may be the only information you have about your quilt if the ancestor who made it has passed on and didn't leave a written record.

But the folklore of a quilt, while interesting, isn't quite enough. Provenance can run the range of family folklore to precise documentation. The more formal that documentation, the better the provenance of the quilt, and the more collectible and valuable it becomes. If you can locate a birth certificate, wedding certificate, notations in the family Bible, letters mentioning the quilt, or, the best documentation, a photograph of the maker with the quilt, these items create the best form of provenance. Add to your provenance a list of the people who owned the quilt between the time the maker finished it and you acquired it and your documentation is complete.

Your provenance, including any or all of the above documents, adds to the value of a quilt today. Knowing the maker's name, an accurate date, or the history of ownership of a quilt can increase the price by anywhere from a third to double its value-based on other criteria. One quilt we saw was not particularly colorful or well done. But the fact that it was finished the same day as the Battle of the Alamo by women whose male relatives died there, made it a unique, and therefore valuable one. Another quilt included embroidered coffins and the names and death dates of the maker's relatives. Other quilts have been made from military uniforms, nursing uniforms, wedding gowns, and christening outfits. Quilts that are both dated and signed by the maker also increase in value because their history is known. Remind the current quiltmakers in your family and circle of friends that they should always sign and date their quilts. They are, after all, the collectibles of the future!

Another trend is to overlook fair or poor condition. Ideally, to be of optimum value, a quilt should be in excellent condition with no wear, a good binding, and no stains or deteriorated fabric. But, if the quilt appropriately represents a certain time period, is of excellent design and visually pleasing, or has an interesting history, condition considerations should be secondary. And, as the pool of antique quilts available for sale decreases—there are, after all, only so many antique quilts that exist today!—quilts with condition problems will increase in value to meet the steady demand. Fortunately, we are in a time period that values all quilts. The belief that all examples of history should be preserved will continue to encourage collectors and museums to overlook condition flaws.

At one time any quilt with machine quilting or appliqué was considered of much less value than those done completely by hand. But sewing machines became popular after the Civil War and sewers took great pride in using them. The early machines were capable of sewing tiny stitches, and their owners used them to assemble, stitch down appliqué pieces, and quilt the finished tops. So enamored were they with the machines that they even appliquéd their pieces using a contrasting thread so the machine stitches would easily show. So don't pass up that obviously machine-made quilt. If you can date it to the period just after the Civil War, the quilt can be a valuable example of the advent of a new technology and its use in the home.

Probably the most important addition to the market is the use of the Internet. Not available when we did this book 12 years ago, it is an addition that seems to have wiped out regional pricing differences. We saw no indication that values and prices changed depending on the ground location of a quilt dealer. Prices seemed stable and uniform from site to site determined by the factors of age, condition, workmanship, and rarity. The advantage to shopping for antique quilts on the Web is the same as shopping for anything else. It's convenient, time-saving, affordable, many times backed with return guarantees if the buyer is not satisfied, and it simply abounds with sources. A simple search using only the MSN search engine and the words "antique quilts" returned 37,125 listings! When we used the words "antique quilts retail" we received 5,231 sites to view! "Miniature antique quilts" led us to 5,275 sites, and 3,876 sites appeared to our request using the words "African American quilts." Amazon, eBay, Bid, and more offer online auctions that include tutorials on how to participate and regularly list antique quilts for sale. New protection measures make using your credit cards online as safe as possible. Once again, the use of computers has increased the possibilities available to us all.

Another trend we've noted isn't in the marketplace—it's the research currently under way on the history and significance of quilts as more than bed coverings. New evidence and ongoing study into the use of quilts in the Underground Railroad activities leading up to the Civil War show that there are many questions yet to be answered. Research is also being done on Native American quilts and quilting. The expansion of American quilt techniques to other countries, such as Liberia is also being studied. Textile manufacture and dye technologies continue to be researched. Quilts have played, and continue to play, a significant role in the U.S. economy; after all, the very beginnings of the Industrial Revolution are imbedded in textile manufacturing, among other technologies. We find the increasing trend toward concentrating research on specialized categories of quilts a remarkable, and required, development. It can only increase the marketability and value of antique quilts.

What's collectible and what sells, what appeals to a dealer or a collector and what appeals to the first-time buyer may never be the same. Just because a dealer recognizes the value of the unique quilt doesn't mean that quilt is easy to sell.

It's that curiosity, that wonder in the heart and mind of the quilt buyer that really determines the value and sale of a quilt. Even with poor workmanship, shoddy fabrics, and poor condition, the truly unique quilt with a story to tell will always be valuable.

11 How to Use This Price Guide

In the previous chapters, we told you about the many aspects of quilt collecting and what you need to know to be successful at it. The following chapters are educational, too, but in a different way, as they list nearly 750 quilts and related items, with their associated asking prices.

Over the course of six months, we looked for quilts and recorded the details, so we could share that information with you. Only quilts that are actually for sale are listed; anything in a museum or being held in a private collection is not.

The quilts listed here come from all over the country, at flea markets and on the Internet, at big antique markets and small regional antique shows, at auction houses and online auctions, at estate sales and yard sales, at sophisticated metropolitan antique stores and quaint country antique shops, and, most certainly, at specialty antique quilt shops. During our travels we learned a few simple truths: Looking at quilts is fun and writing about quilts is fun. Categorizing quilts is *not* fun!

In organizing these quilts, we tried numerous options. We considered every way of grouping our finds, from predominant color to price. It was suggested that the only logical way was to organize by date, so we tried that. An expert quilt collector told us that organizing couldn't be done using the pattern name so we crossed that off the list. When we ended up with no easy way, we went back and looked again and decided the only logical way to group the quilts was, in fact, by pattern name.

Even that wasn't foolproof, for nearly every quilt pattern ever used has more than one name. Even if a pattern is known by a common name, a tiny change in, say, a color arrangement or the size of a triangle can make a different pattern. You'll probably never see the word "*variation*" used more often than in naming or identifying quilt patterns!

So the pattern name is where we start, and it's only the first of the many ambiguities we encountered in organizing these quilts. The only thing scarier than two experts discussing the proper name of a particular quilt pattern is the same two experts discussing whether a particular pattern should be considered a one patch or a two patch. Conflict! Stand back!

Barbara Brackman, in her book *"Encyclopedia of Pieced Quilt Patterns"* has 22 chapters describing over 4,000 patterns in piecework alone. Add appliqué and other kinds of quilts, and the total number of patterns could be 6 thousand or more. That's a lot of organizing.

We used Brackman's book a lot while we looked at quilts, and we suggest that you also use it, or rely on one of the other excellent quilt pattern books available. While many people selling quilts may be knowledgeable, they may not have the time to research a pattern in depth, or may just name a quilt for the pattern it most closely resembles. You might be surprised to know how many quilts we found labeled "pinwheel" that were, in fact, waterwheel, windmill, or turnstile.

So, we have listed the quilts alphabetically, within each chapter, by **pattern name**, the first fact in the listings. We tried to use the name given by the seller, if it was reasonably accurate, but we used Brackman's book to review the given name and to settle any conflicts.

The next fact in the listings is the quilt's **date.** We accepted the date given to us by the seller, except where we felt it was way off. Unless a quilt was actually dated, we found a range, usually a decade, to be acceptable. In general, we found that most people selling quilts are fairly accurate, although we did find a couple of quilts labeled 1800s—an entire century! In such cases we tried to narrow it down.

The next item is **color**, by which we mean the predominant color or colors, the ones that jump out at you when you take in the entire quilt. There may be other colors on the quilt; in fact, especially in piecework, there usually are. We try to list as many of the major colors as seem appropriate. Under color we also list if the fabrics are solid colors or prints, and if possible what other colors are in the prints. *Multicolored* means that there are just too many colors to list, and you can find just about every color under the sun on the quilt. You wouldn't think color could be an area for heated debate, but if you've ever heard two experts discussing whether a particular yellow is butter or lemon, well. . .

The next item noted in each listing is **features.** This includes such things as sashing, set, borders, odd configurations of blocks, spectacular color arrangements, horrible color arrangements, and any other thing we thought would be helpful. Also listed in features are the kinds of fabrics used in the quilt—unless they are all cotton. In order to save space, we note only fabrics other than cotton.

After features comes the quilt's **provenance,** or history, if it is available. Most often, the seller won't know exactly where a quilt was made, as it may have come through many hands. The seller is even less likely to know who made the quilt, unless it came directly from a family member or is signed. Any information that can be verified will be listed here.

Information about the **quilting** on the quilt will be listed next. *Quilting*, of course, means the stitches that go through all of the layers of the quilt and basically hold the "sandwich" together. Sometimes the "quilt" is really just a top and is unfinished, or is tied and there is no quilting. We'll tell you that, too. We'll also say if there is a lot more or a lot less quilting than would be generally required to just do the job of holding the quilt together.

In general we try to give the kind of quilting and where it is located, such as outline quilting in the blocks or cable quilting on the border. Also, we tell how well the quilting is done. Sometimes we can provide the number of stitches per inch, and that can be used to determine the quality of the quilting. In general, 6 to 8 stitches per inch is standard, while 8 to 10 is very good, and 10 or more is excellent.

It takes an expert quilter to produce tiny stitches, but it takes one even more expert to produce even stitches. Large but even stitches may be more impressive than small, wobbly ones.

The next item in our listings is crucial, as it involves **workmanship,** which includes **assembly.** To rate a "good" in this category, a quilt must have most seams flat, not puckered, and the preponderance of points, junctions, and/or corners should match and be assembled evenly. To save space, we consider all quilts to be hand pieced; if they are not, we will say so.

To rate a "good" in appliqué, the stitches must be small, even, and inconspicuous. Also, the edges of the appliqué pieces should be straight, curved, or pointed where they are supposed to be straight, curved, or pointed. Points are taken off for puckers, bumps, and corners where there should be curves. Other types of quilts may rate other comments, and we have tried to give as much information as possible.

There is no accepted standard for **condition** in antique quilts, although many appraisers and dealers have set their own. Words like *pristine* and mint are sometimes used to characterize condition, but they are not used universally, nor always with the same meaning.

So we put together our own grading system for condition. We use as our benchmark a pristine quilt that is as perfect as the day it was made: crisp and unwashed fabric, no soiling or stains, no wear or tears, pure and strong colors, the quilt basically unused, often with quilting lines remaining. Such a quilt would be rated a 10, or excellent. We do give a little and allow an excellent quilt to have been washed once, simply to remove settled dust or the soil left by the hands that quilted it. From there we take away one point, from the perfect 10, for each less-than-perfect thing we can see on the quilt, such as:

- overall wear

- spot wear such as a frayed or torn binding

- repairs, such as a cut down chin edge

- overall color fade, such as from repeated washings

- color changes such as green degraded to khaki

- tears and/or rips

- fabric split or shattered from age or poor storage

- fabric disintegrated and missing from age

- holes such as from moths or punctures

- stains, like water or age, overall or localized

- spots, such as from mildew, spills, or other

- soiling, overall or in some places, like fold lines

- stitches broken or missing, on embroidery or appliqué

- seams split or separating

- unpleasant or musty smell that won't wash out

After figuring the bottom line number, we break the condition score down like this: 10 = Excellent, 9 = Very Good, 8 & 7 = Good, 6, 5 & 4 = Fair, 3, 2 & 1 = Poor, 0 or less = ? A study piece maybe.

We weren't so picky as to take off a point for *every* spot on a quilt, but rather for the fact that it *has* spots. As with anything, there are degrees.

We certainly would start a conflict if we insisted this system was perfect. It isn't, but it helps give you a feeling for the condition of a quilt. We've tried to explain in words the condition of any quilt we list, and we hope you get the information you need.

The most important thing to remember about condition information is that it is *only* a description. The fact that spots are present on the quilt is what affects its value, not the rating we gave it.

The one thing that rankles some quilt sellers is the thought that something like condition will affect the *value* of a quilt, since that dictates how much money they'll make on a sale. The truth is that the real value of a quilt is what someone is willing to pay. A dealer may think that a quilt is worth (and they should be paid) $1,000, but if no buyer is willing to pay that price, the quilt is, in fact, of lesser value than the dealer's asking price.

The **size** of the quilt is given in inches, and it is exciting to find something that is without conflict. Well, almost without conflict. We did hear a discussion about whether a prairie point edge should be measured from tip to tip, or left out of the quilt's dimensions entirely.

The one thing that is absolutely without conflict is the **price!** We list exactly the price being asked by the seller. We may not agree with the price set by the dealer, but that always leaves room for the collector to negotiate.

This guide is a tool to be used in looking for your quilts, but there are some other tools you should take with you in your search, if you are looking in person. First, take a measuring tool—ruler, yardstick, tape—so you can verify the size of a quilt. We know one collector who came home with a quilt stated to be a certain size that didn't even cover her bed.

Second, take four strips of cardboard, each one about 14 inches long and 4 to 6 inches wide. If you are having trouble identifying a pattern block, these strips will be very helpful in isolating any block. Just arrange them in a square and move them around the quilt, looking for the block pattern.

Third, if you have any absolutes about color, take a sample with you of what you are trying to match. One collector was quite disappointed when the quilt she bought for her living room was a terrible clash with her gold painted walls. Of course, we would have repainted the walls rather than take back the quilt, but that's just us!

Next, bring paper and pen. Take notes and be specific, especially if you are viewing more than one quilt. If you need to think about a quilt, you'll have plenty of information to digest. You might want to consider a camera as well, although some dealers won't allow pictures.

Finally, take this book with you. While we may not have an example of every quilt you may run across in the marketplace, this will give you a place to start, and invaluable information during your search.

In each listings chapter that follows, there is additional useful information about what quilts are included in it and why and some general ideas about each group of quilts. The price listings should be used as guidelines, for, as we have learned, many factors affect the value and desirability of a quilt. Good luck in your search; we are sure you'll find the perfect quilt to warm your heart.

12 One-Patch and Two-Block, Including Irish Chain

The most basic definition of a quilt is two pieces of fabric with some sort of stuffing in between, and stitches going from the top piece through the backing holding it all together. Quilts may have started that way, as a stuffing sandwich, and have been around in that form for hundreds of years, but once they landed on the shores of America, they went all to pieces!

Pieced quilts are most truly an American art form. Perhaps, as we've been told about quilting, piecework began as a way to use up those leftover scraps of fabric in a land so far from known civilization that nothing could be wasted. Maybe it began in an effort to find something in the guise of the practical, that was in fact mentally stimulating. However it started, piecework quickly became a way for a quilter to express her creativity, and maybe even outshine her neighbor at the county fair. And ever since the square was cut into two triangles and sewed together with two other triangles, all sorts of small fabric pieces have been put together to make interesting patterns.

The first pieced quilts were probably one- or two-patch varieties that used the most basic of blocks, a square, a rectangle, or a triangle. Even that simplicity didn't deter the adventurous quilter, for she could arrange those simple pieces in a way that alternated lights and darks to make a wavy look or use just one piece of every kind of fabric she could get her hands on for a unique look. Many quilt patterns lend themselves to the one-patch style, including Tumblers, Bars (made of rectangles), Thousand Pyramids (made of triangles), Roman Stripes, Postage Stamp (made of squares), and Flying Geese in all its variations. *See illustration #37.*

One-patch quilts were also made as Charm Quilts, in which the quiltmaker would not only use just one of each fabric, but might cut the pieces in a way to show off a particular print. We've seen one-patch quilts with squares showing a printed bird, a teddy bear, George Washington's face, and an old house.

The most easily recognizable one-patch design is the Grandmother's Flower Garden, which is assembled from hexagons into a complete hexagon garden. Traditionally, the center hexa-

37 Made by a boy who was recovering from a long illness, this blue and rust stripes Bar Quilt is from the 1930s. A simple looking one-patch pattern, it nonetheless has many block junctions to be matched. He did a pretty good job! Quilt courtesy of Pam Sperry.

gon of a Grandmother's Flower Garden piece is yellow, with anywhere from three to five rings around it; a row of green diamonds surrounds the pieces as they are assembled, making pathways around the gardens. As happens with all quiltmaking, after the first grandmother's flower garden was created, the variations began. The color of the center hexagon could be changed, the green paths could be left out or replaced with white hexagon paths, the rings could alternate light and dark, or printed and solid. The quilter might change the assembly in such a way that the hexagon gardens became a diamond shape and make the Diamond Field pattern. *See illustration #38.*

Flower Garden quilts and their variations have been popular since 1800, reaching a peak in 1925 and still going strong. When first made, the English method was used, where the fabric is pressed around a paper template, the pieces overcast stitched together, and the paper removed. Although that method is rare nowadays, quilts have been found with some of the paper templates still in place—a sure sign the quilt was made in the 1800s. In the early 1900s, pieces were stitched together like any other pattern pieces, without templates. A new method has gone back to using templates, but these are made of plastic and are removed after the quilt is pieced together. Even in quilting, trends may go in cycles.

You'd think the next evolution of quilt pieces was probably a Two-Patch, but if you take two square blocks and put them together, you get a rectangle, two more blocks to make another square and then you've got a Four-Patch. That's what happens with the Drunkard's Path pattern and its variations, and we've decided to leave that pattern, since it has so many variations, in with the Four-Patches in Chapter 14.

For the rest of this chapter, we'll look at what is really a two block, the Irish Chain.

There are many two-block patterns, such as Flagstones and Suspension Bridge, but the Irish Chains have a unique twist, a slight of hand that requires us to look closely to see the block

38 The one-patch Grandmother's Flower Garden block is taken to its limits to make this Trip Around the World style hexagonal throw. This 1930s piece shows alternating light and dark rows, and contains a large variety of colors. Quilt courtesy of Lois Belden.

39 Made around 1860 in Massachusetts, this Compass and Birds applique quilt would be beautiful and skillfully done with just the four compass medallions but the maker added a remarkable border comprised of flowers, vines, leave and bud applique. The simple crosshatch style quilting was chosen to further emphasize the applique.

from which they are really made. Part of the appeal of this pattern is the optical illusion created that makes us think the block is something else. *See illustration #39.*

To make an Irish Chain, the quilter starts with a simple Nine-Patch, usually a dark color and white, with the squares arranged so the dark color is in the corners. She then takes a plain white block and appliqués a small square in each corner. Make a whole bunch of both blocks, assemble them in an alternating design, and you have an Irish Chain.

The Double Irish Chain is made the same way, but a five by five grid block (a 25-patch) and two colors with white are used instead of the Nine-Patch and one color. Again the darkest color is appliquéd on the plain block corners and the optical illusion occurs. To get a Triple Irish Chain, add a third color and a seven by seven grid block, and you are good to go.

Except for quilting, the large white blocks with the appliqués in the corner are usually left plain, which leaves a lot of light space around the chains so one can see the rows of diamonds running back and forth across the quilt. This gives the pattern a clean and contemporary look that goes with much modern decor, proving that a very old pattern can certainly stand the test of time.

It also proves that categorizing quilt patterns is quite a challenge.

One-Patch Quilts

BARS: 1880s; yellow on yellow print, browns with pinks, creams with browns, other browns in prints and florals; six pieced vertical bars with five yellow bars between, cream with brown floral border, brown print backing; from Pennsylvania; minimal outline quilting, neat stitches; good assembly; good condition, some overall color fade; 74" × 86"; $2,600.

CATHEDRAL WINDOW, POSTAGE STAMP: 1940–50; tiny (just over one inch square) windows, multicolored, set on point on cream background; from Kentucky; excellent assembly; excellent condition; 76" × 92"; $3,000.

DIAMOND FIELD: 1929; bright reds and white; similar to grandmother's flower garden with four rows of hexagons around a center, but in shape of diamond, red and white prints alternating with solid white and solid red "paths"; from Oklahoma, via Colorado, maker known; excellent line quilting overall, small, even stitches; excellent assembly, excellent condition, unused, possibly washed once, some areas where color may have faded slightly; 74" × 78"; $850.

DIAMOND FIELD: 1930s; yellow, multicolored pastels, and brights in prints, stripes, checks, plaids; each diamond field has yellow center with white and yellow outside path, cream white backing, white binding; each hexagon piece is just over one inch; outline quilting overall, 6–7 stitches per inch; good assembly, most corners match; very good condition, a couple of small stains in one area; 70" × 80"; $425.

DIAMOND FIELD: 1930s; pure white, pastels, and brights in solids, prints, florals, checks; each diamond field has solid center and outside row with color-coordinated print/patterned fabric row between, white row around each field; fields are arranged so that close up, they form a six point star shapes and from afar, the whole quilt looks like "tumbling blocks"; wide white border, white backing, green binding; from Pennsylvania; outline quilting in the hexagons, floral quilting on the border, 6 stitches per inch; excellent assembly; excellent condition; 68" × 90"; $395.

DIAMOND FIELD: early 1900s; solids of dark green, red, cheddar yellow, and white; each field has cheddar hexagon center, tiny red diamond pathways between, edges are straight with narrow double border, white, then red; very, very thin muslin backing; from Tennessee; outline quilting overall at 5–6 stitches per inch; good assembly, most points and corners match; fair condition, many dark and pale stains on front, many dark stains on back; 40" × 66"; $125

GRANDMOTHER'S FLOWER GARDEN: 1930s; dark green, white, yellow, and many period colors and prints; gardens do not have traditional tiny diamond pathways, just green hexagon rows all around, yellow centers, white binding, straight edges on two sides, edges that follow garden shape on other two sides; outline quilting, 8 stitches per inch; excellent assembly and color coordination; excellent condition; 73" × 82"; $495.

GRANDMOTHER'S FLOWER GARDEN: 1930s; dark green, white, yellow, and many period colors and prints; gardens do not have traditional tiny diamond pathways, just green hexagon rows all around, yellow centers, straight edges on all sides, green binding; triple border, white, then green, then white; outline quilting in garden hexagon, cable quilting in all three borders, tiny and even, 12 stitches per inch; excellent assembly and color coordination; excellent condition; 73" × 82"; $575.

GRANDMOTHER'S FLOWER GARDEN: 1930s; green and period pastels in prints and florals; traditional green pathways between gardens, green binding on "scalloped" edge that follows gardens on all sides; outline quilting overall, 7–8 stitches per inch; good assembly, most edges and corners match; good condition, has been washed; 60" × 90"; $960.

GRANDMOTHER'S FLOWER GARDEN: 1930s; green, white, lavender, multicolored period colors and prints; traditional rendition, with yellow garden centers, tiny green diamond pathways; lavender backing and binding; outline quilting, 5 stitches per inch; excellent assembly; very good condition, has been washed; 70" × 82"; $200.

GRANDMOTHER'S FLOWER GARDEN: 1930s; green, white, yellow, many period prints and colors; gardens have traditional tiny diamond pathways between, yellow centers, all four sides follow the shape of the gardens, as does pieced green border and yellow binding made of tiny yellow triangles; outline quilting overall, 8 stitches per inch; excellent assembly, and color coordination; very good condition, has been washed; 63" × 76"; $550.

GRANDMOTHER'S FLOWER GARDEN: 1930s; green, yellow, multicolored period prints and florals; green paths between gardens, green binding along scalloped edge that follows garden edges; outline quilting overall, small stitches; very good assembly, nearly all junctions match; good condition, some slight overall color fade, few stains; 78" × 84"; $500.

GRANDMOTHER'S FLOWER GARDEN: 1930s; multicolored prints, stripes, plaids, checks, and florals, pure white, green; traditional pattern with four hexagon row gardens, white centers, green diamond pathways; the two sides have an additional row of hexagons as border, edges follow shapes of gardens, top and bottom edges are straight; thin batting, white backing, green binding; outline quilting overall, 8 stitches per inch; excellent assembly, excellent condition, minimal washing; 78" × 82"; $625.

GRANDMOTHER'S FLOWER GARDEN: 1930s; white, green, yellow, multicolored period prints, designs, checks, florals, and stripes; traditional arrangement with green diamond paths, yellow centers, white fences, top and bottom are straight, sides are curves to follow garden edges, white binding; outline quilting overall, small and even stitches; good assembly, few puckered piece edges, some corners don't match; good condition, some slight overall color fade, top binding worn; 64" × 76"; $450.

GRANDMOTHER'S FLOWER GARDEN: 1930s; white, green, yellow, multicolored period prints, designs, checks, florals, and stripes; traditional arrangement with green diamond paths, yellow centers, white fences, top and bottom are straight, sides are curves to follow garden edges, yellow backing and binding; outline quilting overall, small and even stitches; excellent assembly; very good condition, never washed or used, one corner has some slight color fade; 77" × 90"; $545.

GRANDMOTHER'S FLOWER GARDEN: 1930s; spring green, pastels in solids and prints; each garden has five rows, solid center of hexagons, paths are solid green hexagons; top and bottom edges are shaped by garden sides, sides have additional row of green hexagon with gold hexagon creating an additional "bump" on the indent of the original gardens; outline quilting overall, 8 stitches per inch; very good assembly, most points match; good condition, some minor color loss, few stains; 62" × 80"; $500.

GRANDMOTHER'S FLOWER GARDEN, PAIR: 1934 and 1935; off-white, with brights and pastels of greens, blues, golden browns, tans, pinks, yellows in prints and solids; ten rows of nine gardens with bright green paths between; each garden has solid yellow center, surrounded by row of solid color hexagons, surrounded by row of coordinating color print hexagons, surrounded by row of off-white hexagons, then green pathway; quilt's edges shaped by gardens, triple border of solid color hexagons, blanket stitch edging; dated and initialed; outline quilting overall, on each hexagon; excellent condition, minimal use and washing; 73" × 91"; $1,200 for the pair.

GRANDMOTHER'S FLOWER GARDEN: 1910–20; pale green, multicolored prints; all four edges curved following sides of gardens, green "paths" and border; outline quilting overall, 7–8 stitches per inch; good assembly, most corners match, some patches misshapen; good to excellent condition, minimal use; 78" × 80"; $775.

GRANDMOTHER'S FLOWER GARDEN: 1920s; green and multicolored period prints; top and bottom are straight, sides follow edges of gardens, no diamond pathways, gardens defined by hexagon shapes; from California; outline quilting overall; good assembly; excellent condition; 70" × 72"; $1,200.

GRANDMOTHER'S FLOWER GARDEN: 1920s; green, pink, yellow, multicolored period prints, florals and designs; green diamond paths between gardens, edge is wavy, following the sides of the gardens, green binding; outline quilting overall, uneven stitches, 5–6 stitches per inch; fair to good assembly, many uneven edges, corners don't match; fair condition, very faded, well washed and used, overall wear, no tears or splits; 78" × 80"; $640.

GRANDMOTHER'S FLOWER GARDEN: 1920s; greens, lavender; traditional green "paths," two side edges curved and follow sides of gardens, top and bottom edges straight; outline quilting overall, 7–8 stitches per inch; good assembly, most corners match, some centers misaligned; excellent condition, minimal use and washing; 88" × 100"; $950.

GRANDMOTHER'S FLOWER GARDEN: 1930s; green, yellow, blue, pink solids, multicolored period prints, designs, florals; light green binding and backing, yellow centers to gardens, no diamond pathways, green pathways of hexagons, scalloped edges follow sides of gardens on all four sides; outline quilting overall, large stitches; fair assembly, many corners don't match, many pinched fabric on edges of pieces, many pieces misshapen; excellent condition, unwashed and unused; 70" × 78"; $550. *See illustration #40.*

GRANDMOTHER'S FLOWER GARDEN: 1930s; solids of green, white; prints of blues, greens, reds, pink, yellow, many others; four gardens by seven whole or partial gardens, white hexagons around each garden, green paths between all gardens; narrow green border, slightly wider white border, unusual edging border of alternating green and multicolored "wedges"; outline quilting overall; 68" × 98"; $500.

GRANDMOTHER'S FLOWER GARDEN: 1930s; white, green, pastel solids and coordinating floral prints; 11 gardens by 10½ gardens, with tiny green diamond paths between; each garden has yellow gold center, row of floral hexagons cut to have one flower in each piece, row of coordinating solid color hexagons, and row of white hexagons, then green paths; edge shaped by the gardens and half gardens; outline quilting overall, 8 stitches per inch; excellent condition, probably never used, never washed; 73" × 81"; $550.

GRANDMOTHER'S FLOWER GARDEN; 1930s; multi-pastels and pastel prints/plaids, white around each "garden," tiny green diamond pathways between "gardens," all golden yellow

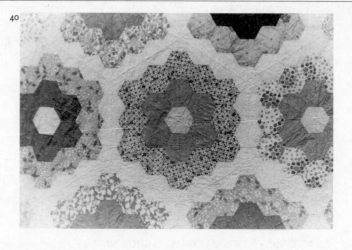

40 This traditionally assembled Grandmother's Flower Garden reveals minimal but precise straight line machine quilting. The wide variety of wonderful 1930s prints is captivating. Quilt courtesy of the Warner Family.

centers, narrow pink binding; excellent example of the pattern style, straight on top and bottom, scalloped from the shape of the gardens on sides; from Kentucky; row-by-row quilting overall; very good assembly, most corners match; excellent condition, minor age discoloration; 74" × 83"; $1,250.

HONEYCOMB: 1870s; browns, pinks, reds, cranberry, blues, greens, many others in tiny prints, checks, stripes, designs; "charm" quilt, all fabrics seem to be unique, many hexagons have figures in them (cats, birds, butterflies, etc.); from the Midwest; minimal outline quilting, about a third of the pieces only, 6 stitches per inch; fair to good assembly, many pieces are misshapen, many corners don't match; very good condition, slight overall color fade; 70" × 78"; $1,050.

MOSAIC SQUARES: 1850s; all silks in Prussian blue and other jewel tones; three-inch squares, blue backing, binding, and very wide border, small flowers embroidered along border in black silk thread; from North Carolina; tied with black silk, no quilting; good assembly, most corners match; fair to good condition, many fabrics have shattered or become brittle, many fabric splits in the border; 78" × 88"; $10,025.

OCEAN WAVE: 1880s; indigo blue and white; very wide white border; feather and straight line quilting overall, 9 stitches per inch; very good assembly; 80" × 80"; $850.

OCEAN WAVES/SAWTOOTH VARIATION: 1840–80; browns, tans, grays, solids, calicoes, prints, plaids, checks, with large cream-color center squares; set on point with brown/gray print sashing and border; overall line quilting, 7 stitches per inch; very good assembly, most corners match, some sashing wavy, possibly due to washing; very good condition, some small stains/spots, few small holes, small repair on back; 71" × 79"; $2,600.

OCEAN WAVES: 1880s; blue and white; pattern blocks are blue with tiny white stars print and white, with white squares in the center; triple border, blue, white, then blue, blue binding;

outline quilting in the pattern blocks, grid quilting on the white blocks, 9 stitches per inch; excellent assembly; excellent condition, has been washed once or twice; 64" × 70"; $895.

OCEAN WAVES: 1880s; dark green, multicolored lights and darks in prints, designs, checks, stripes, plaids, dots; some of the quilting is done in dark thread, green ground, border, and binding, dark rose and red print backing; outline quilting on the pieces, diamond grid in the center blocks, very small and even stitches; very good assembly, nearly all points and corners match; very good condition, never washed, very slight fade in fold lines; 70" × 87"; $975.

OCEAN WAVES: 1880s; green with tiny yellow print and off-white; "ocean waves" sections surround plain white blocks, double border, one narrow green, one narrow white, green binding; outline quilting in waves pieces, grid quilting in white blocks, 7–8 stitches per inch; excellent assembly; very good condition, few tiny spots in one area; 68" × 76"; $695.

OCEAN WAVES: 1900–1910; three different smoky blacks with tiny white dots and flowers prints on white ground; outline quilting in waves, diamond grid quilting in center blocks, very small stitches; excellent assembly; excellent condition; 76" × 78"; $2,500.

OCEAN WAVES: 1920s; solids and prints in blues and greens, with white; outline quilting overall, 8–9 stitches per inch; excellent assembly, excellent condition, unused, unwashed; 60"x 72"; $750.

OCEAN WAVES: 1930s; red and blue solids, multicolored prints, and florals, white; "waves" are red or blue triangles with multicolored triangles, with white center blocks; outline quilting overall, 8 stitches per inch; good assembly, most waves are even, points match; good condition, minimal use and washing; 70" × 80"; $965.

OCEAN WAVES: 1944; yellow solids and multicolored prints; half blocks on the diagonal, one half solid yellow, the other half print; from Kansas, dated, maker known; outline quilting overall, 8 stitches per inch; excellent assembly; good condition, minimal use and washing; 66" × 82"; $1,100.

ONE-PATCH, SQUARES MAKE DIAMONDS: 1930s; white and multiple period colors and prints; approximately four-inch print/patterned squares are set on point with white squares between, edges are straight with white triangles; outline and straight-line quilting, 6 stitches per inch; excellent assembly; excellent condition; 70" × 72"; $395.

POSTAGE STAMP: 1880s; prints and solids in dozens of blues; from New Mexico; minimal quilting overall, 5–6 stitches per inch; good condition, some overall fade, has been used and washed; 42" × 48"; $500.

POSTAGE STAMP: 1890s; red, white, blue; solid colors, red/white/blue narrow triple border, over 4,000 one-inch blocks; from Pennsylvania; straight-line quilting overall, through center of each row of blocks, slanted three-line echo quilting on the border, 8 stitches per inch; good assembly, most corners match; good condition, some overall color loss, minimal washing; 70" × 70"; $950.

POSTAGE STAMP: 1930s; deep blues, many other multicolored prints and stripes; nearly 5,000 one-inch squares, five outside rows of striped fabric so similar they seem to form borders; found in Oklahoma; straight-line quilting overall, 7–8 stitches per inch; very good assembly for so many small pieces, most corners match; good condition, some wear, some overall fade; 60" × 68"; $1,200.

POSTAGE STAMP: 1930s; multicolored in period prints; outline quilting, 7–8 stitches per inch; excellent assembly; excellent condition; 80" × 88"; $925.

ROMAN STRIPES: 1910; blacks, reds, several grays; all silks, very bold graphics; from Colorado, maker known; tied, no quilting; good condition, but very delicate, some small areas of restoration with later fabrics; 65" × 75"; $800.

ROMAN STRIPES: 1940s; red, black, blue; all wool fabrics in worsteds and basket weaves, solids and prints; blocks of three bars alternate with plain blocks, tied, some machine quilting in star pattern in plain blocks; from Ohio; fair assembly, many blocks misshapen, many corners mismatched; good condition, minimal use; 54" × 70"; $650.

SPOOLS: 1900–30; multicolored solids and prints, scrap bag of three decades of fabrics; one-piece red, blue, and white floral backing, very thick batting; shell quilting overall, 5 stitches per inch, uneven; good assembly, most edges and corners match; good condition, some color loss, overall color fade; 71" × 87"; $200.

STRING SQUARES: 1923; pink with tiny floral print, blue with tiny print, multicolored prints and stripes; five rows by six rows of square string pattern blocks, set square with pink print sashing between and blue print squares at set corners; blue print binding and backing, striped flannel sheet as batting; dated; minimal quilting; good assembly, most corners match; good condition, few rusty stains; 72" × 78"; $225.

SUGAR LOAF: 1890s; red with tiny yellow squares and black dots as ground, yellow, green, white, pink, others all in prints, stripes, designs; gray print border, white backing; from Pennsylvania; outline quilting overall, small and even stitches; excellent assembly and color arrangement; excellent condition; 72" × 80"; $775.

THOUSANDS OF TRIANGLES, POSTAGE STAMP: 1930s; darks and lights of burgundy, grays, creams, yellow, blues, greens, pink, black, many others in stripes, prints, dots, plaids, checks, solids; very thick batting; reverses to completely different quilt: four-patch; blues, red, green predominate; print sashing with red squares at set corners; no quilting, abundance of red string ties, good assembly, good condition with slight batting shift; 70" × 84"; $150.

TRIP AROUND THE WORLD, POSTAGE STAMP: 1920s; multicolored prints, designs, florals, checks, stripes, plaids; thousands of one-inch pieces, dozens of fabrics; no quilting, lots of yarn ties, almost square, one extra row top and bottom; good assembly, most corners match; fair to good condition, overall color fade, well washed and used, very worn binding; 68" × 70"; $635.

TRIP AROUND THE WORLD, POSTAGE STAMP: 1930s; period prints and patterns, primarily in blues; from Colorado, via Oklahoma; outline quilting overall, 5–6 stitches per inch; excellent assembly; good condition, has been washed and used; 70" × 77"; $700.

41

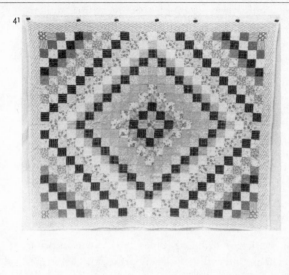

41 This beautiful example of a Trip Around the World quilt shows great use of the lights and darks and has a print border that pulls it all together. Made in the 1940s, the quilt is machine quilted in straight lines. Quilt courtesy of Brian Comstock.

TRIP AROUND THE WORLD, POSTAGE STAMP: 1930s; multicolored period prints, solid rose pink and white; around 6,000 pieces, large center trip around the world square, surrounded by triple border, inner rose pink solid, then postage stamp pieced, then another solid rose pink; very narrow white border on sides, wide white border on top and bottom, green prairie point binding, thin batting; straight-line quilting in the pieces, overlapping circles quilting in borders, 5–6 stitches per inch; fair assembly, many misshapen and misaligned pieces, color balance not well considered or executed; good condition, has been washed and used; $650.

TRIP AROUND THE WORLD, POSTAGE STAMP: 1945–50; carefully coordinated cotton prints and solids of cream, white, bright pink, pale pink, rose, three shades of green, three shades of yellow, two shades of blue, violet, purple, others; from Illinois, maker known; grid quilting overall, well executed; excellent condition, unwashed and unused; 90" × 90"; $650.

TRIP AROUND THE WORLD: 1890s; prints, checks, stripes of double pink, blue, browns, yellow, wine, others; double pink wide border and binding, backing of red and black print; from Pennsylvania; outline quilting on the squares, chevron quilting on the border, 6 stitches per inch; excellent assembly; excellent condition, unused; 90" × 90"; $550. *See illustration #41.*

TRIP AROUND THE WORLD: 1920s; blues and greens in solids, prints; straight line quilting crossed in center of squares, 6–7 stitches per inch; good assembly, most corners match; good condition with some overall fade; 68" × 70"; $600.

TRIP AROUND THE WORLD: 1930s; pastels and darks in reds, yellows, greens, blues; mostly solids, some prints; traditional diamond pattern in rainbow and reverse rainbow effect; from Vermont; diamond straight-line quilting overall; large stitches, 6 stitches per inch; very good assembly, nearly all corners match; 78" × 92"; $600.

TUMBLER: 1880s; multicolored (predominantly browns, blues, creams) prints, designs, stripes, dots, plaids, checks; scrap bag look, black and white floral binding and backing; straight-line quilting across tumblers; good assembly, most corners match, edges straight, pleasing color arrangement; good condition, a few small, light stains; 74" × 86"; $450.

TUMBLING BLOCKS: 1860s; browns, blues, pinks in prints and designs; floral binding, brown print backing; from Pennsylvania; outline quilting overall, small and even stitches; good assembly, colors are arranged to give good optical illusion, most points and corners match; good condition, some overall wear, slight overall color fade; 85" x 100"; $2,375.

TUMBLING BLOCKS: 1880s; burgundy, medium blue, creamy white; blues are all the same blue, but with two different tiny white prints, white solids, burgundy has tiny rose print; burgundy border, blue border, burgundy binding; outline quilting overall, 6 stitches per inch; excellent assembly, very good condition, one small area of fading on one border; 68" × 77"; $800.

TUMBLING BLOCKS: 1890s; double pink, darks are primarily blues and browns in prints, florals, solids, checks, stripes, lights are cream and off-white with tiny prints, checks, stripes; tops of blocks are double pink, dark green binding, no batting; from Pennsylvania; outline quilting overall, 9 stitches per inch; excellent assembly and color arrangement to form optical illusion; excellent condition; 66" × 78"; $1,195.

TUMBLING BLOCKS: 1890s; white, blue prints, red prints; blue border and backing; outline quilting overall, 6 stitches per inch; very good assembly, nearly all points and corners match; fair to good condition, overall wear and fading, few tears on top and binding; 73" × 78"; $950.

TUMBLING BLOCKS: 1920s; solid red, multicolored prints and solids; fairly good rendition, although in several sections, stars stand out more than the optical illusions blocks; red plaid backing, red binding; from Ohio; outline quilting overall, small and even stitches; excellent assembly; excellent condition; 72" × 88"; $1,100.

WILD GOOSE CHASE VARIATION: 1930s; white, green solids, and multicolored prints, checks, plaids; green and multicolored flying geese strip as sashing surrounds white blocks; green border; from Vermont; diamond and outline quilting overall; good assembly, most corners match; good condition, slight fading overall; 70" × 80"; $600.

WILD GOOSE CHASE: 1928; white and several cornflower blue prints; 15 two-inch-wide "goose" strips of blues on white, with two-inch-wide white strips between, very wide white border, white binding; dated; outline quilting in pattern strips, cable quilting in white strips and on border, 8–9 stitches per inch; excellent assembly; very good condition, slight overall color fade from washing; 80" × 86"; $645.

Irish Chain Quilts

DOUBLE IRISH CHAIN: 1840s; rose red and white; from West Virginia, via Colorado, maker known; excellent quilting and assembly; excellent condition, unwashed, unused; 74" × 82"; $1,550.

DOUBLE IRISH CHAIN: 1850s, backed and quilted in 1920s; cottons, red, blue, olive on natural cream background, yellow binding and backing; from Kentucky; well-done crosshatch quilting overall; very good assembly, matching points/squares; large areas of color loss/fading in the natural vegetable dyes in the top, some minor age/use discoloration; 68" × 78"; $1,050.

DOUBLE IRISH CHAIN: 1860s; indigo blue and pale pink solids; woman's name embroidered on front; straight-line quilting overall; good assembly, most points match; some fabric deterioration and wear; 72" × 98"; $400.

DOUBLE IRISH CHAIN: 1860s; white ground, rusty red with tiny white dots, green on green; white binding and backing; from Ohio; outline quilting in chains, double wheel in white centers, small and even stitches; very good assembly, most corners match, very small appliqué stitches; very good condition, slight overall color fade; 76" × 82"; $1,400.

DOUBLE IRISH CHAIN: 1890s; white with light blue and dark blue solids; center chain is dark, outside chains are light blue, dark blue binding; outline quilting overall, diamond grid in white areas, 8 stitches per inch; excellent assembly; very good condition, few small stains; 70" × 70"; $1,000.

DOUBLE IRISH CHAIN: 1900–10; red and white, with white central squares; outline quilting in chain squares, florals in center squares; good assembly; good condition, overall color fade; 70" × 76"; $700.

DOUBLE IRISH CHAIN: 1900–10; red, green, white; red chains and green chains parallel and crossed on white ground, red binding on two sides, green binding top and bottom; from West Virginia; diamond grid quilting overall, small and even stitches; very good assembly, most corners match; excellent condition, unwashed; 65" × 84"; $645.

DOUBLE IRISH CHAIN: 1920s; blue and white; double border, one blue, one white; straight-line and outline quilting, 6 stitches per inch; good assembly, most corners match; good condition, some use, some washing; 78" × 80"; $475.

DOUBLE IRISH CHAIN: 1930s; lavender on white ground; from Pennsylvania; outline quilting on pieces, feather wreath quilting on white blocks, 8 stitches per inch; excellent assembly, corners match, edges are even; very good condition, minimal use, some washing; 86" × 77"; $525.

IRISH CHAIN: 1846; indigo blue on white; dated; outline quilting in squares, half moons and stars in white blocks, inspired by the "Great Comet" of 1848, small and even stitches, 8 per inch; very good assembly, most all corners match; good condition, slight overall wear, some overall color fade; 75" × 80"; $3,200.

IRISH CHAIN: 1890s; tiny prints of red, yellow, blue; inside chain of yellow, outsides chains of red, center blocks of blue; double border, narrow red, very wide blue, red binding and backing; from Pennsylvania; outline and inch grid quilting in the pattern and center blocks, ¾ inch chevron quilting on the border, 8 stitches per inch; excellent assembly; excellent condition; 88" × 88"; $550.

SINGLE IRISH CHAIN: 1860s; white, blue print; chains are two blue around white, on white ground, very narrow blue print and white triangle border; from Ohio; square grid quilting overall, small and even stitches; good assembly, most corners match; very good condition, has been washed, slight overall color fade; 86" × 86"; $1,900.

SINGLE IRISH CHAIN: 1870; primarily browns, in prints and calicoes, some blues, pale greens, grays, pink, shirtings; true scrap bag quilt; cotton, summer quilt, no batting or quilting; from Pennsylvania; good assembly; excellent condition; 80" × 80"; $600.

SINGLE IRISH CHAIN: 1900–1910; white on solid blue; outline and straight line quilting overall, diamond grid in blue blocks, very even stitches, 7 per inch; very good assembly, nearly all corners match; fair to good condition, very faded overall, binding very worn; 80" × 80"; $570.

SINGLE IRISH CHAIN: 1930s; pink and white; narrow pink border, wide white border, pink binding; straight line and cable quilting overall, 8 stitches per inch; good assembly, most corners match; excellent condition; 44" × 60"; $250.

SINGLE IRISH CHAIN: 1930s; solid blue and white; very wide blue border, scalloped edge, white binding; diamond and serpentine quilting overall, 8 stitches per inch; excellent assembly; excellent condition; 41" × 55"; $450.

SINGLE IRISH CHAIN: 1930s; cornflower blue on white; blue binding; from Pennsylvania; straight line quilting overall, 7 stitches per inch; good assembly, most corners match, edges even; very good condition, some overall color fade; 79" × 79"; $1,000.

SINGLE IRISH CHAIN: mid-1800s; indigo and red calicoes, also browns, cranberry; homespun, home dyed backing; from Kentucky, signed; overall line and outline quilting; good assembly, most corners match; some stains, some fabric splits; 56" × 76"; $1,350.

TRIPLE IRISH CHAIN: 1870s; indigo and white; indigo with tiny white rice shaped dots print, white/indigo print/white triple border, indigo print binding; crisscross and straight-line quilting overall, 8 stitches per inch; good assembly, most corners match; excellent condition, minimal washing and use; 68" × 76"; $950.

TRIPLE IRISH CHAIN: 1890s; white, with green solid; green binding and backing; minimal outline quilting, large stitches; corner appliqué squares are misshapen; fair to good condition, overall color fade, overall wear, binding very worn; 72" × 78"; $385.

TRIPLE IRISH CHAIN: 1940s; white, red with tiny white dot print, multicolored prints and patterns; center chain is red with white dot, white ground, rest of chains are various and assorted multicolored period prints; triple border, white, red dot, white; diamond quilting overall, along chains, 5 stitches per inch; excellent assembly and color arrangement; excellent condition; 66" × 80"; $300.

TRIPLE IRISH CHAIN: 1940s; solid cottons of bright blue, and red with pale salmon pink background; narrow blue and wide red border, thin batting; Pennsylvania Mennonite; grid quilting overall, twisted rope quilting on borders; very good assembly, nearly all corners match; excellent condition, unwashed; 84" × 84"; $800.

13 Three-Patch and Square in a Square

This may seem like an unusual pairing, the Three-Patch and Square in a Square patterns, but in fact, they are, in many ways, alike.

A square in a square is just as the name states: take one square, put it inside another, larger, square, either straight or turned on point, put those two inside another even larger square, and you pretty much have your pattern. Most of such blocks have three layered squares, but there can be more or less. Sawtooth Diamonds often have only the center diamond and one outer square, with the interest added by the sawtooth around each.

Many people consider an Ocean Waves block as a Square in a Square, since the "waves" simply surround a center square. Log Cabins can also be considered a Square in a Square, as can the Double Wedding Ring. We put those in categories by themselves, but you should be aware that you might find quilt patterns categorized many different ways.

A Three-Patch is, of course, a square that is divided into three pieces, but as we have already found out, nothing is that simple in quilt patterns. The two seams on a Three-Patch square can run parallel, they can intersect, or they can sort of run around a center square, and the whole thing can be just as confusing as the square in a square, or any other quilt pattern, for that matter.

It would seem that a Three-Patch is just a precursor to a Nine-Patch, but it isn't. Take a look at a Garden of Eden Three-Patch and you'll see something that looks like a Nine-Patch, until you look closer and see that the center strips cross rather than intersect. Look at a Three-Patch Mrs. Taft's Choice and it looks a lot like the Four-Patch Crosses and Losses or Old Maid's Puzzle.

It gets a little confusing, but that's one thing that makes quilt patterns interesting.

42 The arrangement of the strips in this quilt, with the same color diagonally across each block, gives the look of narrow sashing—an interesting way to get this effect. Brackman's *Encyclopedia* categorizes the pattern as a Square in a Square because four blocks placed together will match the center strips and form a square. This 1947 quilt has scrap bag fabrics and straight line quilting. Quilt courtesy of Brian Comstock.

Square In A Square

CARPENTER'S SQUARE: 1930s; blue and white; wide white border; straight-line, criss-cross quilting overall, twisted rope quilting on border, 10 stitches per inch; 70" × 84"; $670.

ECONOMY PATCH VARIATION: 1920s; multicolored period prints, designs, checks on white ground; pattern blocks in groups of four with white sashing between groups, print squares at sashing corners, white binding and backing; square and diamond grid quilting overall, small and even stitches; excellent assembly; very good condition, has been washed, minimal use; 86" × 86"; $345. *See illustration #42.*

ECONOMY PATCH: 1890s; solid red, whites with blue dots, prints, blues with tiny white print, white with red print, few browns, double pink; pattern blocks are set square with solid red blocks between; triple border, white print, solid red, then white print, and red binding; from Pennsylvania; outline quilting in pattern blocks, diamond grid in red blocks, double echo zigzag in borders, mostly even stitches; good assembly, most corners match; excellent condition; 86" × 86"; $1,875.

RIGHT AND LEFT: 1880s; several blue with tiny white prints on white ground; four by five pattern blocks, set on point with white blocks between and around, blue border, white binding; from Pennsylvania; double outline quilting in pattern blocks, diamond grid in white blocks, 7 stitches per inch; very good assembly, most points and corners match; excellent condition; 66" × 88"; $700.

ROAD TO JERUSALEM: 1920s; white, purple, and lavender solids, lavender and red print on white; four rows by five rows of pattern blocks, lavender print and purple solid on white ground, set square, with lavender sashing between, wide lavender border and backing; minimal quilting, large zigzag on border and sashing, double outline in pattern block pieces, mostly even stitches; good assembly, most corners and points match; good condition, one tiny rusty spot, minimal washing; 72" × 83"; $175.

SAWTOOTH DIAMOND IN SQUARE: 1890s; rose pink and white; large white center diamond with sawtooth edges on rose square, wide double sawtooth borders, white then rose; from Ohio; outline, starburst, oval, straight-line quilting, very small and even stitches; good assembly, most corners and points match; very good condition, has been washed, slight discoloration on back; 74" × 80"; $800.

SAWTOOTH DIAMOND: 1930s; lemon yellow and white; three layers of squares, thin batting, white backing, yellow binding; quilted with large center wreath, cables, florals, leaves, vines, scrolls, grid, 8 stitches per inch; excellent assembly, sharp points, corners and edges match; excellent condition, unused, unwashed; 78" × 88"; $650.

SAWTOOTH DIAMOND: 1930s; solid peach and white; diamond in square, with three squares, with wide white border, all with sawtooth edges, wide peach border, peach binding, thin batting, white backing; large, elaborate feather wreath medallion and grid quilting in center square, outline quilting on teeth, florals, feather chains, cables, butterflies on borders and elsewhere, 8 stitches per inch; excellent assembly; excellent condition; 74" × 74"; $750.

SNAIL'S TRAIL: 1930s; green and white; pattern blocks alternate with plain green and white blocks to make the traditional overall look, white binding, muslin backing; from Texas; outline and straight-line quilting overall, 8 stitches per inch; very good assembly, nearly all points and corners match; excellent condition, has been washed; 72" × 80"; $735.

TWELVE TRIANGLES: 1930s; predominantly red, pink, yellow and blue solids, with some additional colors in prints, plaids, checks; each pattern block has red center square with four print or otherwise patterned-fabric triangles, then four yellow triangles, then four otherwise patterned-fabric triangles, to make the total blocks; blocks are set straight with blue sashing, with pink squares at the set corners; thin batting, plain muslin backing; from Texas, maker known; fan quilting overall, large stitches, 5 per inch; excellent condition, never used, minimal washing; fair to good assembly, many corners or points mismatched; 70" × 82"; $250.

Three-Patch

CHIMNEY SWEEP: 1850s; browns, greens, pinks, blues, others in various prints, designs, stripes, checks; six rows by six rows of pattern blocks, on white ground, set on point with brown print squares between, brown print binding, muslin backing; from New York State; outline and square grid quilting overall, small and mostly even stitches; very good assembly, most corners match; very good condition, strong colors, two tiny age spots on front, stained area on backing; 84" × 84"; $2,300.

CHIMNEY SWEEP: 1860s; various shades and tones of browns, reds, purples, others in prints, designs, checks, and stripes, green with black and yellow dots, white; six rows by six rows of pattern blocks, each on white ground, with narrow green sashing between, green border and binding; grid quilting overall, small and even stitches; excellent assembly; very good condition, few small spots; 76" × 77"; $1,195.

CHIMNEY SWEEP: 1870s; white, pinks, lavenders, grays, greens, reds, blues, in various designs, stripes, and prints; pattern blocks, on white ground, set on point with narrow white sashing and border, white border; from Pennsylvania; outline quilting in pattern blocks, chevron quilting in sashing and border, small and even stitches; excellent assembly; excellent condition, has been professionally washed; 81" × 81"; $595.

OLD GRAY GOOSE VARIATION: 1870s; reds, tans, blues, cream, greens in prints, stripes, checks; pattern blocks set on point with plain blue-green print blocks between, same fabric as edging; large stitches, 5 per inch, shell quilting overall; some color loss, deterioration, several pieces have obviously been replaced; 62" × 80"; $500.

14 Four-Patch, including Drunkard's Path

When early quiltmakers split one square into four, and sewed them back together, they had effectively created the first Four-Patch block. In most Four-Patch squares each of the four pieces is itself split in some way, either into more squares or into triangles, to contribute to the developing pattern. There are almost as many ways to change the basic Four-Patch as there are kinds of fabric, which makes this versatile square a perennial favorite. One-quarter of all pieced quilt patterns are based on the four patch. *See illustrations #43–43G.*

Some experts consider the Drunkard's Path pattern to be a Two-Patch or a Two-Square, but it is really a Four-Patch with curves on the corners. Because it involves curved piecing, this block is a challenge to the quiltmaker. Traditionally, this square is made in just two colors, usually white and another—its appeal is in its assembly. An almost quarter circle is taken out of the white block and replaced by the same quarter circle taken from the colored block. Hence the pattern is also known as one of the Robbing Peter To Pay Paul variations. The blocks are arranged in two groups, one with the white quarter circles along the edge of the four squares, causing a look like a windmill, the second with the four colored quarter circles all turned to the center. When each of these two sets of blocks is alternately joined, the overall visual look is easily identified as a horrible trail (or trial, perhaps) for the inebriated.

Like the Log Cabin, the Drunkard's Path pattern can be assembled different ways. The Falling Timbers looks like the Log Cabin's Straight Furrows, and the Love Ring looks like Barn Raising. One of the best books for review of the assembly variations for Drunkard's Path is Marguerite Ickis's *The Standard Book of Quilt Making and Collecting*, as listed in the Bibliography.

The Drunkard's Path pattern was supposedly first given that name in association with the women's temperance movement. Since many quilters wanted to use the pattern without its association with overindulgence, it has often been called Pumpkin Vine, a name that probably suits it better anyway. *See illustration #44.*

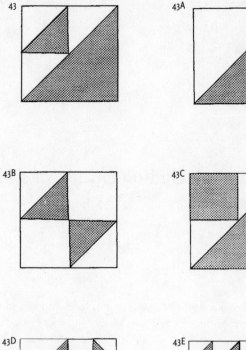

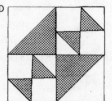

43-43C: Basic Quilt Block Assembly. These four pieced squares can be assembled into many different blocks. Sometimes just a simple twist makes all the difference.

43D: The simplest arrangement, using two of the pieces, makes Crosses and Losses.

43E: Add two corner triangles and the block becomes Old Maid's Puzzle.

43F: Twist the hour-glass shaped corners and the block becomes Fox and Geese.

43G: Change the corner triangles into squares and you now have Double X #3. Confused? What makes things worse is the fact that each of these blocks has anywhere from two to six other names!

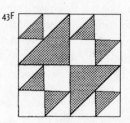

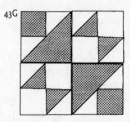

44 The pinwheels on his Flying Dutchman Variation quilt are shades of blue stripes, gray prints, yellow prints and gold solids. The border and sets are orange. A very graphic look. The quilt was made in the 1940s, shows excellent assembly and straight-line quilting. Quilt courtesy of Brian Comstock

BARRISTER'S BLOCK: 1910–1920; solids of pink, green, red, blue on white; pattern blocks are solid color and white, set square with green sashing vertical and pink sashing horizontal, white squares at set corners; straight-line quilting overall, 8 stitches per inch; good assembly in difficult pattern, most points match, most corners are square; very good condition, minimal use and washing; 80" × 82"; $750.

BIG DIPPER: 1830s; golden yellow plaid print, dark blue and white twisted rope print, golden yellow plaid binding; from Massachusetts; outline quilting overall, large stitches; good assembly, most corners match; very good condition, has been washed; 32" × 36"; $600.

BIG DIPPER: 1900–1910; blue and white; pattern blocks set on points with white blocks between, wide white border, white binding; straight line quilting in pattern blocks and border, feather wreath quilting on white blocks, 8 stitches per inch; excellent assembly; excellent condition, unwashed, unused; 70" × 80"; $900.

BIRDS IN THE AIR: 1870s; lights are white, darks are reds, blues, black, few others in prints and solids; from Pennsylvania; diamond grid quilting overall, large but even stitches; very good assembly, nearly all points and corners match; excellent condition, has been washed once; 71" × 82"; $2,450.

BONNIE SCOTSMAN VARIATION: 1930–50; cotton feed sacks, cottons, and silk fabric in purple and white, and green and white prints, sage green solids, tiny touches of black and red; pieced feed sack backing; from Kentucky; fan quilting overall, large stitches, 5 per inch; fabric fracture in some silk, some age discoloration; 70" × 80"; $400.

BOW AND ARROWS: 1890s; white and dark blue with tiny white dots; wide white border, white binding; outline quilting overall, cable in border, very small and even stitches; excellent assembly; very good condition, has been washed, several tiny spots in a couple of places; 29" × 33"; $875.

BOW TIES: early 1900s; blues in prints, checks, and white; blue sashing and border; curves and straight-line quilting overall, even stitches, 8 stitches per inch, excellent assembly with matching corners and straight edges; fair to good condition, with some overall fading, washed and some use and wear; 72" × 78"; $575.

BOW TIE: 1890–1930; blue bow ties, around pink octagons; cottons, narrow blue binding/border, feed sack backing; from Kentucky; line quilting overall; few small tears, some slight color loss overall; 76" × 85"; $1,299.

BOW-TIE: 1900–20; cottons checks, stripes, prints, dots, plaids in blues, grays, reds, others; Tennessee; straight line grid quilting overall, 7 stitches per inch; good assembly, nearly all points and corners match; minor discoloration, few small tears; 70" × 78"; $900.

BROKEN DISHES: 1890s; solid and print blues and white; blue border; straight line quilting overall, 6 stitches per inch; good assembly, most points match; good condition, some overall fade, from washing; 72" × 76"; $625.

BROKEN DISHES: 1890s; blue and red in tiny prints, on white ground; double border, blue and white; feather wreath quilting in the pattern blocks, diamond grid on borders, small and even stitches; very good assembly, nearly all corners and points match; excellent condition, un-washed and unused, quilting lines remain; 70" × 78"; $800.

BROKEN DISHES: mid-1800s; cotton in calicoes of browns, tans, indigo, rust; blocks set on point with cranberry calico squares set between; from Kentucky; few small fabric fractures; 68" × 80"; $2,750.

COLT'S CORRAL: 1930s; burgundy, multicolored period prints, designs, florals; three stripes in each piece of four patch are burgundy, others vary, lots of yellows, burgundy border and binding; from Pennsylvania; outline quilting overall, small stitches; good assembly, most corners match, most stripes even; fair to good condition, much overall color fade, multiple washings, few small holes in two areas; 60" × 76"; $700.

CROSSES AND LOSSES: 1850s; brown, red, blue; floral chintz prints, tiny prints, stripes; six rows by six rows of pattern blocks with red floral chintz sashing and binding, which is pieced; red and cream white squares at the set corners, pieced back; from upstate New York; minimal straight-line quilting, different color threads, 5 stitches per inch; good assembly, most corners and points match; fair to poor condition, some fabrics feel brittle/fragile, some pieces have splits, one split on binding, several seam separations, few small spots; 86" × 86"; $495.

CROSSES AND LOSSES: 1920s; lavender on white; pattern blocks set square, with white blocks between, lavender border and binding; outline quilting on pattern blocks, circular flowers on white blocks, small and even stitches; very good assembly, nearly all corners match; very good condition, slight overall color fade, few stains in one area; 80" × 90"; $500.

CROSSES AND LOSSES: 1930s; cottons in solids, prints, checks, stripes of blues, lavender, pink, yellow, red, greens; pieced feed sack backing; Kentucky; straight line and outline quilting, 7 stitches per inch; some minor color loss, staining; 74" × 90"; $650.

DELECTABLE MOUNTAINS: 1880s; red on white; pattern blocks set square, narrow red border, cutout corners for bedposts; lots of outline and straight-line quilting overall, very small and even stitches; excellent assembly; good condition, some overall soiling and age discoloration, few stains; 64" × 80" (100" × 92" with 18" drop on two sides and bottom); $775.

DELECTABLE MOUNTAINS: 1890s; red on white; triple border, red, white, red, red binding; outline quilting overall, 8 stitches per inch; very good assembly, most points match; fair to good condition, very faded overall, well washed, binding very worn, few small stains; 70" × 78"; $950.

DELECTABLE MOUNTAINS: 1930s; pattern squares of solid dark green and white, with plain white squares between; straight line echo quilting overall, 7 stitches per inch; excellent assembly; excellent condition, unused, unwashed; 68" × 78"; $900.

DIAMONDS AND SQUARES: 1890s; lavender and cream plaid squares, around diamonds of indigo blues, reds, maroons, many other colors in calicoes and prints; homespun and home-dyed backing; optical illusion due to plaid squares, almost seems to pulsate; very heavy, thick batting; from Kentucky; minimal line quilting; good assembly, excellent condition, with one tiny stain; 74" × 86"; $1,750.

DRUNKARDS PATH: 1900–10; solid red and off-white; double border, red then white, red binding; from Indiana; diamond grid quilting overall, straight line diagonal on border, 6 stitches per inch; very good assembly, a few puckered pieces; excellent condition; 80" × 80"; $1,095.

FLYING BATS/DIAMOND FOUR-PATCH: mid-1800s; cotton solids of green, white, red, peach; from Kentucky; outline and grid quilting, 5 stitches per inch; very good assembly, nearly all points match; fair condition, slight overall fade, some seam separations, home-dyed green has deteriorated to brown in large, splotchy areas, looks like along sides and fold-line; 79" × 92"; $1,150.

FOUR-PATCH IN A SQUARE: 1890s; predominantly prints of dark green, double pink, blue with multicolored prints, stripes, checks, dots; seven rows by eight rows of pattern blocks on dark green ground with zigzag sashing between, blue triangles around outside edge of pattern blocks and sashing, dark green border on four sides, then double pink border on three sides, dark green binding; backing is pieced "bars" pattern of red and brown on white calicoes; from Pennsylvania; 1½-inch grid quilting overall, 6 stitches per inch; excellent assembly; excellent condition; 85" × 98; $675.

HEARTS AND GIZZARDS VARIATION: 1920s; double pink calico on white; wide zigzag border is double pink on white, wide white border, rose pink binding in different hue/value than double pink print; two rows by three rows of pattern blocks; from Pennsylvania; outline quilting in pattern blocks, straight line echo quilting on zigzag border, close grid quilting on white border, small stitches; fair to good assembly, most corners in pattern blocks match, but zigzag border does not line up, nor look well planned; excellent condition; 40" × 42"; $195.

HEARTS AND GIZZARDS: 1928; bright pink and white; pattern blocks alternate with plain white blocks; from South Dakota, maker known, dated; lots of outline quilting in pattern blocks, florals in plain blocks; excellent assembly; very good condition, minimal use, has been washed, very slight overall color fade; 72" × 76"; $965.

HEARTS AND GIZZARDS: 1930s; pink gingham check and white; from Oklahoma; large and awkward line quilting overall; fair to good assembly, many junctions don't match, edges uneven; very good condition, some overall color fade; 63" × 71"; $570.

HEN AND CHICKS: 1880s; black and red on white; homespun backing, very graphic, black fabric is tiny floral on white, several reds with tiny white florals; found in Texas; circular quilting overall, 6 stitches per inch; good assembly, most corners match, squares are even; good condition, minimal use and washing, some overall color fade; 68" × 74"; $1,300.

HOURGLASS: 1930s; solids of white, red, bright blue; seven rows by eight rows of hourglass blocks, red and blue, with white sashing between, triple border in white, red, white; white backing, blue binding; from Indiana; straight-line, outline, and simple cable pattern quilting overall, 6 stitches per inch; excellent assembly; fair condition, one tear, one area where sashing was replaced, some triangles replaced, few small holes, never used, minimal washing; 80" × 86"; $125.

HOVERING HAWKS: 1930s; medium green solid, black with tiny white dots print; pattern blocks set square, six rows by seven rows, narrow black and green sawtooth border, wide green outside border, green binding; outline quilting overall, 10 stitches per inch, very even; excellent assembly, nearly all points and corners match; very good condition, unused, few small stains; 72" × 82"; $830.

JACK AND SIX: 1940s; medium blue and white; four pattern blocks on each of two sides, two additional blocks in center, all on white ground; no batting, wide blue border, white binding, white backing; outline quilting overall, wreath quilting in white areas, 8 stitches per inch; good assembly, some corners don't match; very good condition, few small spots; 22" × 22" doll quilt; $145.

JACK IN THE PULPIT: 1910–20s; multicolored pastels and brights in solids, plaids, checks, prints, and stripes, on yellow/green/white daisy print; colors within each pattern block are coordinated, pattern blocks set on point with daisy print blocks between, nine rows by eight rows of pattern blocks; daisy print border and bonding; from Indiana; grid quilting overall, 8 stitches per inch; very good assembly, nearly all corners match; excellent condition, unwashed; 74" × 86"; $550.

JACOB'S LADDER VARIATION: 1830–70; cottons, in greens (some of which have faded to gray) and black dots on white; different borders on three sides, one sawtooth, one striped, one plain; no border on fourth side; from Kentucky; straight-line and outline quilting overall; good assembly; uneven fading overall, some fabric tears; 66" × 82"; $800.

JACOB'S LADDER: 1900; gray/green and white cotton, green has probably faded from deeper color, home-dyed backing; from Kentucky; crosshatch quilting overall, 7 stitches per inch; overall soiling and spotting, some fabric tears; 82"x 92"; $600.

JACOB'S LADDER VARIATION: 1870s; green on green print, with pinks, grays, blues, and browns in prints and plaids; linen backing and quilting thread, green on green binding; from Indiana; excellent outline and diamond grid quilting overall, very small, even stitches; very

45

45A

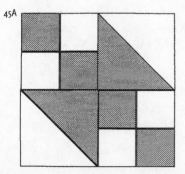

45 & 45A Jacob's Ladder—Four Patch. The traditional "Jacob's Ladder" is a four patch, but, when assembled, it can easily fool the eye into seeing a nine patch. Several different patterns are called Jacob's Ladder and one of them *is* a nine patch. Add a different color or a print (lower left corner of the quilt) and the blocks become even harder to identify.

good assembly, though color arrangement is not appealing, very haphazard; very good condition, has been washed, slight overall color fade; 70" × 86"; $1,400.

JACOB'S LADDER VARIATION: 1920s; white ground with light blue on white print of flowers and dots; from New Hampshire; straight-line and crisscross quilting overall, small and even stitches; good assembly, some corners don't match; excellent condition; 66" × 84"; $1,400.

JACOB'S LADDER: 1920s; pink and white; wide pink border; minimal quilting overall, straight-line and outline, even stitches, 6 per inch; fair assembly, many corners misaligned; excellent condition, unused, unwashed; 70" × 80"; $575.

JACOB'S LADDER: 1930s; off-white and solids in rose, medium, blue/gray, peach, spring green, tan, medium brown, orange, others; golden yellow border on two sides and bottom; from Texas; outline quilting along each pieced seam, and slanted straight-line quilting in the borders, all of large, awkward stitches, 5 per inch; poor to fair assembly, with many misaligned junctions; very good condition, minimal use and washing, few small spots in one area; 68" × 80"; $195.

JACOB'S LADDER: 1930s; solid blue and white; narrow blue and white sawtooth inner border and wide white outer border; straight-line and double straight-line quilting overall, 8 stitches per inch; fair to good assembly, several corners/points don't match; has been washed, some wear on binding; 78" × 80"; $550. *See illustrations #45 and 45A.*

KANSAS TROUBLE: 1880s; red and white; pattern blocks set straight with plain white blocks between, red binding; $3/4$-inch diamond grid quilting overall, 11 stitches per inch; excellent assembly; very good condition, has been washed, some overall color fade; 70" × 84"; $695.

LOST SHIP: late 1800s; bold red calico and white with tiny black print; red calico border, white with black print binding, home-dyed backing; from Kentucky; outline quilting overall, 7 stitches per inch; good assembly, most points and corners match; overall soiling, needs cleaning, some color loss and change; serious fraying and deterioration on top and bottom edge; 70" × 80"; $2,000.

LOVER'S KNOT: 1880s; indigo blue and white; indigo blue border, binding, and backing; from Pennsylvania; excellent quilting, triple echo line in blocks, feather quilting on border, small and even stitches; good assembly, most corners and points match; excellent condition, unwashed and unused; 70" × 80"; $1,150.

OLD MAID'S PUZZLE: 1920s; solid pink and white; wide pink border; straight and outline quilting overall, 6 stitches per inch; good assembly, most corners and points match; fair to good condition, very worn binding, overall color fade, used and well washed; 72" × 80"; $650.

OLD MAID'S PUZZLE: 1930s/1960s; peach and off-white; pattern blocks set square with plain white blocks between, triple border, medium wide white, narrow peach, very narrow white; 1930s top, quilted more recently; from Texas; straight-line quilting in plain blocks, outline quilting in pattern blocks, 5 stitches per inch; excellent assembly; very good condition, one pale stain; 74" × 84"; $165.

OLD MAID'S RAMBLE: 1930s; dark red and white; pattern blocks are four in a square, set straight with white sashing between, and eight-point star squares in the set corners, red binding; straight-line quilting in the pattern blocks, feather quilting on the sashing, even stitches at 8 per inch; excellent assembly; excellent condition; 71" × 71"; $1,195.

ORANGE PEEL: 1920s; red and white; double border, white then red; very minimal outline quilting, large stitches; excellent assembly; excellent condition, unwashed, unused; 68" × 76"; $900.

ORANGE PEEL: 1930s; white with multicolored prints; white border, white prairie points edging; outline quilting overall, small and even stitches; good assembly, curved edges are mostly flat and even; fair condition, many loose seams, several stains, one very large water stain, much use and washing; 78" × 84"; $385.

PATHS TO PIECE: early 1900s; cotton feed sacks, in many, many colors, primarily pastels; some printing still visible on sacks; from Kentucky; line quilting overall, large inept stitches, 9 per inch; unskilled assembly, poor matching of pieces, possibly made by a child; slight discolorations on some pieces, probably before sacks were cut for piecing, much seam separation; 72" × 84"; $750.

ROB PETER TO PAY PAUL: 1920–40; cotton solids and prints, feed sacks; multicolored, blues, browns, tans, yellows, natural; narrow tan print binding; from Kentucky; outline quilting; some minor color loss; 68" × 80"; $450.

ROSE DREAM: 1930s; solids of cream and medium blue; five rows by five and a half rows of pattern blocks, set square, different shade of cream borders on each end; from Kentucky; outline and straight-line quilting, small, even stitches; very good assembly, nearly all points and corners match; very good condition, has been washed; 78" × 83"; $1,750.

SIXTEEN-PATCH: 1900–10; white, blues in solids and prints; four rows by five rows of pattern blocks, set square with solid blue blocks between, blue binding, very heavy batting; minimal and awkward straight-line quilting overall, large and uneven stitches; fair assembly, many puckered edges, most corners don't match; fair to poor condition, much used and washed, some fabric loss, few tears, overall color fade; 40" × 60"; $275.

SPIRIT OF ST. LOUIS: 1920s; red, white, blue; five rows by five rows of pattern blocks, set square, with red sashing between white squares at set corners, very wide red border, white binding; from Maryland; straight-line and in-the-ditch quilting in pattern blocks, concentric circles in the border, small and very even stitches; excellent assembly; excellent condition; 82" × 82"; $975.

SUGAR CONE VARIATION: late 1800s; multicolored, but predominantly reds, pinks, blues, gray, green, and black; cottons and shirtings in solids, prints, dots, stripes, plaids; center block of cones consists of four triangles, two of one color/print, two of another; outer four cones ("star" arms) are thin strips of various colors, mostly stripes, some prints, sewed together to make thin horizontal bars; pattern blocks are set on point, with plain blocks of green, cream, and black plaid fabric between; feed sack backing, looks hand dyed; very graphic, very unusual; from Kentucky; curved echo quilting overall, good assembly in difficult pattern, most corners, edges match; excellent condition, few stains on backing that seem to be pre-dying; 64" × 82"; $19,500.

THE "H" SQUARE QUILT: 1930s; light green on white; pattern blocks set on point with white blocks between, double border, white then green, green binding; outline quilting in pattern blocks, feather wreath quilting in white blocks, cable on borders, 7 stitches per inch; good assembly, most corners match, edges even; very good condition, slight overall color fade; 82" × 90"; $865.

TRUE LOVERS' KNOT: 1930s; white ground with various period prints, checks, solids, stripes, plaids, dots; white binding and backing; outline quilting overall, even stitches; good assembly, most corners match; excellent condition; 78" × 78"; $350.

TURKEY TRACKS VARIATION: 1870–90; cottons in red checks, dark indigo and brown prints, gray and golden orange solids; triple sashing of one dark indigo center stripe, with two golden orange stripes; double border, dark indigo and golden orange, printed feed sack backing; from Kentucky; straight-line quilting overall, with scallop shell quilting in borders; large stitches, 5 per inch; some color loss, a few small tears; 66" × 90"; $3,250.

TURKEY TRACKS: early 1900s; solid red and green on white ground; outline quilting overall, 8 stitches per inch; good assembly, most corners and points match; good condition, some overall color fade, has been used and washed many times, slight wear on binding on one side; 72" × 84"; $835.

WATERWHEEL: 1870s; solid white, pink, and blue with tiny white star print; eight and two halves of 2½-inch pattern squares are set on point with pink sashing between, wide white border, white binding; straight-line and curved quilting overall, large stitches; fair assembly, many points don't match, sashing is uneven, doll quilt probably done by a child or inexperienced quilter; fair to good condition, some overall wear, some age discoloration; 13" × 15½"; $395.

WATERWHEEL: 1900–10; menswear wools of grays, purple, browns, blues, tans, creams; six vertical rows of pattern blocks, set on point with zigzag sashing between, striped flannel backing; diamond grid quilting overall, large but even stitches; fair to good assembly, many points and corners are mismatched; very good condition; 68" × 77"; $775.

WATERWHEEL: 1920s; white and blue; blue binding and backing; from Ohio; chevron quilting overall, small and even stitches; good assembly, most points and corners match; excellent condition; 62" × 68"; $1,600.

WATERWHEEL: 1925; yellow solid on white; five rows by six rows of pattern blocks set square with white blocks between, with yellow blocks at set corners, yellow binding, chin edge cut down and rebound; dated, from Ohio; diamond grid quilting overall, small and even stitches; very good assembly, most corners and points match; fair condition, worn binding, chin edge rebound, much overall wear and use; 64" × 82"; $250.

WATERWHEEL: dated 1905 and initialed; pink/gray plaid, with browns, tans, blues in various prints, stripes, checks and plaids; pattern blocks are various patterned fabrics and white, six rows by six rows of pattern blocks, set on point with plain pink/gray plaid blocks between; wide gray/pink plaid border on three sides; fabrics seem to be 10 to 15 years older than the quilt; echo outline quilting in pattern squares, grid quilting overall, 8 stitches per inch; excellent assembly; poor to fair condition, unused, unwashed, with several significant large and small holes, some areas that may be rust stains, or may be fabric deterioration; 75" × 80"; $100.

WATERWHEEL: early 1900s; blue and white; blue border and backing; straight-line and circle quilting overall, 7 stitches per inch; good assembly, most corners and points match; good condition, minimal use, overall color loss/fade; 78" × 84"; $965.

WHIRLWIND/PINWHEEL: 1930s; solids of pale peach, light blue, pink; five rows by seven rows of pattern blocks, each pink on light blue ground, with narrow peach sashing between, very wide peach border, peach binding; from Maine; flower petal quilting in pattern blocks and sashing, curling ocean wave quilting on border, very small stitches; very good assembly, nearly all corners and points match; excellent condition; 62" × 76"; $800.

WINDING WAYS: 1930s; peach and cream white; graphic, optical illusion; curved edges, peach binding; outline quilting, 9 stitches per inch; fair to good assembly, many junctions misaligned; good condition, slight color loss in a few areas, few tiny spots; 70" × 78"; $350.

WINDING WAYS: 1930s; solids of orange and yellow; outline quilting in large stitches, 6 stitches per inch; fair assembly, many corners don't match; some fading; 64" × 80"; $495.

WINDMILL FOUR-PATCH: 1930s; cottons in pure white, lavender print with white and purple florals, and golden yellow print with white and red florals; pattern blocks set straight with plain white blocks between; white scalloped border with lavender print binding; outline quilting on the pattern blocks, elaborate and detailed medallion patterns quilted in the white blocks, 8 stitches per inch, in yellow thread; very good condition, probably never used or washed; few small stains on front, few on back; 75" × 92"; $495.

WINDMILL VARIATION: 1880s; black, teal, dark red; eight rows by eight rows of pattern blocks, each pattern block with red center, triangles move away from center rather than toward as in traditional rendition; very wide teal border with narrow black zigzag through it, pattern blocks at each corner, dark red binding; Pennsylvania Mennonite; excellent straight-line quilting overall; excellent assembly; excellent condition; double bed size; $2,700.

WINDMILL: 1890s; indigo blue and white; double border, blue then white, blue binding; feather quilting overall, 6 stitches per inch; good assembly; fair to good condition, some overall color fade, slightly worn binding, some loose and broken quilting stitches; 74" × 78"; $650.

WINDMILL: 1890s; indigo blue and white; navy blue border with tiny white pattern; lots of straight-line quilting overall, small and even quilting stitches; good condition, some use, some slight color loss; 76" × 80"; $635.

Drunkard's Path

CHAIN QUILT VARIATION OF DRUNKARD'S PATH: 1951; cottons, in red, light red on white; red with tiny white dots border; signed and dated; from Pennsylvania; excellent assembly and design, outline quilting, 7 stitches per inch; small frayed area on binding, stain on backing, has been washed but quilting lines remain visible; 86" × 93"; $900.

DRUNKARD'S PATH, LOVE RING VARIATION: 1940s; solids in pink and tan, with various prints and patterns in blues, reds, burgundy, grays, browns, others; five rows by six rows of pattern blocks, set square, with pink sashing and tan squares at the set corners, red feed sack

46 This Drunkard's Path Quilt, circa
1880, is the best example we saw
of this two-patch design—with a
twist! In this case, both fabrics are
prints where traditionally the
background for the 'path' part of
the design is done in a solid
fabric. A stunning quilt. Quilt
courtesy of Stella Rubin. Photo
courtesy of Steven Goldberg.

backing; from Kentucky; diagonal straight-line quilting overall, even stitches; good assembly; excellent condition, quilting lines remain; large double bed size; $700.

DRUNKARD'S PATH: 1880s; blue with tiny white stars, white with tiny rose gray flowers; double border, blue, then white, blue binding; from Pennsylvania; straight-line quilting overall, cable on blue border, very small and even stitches; very good assembly, most corners match; excellent condition; 82" × 82"; $775.

DRUNKARD'S PATH: 1880s; white and dark indigo with tiny white dots; triple inner border, blue, white, blue, then very wide outer border; one-half-inch grid quilting overall, 8 stitches per inch; excellent assembly; excellent condition; 74" × 74"; $1,100.

DRUNKARD'S PATH: 1890s; white with tiny brown print, red with tiny white leaves print; outline quilting overall, even stitches, 8 per inch; excellent assembly, nearly all corners match, edges are smooth; very good condition, minimal use, slight overall color fade in red; 72" × 80"; $365.

DRUNKARD'S PATH: 1920s; blue and white; double border, white then blue, blue binding; lots of straight and outline quilting overall, small flowers in white areas, very small and even stitches; excellent assembly; fair to good condition, overall soiling, binding worn, very faded overall; 70" × 80"; $900.

DRUNKARD'S PATH: 1920s; indigo blue and white; traditional assembly of pattern; minimal outline quilting overall; excellent condition, unused, unwashed; 78" × 84"; $750.

DRUNKARD'S PATH: 1920s; white and lavender solid; white border, lavender binding; outline quilting overall, 8 stitches per inch; good assembly, most corners match, few pieces are puckered; good condition, slight overall color fade, very slight wear to binding, few small stains in one corner; 70" × 74"; $700.

DRUNKARD'S PATH: 1930s; dark green and white; outline quilting overall, 6 stitches per inch; good condition, used and washed, some color fading; 72" × 76"; $375.

DRUNKARD'S PATH: 1930s; white and three lavender prints; lavender binding, white backing; outline quilting overall, 7 stitches per inch; good assembly, few puckers in some pieces; good condition, overall color fade, binding very worn; 68" × 90"; $600. *See illustration #46.*

DRUNKARD'S PATH: early 1900s; pink print and white; outline quilting overall, 6 stitches per inch; excellent condition, never used, washed once; 74" × 78"; $700.

DRUNKARD'S PATH: early 1900s; solid pink and white; outline quilting overall, some quilting stitches uneven, 5 per inch; good condition, some overall fading, has been washed and used; 72" × 80"; $500.

DRUNKARD'S PATH VARIATION: 1930–40; cottons of white, blue, yellow/gold solids, teal/blue stripes; blue and yellow/gold blocks made of four groups of four squares of traditional drunkard's path squares, arranged so paths appear to make circle around the blocks; blocks set square between teal/blue sashing with white squares at the set corners; wide teal/blue border; Kentucky; outline quilting overall, 6 stitches per inch; some color loss, some minor fabric deterioration; 72"x 78"; $500.

DRUNKARD'S PATH: 1890s; clear red on white; same red backing and binding; outline quilting overall, very good, even stitches, 8 per inch; fair to good assembly, not all junctions match; good condition, minimal use and washing, minimal fading; 74" × 82"; $525.

DRUNKARD'S PATH: 1910–20; red print and light blue; paths are red print; flower quilting in blue squares, outline and double echo straight-line quilting in red paths, 10 stitches per inch; good assembly, most corners and edges match; excellent condition, unwashed and unused; 70" × 80"; $830.

DRUNKARD'S PATH: 1920s; white with white on red print; same red print binding and backing; from Ohio; outline quilting overall, feather quilting in white blocks, 8 stitches per inch; excellent assembly; excellent condition, never washed; 70" × 82"; $800.

DRUNKARD'S PATH: 1930–40; classic, traditional pattern in cottons, golden yellow and bright green; self binding; from Kentucky; line quilting within each block, along "paths"; nice assembly; excellent condition, some minor color changes, minimal washing/use; 68" × 80"; $800.

DRUNKARD'S PATH: 1930s; medium blue and pure white; double border, one white, one blue; outline and straight-line quilting overall, 6 stitches per inch; good condition, has been washed, some color loss overall; 72" × 82"; $425.

DRUNKARD'S PATH: 1930s; medium blue and white, blue border; outline quilting overall, small stitches, good assembly; 70" × 76"; $625.

15 Nine-Patch

As squares were divided again and again by enterprising quiltmakers, the Nine-Patch became a favorite. Easy enough to not overwhelm a new quilter, yet challenging and versatile enough to be interesting, this patch is one of those most often found in the marketplace. From the simple three squares by three squares to the much more intricate Beggar's Blocks, everyone can find a Nine-Patch to love. Even the names enchant: Path and Stiles, The Queen's Petticoat, Summer Winds, and Cat's Cradle. Of course there is also Broken Windows, Wandering Lover, and Devil's Claws. Everything has its up side and its down. *See illustrations #47 and #47A.*

AUNT SUKEY'S PATTERN: 1920s; yellow, yellow print, medium blue; five rows by six rows of pattern blocks, set square with blue sashing between, blue binding and backing; straight-line quilting overall, cable quilting on sashing and border, 8 stitches per inch; good assembly, most corners and points match; excellent condition, never washed, never used; 83" × 96"; $500.

BEAR'S FOOT: early 1900s; white and solid pink; three rows by four rows of pattern blocks, set straight with white sashing between and around, three slightly different shades of pink, wide pink border, pink binding; cable quilting on border and on sashing, straight-line, diamond grid, and floral on pattern blocks, even stitches; very good assembly, nearly all corners match; good condition, has been washed, some slight overall color fade, few tiny stains; 73" × 84"; $72.

BEAR'S PAW: 1890s; pattern blocks of red on white; outline quilting overall, 6 stitches per inch; excellent assembly; good condition, some overall color fade; 78" × 82"; $600.

BEAR'S PAW: 1920s; red, pinks, white; white sashing and border; feather quilting overall, 6 stitches per inch; slight fade overall, some wear on binding; 70" × 82"; $450.

BEAR'S PAW: 1910–20; indigo blue on white; indigo blue border; lots of very good quilting, twisted cable on border, outline and straight-line in pattern blocks, very small and even stitches; excellent assembly; excellent condition, had been washed; 70" × 78"; $955.

47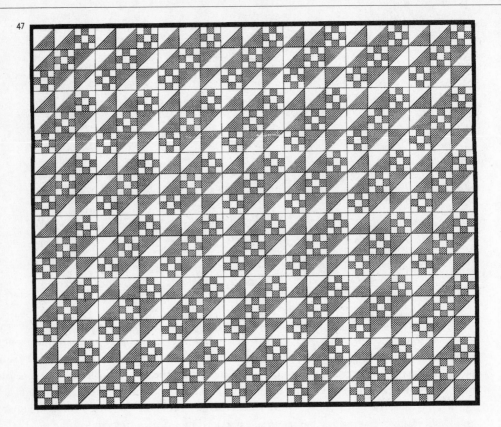

47A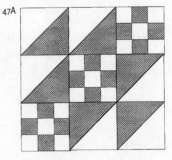

47 & 47A Jacob's Ladder—Nine
Patch. This is the nine-patch
Jacob's ladder block. Set it square
with lots of the same blocks and it
is easy to see how it can be
confused with the four-patch
version.

1 & 1A This silk, satin and velvet Crazy Quilt is over 100 years old and an excellent example of the style. The piece has lots of interesting embroidery and topstitching, pointed edges of wool challis, and some of the features that typify the style. The close-up shows the tiny tulips embroidered on one piece, and a Christmas ribbon that has been included in the design. All perfectly planned to look completely random. *Quilt Courtesy of Helen Warner.*

2 The yellow "sashing" on this Yo-Yo Quilt is an interesting variation, and a great way for the maker to show off her ability and creativity. The yo-yo's are very well made, the assembly superb and the overall look pleasing. While it might not keep you physically warm, it certainly would warm your heart. *Quilt Courtesy of Joan Halla.*

3, 3A Some key dating characteristics stand out in this Cactus Basket quilt. The green in one basket has faded to tan, an indication of dyes used in the early 1800s, and the Turkey red fabrics are deteriorating. Most important, the quilt is the best example we found to illustrate the importance of signing a quilt. The woman who finished the quilt knew her ancestor who pieced it, so she embroidered his name and the date on the quilt. She also added the year she quilted it, completing the provenance and adding value to the quilt. *Quilt Courtesy of Dottie Whitner.*

4 Everything about this Barn Raising
Log Cabin Quilt makes it
remarkable. The color
arrangement of the tiny, light and
dark silk logs is a perfect example
of the assembly variation, and the
black velvet border sets off the
colors superbly. This quilt shows
why Log Cabins are so popular
and interesting. *Collection of the
Torrington Historical Society,
Torrington, Connecticut. Photo by
David Stansbury.*

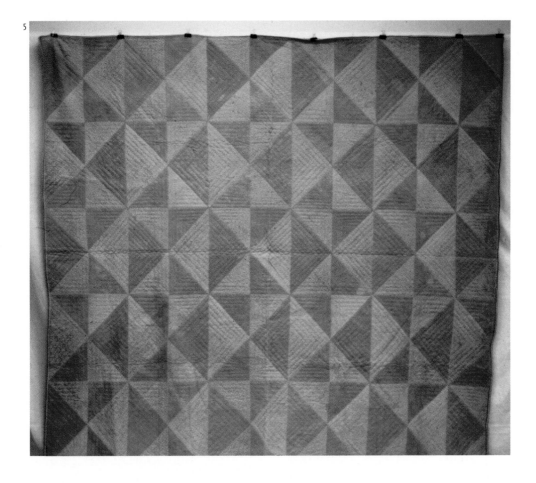

5 This pink and green Diamonds Quilt is a good example of how appealing a simple pattern can be. It is covered with excellent straight-line echo quilting, and has near perfect assembly—all the points and corners match. Even with some minor color loss this is quilt is very attractive and charming. *Quilt Courtesy of Betty Wilson.*

6 & 6A Although made in the early 1800s, of all colors of wools, this Triangles Make Diamonds Quilt has maintained its color and condition, proof of what care in handling and the proper storage techniques can do for a potentially fragile quilt. The sashing supports the colors and the overall pattern very well. Details, such as fine feather topstitching, can be seen in the close-up photograph. *Quilt Courtesy of Betty Wilson.*

6

6A

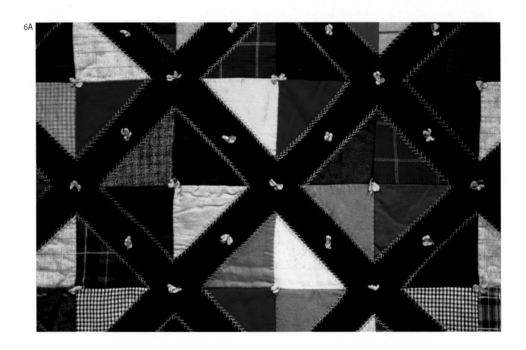

7

7 The red, green, and yellow of the gorgeous Rose Wreath Appliqué Quilt really stand out. Made in the 1860s, this quilt has superb appliqué, tiny quilting stitches in cable and other patterns, and a truly unique design. An incredible addition to any collection. *Quilt Courtesy of americanquilts.com.*

8

8 This is the second Bible Story
Quilt made by Harriet Powers, the
"mother" of African American
quilting. This quilt was completed
in 1898 and was a commissioned
work. Powers' first Bible quilt is on
public display at the National
Museum of American History and
this quilt is in the permanent
collection of the Museum of Fine
Arts, Boston. There is a large
amount of written material on the
design, interpretation, and intent
of the Powers Bible story quilts. A
study of the life and quilting of
Harriet Powers is fascinating and
well worth the time.

BEAR'S PAW: 1920s; solid red on white; white backing, red border; clamshell quilting overall, some outline, 6 stitches per inch; good assembly, most corners and points match; good condition, slight overall color fade, few stains in one area; 68" × 78"; $515.

BROKEN WHEEL: 1870s; two different dark red with tiny yellow prints or dots, three different cheddar yellows with tiny red prints, medium blue with tiny dark blue print; very wide border of red calico zigzag on medium blue print fabric; backing of rusty red print, thin batting; from Pennsylvania; outline quilting in blocks, grid quilting in border, all blue thread, 6 stitches per inch; many pieces pulled out of shape, border misaligned, less-than-perfect assembly; unwashed, unused, excellent condition; 82" × 98"; $750.

BROKEN WHEEL: 1900–10; red with tiny white print, cream white; prints of gray, black, double pink, blues; pattern blocks are set on point, touching horizontally, with wide red print sashing between rows; thin batting, red print backing; fair to good assembly, with some pieces misshapen, misaligned; fair to good condition, with some areas showing some wear, has been well used and washed; 70" × 79"; $265.

CATS AND MICE: early 1900s; red solid on white; minimal line quilting, 6 stitches per inch; good assembly, most corners match; excellent condition, never used, minimal washing; 66" × 72"; $850.

CHURN DASH NINE-PATCH, POSTAGE STAMP: 1930s; various white solids, with blues, grays, reds, greens, yellows, golds, and many others in prints, stripes, checks, plaids; nine-patch blocks with 3½-inch squares, five churn dash squares and four plain white squares; various whites used, from cream to pure, white sashing and border, thin batting; straight-line quilting overall, large stitches, 6 per inch; unwashed, faint quilting lines remain; 70" × 83"; $500.

CHURN DASH: 1890s; red on white; straight-line quilting overall, 6 per inch; good assembly; well washed and used, some overall color loss/fade; 68" × 70"; $675.

CHURN DASH: early 1900s; solid red, red and white print, white with tiny black dots; back pieced of white with black dots fabric, self edging of red and white print; pattern blocks alternate with solid red blocks; very heavy, thick batting; from Connecticut; tied, no quilting, batting shifting overall; condition poor, edging badly worn, almost missing in some spots; reds fading in places, many stains both front and back; 68" × 70"; $375.

CROSS AND CROWN: 1920s; mint green and white; five rows by six rows of pattern blocks, mint green on white ground, set square with green sashing between, green border, white binding and backing; from Ohio; diamond grid quilting in pattern blocks, cable quilting in border and sashing, very small and even stitches; excellent assembly, excellent condition; 74" × 86"; $1,800.

CROWN AND THORNS VARIATION: 1800s; white, indigo with tiny white print, black and white stripe, double pink; pattern blocks are stripes on double pink, with indigo centers, three rows by three rows, with white sashing between, white border and binding; from the Midwest; outline quilting in blocks, feather quilting in sashing and border, small even stitches;

very good assembly, all but a couple junctions, points match; excellent condition; 80" × 80"; $395.

DOE AND DARTS: 1930s; white and various period prints in primarily yellows; five rows by six rows of pattern blocks; solid yellow border on two side, yellow binding; outline quilting in pattern blocks, cable on border, 6 stitches per inch; good assembly, most points and corners match; good condition, slight overall fade and wear, binding has been replaced; 78" × 78"; $555.

DOUBLE MONKEY WRENCH: 1890s; primarily reds, with blues, tans, grays, others in prints, stripes, checks, plaids, and solids; red calico background in pattern blocks and plain blocks set between, and border; from Ohio; straight-line quilting overall, 8 stitches per inch; thin batting, good assembly, with some corners misaligned; unwashed and unused, some discoloration and creases where folded; 69" × 72"; $400.

DOUBLE NINE-PATCH: 1860s; cottons and homespun of browns, blues, cream, reds, others in prints, dots, stripes, checks; each nine-patch block assembled of five small nine-patch block of patterned fabrics and dominant fabric blocks, and four whole blocks of dominant fabric; wide, brown sashing, binding and border; straight-line quilting overall, large stitches, 7 per inch; very good assembly, most corners match, sashing straight; some wear/fraying of binding; 70" × 70"; $400.

DOUBLE NINE-PATCH: 1850–80; green and salmon red solids, multicolor of blues, reds, browns, grays, in prints and solids; four nine-patch blocks by five nine-patch blocks, set on point with solid salmon red blocks between; home-dyed indigo border; from Kentucky; scallop quilting overall; good assembly, most corners match; some small tears in binding, some color loss and change, especially in obvious fold lines; 66" × 89"; $1,950.

DOVES IN THE WINDOW: 1920s; solid blue and white; minimal outline quilting, large stitches; fair to good assembly, many junctions don't match; fair to good condition, overall color fade and wear, binding worn; 76" × 70"; $750.

DOVES IN THE WINDOW: 1930s; white and two shades of green; pattern blocks are green on white, set square with white sashing between and green squares at the set corners; white border and binding outline quilting on the pattern blocks, feather quilting on the border, 7 stitches per inch; good assembly, most points and corners match; good condition, slight overall color fade and wear; 72" × 86"; $500.

DUTCH NINE-PATCH: 1950s; white, some solids, mostly multicolored prints, florals, designs; seven rows by eight rows of pattern blocks on white ground, with blue on white floral print sashing and border, with yellow print squares at set corners; from Illinois; diamond grid quilting overall, small and even stitches; good assembly, most corners match; excellent condition; 82" × 94"; $450.

EIGHT POINTED STAR VARIATION: 1920s; solids of red, white, blue; five rows by six rows of pattern blocks, triple border, red, white, blue with blue binding; from the Midwest; outline and straight-line quilting overall, 6 stitches per inch; good assembly, most corners and points match; excellent condition; 75" × 84"; $1,200.

EVENING STAR: 1880s; double pink, green prints; pattern blocks are in groups of four to make 13 larger squares, which are set on point with green on green print sashing, narrow pink and green sawtooth border on top and bottom, very wide green border, pink binding; from Pennsylvania; outline quilting in pattern blocks, clamshell on border, diagonal line in sashing, very small and even stitches; very good assembly, nearly all corners match; very good condition, slight overall color fade; 80" × 86"; $2,500.

FEATHERED STAR: 1860s; rose red and white; four rows by five rows of pattern blocks, rose red stars on white ground, white binding; from Maine; large florals and overlapping circle quilting overall; very good assembly, nearly all points match; excellent condition; 72" × 92"; $1,600.

FIVE CROSSES VARIATION: 1860s; multicolor, pink on pink, creams, darks of blue, purple, reds, greens; all in prints, florals, checks, stripes, plaids; pattern blocks alternate with plain blocks, rusty red print border; straight-line quilting overall, 7 stitches per inch; excellent assembly; fair to good condition, two areas of damage, some wear on binding; 80" × 82"; $550.

FIVE CROSSES: 1870s; natural white with tiny black print, browns, double pinks, blues in plaids, prints, shirtings; set on point with natural white print sashing and top and bottom border, side bindings; from Ohio; straight-line quilting overall at 7 stitches per inch; few tiny spots and discolorations, unwashed, quilting line remain; 68" × 76"; $450.

FLUTTER WHEEL: 1880s; white on red print, tans, blues, grays, browns, many other period colors in prints, patterns, stripes, checks, plaids; four rows by four rows of pattern blocks, set on point, with white on red zigzag sashing between, and with half block triangles around the edges to make a straight edge; thin batting, gray and white stripe backing, white on red print binding; from Pennsylvania; straight-line quilting overall, 5 stitches per inch; excellent assembly; excellent condition; 88" × 88"; $750.

FRIENDSHIP CHAIN: 1850s; white ground, gray and maroon tiny print with maroon stripe, green on green print, grays, maroons, browns, chrome yellow; pattern blocks are set on point with gray print sashing; from Maine; outline quilting overall, small stitches; good assembly, most corners match, edges even; very good condition, has been washed; 82" × 84"; $1,400.

GREEK SQUARE: 1930–40; multicolored prints, stripes, checks, plaids of cotton and cotton feed sacks; five squares by six squares with solid pink sashing between and lavender sets at corner junctions; striped backing; from Kentucky; outline quilting; fair assembly; some overall fading; 68" × 84"; $550.

HONEY BEE: 1860s; white and dark blue with tiny white dots; pattern blocks set square with plain white blocks between; wide white border, circular flowers with stem and two leaves appliquéd around the edge, on the border, blue binding; diamond and straight-line quilting overall, 9 stitches per inch; excellent assembly; excellent condition; 84" × 88"; $1,650.

HONEY BEE: 1890s; dark green with white dot calico, cream white solid, rusty/peach/tan solid that may have originally been darker, redder; four rows by four rows of pattern blocks, set on point with white blocks between, white backing; "bees" in the four corners of the pattern blocks are appliquéd; narrow rusty/peach border, wide white border, rusty/peach binding; from Missouri; outline, grid, straight-line quilting, large feather wreaths in plain white blocks, 5 stitches per inch; good assembly, few corners don't match; good condition, unwashed, quilting lines remain, few tiny age spots in some areas; 85" × 90"; $450.

IRISH CHAIN DOUBLE NINE-PATCH, POSTAGE STAMP: 1940s; blues, pinks, multicolored prints on pure white; pattern blocks are made of one-inch squares, set straight on white ground, with white sashing, nine-patch squares in set corners; triple border, very wide white strip, then row of multicolored squares set on edge to form diamonds of same size as in pattern blocks, then another wide white strip, blue binding; clamshell quilting overall in the white, grid quilting on the borders, outline quilting in the print squares, 9 stitches per inch; excellent assembly; poor to fair condition, unused, unwashed, with several significant tears in the binding, two large holes that go completely through, front to back, some small tears on the back; 71" × 84"; $195. *See illustrations #48 and #48A.*

JACKS ON SIX: 1880s/1930s; deep red, deep blue, white; probably backed and quilted in the 1930s; deep blue with tiny dots, white with tiny blue dots, deep red with tiny red and black circles and dots; double border, white inner, red outer; six rows by seven rows of pattern blocks, with plain red blocks between; backed with plaid flannel blanket; diamond, straight-line and other quilting overall, 9 stitches per inch; very good assembly, nearly all corners match; excellent condition; 74" × 82"; $600.

MILLER'S DAUGHTER/WEATHERVANE VARIATION: 1890s; cream white, blue gray on gray stripe, yellow with tiny red flowers print; pattern blocks of gray and yellow stars, five rows by five rows of pattern blocks, set on point on cream ground with cream blocks between; triple border, gray, yellow, white, with gray binding; from Ohio; large floral wreaths quilted in the cream blocks, straight-line quilting on the border, outline in the pattern blocks, 8 stitches per inch; very good assembly, nearly all points and corners match; good condition, some slight overall color fade, soiling and staining in the fold lines; 80" × 84"; $400.

MONKEY WRENCH, POSTAGE STAMP: 1900; cottons of reds, yellows, blues, pinks, many others in prints, plaids, stripes; thirteen squares by thirteen squares, set on point with tan blocks between, indigo calico backing; double border, narrow tan and red pieced latticework border, with wider tan border outside; Pennsylvania Mennonite; twisted rope quilting on border, 9 stitches per inch; some fabric deterioration, some stains, few small holes, overall soiling, needs cleaning; 82" × 82"; $2,000.

MONKEY WRENCH: 1880s; dark red solid and white; from Colorado; outline quilting overall, small stitches; excellent assembly; good condition, some overall color loss from washing, has been used; 63" × 77"; $775.

MONKEY WRENCH: 1890s; blue and white; feather quilting overall; good assembly, most edges and corners match; good condition, some overall color fade; 72" × 78"; $800.

MONKEY WRENCH: 1890s; blues and browns in prints, checks, stripes on white; pattern blocks set on point with white blocks between; outline quilting in pattern blocks, feather wreath quilting in white blocks, 8 stitches per inch; very good assembly, nearly all corners and points match; very good condition, very slight overall color fade, probably from washing, minimal use; 78" × 82"; $575.

48

48A

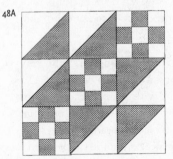

48 & 48A Jacob's Ladder—Nine-Patch Different Assembly. Take the same nine-patch block, turn it a couple of different ways, join it with other groups of blocks, add some sashing and the look is completely different. And unique!

MONKEY WRENCH: 1890s; red, white, browns, grays, tans, dark blues in prints, stripes, plaids; wrenches in pattern blocks mostly dark colors with white or light on sides of block and red print center square; pattern blocks set on point with red print blocks between; red print border; from Oklahoma; curved line quilting overall, 5 stitches per inch; unused, unwashed, many stained and soiled areas, one small repair; 71" × 80"; $475.

NINE-PATCH CHECKERBOARD: 1930s; pink, green, multicolored prints, patterns, plaids, checks, and solids; four rows by fours rows of pattern blocks, set square with pink sashing and green squares at the set corners; blue border on sides, feed sack backing; from Kentucky; fan quilting overall, even stitches; very good assembly, most corners match; very good condition, has been washed; 72" × 76"; $550.

NINE-PATCH, LARGE CENTER BLOCK: 1900–10; cottons in multicolored calicoes, prints, checks, stripes; blues, greens, tans, grays, burgundy, true scrap bag; squares set on point, with burgundy striped sashing, wide tan calico border; from Kentucky; outline quilting; good assembly; some overall and splotchy fading; 65" × 79"; $450.

NINE-PATCH: 1850s; predominantly browns, some burgundies, indigo; fabrics look home dyed; from Texas, maker known; outline quilting overall, uneven stitches, 5 per inch; fair to good condition, overall fade, few small repairs of holes; 62" × 80"; $3,450.

NINE-PATCH: 1870s; dark reds, grays, blues, in prints, checks, stripes, yellow solids, cream prints, many others; blocks set on point with whole blocks of dark gray print between, dark gray print border; from Vermont; crosshatch quilting overall; good assembly, though some corners out of line; good condition, slight fading in tiny areas; double bed size; $500.

NINE-PATCH: 1880s; blue, burgundy, teal green, cream, white in checks, prints, stripes; nine-patch blocks set on point with teal green print blocks alternating between; straight-line quilting overall, large stitches, 5 per inch; good assembly, most corners match; 66" × 76"; $200.

NINE-PATCH: 1890s; browns, tans, cream; pattern blocks of brown prints with cream or tan ground, actually two quilts sewn together before batting and backing, one with 12-inch blocks, one with 9-inch blocks; from Connecticut; very thick batting, tan print backing, tied, not quilted; fair assembly, many misshapen blocks, misaligned corners; poor to fair condition, many split seams, overall color fade, much wear overall; 72" × 72"; $25.

NINE-PATCH: 1890–1910; dark red with tiny white print, pales of cream, tan, light gray stripes, darks of greens, maroon, black plaid and striped shirtings; nine-patch pattern blocks are four dark and five light squares; pattern blocks set straight with plain dark red print blocks between; dark blue floral print backing, dark gray/green print border and binding, thin batting; from Pennsylvania; one inch grid quilting overall in black thread, 6 stitches per inch; very good assembly, nearly all corners and points match; unwashed, some slight fade in places on the border; 72" × 72"; $450.

NINE-PATCH: 1890s; indigo blue with tiny white dots and white cotton; blue print and white nine-patch pattern blocks set on point with white blocks between creating crisscross chains of blue print squares; thin batting, wide blue border, with very wide white border, and blue binding; grid and straight-line quilting overall, 6 stitches per inch; good assembly, nearly all

49 A close-up of this Nine-Patch set on point with zigzag sashing reveals the striped material of the sash and some interesting prints as well. Quilt courtesy of the Warner Family.

corners match; good condition, has been washed, with slight color bleed into the white from the blue, few tiny spots in one area; 77" × 82"; $675.

NINE-PATCH: 1900–10; red on white, prints and florals, and white; wide red border; straight-line and cable quilting; good assembly, most points and corners match; good to excellent condition, never used, never washed, few tiny stains in one area; 70" × 76"; $995.

NINE-PATCH: 1920s; predominantly reds in prints and solids, with blues, grays, whites in prints and designs; eight rows by nine rows of pattern blocks, set on point with red print sashing and binding, white backing; outline and straight-line quilting overall, small and even stitches; very good assembly, nearly all corners match; excellent condition; 68" × 73"; $295.

NINE-PATCH: 1930s; dark green and white; four rows by five rows of the pattern blocks, set straight with white sashing between, nine-patch blocks at the set corners, green and white check backing, wide green border; straight-line and crisscross quilting, 7 stitches per inch; good assembly, most corners and edges match; good condition, has been washed and used, some slight overall color fade; 70" × 85"; $200.

NINE-PATCH: 1930s; multicolored prints and florals on white ground; four rows by five rows of pattern blocks, set square with white blocks between, white binding and backing; straight-line quilting in pattern blocks, hearts and florals in white blocks, small and even stitches; very good assembly, nearly all corners match; very good condition, has been washed, minimally used; 55" × 69"; $150.

NINE-PATCH: early 1900s; browns, pinks in prints and checks, multicolors in prints; outline quilting overall, some stitches uneven, 5 per inch; fair to good assembly, many corners don't match; very worn overall, binding worn and torn in spots, much used; 60" × 78"; $390.

NINE-PATCH: late 1800s; navy, bright red on white; white sashing and border; straight-line quilting overall, small, even quilting stitches; very good assembly, nearly perfect corners and junctions; minimal use and washing, slight fold lines evident; 72" × 78"; $1,150.

NINE-PATCH CHECKERBOARD: 1840–1880; cottons, gray stripe and dark red/black check squares, with indigo calico print sashing; blocks set on point with sashing in rail fence pattern; straight-line quilting, 6 stitches per inch quilt stitches; good assembly, very graphic; excellent condition, some very slight discoloration on backing; 75" × 92"; $1,900.

NINE-PATCH, LARGE CENTER PATCH: 1890s; cottons of blues, yellows, burgundy, grays, tans, many others of stripes, checks, prints, plaids; squares set straight, with double pink squares between; six rows of nine-patch blocks, with indigo and white sashing vertically between each row, no horizontal sashing; narrow double border, yellow, then double pink; from Kentucky; echo and scallop shell quilting overall, large 5 stitches per inch; some discolorations, some fabric tears, small repair; 70" × 80"; $900.

NINE-PATCH: 1860–90; cotton in grays, indigo, blues, double-pink of prints, stripes, calicoes; set on point with squares of four triangles set between; gingham backing; from Kentucky; line quilting overall; slight color loss, some discoloration; 70" × 74"; $2,750.

PEEK-A-BOO VARIATION: 1930s; green solid, with pinks, blues, grays in prints, plaids, and checks; three rows by four rows of pattern blocks, with green sashing between, double border, wide green, narrow pink, pink binding; from Arkansas; straight-line quilting overall, small even stitches using green thread; good assembly, most corners and edges match; very good condition, slight overall color fade; 64" × 80"; $350.

ROCKY ROAD TO KANSAS/KITE VARIATION: 1880s; reds, whites, and blues, all in prints, checks, stripes and solids; each star has blue and white "x" block in center, star arms have stripes of various widths, large dark blue diamonds between stars, print backing; from Kentucky; curved-line and fan quilting overall; excellent assembly; excellent condition; 70" × 80"; $3,550.

ROLLING STONE: 1870s; dark green, yellow, brown, orange, double pink; pattern blocks have yellow with tiny dark print center squares, four rows by five rows of pattern blocks with wide double pink sashing between; wide green calico border, one piece print backing, brown binding, thin batting; from Pennsylvania; curved-line and echo quilting overall, 6 stitches per inch; good assembly, most corners match; excellent condition, unused; 75" × 90"; $495. *See illustration #49.*

ROLLING STONE: 1890s; red on white; three rows by four rows of pattern blocks, set on point with white squares between, very thick batting; feather quilting on white squares, double straight-line quilting on pattern blocks, even stitches, 7 per inch; poor assembly, most corners and points are mismatched, sides of blocks puckered, machine assembled, maybe a beginning user; fair to good condition, minimal use, overall age discoloration, slight overall color fade, some red areas have disintegrated; 54" × 60"; $530.

ROLLING STONE: 1920s; white, prints predominantly of blues, reds, grays; pattern blocks set on point with blue print zigzag sashing and border, border follows sides of blocks on sides and bottom, straight on top edge; outline quilting in pattern blocks, diamond chains in sashing and border, 7 stitches per inch; hand and machine pieced, very good assembly, nearly all points and corners match; good condition, slight overall color fade, slight overall wear; 70" × 84"; $400.

ROLLING STONE: early 1900s; blue with white polka dots, and white; blue with white polka dot border; outline quilting overall, 7 stitches per inch; good assembly, most corners match; good condition, has been washed, few stains in one area; 66" × 80"; $1,350.

SAWTOOTH PATCHWORK: 1870s; grays on white; several grays, all with tiny prints; from Missouri, maker known; straight-line quilting overall, 9 stitches per inch; excellent assembly, nearly all corners/points match; good condition, some overall color loss/fade; 64" × 74"; $1,000.

SAWTOOTH STAR: 1920s; red and white; outline and straight-line quilting overall, 8 stitches per inch; good condition, overall color loss/fade; 72" × 80"; $650.

SHOO-FLY NINE-PATCH: 1850–80; cotton of bright Turkey red, olive green, burgundy, blues, calicoes, plaids, stripes, and solids; straight set, four blocks by five blocks with olive green sashing between, and red squares at set corners; from Kentucky; home-dyed backing; outline and straight-line quilting overall; good assembly, most corners match; slight color loss, binding worn and split in a few small places, few small tears; 67" × 84"; $1,250.

SHOO-FLY: 1890s; tiny prints of red, green, yellow and double pink; pattern blocks are pink and green with yellow center, five rows by six rows, set on point with green blocks between; solid Turkey red border follows edge of the pattern blocks forming zigzag; double border, narrow yellow, very wide red, dark green binding, backing is pieced "bars" pattern in double pink and dark green; from Pennsylvania; one inch grid quilting in plain and pattern blocks, cable quilting in border, 7 stitches per inch; excellent assembly; excellent condition; 78" × 86"; $650.

SHOO-FLY: 1930s; white with multicolored period prints, designs, checks, and stripes; pattern blocks are set on point with white zigzag sashing between, white border and binding, each block uses one fabric on white, some feed sacks; from Vermont; fan quilting overall, small and even stitches; excellent assembly, points and corners match; excellent condition; 74" × 74"; $290.

SHOO-FLY: 1930–40; cottons of solid red, red and white, and cream and white prints; solid red sashing with cream and white squares at the set corners; from Kentucky; straight-line quilting overall, 9 stitches per inch; some minor discolorations; 72" × 82"; $1,450.

SISTER'S CHOICE VARIATION: 1920–40; all cotton solids in pale pink, burgundy, blue, green, white; narrow green border, wide pink border, green binding; from Ohio; extensive well-done quilting in patterns of spider webs, scrolls, swirls, ropes, flowers, 9 stitches per inch; excellent condition, minimal use and washing; 70" × 72"; $900.

SNOWFLAKE: 1920s; white and multicolored period prints; five rows by six rows of pattern blocks, white center squares, wide white border; from Pennsylvania; outline and diagonal straight-line quilting, small even stitches; excellent assembly; excellent condition, quilting lines remain; 72" × 84"; $395.

TEXAS PUZZLE VARIATION: mid 1800s; prints, stripes, checks, and plaids in browns, tans, grays, blues; six rows by seven rows of pattern blocks, set on point with blue with tiny white and light blue flower print blocks between; from Kentucky; excellent assembly; excellent condition; 68" × 81"; $9,500.

THRIFTY NINE-PATCH VARIATION: early 1900s; pink on lavender/pink with white large floral print, white with rose dots print, red with white and black print; pattern blocks are nine-patch with large center square and small four-patch blocks in corners, five rows by six rows of pattern blocks with red/white/black print sashing and border, peach print backing, thin batting; from Pennsylvania; straight-line quilting overall, 5 stitches per inch; good assembly, most corners match; very good condition, unused, minimal washing; 86" × 98"; $425.

YOUNG MAN'S FANCY: 1930s; medium blue and white; three rows by four rows of pattern blocks, five-strip border, blue, white, blue, white, blue with white binding; excellent straight-line quilting in the pattern blocks, cable quilting on the border, wreath and feather quilting on the solid white parts of the blocks, 11 stitches per inch; excellent assembly; excellent condition; 70" × 87"; $775.

16 Crazy Quilts

The style used in Crazy Quilts was one of the first piecework styles ever used, as it truly was a way to use up those leftover scraps, even more efficiently than a one patch. Stitching pieces together in their original size and shape would allow the quilter to make a large piece of fabric from practically nothing. These first quilts were tied rather than quilted, making them "comfortables" or comforters.

The quilts that we actually think of as Crazy Quilts, those lavish pieces of velvets and silk, those elaborately embroidered bits of whimsy, didn't really come to be until the mid 1800s in the Victorian era. A look at the types of fabrics preferred for these beauties shows that these quilts were the province of the upper and middle class, the Victorian quilter's way of "keeping up with the Joneses."

Or even surpassing them, as the best fabrics, such as brocades, satins, velvets, silks, and fine, silky wools were often purchased just for these quilts—no leftovers here! Special adornments were saved or purchased as well. The quilter might include pieces of Christmas ribbon, strips of fine lace, a length of twisted gold braid or a section of fringe. After all of the base pieces were put together in a "random" looking pattern that was anything but, they were adorned with some degree of fancy embroidery, and sometimes even other embellishments such as small paintings.

One style of Crazy Quilt is even more elaborate, as it is appliquéd, not pieced. The quilter would take black ground fabric and appliqué pieces of silk and velvet onto it, leaving a thin strip of the black to show through, making the entire quilt look like a stained glass window.

Crazy Quilts were also made of perfectly utilitarian fabrics, just like any other quilt, but the jewels we most often look for are the fancy ones. Unfortunately, the wonderful fabrics, even if they were well cared for and carefully stored, did not stand up to the passage of time. Mostly due to the dyes of the day, they tended to split, shatter, and deteriorate, leaving only dust be-

50

50 This wool Crazy Quilt has the usual scattered assembly of pieces and added yellow topstitching. Made in 1916, the quilt also features fans in the corners, a nice touch. Quilt courtesy of the Warner Family.

hind. If this had not happened, many more of these highly desirable quilts would probably be available today.

As the 1900s began, the fancy fabric phase started to wane, and more wool and cotton Crazy Quilts were made, using simple embroidery on the seams only. One historian attributed this decline of gaudiness to a societal rejection of the overindulgence of the Victorian era.

Even if the crazy quilt you find is not in perfect condition, it may benefit from stabilization and become your prize quilt. In any case, you'll want to display your treasure in some sunlight-free area and not use it on a bed. *See illustration #50.*

CRAZY QUILT: 1880s; black, browns, burgundy, blue, red, other darks in velvets, silks, satins with lace, ribbons, glass beads, other embellishments; yellow featherstitch embroidery over all seams and piece junctions, very precise and small stitches, expertly done, tiny flowers, other patterns embroidered in some pieces; excellent assembly, very well balanced color arrangement; excellent condition, has been well cared for, no fabric loss or breakdown; 60" × 60"; $17,500.

CRAZY QUILT: 1880s; darks and lights in velvets, satins, brocades, silks; featherstitch embroidery overall, not heavily detailed; good assembly; very good condition, two fabrics seem brittle; 40" × 40"; $1,525.

CRAZY QUILT: 1880s; darks and lights in velvets, satins, silks; simple and minimal featherstitch embroidery on piece seams; good assembly; fair condition, some fabric deterioration, several seem brittle, several broken embroidery stitches; 58" × 58"; $485.

CRAZY QUILT: 1885; black, blue, burgundy, other darks, and jewel tones of fuchsia, turquoise in silks, velvets, satins; several ribbons, many fan-shaped pieces that seem to be arranged for balanced look, several different embroidery stitches used on seams and on pieces, depicting flowers, birds, kittens, others; dated; excellent workmanship; excellent condition, fabrics seem sound, no brittleness; 72" × 72"; $4,875.

CRAZY QUILT: 1887; blacks, burgundy, several other dark colors; all wools, looks unplanned, signed and dated, one piece backing, black and red wool; herringbone embroidery on all seams, many figures in larger pieces: pigs, dogs, cats, others; tied, very good assembly and embroidery, even and consistent; good condition, few small tears, holes, scuffed spots; 90" × 110"; $5,300.

CRAZY QUILT: 1890s; all wools in blues, red, pink, grays, burgundy, cream, brown, mostly solids, a few plaids and stripes; five rows by five rows of pattern blocks, set square with gray sashing between, electric blue squares at set corners, dark blue border; herringbone embroidery in light thread in the pattern blocks' seams; Pennsylvania Mennonite; diamond grid quilting overall, small and even stitches; excellent assembly and color arrangement; good condition, few tiny spots, some damage to backing; 75" × 75"; $875.

CRAZY QUILT: 1900–10; multicolored darks in velvets, silks, satins; narrow black velvet border, yellow herringbone embroidery on all piece junctions; tied, no quilting; good assembly and embroidery; fair condition, several fractured silks, satins disintegrating, very worn velvets; 30" × 60"; $130.

CRAZY QUILT: 1900–10; multicolored, satins, silks, velvets, few cottons; nine blocks joined in three rows by three rows, each block with dozens of small pieces; mostly herringbone topstitching where pieces join; double border, medium wide pale pink satin, wide butter yellow satin, rose red binding; fair condition, some fabrics have shattered, some frayed; 68" × 70"; $350.

CRAZY QUILT: 1910–20; browns, blues, many others in velvets, silks, satins; no quilting, yellow featherstitch on block joints and elsewhere, good assembly, pleasing arrangement of fabrics; some wear, some fabric loss, some fractured fabric pieces, especially in silks; 68" × 70"; $500.

CRAZY QUILT: 1916; wools, cottons, velvets in reds, blacks, many others; white yarn embroidery on seams, and in various spaces, in figures such as butterfly, flowers, caterpillar; red linen backing and ruffled edge; from Pennsylvania, signed, dated and addressed; two damaged areas on front; 80" × 82" including 4½-inch ruffle; $425.

CRAZY QUILT: early 1900s; velvets, silks, satins in black, burgundy, other darks; large and small pieces, yellow topstitching; tied, no quilting; fair to good assembly, many uneven edges, uneven and inconsistent herringbone topstitching; fair condition, some fabric loss and deterioration, broken and loose stitches; 78" × 80"; $575. *See illustration #51.*

CRAZY QUILT: early 1900s; velvets, silks, satins, ribbons, in blues and other darks; yellow herringbone topstitching overall; tied, no quilting; excellent assembly and embroidery, tiny stitches; fair to good condition, some fabrics have shattered, some pieces are gone, backing torn in two places; 72" x 80"; $650.

CRAZY QUILT: late 1800s; velvets, satins in blacks, golds, greens, blues, other darks; minimal yellow feather topstitching in some areas, several circular shaped pieces; tied, no quilting;

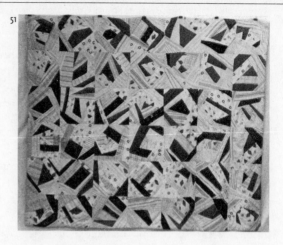

51 A 1930s version of a Crazy Quilt, this piece shows a variety of flannel fabrics, and the simple style possible for this type of quilt. The darks and the light balance for an interesting abstract look. Quilt courtesy of Laura Caro.

good assembly and embroidery; good condition, with some pieces having fabric loss; 68" × 68"; $960.

CRAZY QUILT: late 1800s; velvets, silks, satins in blacks, blues, other darks; lots of ribbons and other inclusions, wide black velvet border; embroidered fans in corners, yellow topstitch embroidery on all seams in a variety of patterns, biblical symbols in many blocks; from California; tied, no quilting; very good assembly and embroidery, very creative in coordinating topstitching to shape and size of the fabric piece; poor to fair condition, many pieces missing, much fabric deterioration; 69" × 69"; $1,200.

17 Double Wedding Ring

The Double Wedding Ring pattern is one that collectors and dealers either love or hate. This easily identifiable quilt dates from the 1920s, when quilters first moved away from traditional geometrics and started using curved designs. It quickly became so popular, either from its unique look or its romantic name, that thousands of quilt kits in the pattern were sold. Because it is a scrap bag type quilt, and any fabric could be included in a kit, it is hard today to tell if the quilt was made from a kit or from the quilter's own scraps. For that reason alone, many dealers don't like to carry Double Wedding Rings, and many collectors avoid them. But they remain the most popularly selling antique quilts on the market, and are usually given as surprise wedding gifts!

Many collectors' first acquisition is a Double Wedding Ring, since they do have a certain uniqueness and charm. The colors and fabric prints are often appealing, they are usually in good condition, and they are not all that old, dating from the 1920s and 1930s. If you want to add a Double Wedding Ring to your collection, speak to your favorite dealer about finding one for you.

In the hands of an experienced quilter, the white areas between the rings became a canvas for elaborate feather wreath or other round-pattern quilting. The quilting may be what catches your eye and brings you to own one of these quilts. Because of the name, many were made as bridal quilts or gifts, and you might like the pattern for that reason.

Some variations of the Double Wedding Ring are the Pickle Dish, Robbing Peter to Pay Paul, Pincushion, and the Endless Chain. We wonder, were those made *after* the honeymoon? *See illustration #52.*

DOUBLE WEDDING RING VARIATION: 1940s; white, red, blue; rings are composed of alternating color pieces, four-patch where rings cross are blue and red, five-point red stars appliquéd in ring centers; outline quilting overall, black thread on blue, white on red and white, 8 stitches per inch; very good assembly, nearly all junctions are even and match; excellent condition; 72" × 92"; $7,050.

52 This rosebud applique quilt is signed "GWS" in all four corners and dates to about 1860. Made in Pennsylvania, each medallion has a rose center surrounded by rose buds and leaves. It is elaborately quilted and never washed—the pencil markings for the quilting are still visible.

DOUBLE WEDDING RING: 1930s; rose pink, teal green, multicolored pastels and brights in prints, checks, plaids, stripes; multicolored pieced rings, with rose and green four-patch squares at corners where rings cross on muslin, muslin backing and binding, very thin batting; maker known, from Ohio; four-point star and circle quilting overall, 7 stitches per inch; excellent assembly; excellent condition, never used, pencil lines for quilting remain, stored well, few tiny spots in one corner; 88" × 102"; $500.

DOUBLE WEDDING RING: 1920s; white, pink, multicolored period prints, designs, checks, dots and florals; white ground, pink and yellow four-patch squares where rings cross, scalloped edges on all four sides, pink binding; outline quilting in the ring pieces, florals in the ring centers, 8 stitches per inch; very good assembly, few puckered piece edges; very good condition, minimal use, few stains, two tears on backing; 68" × 82"; $600.

DOUBLE WEDDING RING: 1920s; greens, pinks, other pastels in prints and solids; solid pinks and greens at ring junctions, scalloped edge follows shape of the rings; outline quilting overall, with curved lines and circles inside the rings, large quilting stitches, some uneven; good assembly, most edges and corners match; overall fading, chin edge binding very worn, with some tears; 60" × 70"; $650.

DOUBLE WEDDING RING: 1920s; greens, yellows, other multicolored prints; edges curved, following rings; outline quilting overall, 7 stitches per inch; good assembly, most corners match; fair to good condition, some wear on edges, overall fading, much use; 76" × 88"; $600.

DOUBLE WEDDING RING: 1920s; pastels, multicolored prints; four curved edges following rings; outline and straight line quilting overall, 7 stitches per inch; good assembly, some corners don't match; good condition, some overall fade, few age stains; 76" × 78"; $650.

DOUBLE WEDDING RING: 1920s; pinks and blues, solids and prints; four curved edges following the rings; outline quilting overall, 7 stitches per inch; good assembly, most corners match; good condition, little wear, much washing, overall color fade; 76" × 76"; $700.

DOUBLE WEDDING RING: 1920s; white, yellow, pink, multicolored period prints, designs, florals; yellow and pink four-patch squares where rings cross, white ground, wavy edges that follow ring sides; feather wreath quilting in ring centers, outline overall, tiny and even stitches, 10 per inch; very good assembly, nearly all corners match; excellent condition, never washed; 70" × 78"; $770.

DOUBLE WEDDING RING: 1930s; "depression" green, pink, multicolored pastels and brights in prints, dots, stripes; depression green binding, quilt sides follow the curve of the rings, white backing, thin batting; outline quilting overall, 5 stitches per inch; good assembly, even curves, most corners match; excellent condition, never used, minimal washing; 76" × 76"; $600.

DOUBLE WEDDING RING: 1930s; blues, golden yellow, multicolored period prints, designs, solids, florals, checks; white ground and backing, dark blue binding, blue and yellow squares at ring crossings, quilt sides are scalloped following ring edges; triple curved-line quilting on the rings, five row echo on ring centers, double echo in ring overlaps, small and even stitches; good assembly, most corners match; very good condition, has been washed, minimal use; 65" × 77"; $285.

DOUBLE WEDDING RING: 1930s; lavender and pink solids, multicolored period prints, patterns, florals, checks, plaids, stripes; four rings by five rings, curved edges that follow the rings, yellow binding, four-patch lavender and pink squares where the rings cross, white backing; from Missouri; lots of outline quilting around each piece and entire rings, four-petal flowers in center of rings, small and even stitches; excellent assembly; good condition, slight overall soiling from handling, one small tear, some fabric wear in a few areas; 70" × 85"; $500.

DOUBLE WEDDING RING: 1930s; pink, green, white, multicolored period prints, designs, florals, and checks; white ground, pink and green four-patch squares where rings cross, scalloped edges on all four sides, white scalloped border, white binding and backing; outline quilting in ring pieces, cable quilting on border, scroll-like patterns in ring centers, even stitches, 8 per inch; very good assembly, most corners match, flat edges; excellent condition, never washed, minimal use; 73" × 88"; $645.

DOUBLE WEDDING RING: 1930s; pink, multicolored florals, prints, checks; rings are set on pink ground, with pink squares at ring crossings, white binding and backing; outline quilting overall, double outline in ring centers, small and even stitches; good assembly, most corners match, piece edges are even; quilt sides are scalloped, following rings sides; very good condition; 74" × 86"; $350.

DOUBLE WEDDING RING: 1930s; white, pink, blue, innumerable period colors and prints; pink and blue four-patch squares at ring connections, very small pieces form the rings, pink binding; outline quilting on the ring pieces, diamond quilting and wreath quilting in the large white areas, 9 stitches per inch; excellent assembly; excellent condition; 80" × 90"; $695.

DOUBLE WEDDING RING: 1930s; white, pink, green, multicolored period prints and florals; rings are multicolored with green and pink squares where the rings cross, white ground; scalloped edge follows the sides of the rings; excellent outline quilting on rings, floral quilting on white ground between rings, small and even stitches, 10 per inch; excellent assembly; good condition, slight overall color fade, some wear on back; 72" × 72"; $635.

DOUBLE WEDDING RING: 1930s; white, pink, green, multiple period prints and colors; multiprint rings with four-patch pink and green squares at the ring junctions; straight edges, narrow triple border, green, pink, green, very wide white border; from Missouri; cable quilting on the white border, grid quilting in the ring centers, small stitches; very good assembly, almost all junctions match; very good condition, has been washed, small rust stain on one edge; 70" × 72"; $550.

DOUBLE WEDDING RING: 1930s; white, purple, green, and multicolored period prints and florals; multicolored ring pieces, solid purple and green four-patch in corners where rings cross, all on white ground; scalloped edges follow rings; outline on rings and curved-line quilting in center of rings, 6 stitches per inch; excellent assembly; excellent condition; 72" × 94"; $595.

DOUBLE WEDDING RING: 1930–40; very pale pastels, pale oranges, greens, and lavender prints on white background; outline quilting overall; good condition; 54" × 72"; $300.

DOUBLE WEDDING RING: 1930s; classic, traditional pattern in creams, pastels, and prints, pink and green squares at ring junctions; half circle edges formed by rings; crosshatch quilting, 7 stitches per inch; very nice assembly; excellent condition, nearly unwashed, minor color fading, minor binding fraying; 80" × 93"; $1,300.

DOUBLE WEDDING RING: 1930s; gold, medium blue, and rose pink solids, various multicolored prints, stripes, checks, plaids, others; rings in multicolored and multipatterned pieces on gold background with blue and rose four-patch squares at the ring junctions, blue binding; outline and straight-line quilting overall, four-petal flowers in centers of the rings, 8 stitches per inch; small hole in binding, good condition, minimal use, minimal washing; 64" × 75"; $325.

DOUBLE WEDDING RING: 1930s; golden yellow solid, mint green, with prints, checks, plaids and solids of every color possible; multicolored pieced rings with golden yellow between and around the rings; plain muslin backing, mint green binding; thin batting; from Texas; outline quilting overall, flower patterns in centers of the rings, large stitches, 5 per inch; unused, unwashed, one small area soiled, some color loss overall; 72" × 85"; $325.

DOUBLE WEDDING RING: 1930s; interesting interpretation of all solids, bright blue, cheddar yellow, hot pink with white background in ring centers; horizontal ring segments are alternating pink and cheddar pieces, with blue in the space where the rings overlap, vertical ring segments are alternating pink and bright blue with cheddar in the space where the rings overlap; four-patch squares in ring corners of bright blue and cheddar; five rings by four rings, edges shaped by the rings; outline quilting in the ring pieces, with quilting of eight-petal flowers in the centers of the rings, two-petal flowers in the spaces where the rings cross, 8 stitches per inch; very good assembly, pieces well matched; good condition, has been washed, very slight color loss in some pieces; 63" × 75"; $400.

DOUBLE WEDDING RING: 1930s; multicolored pastel prints, checks; curved edges follow rings; outline quilting overall, simple medallions in centers of rings, 6 stitches per inch; good assembly, most corners match; excellent condition, minimal use and washing; 80" × 82"; $845.

DOUBLE WEDDING RING: 1930s; mustard yellow, black sateen, various multicolored prints, stripes, checks, plaids, others; rings in multicolored and multipatterned pieces with black background in the ring centers and mustard yellow in space where rings overlap, with black and mustard yellow four-patch squares at the ring junctions; edge has shape of the sides of the rings, with black binding; outline quilting overall, six petal flowers in centers of the rings, 6 stitches per inch; small hole on back, some seam separation, has been washed, few spots/stains; 82" × 96"; $325.

DOUBLE WEDDING RING: 1930s; pure white background, four-patch squares in ring corners of spring green and lavender solids, rings pieced of prints, plaids, and checks of nearly every color possible; five rings by six rings, edges shaped by the rings; from Ohio; outline quilting in the ring pieces, with quilting of four petal flowers in the centers of the rings, two-petal flowers in the spaces where the rings cross, 8 stitches per inch; good assembly, although some areas are slightly pulled out of shape; good condition, has been washed; 69" × 78"; $450.

DOUBLE WEDDING RING: 1930s; yellow prints, checks, florals; curved edges follow rings on all sides; outline quilting overall, 6 stitches per inch; good assembly, most corners match; 45" × 80"; $700.

DOUBLE WEDDING RING: 1930s; yellow, gold, blue, multicolored period prints and florals; rings on yellow ground, with blue and gold four-patch square where rings cross, two sides have scalloped edges that follow rings, top and bottom are straight, yellow backing and binding; outline quilting on rings, large daisylike flowers in ring centers, 8 stitches per inch; good assembly, most edges are even, corners match; fair to good condition, slight overall color fade, well used and washed, some overall wear, top edge binding is very worn; 76" × 80"; $500.

DOUBLE WEDDING RING: 1930s; yellows, peach, other multicolored prints; curved borders on four sides follow rings; outline quilting overall, 6 stitches per inch; good assembly, most corners match; excellent condition, unused, minimal washing; 80" × 114"; $1,550.

DOUBLE WEDDING RING: 1940s; white ground with multicolored period prints, designs, checks, stripes, plaids; all four sides are scalloped following the edges of the rings, lavender binding, light blue floral backing; outline quilting on rings, four-point medallions in ring centers, small and even stitches; good assembly, most corners match, some piece edges are uneven; excellent condition, quilting lines remain; 76" × 88"; $395.

DOUBLE WEDDING RING: 1940s; white with blues, navy and light, and multicolored period prints and florals; rings are multicolored with navy and light blue squares where the rings cross, white ground; poor to fair quilting, large, sloppy stitches, not much quilting, straight-line and outline; poor to fair assembly, much misalignment in pieces, uneven edges, rings look

167

misshapen overall; good condition, slight overall color fade, slight wear to binding; 86" × 92"; $300.

PICKLE DISH VARIATION OF DOUBLE WEDDING RING: 1930s; green, rusty/red, rose pink solids, several multicolored prints; plain rusty/red squares in ring corners; solid green centers in rings, narrow double border, green inner, rusty/red outer; good assembly, most corners match, although several ring edges are wavy; good condition, two areas repaired with same green fabric by appliqué; 68" × 84"; $160.

18 Log Cabin Quilts

Log Cabin blocks were inspired by pioneer homes, with the red "hearth" in the center. Around the hearth, "logs" are placed, one after another, just like building a real log cabin. From the basic Log Cabin block arose dozens of variations.

The traditional Log Cabin block is easy and fairly quick to assemble, since the log strips are placed around the central square, one at a time, and sewed down to a foundation fabric. After each strip is added, the block is turned one-quarter turn and is ready for the next strip. Most Log Cabin blocks, as they are assembled, are split on the diagonal, with light-colored logs on one side, and dark-colored logs on the other. Once the blocks are put together with other blocks to make the whole quilt, the value of this can be clearly seen. *See illustrations #53 and #53A.*

Just by turning each block in relation to its neighbor, different optical effects can be seen. The Streak of Lightning arrangement places the light and dark sides of the blocks in jagged rows, while Barn Raising creates diamond-shaped rings that rise from the center of the quilt. The accompanying illustrations show how the different assemblies are achieved using this most versatile block.

Two other variations of the basic Log Cabin block make for even more versatility. Each uses the strip method of assembly, but places the logs in a different order. In Courthouse Steps, instead of adding the strips in a circular way around the central square, the strips are added two lights at one end, then two darks on the sides, which is much harder than working in a circle. Many a quilter has found herself ripping out stitches when she discovers that she has slipped and put the wrong strip in the wrong place. The symbolism of the Courthouse Steps is different, too, with the central square representing the building, and the strips representing the steps leading up to it.

The other very popular variant of the Log Cabin is the Pineapple or Windmill Blades style. In this version, the central square is set on point and the strips arranged around it alternating

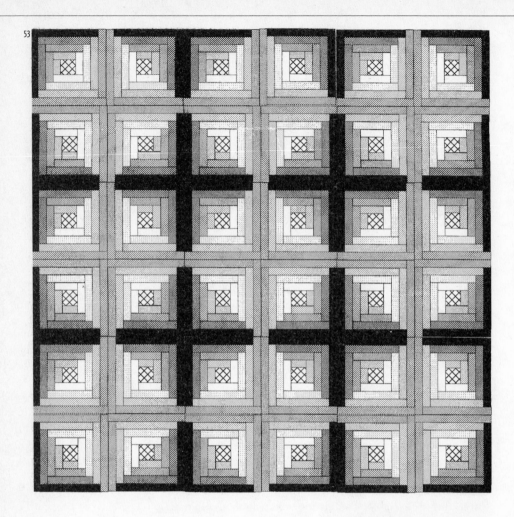

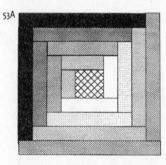

53 & 53A The Versatile Log Cabin Block: Sunshine and Shadows. Log Cabin blocks are made up of strips of fabric around a center square, traditionally with dark colors on one side and light colors on the other although many variations are possible. Completed blocks may be assembled in several ways, including the Sunshine and Shadows shown below.

54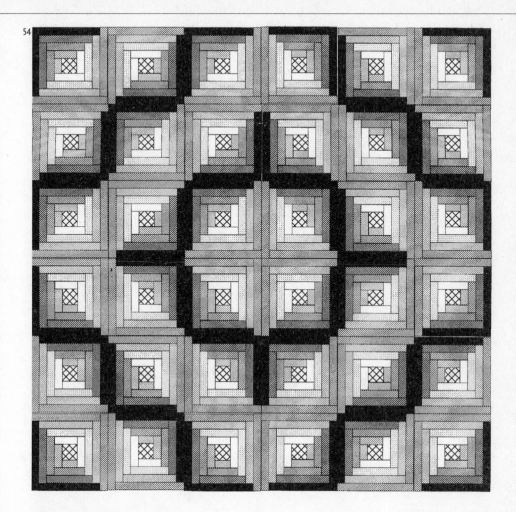

54A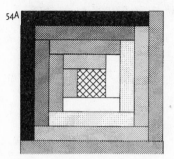

54 & 54A The Versatile Log Cabin
Block: Barn Raising. Just by flip-
flopping the blocks, the assembly
becomes the Barn Raising
variation.

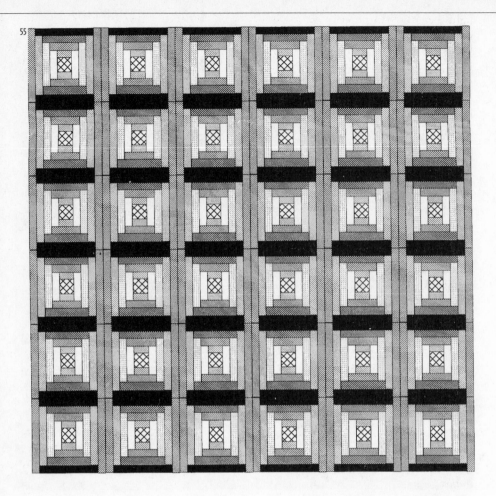

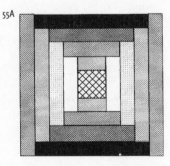

55 & 55A The Versatile Log Cabin
Block: Courthouse Steps.
Move the light and dark logs to the ends
and sides of the cabin and the
block provides the completely
different look of the Courthouse
Step Variation.

light then dark. In order to get the wedge shapes, each strip must be a different size, and shaped with pointed ends. If narrow strips are used, and the finished blocks assembled with lights meeting lights and darks meeting darks on opposite corners, the quilt looks like spinning windmill blades.

Log Cabin blocks are one of those patterns usually made on a foundation fabric, which lets the assembly go fairly quickly. Newspaper was occasionally used as the ground, to eliminate the weight and thickness of the ground fabric; when the block is complete, the paper is torn away. In either case, the ground stabilizes the logs and makes the quilter's job much easier.

Log Cabin quilts were sometimes made of silks and satins, as summer spreads or just show pieces. They were also made of wools for winter warmth; these quilts can be quite striking with the deep colors of wool and its natural texture. In any case, because of the way log cabin quilts are constructed, they are rarely quilted and are usually tied.

Originally, Log Cabin blocks were used between 1840 and 1865 as a border motif, but they quickly grew so popular that they became entire quilts. These became so popular that many country fairs and shows began giving separate prizes for the category.

However they are assembled, into whatever patterns, the Log Cabin quilt is a wonderful reminder of our pioneer heritage.

BARN RAISING LOG CABIN, CRIB QUILT: 1910–20; lights and darks in multicolored prints, plaids, solids, checks; tiny logs make up more than a dozen light and dark rows out from the center of the quilt, red binding, tied with red silk threads, no quilting; fair condition, much wear, some fabric deterioration; 30" × 30"; $200.

BARN RAISING LOG CABIN: 1870–90; wool worsteds, cottons, silks in deep browns, olive, blues, reds, orange, tans; plaids, prints, checks, solids; homespun wool; from Pennsylvania; good assembly; fair condition, fractured silks, some deterioration; 56" × 76"; $1,150. *See illustrations #54 and #54A.*

BARN RAISING LOG CABIN: 1880s; lights are various whites, pinks, light grays and blues in prints, designs and plaids, darks are blues, reds, grays in solids, prints, plaids, and checks; cabins have green on green centers, double border, blue/gray print, red, print, pink print border; from Pennsylvania; diagonal straight-line quilting overall, mostly even stitches; very good assembly and color balance, although in several blocks the center square is misplaced; excellent condition; 75" × 75"; $625.

BARN RAISING LOG CABIN: 1880s; cottons, shirtings, and homespun with lights of greens, creams, yellows, pale blues, many others, and darks of rose, burgundy, blues, many others, in prints, stripes, checks, solids; straight-line quilting overall, large stitches, 5 per inch; fair to good assembly, many junctions not well matched; 63" × 85"; $600.

BARN RAISING LOG CABIN: 1880s; prints, stripes, checks of blues, reds, creams/whites, double pinks; double border; Pennsylvania Mennonite; in-the-ditch and straight-line quilting overall; good assembly; unwashed, some stains and spots; 66" × 66"; $600.

BARN RAISING LOG CABIN: 1890; cotton, red, green and whites, solids, calicoes, prints; wide red/green stripe border, homespun backing, summer cover with no batting; from Penn-

56

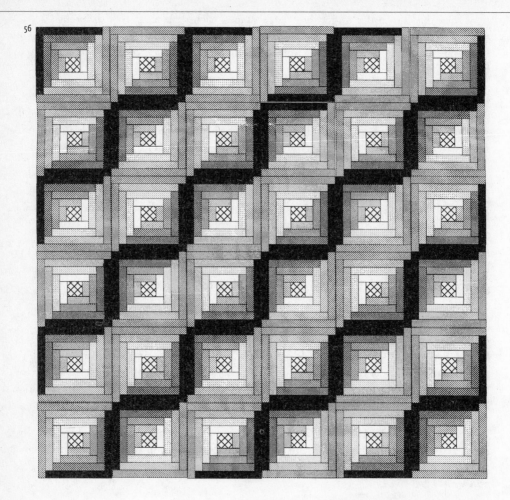

56A

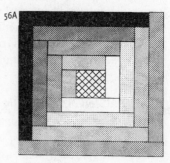

56 & 56A The Versatile Log Cabin Block: Straight Furrows. Flip-Flop a little differently, to again change the assembly, and the overall pattern becomes the Straight Furrows Variation.

57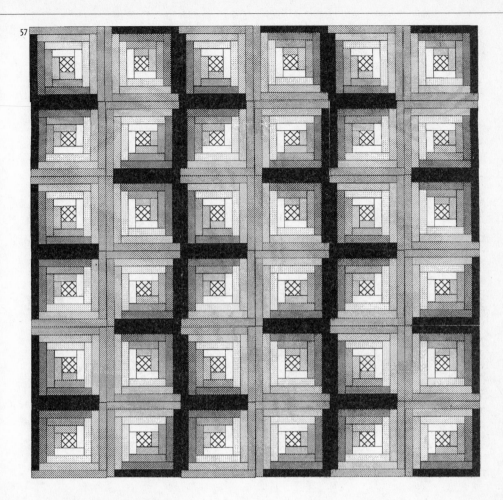

57A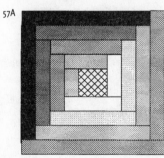

57 & 57A The Versatile Log Cabin
Block: Streak of Lightning. Give
the furrows a little twist and the
assembly now becomes the Streak
of Lightning Variation.

58

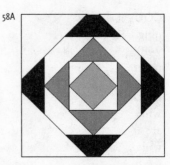

58A

58 & 58A The Versatile Log Cabin
Block: Pineapple. The Log Cabin
Pineapple assembly gives a
completely unique look, as the
strips are arranged on pint around
the center block and triangle
corners are added.

sylvania; excellent in-the-ditch line quilting overall; very good assembly; some minor discoloration, fabric crisp, minimal use/washing; 73" × 80"; $2,950.

BARN RAISING LOG CABIN: 1900; blue-green and red solid dark logs, pinks, pale blues on white prints light logs; from Kentucky; straight-line and cross-hatch quilting overall; very good assembly; slight color loss; 78" × 86"; $1,450.

BARN RAISING LOG CABIN: 1900–10; black, red; thin strip (about ½-inch) logs around red centers, silks and homespun; from Colorado; no quilting, tied; very good condition, few tiny repairs; 66" × 76"; $3,200.

COURTHOUSE STEPS LOG CABIN: 1860–90; wools in black, olive, gray, some red, orange, navy; striped flannel backing; from Kentucky; good assembly; comforter, tied, not quilted; large piece missing from backing, many holes and moth holes; 78" × 82"; $1,250.

COURTHOUSE STEPS LOG CABIN: 1880s; all wools, mostly solids, some plaids and stripes, lights are creams, tans, beige, pink, light blues, darks are browns, blues, burgundy, black, grays; six rows by six rows of pattern blocks, with four borders, first is pieced "bars" of above colors, second and fourth are bright medium blue solid, third is sawtooth of above lights and darks; border and backing are two different blue paisley wools; tied in the pattern blocks and bars border, large zigzag quilting in blue borders, large stitches, but even; fair to good assembly, many piece edges are uneven, many points and corners don't match; excellent condition; 72" × 72"; $775. *See illustrations #55 and 55A.*

COURTHOUSE STEPS LOG CABIN: 1880s; browns, reds, grays, burgundy, cream, many others in stripes, prints, checks; cabins are courthouse steps assembly, but have no specific arrangement of lights and darks, so pattern is not clearly evident; triple border, very wide green with tiny black, blue, and cream dots and flowers print, on each side, with wide center border of red with white dots print and large squares of red dot print in each border corner; blue gray plaid pieced backing and binding; minimal straight-line quilting in large stitches; good assembly, although many logs are uneven; good condition, unused, unwashed, no stains or spots, but several fabric strips are split; 75" × 75"; $340.

COURTHOUSE STEPS LOG CABIN: 1906; greens, blues, pinks on bright white; prize-winning quilt; from Iowa, maker known, signed and dated; excellent outline quilting overall, 9–10 stitches per inch; excellent assembly, all logs even, corners square; excellent condition, never used or washed, carefully stored; 78" × 86"; $1,200.

DOUBLE SQUARES, WITH PINEAPPLE LOG CABIN CENTER BLOCK: 1890s; red and white "double squares" blocks, three blocks on each side; lights of center "pineapple" square are all pale prints on white, darks are small light prints, plaids on black, burgundy, browns; wide red sashing and border, backing is pale colors on white with bird and tree print, solid piece of fabric; minimal outline quilting in red squares and border; very good condition, minimal washing, possibly unused, one small tear, one small pale spot; 42" × 46"; $495.

LOG CABIN: late 1800s; shades of browns, tan, beige; darks are velvets, lights are wools, red satin center squares; tied, no quilting; good assembly, most edges are even and match; fair to good condition, several tears, some fabric loss, some moth holes; 70" × 80"; $1,025.

PINEAPPLE LOG CABIN: 1880s; silks and velvets in black, blues, reds as the darks, and yellow, gold, and cream as the lights; nine log squares, three squares by three squares; pieced, border of red and cream silk stripes, with wide black velvet stripes between; crazy quilt-type embroidery in vine and feathered line styles in the center and edge blocks; from Massachusetts or Connecticut; comforter, tied, not quilted; some fracturing of the silks overall, some deterioration overall; 60" × 60"; $2,500.

PINEAPPLE LOG CABIN: 1900–10; purples, reds, tans, browns, others; all twills and wools, black velvet block centers, red plaid border, different plaid binding and backing; tied, no quilting; good assembly, most edges are straight, corners match; good condition, some fabric deterioration in a few areas, some color fade in some fabrics; 78" × 84"; $1,200. *See illustrations #58 and #58A.*

PINEAPPLE LOG CABIN: 1900–20; cottons in darker pastels, blues, grays, golds, green prints and checks and natural white; all natural white centers, natural white border; seeds and leaves visible in cotton batting; from Kentucky; straight-line quilting overall; good assembly, squares and corners match very well; some stains, some discoloration; 60" × 73"; $800.

PINEAPPLE LOG CABIN: 1930s; fuchsia/rose and cream white; five rows by four rows of pineapple blocks, wide fuchsia/rose border, binding; outline quilting in each "log" of the pineapples, floral and feather quilting in the border, 7 stitches per inch; excellent assembly; very good condition, unwashed, unused, few small spots; 80" × 95"; $695.

PINEAPPLE LOG CABIN: early 1900s; yellows, blues, browns, pinks, mostly in small prints, with off-white; off-white border and backing, foreign material visible in batting, through backing; from Kentucky; straight and outline quilting; good assembly; good condition, some staining overall; 60" × 73"; $800.

STRAIGHT FURROWS LOG CABIN: 1880s; darks are several green prints and stripes, lights are several tan and cream shirtings in stripes, plaids, checks, and prints; double pink backing, solid tan center squares, tied, no quilting; good assembly, most corners match, most block edges even; fair condition, some fabrics have shattered and been lost, some greens have faded to mustard, tan with dark dots print has lost dots due to dye deterioration, binding very worn; 54" × 72"; $175.

STRAIGHT FURROWS LOG CABIN: 1880s; reds, greens, browns, yellows, pinks, whites; wide border of white with blue print in delicate ribbon pattern, batting is thin blanket; minimal outline quilting; good assembly, most logs even and most corners match; excellent condition, unwashed, unused; 80" × 80"; $1,800.

STRAIGHT FURROWS LOG CABIN: 1900–10; lights of tans, white, light blue, cream with prints and patterns, darks of blues, browns, grays in prints and solids; from Connecticut; very thick batting, tied, not quilted; fair to good assembly, many uneven edges, mismatched corners; fair condition, much use and washing, overall color fade, worn edges; 70" × 78"; $100. *See illustrations #56 and #56A.*

STRAIGHT FURROWS LOG CABIN: 1920s; predominant color is red; lights are whites, grays, pastels in prints, solids, checks, stripes; darks are reds, rusts, blues, grays, green, black in checks, solids, stripes, plaids; light orange square in center of each "cabin," spring green border at one end only; from Texas; awkward fan quilting at 5 stitches per inch; fair condition, lots of use and washing evident, few small holes, some spots/stains; 72" × 74"; $150.

STREAK OF LIGHTNING LOG CABIN: late 1800s; lights are white and creams with blue, black, other darks in stripes, dots, prints; darks are reds, blacks, grays, browns in prints, dots, stripes; center squares are bright red with black dots; black and white stripe backing in a solid piece of fabric, gray floral pattern binding; straight-line quilting overall, 6 stitches per inch; excellent assembly; fair to good condition, many stains and soiled areas, slight overall color fade; 70" × 76"; $375. *See illustrations #57 and #57A.*

SUNSHINE AND SHADOWS LOG CABIN, CRIB QUILT: 1900–10; light logs are tan and cream plaid shirting, dark logs are four different blacks with white prints, center squares of log cabin blocks are oversized, of double pink print; wide black with white dot border; outline quilting overall, 7 stitches per inch; excellent condition, unwashed, unused; 43" × 43"; $300.

SUNSHINE AND SHADOWS LOG CABIN: 1880s; predominantly whites, reds, browns, blacks grays, blues; lights are whites and creams with tiny prints in reds, grays, browns, blacks; darks are browns, blacks, dark blues, dark reds with tiny white or cream prints or plaids; central square of each block is dark double pink, triple border of two dark double pink, and one Yale blue print; from New York, history known; grid quilting overall, 7 stitches per inch; very good assembly, excellent pattern balance; unused, unwashed, two small faded areas in blue border; 72" × 84"; $900.

TRIP AROUND THE WORLD LOG CABIN: 1890; golds, reds, greens, blues in bright solids and print cottons; four narrow borders of gold, red, blue, green; backing pieced in bars; from Pennsylvania; overall line quilting; very good assembly of 1½-inch squares; fabric crisp; excellent condition; 83" × 83" square; $8,950.

WASHINGTON PAVEMENT, PINEAPPLE LOG CABIN VARIATION: 1930s; green and multicolored prints, designs, checks, florals on white ground; green prairie point edging, green backing; outline quilting overall, double outline and cross quilting in white blocks; small and even stitches; machine pieced, very good assembly, nearly all points and corners match; very good condition, minimal washing and use; 72" × 86"; $295.

19 Shapes, Including Baskets and Such

The images that can be made using squares and triangles are incredible and numerous. Besides the entire alphabet, quilters have fashioned buildings, airplanes, all sorts of animals, various people, lanterns, umbrellas, household items, insects, boats, all kinds of trees, dozens of kinds of flowers, and, of course, baskets.

The latter is a very popular group, and there are probably two dozen named basket patterns to be found. Some baskets are plain, some have pieced flowers in them, and some have appliquéd fruits. Whatever way they look, basket quilts are interesting and desirable.

The key to making a basket quilt or any other shape quilt is to plan ahead. Use of a paper grid helps the quilter visualize how the final pieces should go together and allows her to see potential defects before she does all the piecework.

Most of the quilts depicting shapes are made of some multiple of five-seven, or eight-patch squares. In order to get the detail she needs, a quilter may have to divide a square with ten or more pieces. That's a lot of pieces for patterns like Cone Tree, Dancing Bear or Ching and Chow.

Imagine the first quilter who created one of these blocks. She must have been very pleased. And probably very tired!

ALPHABET SQUARES: 1916; yellow, greens; yellow border around and between each block; from Pennsylvania, signed and dated; line and chain quilting overall, small, consistent sized quilting stitches; excellent assembly, alphabet blocks even, corners square; excellent condition, never used or washed, pencil lines for quilting remain; 80" × 100"; $12,200.

BASKET: 1890s; red and white; six rows by seven rows of pattern blocks, red and white baskets on white ground, appliquéd red handles, set square, red border and binding; uneven outline quilting on baskets, hand done, 7 stitches per inch, machine quilting in simple cable on border; fair assembly, many points mismatched, handles uneven, large appliqué stitches; very good condition, minimal use, few tiny stains in one area; 76" × 88"; $925.

BASKET: 1930s; polished cotton fabric in shades of pink; 25 baskets, five down and five across, appliqué handles; from Kentucky; crosshatch and straight-line quilting overall, rather large stitches, 7 stitches per inch; some seam separations, some discolorations and color loss, frayed binding, has had some repairs, some soiling overall; 78" × 80"; $1,450.

BASKET: 1840s; reds and greens; all print fabrics, baskets have appliquéd handles; excellent line and pattern quilting, hearts under basket handles, small, even stitches, 8 per inch; excellent assembly; good condition, slight overall color loss/fade; 70" × 74"; $1,500.

BASKET: 1870s; solid red on white; simple baskets, no handles, set on point with white squares between; from Maine, signed in ink; outline quilting overall, 6–7 stitches per inch; good assembly, most points/corners match; good condition, some overall fade, has been used and washed; 72" × 84"; $1,200.

BASKET: 1870s; white, green, pink print; pattern blocks are set on point, on white ground, baskets are pink and green on white, with green appliqué handles, narrow pink and green sawtooth border; outline quilting overall, 8 stitches per inch; excellent assembly; fair to good condition, few stains in several areas, several areas of splotchy color loss, especially in pink fabric, some wear to binding; 60" × 70"; $380.

BASKET: 1880s; rose red and white print, white; appliqué handles, rose red print sashing, pattern blocks set on point; good condition, minimal use, small area of repair; 81" × 81"; $1,150.

BASKET: 1890s; browns and pinks, prints and solids; each basket a different pink fabric, no handles on baskets; minimal straight-line quilting, fair assembly; some wear and fading, primarily in browns; well used and washed; 72" × 78"; $425.

BASKET: 1920s; browns and greens in solids and prints; baskets have no handles; minimal straight-line quilting around baskets, 6 stitches per inch; good assembly, most corners/points match, a few uneven edges on some squares; well used, washed, some overall color loss/fade; 78" × 80"; $645.

BASKET: 1930s; solids of electric blue, white, red; red, white, and blue baskets on blue or red ground, white appliquéd handles; three rows by three rows of pattern blocks, set square, narrow red and white sawtooth border, wide blue border, blue binding; outline, starburst, simple cable quilting in pattern blocks, double cable quilting on blue border, white thread very prominent, small and even stitches; very good assembly, nearly all corners and points match; excellent condition; 72" × 72"; $975.

BERRY BASKET: 1865–75; dark green on green calico, several double pink prints, several pink and dark red prints; eight rows of five basket blocks each, set on point with green calico sashing; empty baskets of red prints and double pink prints on red print ground with appliquéd double pink handles; brown on cream whole cloth print backing; from Pennsylvania; outline and straight-line quilting at 6 stitches per inch; excellent assembly; mint condition, unwashed, unused; 81" × 99"; $1,650.

BETTY'S BASKET VARIATION: 1910–20; solid red, dark pink on pink, yellow with tiny dark red dot print, dark rose/red check; five rows by six rows of pattern blocks, pink and yellow, very wide rose/red border; pattern blocks set straight, with red sashing, yellow squares at set corners, thin batting; from Pennsylvania; one-inch grid and chevron quilting overall, 5 stitches per inch; very good assembly, some edges not straight; excellent condition, unwashed; 70" × 80"; $325.

BREAD BASKET/BASKET QUILT VARIATION: 1930s; yellow, red, rose, green, lavender, blue, all solid colors, on white; pattern blocks set on point so baskets stand level, with white blocks between, basket handles are pointed rather than rounded, double border, narrow yellow, narrow lavender; straight-line, chevron, diamond, and outline quilting overall, 9 stitches per inch; very good assembly, most corners match; very good condition, slight overall fade from washing; 80" × 82"; $450.

BREAD BASKET: 1910–20s; white with tiny blue stars print, very pale tan/green lattice/plaid print, pink on pink, tan with tiny brown flower print, three dark blues with tiny white floral/dot print; basket blocks are set straight with tan/green sashing and pink on pink squares at the set corners, basket handles are machine stitched on, muslin backing and binding; lots of ¾-inch echo quilting overall, 7 stitches per inch; excellent assembly; fair to good condition, small hole in border, several age discoloration spots, slight fading in one area; 68" × 76"; $295.

CACTUS BASKET VARIATION: 1860–90; cottons in plaids, prints, stripes, checks of reds, rust, golds, wine, blues, grays; bright Turkey red with gold squares at the set corners, double red border on one end and one side, indigo calico border on other side, home-dyed gray backing: from Kentucky; straight and outline quilting overall; some stains, some minor color loss; $2,650.

CACTUS BASKET: 1930s; solid pink on white; appliqué handles, pink border; outline quilting overall, 6 stitches per inch; good assembly, most corners and points match; good condition, minimal wear but much washing, some yellow areas on whites; 78" × 82"; $550.

CACTUS BASKET: 1940s; solids of pink and green, multicolored prints and solids; six rows by seven rows of pattern blocks, set square, with pink sashing with green squares at set corners, plaid backing; from Kentucky; fan quilting overall, even stitches; very good assembly, nearly all corners and points match; excellent condition, quilting lines remain; large double bed size; $700.

CACTUS BASKET: Late 1800s; Turkey red, cheddar yellow, with plaids, dots, stripes, prints in blues, burgundy, tan, whites, others; four rows by five rows of pattern blocks, set square, with solid red sashing, and cheddar squares at the set corners, red border on one end, blue border on one side, red border on other side; from Kentucky; outline and straight-line quilting; very good assembly, nearly all points/corners match; good condition, minimal washing and use, some stains in few areas; 67" × 88"; $2,650.

CAKE STAND VARIATION: 1890s; solid dark blue, medium blue on blue print, cream with brown and pale pink round splotches print, white with tiny black dots; five rows by six rows of pattern blocks, set on point with white dot blocks between; pattern blocks have dark blue "basket," blue print "cactus" on cream print ground, cream print border and binding; from

Ohio; diamond grid quilting on pattern and plain blocks, diagonal-line quilting on border, 6 stitches per inch; very good assembly, nearly all points and corners match; fair to good condition, some soiling along fold lines, large area of faint oily stain, one small rusty stain; 64" × 80"; $153.

CAKE STAND/BASKET VARIATION: 1890s; solids of Turkey red, cheddar yellow, dark green, double pink; pattern blocks are dark green and red on cheddar ground, set on point with double pink blocks between; five rows by five rows of pattern blocks, white muslin backing, wide dark green border and binding, thin batting; from Pennsylvania; straight double echo quilting in the pattern blocks, one-inch grid quilting in the pink blocks, chevron quilting in the border, 7 stitches per inch; excellent assembly; excellent condition; 77" × 77"; $850.

CAKE STAND: 1920s; white and tiny pink floral on white; five rows by five rows of pattern blocks, set on point with white blocks between, double border, pink then white, pink binding, pink backing; from Pennsylvania; feather wreath and diamond grid quilting in white blocks, outline and straight-line in pattern blocks, very small and even stitches; excellent assembly; excellent condition; 76" × 78"; $875.

CAKE STAND: 1930s; white, orange, brown; pattern blocks, of orange and brown stands on white ground, set on point with white blocks between, white border, orange binding; outline and square grid quilting overall, 7 stitches per inch; very good assembly, nearly all points and corners match; fair to good condition, well worn and washed, very faded overall, binding worn; 75" × 100"; $300.

CHERRY BASKET VARIATION: 1890s; solids of cheddar, maroon, dark teal green; five rows by six rows of basket blocks, set on point with maroon blocks between, wide maroon border, cheddar binding, light blue print backing; baskets are dark teal green and cheddar on maroon ground, are assembled from maroon and cheddar squares, and cheddar triangles on dark teal green ground, have machine appliquéd cheddar handles; Pennsylvania Mennonite; lots of excellent, detailed quilting, pomegranates in maroon set blocks, wheel and hearts in pattern blocks, feather vines in border, very small and even stitches; excellent assembly and color arrangement; excellent condition; 80" × 90"; $2,700.

CHINESE LANTERN: 1933–34; white, dark green, multicolored prints; pattern blocks are set on point with large white squares between and green quarter circle in each corner; each lantern is on white ground, has green band at top and bottom, is composed of 14 diamond-shaped pieces; quilted with green thread, medium wide green border, dates embroidered on one edge; outline and patterned quilting overall, 9 stitches per inch; excellent assembly; very good condition, one small stain; 68" × 78"; $495.

CHIP BASKET VARIATION: 1880s; dark red, dark green, gold, on white; all solids, white with tiny print backing, red sashing and border; straight and outline quilting overall, 5 stitches per inch; excellent assembly; excellent condition; 66" × 74"; $600.

CHIP BASKET: 1890–1910; pure white, gray/green with white dots, dark double pink print, cheddar yellow with tiny print; pattern blocks with baskets of yellow, on white ground, with gray/green "chips" in the baskets; six rows of baskets by five rows of baskets, pattern blocks set on point with dark double pink print blocks between, yellow print border; probably from

Pennsylvania; straight-line and grid quilting overall, 5 stitches per inch; very good assembly, very good condition, probably never washed or used; one small stain on border; 68" × 84"; $425.

DOGS: 1940s; apple green, white, multicolored prints; cottons and silky cottons; three rows by five rows of pieced "dog" blocks, coordinated so each dog is different print fabric, and each has collar that matches its "toes"; apple green binding, narrow apple green sashing with lavender squares at set corners; from Missouri; outline and in-the-ditch quilting overall, 5 stitches per inch; good assembly, most corners match, edges even; good condition, minimal washing and use, some overall discoloration, probably from storage; 72" × 94"; $1,825.

FLOWER BASKET: 1930s; solid pink and natural white; pieced basket blocks in six rows of six, set on point with wide natural white sashing with pink squares in the set corners, wide pink border; pink handles are machine appliquéd, come to rounded point at handle top; straight-line and outline quilting overall, twisted rope quilting on border; good assembly, most points match; clean, has been washed, very faint color bleed from pink to white, from washing; 76" × 77"; $350.

GRANDMOTHER'S BASKET: 1880s; red and green on white; lots of straight-line quilting, medallion quilting in white half-squares above the baskets; fair to good assembly, some pieces misshapen; good condition, minimal use and washing, but some overall fade, color loss; 70" × 74"; $1,100.

GRAPE BASKET: 1930s; dark red and white; pattern blocks are set square with red sashing between, with white squares at the set corners, red border and binding; outline and straight-line quilting overall, 5 stitches per inch; excellent assembly; excellent condition; 70" × 70"; $495.

HANGING BASKET: 1930s; soft, rusty orange and white; five rows by five rows of pattern blocks, set on point with plain white blocks between; handles machine appliquéd, orange border, white binding and backing; straight-line, cable, and floral quilting overall, 7 stitches per inch; excellent assembly; excellent condition; 76" × 76"; $300.

HANGING BASKET: 1930s; off-white and red, five rows of baskets with appliquéd handles; ice cream cone border of red cones, white backing and binding; extensive quilting of feather chains, diamonds, flowers, 8 stitches per inch; less-than-perfect assembly, many triangle pieces pulled out of shape, many points don't match; never washed or used, quilting lines remain; few tiny stains; 82" × 84"; $950.

OLD HOME/SCHOOLHOUSE: 1910s; red with tiny white and black dot print on white ground; four rows by five rows of house pattern blocks, set square with white sashing between, wide white border, white binding; from Pennsylvania; diamond grid quilting overall, small and even stitches; very good assembly, nearly all corners match; very good condition, minimal washing, one small spot; 67" × 81"; $800.

PINE TREE: 1880s; blue with tiny white print, on white; five rows by six rows of pattern blocks, blue backing, blue binding; outline quilting overall, 9 stitches per inch; good assembly, most corners and points match; very good condition, slight overall color fade; 68" × 72"; $645.

PINE TREE: 1930s; white and solid sea foam green; pattern blocks are green on white, set on point with white blocks between, green binding; edges are alternately scallop and point along sides of pattern blocks; outline quilting in pattern blocks, diamond grid quilting in white blocks, 8 stitches per inch; fair to good assembly, many points and corners are misaligned, many block edges uneven; good condition, slight overall color fade from washing, slight wear on one edge of binding; 74" × 86"; $575.

SCHOOLHOUSE: 1890s; red with black dots, green with black and cream print, cream with tiny brown print; six by seven rows of cream and red schoolhouses with green sashing and border; from Pennsylvania; minimal straight-line quilting overall, large stitches; many of the black dots in the red have disintegrated due to dye action, other areas brittle, binding is frayed, quilt is very fragile; many stains in various areas, many areas of color loss; 70" × 80"; $325.

SCHOOLHOUSE: 1920s; double pinks, brown and tan tiny plaid, deep blue; brown/tan plaid and double pink schoolhouse blocks alternate with plain blue blocks, nine blocks by ten blocks; narrow blue border on sides; grid and straight-line quilting overall, 7 stitches per inch; unused, unwashed, several spots on back, few small spots on front; 66" × 78"; $575.

SCHOOLHOUSE: 1930s; blue, red, white; simple houses with two chimneys, empty windows and door, blue sashing between blocks, red binding; minimal outline quilting around houses, 6 stitches per inch; good assembly, good condition, with some overall color fade, slightly worn binding; 72" × 80"; $900.

SCHOOLHOUSES: 1870s; brown with tiny white print on white ground; five rows by eight rows of pattern blocks, each schoolhouse with two chimneys, one door, three windows, pea soup green border and sashing; from Kentucky; ocean wave quilting on border and sashing, 6 stitches per inch; good assembly, edges are mostly even, most corners match; good condition, slight overall color fade from multiple washing, few small stains in a few areas; 80" × 80"; $2,050.

TREE OF LIFE: 1920s; dark green and white; pattern blocks set on point with white blocks between; from Pennsylvania, maker known; outline quilting in pattern pieces, chevron and diamond grid quilting in white blocks, 8 stitches per inch; good assembly, most points match; excellent condition, never used or washed; 70" × 82"; $1,475.

UNNAMED (FAN) BASKETS: 1930s; pink, white, red, green, rose, purple, and multicolored period prints; six rows by eight rows of pattern blocks, set on point, with solid pink blocks between; baskets are pieced like fans, with pointed handles, each short row the same color combination, different from each other row; from Dallas, Texas; outline and floral quilting overall, 6 stitches per inch; excellent assembly; excellent condition, quilting lines remain; 72" × 90"; $325.

WATER GLASS/GOBLET: 1910–20; primarily tans, browns, various blues with some pink and gray; plaids, checks, stripes, prints; 30 goblet blocks in five rows by six rows, tan print fabric border; goblet blocks set on point so goblets stand upright, with plain tan print blocks between; from Texas; straight-line and diamond quilting overall, 4 stitches per inch; has been washed, some use, several spots and few stains in some areas; 64" × 75"; $225.

20 Patriotic, Political, and Historic

Patriotic and historic themes have long been a part of quiltmaking. When feelings of patriotism run high, during periods of crisis, or around national anniversaries, this trend becomes even stronger. Since the time after the Revolutionary War, fabric has been printed with the images of famous people and events. Quilts have been made that look like flags, and flags have been assembled into quilts. Political party ribbons have found their way into Crazy Quilts.

Just being red, white, and blue doesn't automatically put a quilt in this category, although it is a start. You should look for other clues, like stars, famous faces, and embroidery of slogans.

Certain patterns put a quilt into this category as well: Garfield's Monument, Washington's Choice and Mr. Roosevelt's Necktie fill the bill.

Commemorative quilts, such as those made to honor cancer victims or those who died in the September 11th attacks, can also fit into this category. For more information about all these types of quilts in appliqué, see Chapter 28: Political, Patriotic, and Commemorative.

FLAG QUILT: 1870s; white, red, blue solids; three rows of flag blocks by five rows of flag blocks, each flag block has seven red stripes and six white stripes and one eight point blue star on white background in upper left corner of the flag; three narrow borders of red, white, blue, with white binding and white backing, white sashing between the flag blocks, thin batting; from Iowa; good horizontal straight-line quilting overall, 6 stitches per inch; very good assembly; good condition, some slight color loss, some bleed from washing; 60" × 80"; $2,900.

NAVY STARS: 1930s; six rows by seven rows of large periwinkle-type stars of red and white diamonds, center blocks of dark blue solid; small golden yellow five-point stars embroidered in satin stitch in centers of solid blue blocks, narrow triple border of red, white, blue; outline quilting overall, large stitches, 4 stitches per inch; good condition, few slight stains; 52" × 73"; $525.

TAD LINCOLN'S SAILBOAT: 1920s; white, solid medium green, rusty red with tiny yellow flowers and green leaves print, yellow with tiny rusty red flowers and green leaves print; four rows by five rows of pattern blocks set square with green sashing between, yellow squares at set corners, white binding, pattern block sailboats are red print on white ground; from Oklahoma; cable quilting on sashing, outline in pattern blocks, mostly even stitches; very good assembly, most points and corners match; excellent condition; 70" × 88"; $800.

WHIG'S DEFEAT: 1920s; white, blue, red, multicolored period prints, predominantly reds and rose; five rows by five rows of pattern blocks, set square, on white ground with blue curved corners around the curved pieced sections, narrow red sashing and border, wide white border, blue sashing; outline quilting in the printed sections, small stars in blue corners, large concentric circles in white centers, small and even stitches; very good assembly, most corners match; very good condition, has been washed, some very slight color fade in blue; 72" × 72"; $625.

21 Stars and Wheels

Obviously, we've put these two categories together because they are so similar. They are so similar, in fact, that they add to our confusion, since some stars, like Blazing Stars, are considered wheels, and some wheels, like Pinwheel Star are really stars. The group includes fans, suns, and some other patterns, as well.

Stars, especially the eight-point star created from diamond-shaped pieces, have been popular in quilts since early Colonial times. Because they were more difficult to piece, with their odd angles, they were usually not attempted until a quilter had a few other patterns under her belt. Thus they were often considered "best" quilts, and were well cared for and carefully stored.

Star patterns can have any number of points, from four on up, but when you get to eight, you start to cross over into the realm of wheels. Stars can be made from diamonds, wedges, or triangles, but they can also be cut as one piece. Additionally, half or quarter stars can be used to make completely different patterns, like the lily or peony, which don't look like stars at all. *See illustration #59.*

The LeMoyne star, sometimes called the Lemon Star in a mispronunciation of its name, is the basis for many star patterns, including the Lone Star and the Star of Bethlehem, all of which have remained popular over time. Originally, Star Quilts were assembled from a dozen or more separate blocks; in the late 1800s the "whole top" variety came to be with one large star radiating from the center of the quilt.

Wheels are often a more complicated version of stars, in that they have more points or rays. There's a good chance that more points came about, at least in part, from competition between quilters who wanted to see who could fit the most onto a quilt block. The highest number of points we've seen is 24 on the inside ring of a Double Ring Wheel, which had an incredible 48 on the outside ring. The appliqué Dresden Plate, covered in Chapter 26 is actually a wheel.

59 A good example of a basic Four Point Star pattern, this crib or lap quilt was made in the 1940s, of scrap bag fabrics. As a summer coverlet, it is tied and not quilted. Quilt courtesy of the Belden Family.

Star Quilts

AUSTIN STAR VARIATION: 1930s; white, solid yellow and orange, blue print, stripe and plaid; six rows by six rows of pattern blocks, set on point, with white blocks between, wide orange border, white backing; diamond grid quilting on the border, floral medallions on the white blocks, 8 stitches per inch; very good assembly, most points and corners match; excellent condition; 82" × 82"; $400.

BLAZING STAR: 1860s; yellow/tan, white, double pink, several brown, blue, burgundy prints and checks; all center stars are double pink, with various prints half stars in the block corners, on white ground; pattern blocks are set on point with wide yellow/tan sashing between, very narrow yellow/tan and white sawtooth border, then yellow/tan border and binding; outline quilting in pattern blocks, triple cable quilting in sashing and border, very small stitches; excellent assembly; very good condition, slight overall color fade; 74" × 74"; $1,600.

BROKEN STAR: 1920s; solids of red, pale turquoise, golden yellow, pink on white ground; very narrow candy cane-stripe border of all the colors and white, very wide white border, red binding; from Pennsylvania; outline quilting on star pieces, feather wreath on white ground, feather cable on white border, very small and very even stitches; very good assembly, nearly all points and corners match; excellent condition; 77" × 77"; $1,095.

CARPENTER'S WHEEL: 1920s; red print and blue on white ground; blue backing and binding; outline quilting in block pieces, small medallions quilted in white areas between star pieces, small and even stitches; excellent assembly in difficult pattern; excellent condition, unwashed, unused, quilting lines remain; 80" × 84"; $975.

EIGHT-POINT STAR: 1880s; dark prints and dots in greens, gray, brown, red, wine purple; eight rows by nine rows of pattern blocks, set on point with gray print blocks between, backing is gray/black/blue print; 7½-inch pattern blocks have stars of above colors, on white ground; from Lancaster, Pennsylvania; outline quilting in the pattern blocks, square grid quilting in the plain blocks, 7 stitches per inch; very good assembly, most points and corners match; very good condition, unwashed and unused, some age spots in white areas; 88" × 95"; $950.

EIGHT-POINT STAR: 1900–10; white, double pink, yellow; stars are double pink on white ground, five rows by six rows of pattern blocks, set on point, with double pink blocks between; narrow yellow border, very wide pink border, printed green/white/black plaid backing; outline quilting on pattern blocks, diamond grid quilting on the border, small stitches; very good assembly, nearly all points and corners match; excellent condition; 76" × 86"; $625.

EVENING STAR: 1930s; white, blue and blue floral print; pattern blocks are blue print on white ground, four rows by four rows of pattern blocks, set on point with plain white blocks between, wide double border, solid blue and white; outline quilting in pattern blocks, cable on border, florals and other quilting in plain blocks and pattern block centers, 10 stitches per inch; excellent assembly; excellent condition, has been washed; 66" × 72"; $425.

EVENING STAR: 1930s; tan and blue solids; double border, blue then tan; tan sashing with blue squares in set corners; from Vermont; diamond and swirl quilting in center of stars, straight-line quilting over rest of the quilt; large stitches, 6 stitches per inch; unused, never washed; 62" × 73"; $500.

FEATHERED STAR VARIATION: 1860s; prints of reds, greens, double pinks; large square in center of stars of green print, sashing and border of same green print; straight-line quilting overall, large stitches, 6 stitches per inch; 78" × 78"; $600.

FEATHERED STAR: 1840s; rose red on white; triple border, rose, white, rose, white binding, white linen backing; excellent cable quilting on borders, outline in pattern blocks, 12 stitches per inch; excellent, near perfect assembly; good condition, slight overall color fade, few tiny stains in one area; 80" × 84"; $2,800.

FEATHERED STAR: 1840–60; cottons of blues, pinks, creams, reds, greens in prints, calicoes, plaids, stripes; four-star blocks by four-star blocks, triple sashing and borders of rose and green, with nine patch squares in the set corners; from Kentucky; heavy line and outline quilting overall; some slight color loss, fabric deterioration; few previous repairs; 93" × 94"; $9,500.

FEATHERED STAR: 1850s; prints, florals, dots in pink, purple, tan, red, green, many other colors; four rows by four rows of pattern blocks, multicolored pieces on tan print ground, set square; triple sashing and border, narrow red, green, red, with nine-patch red and green blocks at the set corners; from Kentucky; outline and straight-line quilting overall; very good assembly, nearly all corners and points match; fair to good condition, has had some repairs, needs additional for seam separation and splits; 94" × 94"; $9,500.

FEATHERED STAR: 1860s; red, green, yellow on white background; nine feather star blocks with white blocks between; red vine and flower appliqué around the border; wreath, feather, echo and straight-line quilting overall at 9 stitches per inch; 76" × 80"; $1,300.

FEATHERED STAR: 1880s; teal, red, white; four large pattern blocks with large eight-point teal feathered star, small eight-point red star in center of larger star, on white ground, set square, with red sashing between, narrow red, white, teal sawtooth border around group of four-stars, wide red border, red binding; from Ohio; excellent and even feather quilting on border, scalloped on sashing, diamond grid on pattern blocks, 10 stitches per inch; 82" × 82"; $3,075.

FEATHERED STAR: 1890s; blue and white; one large pattern block in center with wide double border, white, then blue; excellent outline and feather wreath quilting overall, 8 stitches per inch; excellent assembly; very good condition, few small discolorations, minimal use; 72" × 78"; $1,200.

FEATHERED STAR: 1890s; red on white; pattern blocks set on point with white blocks between, wide white border with red criss-cross pattern, red binding; feather wreath quilting in white blocks, diamond grid overall, 8 stitches per inch; excellent assembly; excellent condition, quilting lines remain; 78" × 90"; $2,825.

FEATHERED STAR: 1830s; solids of red, white green; 40 star blocks in red on white, green sashing and border; from North Carolina; outline and grid quilting overall, cable on border and sashing, small and even stitches; very good assembly in difficult pattern with very small triangles for feathering on star edges, nearly all points and corners match; good condition, some overall color fade, some small areas of disintegration in green; 78" × 84"; $5,000.

FOUR-POINT STARS: 1860, reworked in 1920; cottons, shirtings, multicolored in blues, browns, yellows, grays, prints and solids; 1920s backing, true scrap bag; from Kentucky; fair assembly; some discoloration, binding torn/worn, some seams separating; 64" × 76"; $350.

FOUR-POINT STARS: 1880–90; cottons of indigo, Turkey red, wine, white in checks, calicoes, stripes, plaid, prints; points of stars touch, creating light "explosions"; indigo print diamonds between stars; patriotic look; from Kentucky; fan quilting overall; very good condition; 70" × 80"; $3,550.

HIDDEN STARS VARIATION: 1880s; indigo blues, yellow, white; cottons/shirting, blue with tiny white prints, yellow with red and gold print, white with very thin blue line; wide yellow calico border, blue binding; straight-line echo quilting overall, 4 stitches per inch; very good assembly, most corners match; good condition, some areas of fading; 66" × 86"; $500.

HIDDEN STARS: 1880s; browns, reds, indigo, double pinks, many others in prints, solids, plaids, checks, stripes; hexagons are scrap bag multicolored, triangles that make the "stars" are all same double fabric creating very graphic optical illusion; double border, brown with cream print inner, double pink outer; from Tennessee; outline quilting overall; good assembly, most corners/points match; good condition, some overall color fade, age discoloration; 70" × 88"; $2,900.

HIDDEN STARS: late 1800s; cottons in reds, blues, browns, greens of prints, plaids, stripes, others; red with tiny white dots triangles form outside stars and border on sides; home dyed backing; from Kentucky; straight-line and criss-crossed line quilting, 8 stitches per inch; some minor color loss and change, few small holes; 72" × 90"; $2,950.

HIDDEN STARS: late 1800s; cottons in reds, browns, gold, grays, tans of prints, plaids, stripes, others; solid red triangles form outside stars; solid red and gold print border, home-dyed back-

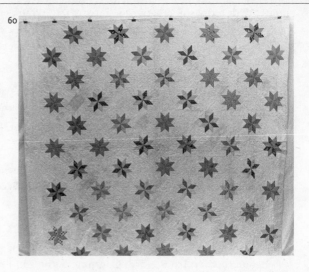

60 This classic LeMoyne Star quilt from the late 1800s shows excellent color balance overall and in the stars all while using scrap bag fabrics. The stars are set on point with white sashing and the quilt has an extra border on the chin edge. Quilt courtesy of the Dean Family.

ing; from Kentucky; straight-line and crossed line quilting, 7 stitches per inch; some staining and discoloration, few holes in backing, border fraying, some seam separation; 78" × 86"; $3,250.

LEMOYNE STAR: mid-1800s; tans, light browns, gray-browns cottons, with stripes, plaids, prints; individual star blocks set on point, between plain blocks; narrow, tan print binding; from Kentucky; overall outline quilting; good assembly, plaids a little uneven in some nonstar blocks, stripes in stars in uniform directions; fair to good condition for age, some fabric deterioration, top worn, some batting showing some repairs with other brighter colors, some discoloration; 72" × 74"; $1,150. *See illustration #60.*

LEMOYNE STAR: 1860–90; calicoes of blues, reds, grays, greens; stars pieced of scraps, set with red squares, olive sashing with red squares in corners of sets; olive prairie point border, home-dyed backing; from Kentucky; fan quilting overall; very good condition, few slight tears; 70" × 86"; $2,650.

LEMOYNE STAR: 1880s; red, white, blue; nine pattern blocks, red, white, and blue on white ground, set square with white sashing, white border; excellent assembly; very good condition, few tiny stains; 36" × 40"; $225.

LEMOYNE STAR: 1890s; blues, greens, white; outline quilting overall, 7 stitches per inch; fair condition, some seam separation, some old repairs in one area, binding worn, overall color loss and fading; 68" × 74"; $450.

LITTLE STAR: 1870s; pink on pink, yellow with tiny dark red dots print, white; four pattern blocks of pink and yellow prints diamonds, on white ground, wide white border, thin batting; from Pennsylvania; cable quilting on border, florals in white areas of pattern blocks, 8 stitches per inch; excellent assembly; good condition, some color fade in a few areas, few tiny spots, one small tear; 48" × 50"; $175.

LONE STAR, WHOLE TOP: 1920s; blues and pinks in solids, prints and florals; blue binding, backing, and wide border; from Massachusetts; outline quilting on star, diamond grid on ground and border, small and even stitches; very good assembly, nearly all points align, edges are even; good condition, some overall color fade, some small stains; 60" × 70"; $575.

LONE STAR, WHOLE TOP: 1940s; solids of tan, beige, gold, yellow on white ground; lots of very good quilting, line quilting across star, medallion and circular on white ground areas, small and even stitches; very good assembly, nearly all points match; very good condition, slight overall color fade from washing; 80" × 84"; $1,200.

LONE STAR: 1920; solids of primarily yellow, various others on white; pattern blocks alternate with plain white blocks, wide yellow border; outline quilting in pattern blocks, medallion quilting in plain blocks, 8 stitches per inch; good assembly, most points and corners match; good condition, slight overall color fade; 66" × 80"; $900.

LONE STAR: 1920–30; natural white background, diamonds that make up the large star in solids of dark red, mint green, yellow, medium blue, red-orange; very graphic, medium blue and yellow double border on top and bottom, medium blue borders on sides; from Kentucky; overall straight-line and outline quilting; very good assembly, nearly all points match; excellent condition with just some minor color loss; 70" × 78"; $1,800.

LONE STAR: 1870s; red, yellow, green solids on white; nine pattern blocks, three of each color on white ground, three rows by three rows, triple border, one of each color; outline and straight-line quilting overall, small and even stitches; good assembly, most points and corners match; very good condition, very slight overall color fade, few very small spots; 86" × 86"; $1,200.

OHIO STAR: 1860s; blue and white; blues are prints of tiny white stars, circles, or dots, binding is blue with tiny red and white flowers print; five rows by six rows of pattern blocks, set on point with plain white blocks between, narrow blue and white sawtooth border, very wide white border with appliquéd swags; some foreign matter felt in the batting; lots of excellent straight-line, triple straight-line, and medallion wreath quilting, 11 stitches per inch; excellent assembly; excellent condition, probably washed once; 77" × 92"; $1,950.

OHIO STAR: 1880s; dark red and white; six red on white pattern blocks, set on point with white block between, wide dark red border, dark red binding; outline and straight-line quilting overall, large stitches; good assembly, most edges straight, corners match; good condition, some wear to binding; 30" × 38"; $395.

OHIO STAR: 1910–20; dark blue on medium blue double dot calico, double pink, cheddar yellow with red double dots; five rows by six rows of pattern blocks with wide blue sashing and yellow squares at set corners; very thin batting, double border, double pink, blue on blue, with slightly scalloped edges; from Pennsylvania; straight-line quilting overall, cables in sashing and borders; 6 stitches per inch; good assembly, most corners and points match; good condition, unwashed, unused, one dark spot, several lighter spots in one area; 82" × 100"; $375.

OHIO STAR: 1920s; blues in solids and prints on white; solid blue border; outline quilting overall, 9 stitches per inch; excellent condition, unwashed, unused; 76" × 78"; $580.

OHIO STAR: 1920s; Turkey red and off-white; pattern blocks set square with off-white blocks between, forming seven rows of five pattern blocks and five white blocks; off-white and red borders on sides, white binding; from Texas; minimal quilting, circles in white blocks, crosses in pattern blocks, 7 stitches per inch; slight soiling along fold lines, few tiny, pale spots, minor yellowing in some white squares; 70" × 82"; $325.

OHIO STAR: 1930s; dark red and white; six rows by seven rows of star blocks, set on point, with white blocks between; double border, red inside, white outside, red binding; large flowers, circle quilting in white blocks, straight and outline quilting in pattern blocks, 6 stitches per inch; very good assembly; very good condition; 78" × 92"; $525.

PERIWINKLE/SNOWBALL: 1930s; white and multicolored period prints in pastels and brights; narrow blue border on two sides, blue backing and binding; outline quilting on stars, florals in the snowball centers, straight-line quilting overall, 5 stitches per inch; good assembly, most corners and edges match; excellent condition; 78" × 82"; $475.

PRAIRIE STAR: 1930s; pure white and scrap bag multicolored, with pinks, yellows, and lavender predominant; eight-point stars created by diamonds, each star with yellow center; row of three stars, by row of four-stars, side by side with points touching; wide border at top and bottom; three of the stars are well balanced color-wise, but others are haphazard, making whole quilt look somewhat disordered; white squares between star blocks quilted with large floral designs, outline quilting in star blocks, about 6 stitches per inch; good assembly, most points match, minor color bleed on back, probably from washing, some binding wear; 71" × 82"; $195.

RISING SUN: 1860s; bright green, cream, and brown, blue, and rose print; blocks consist of 14 print diamonds around print circle on cream background forming a larger circle, on a bright green square; cream sashing between each square; cotton seeds or other material can be seen and felt in the batting; feather, outline and other pattern quilting of large stitches, 6 stitches per inch; very good assembly, most points match; 84" × 88"; $1,100.

ROLLING STAR: 1920s; reds, browns in prints and designs, on white; each pattern block has different print on white ground, set square with red sashing and border; outline quilting on pattern blocks, diamond grid on border and sashing, 8 stitches per inch; good assembly, most corners match; good condition, overall color fade from washing, slight overall wear; 70" × 84"; $510.

ROLLING STAR: 1930s; red, green, white; pattern blocks set on point with white set blocks between, red border, and binding; close diamond grid quilting overall, straight-line quilting in the border, small and even stitches; excellent assembly, most points and corners match; fair condition, much overall fade and wear, much use and washing, binding very frayed; 84" × 92"; $425.

ROLLING STAR: 1930s; yellows, soft greens; from Missouri; excellent line quilting overall, 9 stitches per inch; excellent assembly in difficult pattern, all points and corners match; excellent condition, never used or washed, carefully stored; 64" × 76"; $700.

SEVEN SISTERS: 1850–80; gold, beige, tans, calicoes, and solid cottons, some indigo prints and solids; dark red borders on three sides, tan border on fourth side; nine "seven sister" groups with cream between groups; dark brown home-dyed backing; from Kentucky; large scallop quilting overall; good assembly, most points match; slight color loss, few small stains; 76" × 80"; $1,250.

SEVEN SISTERS: 1860–90; cotton and wools; reds, blues, blacks, grays, maroons calicoes, prints, solids; lavender/pink diamond sets between seven sister patches; dark indigo backing; from Kentucky; line quilting, large stitches; poor to fair assembly, many misshapen patches, and mismatched junctions; few tiny moth holes in wool patches; 76" × 83"; $1,250.

SEVEN STARS/SEVEN SISTERS: 1850–80; blues, grays, browns, solids and prints, all center stars of each group blues and gold/yellows, cream around and between each star and group, pink on pink rectangles around each group of six-point stars; pink on pink border; cotton fabrics, feed sack backing; from Kentucky; straight-line quilting, 8 stitches per inch; good assembly, most corners match in difficult to assemble pattern; some fading, few small stains, slight fraying on binding; 76" × 90"; $2,600.

STAR OF BETHLEHEM: 1910s; red solid, dark double pink print, pink with dark pink print, very pale pink with pink print, and background fabric of white with tiny blue print; half diamond border of all the pink/red fabrics, red binding; from New York/Pennsylvania; outline quilting in the diamonds that form the star, grid quilting overall around the star, 9 stitches per inch; good assembly, though many points don't match; minimal washing, barely used, few faint spots in several areas; 81" × 81"; $500.

STAR OF BETHLEHEM: 1920s; burgundy, blues; lots of straight-line and outline quilting overall, even stitches, 9 stitches per inch; excellent assembly, all matched corners and points; good condition, slight color fade, unused, minimal washing; 50" × 82"; $950.

STAR OF BETHLEHEM: 1920s; white, cream, cheddar yellow, blue, red, teal solids, with one yellow print, and one double pink print; border of five narrow strips, teal, white, yellow, white, red at top and bottom; narrow red border on sides; diamond grid quilting overall, outline quilting in diamonds that form the star; very good assembly, nearly all points match; excellent condition, has been washed, few tiny spots in one area; 73" × 81"; $600.

STAR OF BETHLEHEM: 1930s; solids of lavender, peach, yellow, green on lavender ground; outline quilting in star pieces, square grid quilting on ground, very small, even stitches; excellent assembly, excellent condition; 80" × 88"; $1,900.

SUNRAY'S STAR WITH FANS: 1930s; white, yellow, multiple pastel solids; one eight-point star, yellow on white, fills center of quilt, with five Mohawk trail fan sets, one in center, one at each of four corners of the star; double border, one yellow, one wide white, scalloped edge, yellow binding; outline, straight-line, clamshell, floral quilting overall, 5 stitches per inch; excellent assembly; excellent condition; 76" × 84"; $495.

TEXAS STAR: 1930s; cottons of yellow, pale yellow, yellow-gold, gold, and dark gold solids on white background; triple border, narrow yellow, white with a row of diamonds as compose the star in all the yellows/golds, narrow gold; fourth border, narrow in gold on sides only, yellow binding; from Texas; diamond grid and outline quilting overall, well executed, small stitches, 10 per inch; very good assembly; excellent condition, has been washed at least once, with very slight color bleed to white background; 72" × 77"; $600.

VARIABLE STAR: 1930s; green and brown solids, multiple prints, primarily greens; circle quilting overall, 7 stitches per inch; good assembly, most points match; excellent condition, unused, minimal washing; 68" × 72"; $750.

VARIABLE STAR: 1930s; green and brown solids, multiple prints, primarily greens; circle quilting overall, 7 stitches per inch; good assembly, most points match; excellent condition, unused, minimal washing; 68" × 72"; $750.

WINGED STAR: 1930s; white, pink, green, and yellow solids; pink, green, yellow pattern blocks are set square with wide white sashing, with embroidered flower wreaths at set corners, white border and binding; outline and floral quilting, 11 stitches per inch; excellent assembly; excellent condition; 72" × 74"; $395.

Wheels and Such

ART DECO TYPE FANS: late 1800s; dark red and white; narrow white sashing with red squares at set corners, narrow red border, wider white border; could also be considered a curved four-patch with sashing, or a nine-patch with small center block, no sashing; curved and straight-line quilting overall, 6 stitches per inch; excellent assembly; excellent condition; 62" × 78"; $450.

CHIPS AND WHETSTONES VARIATION: 1840s; yellow on white print, pinks, blues, tans, browns, others in florals, prints, stripes, plaids; seven rows by eight rows of pattern blocks on yellow print ground; from Massachusetts; outline and straight-line quilting overall, very small and even stitches; very good assembly, nearly all points and corners match; excellent condition; 80" × 94"; $2,900.

CROWN OF THORNS VARIATION: 1850s; white, gold solid, rusty red and green, both with tiny dot print; pattern blocks and sashing on white ground, dark blue binding; from Georgia; extensive outline and outline echo quilting, small even stitches; good assembly in intricate patterns, most points and corners match; very good condition, minimal washing, few small stains, one small tear; 84" × 100"; $22,500.

FANS: 1930–40; green and mustard gold solids and various multicolored prints, stripes, checks, plaids, others in blues, greens, reds, many others; fans in multicolored and multipatterned pieces with mustard gold background and green centers; from Texas; straight- and curved-line quilting overall, 6 stitches per inch; unused, unwashed; 72" × 81"; $375.

GRANDMOTHER'S FANS IN PATHS: 1930; multicolored and rose on white; center of fan ("handle") is solid rose fabric, fan "slats" are multicolored fabrics in every pattern and print; fans blocks arranged around plain white to form paths, white sashing, rows of fans along the edges of the quilt; outline, floral, feather wreath quilting, 9 stitches per inch; fair to good assembly, many corners/points don't match, but arrangement is unique; good condition, some overall color fade, some washing; 72" × 88"; $500.

HANDS ALL 'ROUND VARIATION: 1930s; solid pink, blue, lavender on white; three rows by four rows of pattern blocks, set on point with white blocks between, narrow triple border on sides, pink, white, blue; narrow quadruple border on top and bottom, pink, white, blue, white; blue binding, very thin batting, white backing; excellent and expert crisscross, outline and grid quilting overall, feather wreath quilting in the plain white blocks; excellent assembly; unused, unwashed, few tiny spots in one area; 78" × 95"; $650.

HANDS ALL 'ROUND: 1880s; Turkey red on white; pattern blocks set square with red sashing and border; from Pennsylvania; straight-line quilting overall, uneven and awkward stitches; fair to good assembly, many pieces misaligned, fabric puckers, mismatched points; very good condition, unwashed and unused, few tiny spots that look like mildew; 82" × 82"; $1,000.

HARVEST SUN: 1860s; white, yellow with red print, red with yellow print, green with blue print; pattern blocks have yellow sun with yellow and red rays that alternate with white rays; pattern blocks set on point with white blocks between, green sashing, green border and binding; from Rhode Island; outline quilting on pattern blocks, diamond grid on sashing and border, feather wreaths in white blocks, small and even stitches; very good assembly, most corners match; good condition, some slight overall color fade, has been washed and used; 80" × 96"; $985.

MARINER'S COMPASS: 1900–10; light blue with tiny black print, cranberry, camel tan, white; six rows by seven rows of pattern blocks, compass centers of white with blue, tan and cranberry rays on white ground, narrow white border, white binding, very heavy batting; from Connecticut; outline quilting on compasses, echo circles around them, 8 stitches per inch, very even; excellent assembly; excellent condition, unused; 80" × 84"; $890.

MARINER'S COMPASS: 1930s; white and peach solid; peach compasses on white, three rows by three rows, large areas of white between; narrow peach and white sawtooth border, wide white border, peach binding; grid, feather and curved line quilting through and around compasses, grid and florals on white border, 7 stitches per inch; good assembly, neat points; large areas of fading overall, washed many times, faint stains in several places; 78" × 80"; $300.

NOONDAY VARIATION: 1860s; reddish brown twelve point "suns" on white with tiny brown print, on reddish brown ground; white with tiny black bows print binding, border, and sashing, brown gingham check backing; three rows by three rows of pattern blocks; from New England; concentric circles quilting in suns, square grid quilting overall, chevron in border, small and even stitches; excellent assembly; excellent condition; 75" × 76"; $1,095.

NOSEGAY QUILT: 1940s/1990s; green, pink, yellow, lavender, cream white; each nosegay with six points of different print fabric, with five small black points behind, four nosegay blocks, set on point so nosegays stand upright; cream white blocks and half blocks around the nosegay blocks, medium/wide multicolored floral print border, medium/wide green print border; 1940s top, quilted recently; from Tennessee; floral pattern quilting in cream white blocks, straight-line quilting on borders, 7 stitches per inch; excellent assembly, points and corners match; top maker was probably more skilled than quilter; excellent condition; 36" × 36"; $400.

WHIRLING FANS: 1930s; white, primarily blues, pinks, other multicolored period prints, designs, checks, and stripes; pieced fans in both corners of the pattern block, on white ground, pink border; from Pennsylvania; outline and pattern quilting, small and even stitches; good assembly, most corners match; good condition, binding separated from quilt in one area, has been washed; 62" × 80"; $495.

22 Samplers, Albums, and Friendship

The quilts in this chapter are grouped together, not in the specific blocks used to make them, but in how they were made. Friendship quilts were made by groups of people, with each one making a particular block, or with one or more people signing a block. This kind of activity started in New England and the eastern part of the country in the 1840s, and was inspired by the album books that were popular at the time.

Guests who came to a home would write in a blank book, often drawing pictures, writing poems, or offering advice or condolences. Early friendship quilts sometimes had poems or Scripture verses written on them, but as time went on, the idea was to simply sign the blocks, which were usually of the same pattern, although made by different quilters. A variation would be for one quiltmaker to do all the blocks and then have her friends or others sign the blocks. Certain patterns, such as the Chimney Sweep, were often used because the amount and size of the white pieces on them made a perfect canvas for signatures.

When a quilt had every block different, it became an Album Quilt; these could be used as friendship quilts, or they could be simply a way for a quilter to learn how to make different blocks, thus creating a sampler.

Around the U.S. Centennial, album quilts became a 20-year craze, in the form of Baltimore Album quilts. Many of the blocks were appliqué, although piecework and appliqué were freely mixed, and the quilts got just as elaborate as the Victorian Crazy Quilts, as quilters tried more and more difficult quilt patterns. More than 200 Baltimore Album Quilts have been documented, and they are highly prized. Many are in museums and private collections, but it is believed that there are many more tucked away in family trunks and closets.

Over time, Friendship-style quilts were used as fund-raising items, in which a person's name would be written or embroidered on the quilt for a fee. The quilt was then raffled off, to raise more money for the cause, be it library books, church restorations or military memorials. This kind of fund raising activity still goes on today.

CRAZY QUILT SAMPLER: 1909; multicolored wools, worsteds and flannels; mostly solid colors, some stripes, a few prints; six rows by six rows of approximately 10-inch squares, 12 of the 36 squares are fans, four-patch, or nine-patch pieced blocks, the other 24 squares are typical crazy quilt blocks; plaid flannel border, feather-stitch embroidery topstitching over every seam, within blocks, and where blocks join, names embroidered in one block, dated in one block; good assembly, most corners and junctions match; excellent condition; 68" × 74"; $1,500.

FRIENDSHIP SQUARES: 1938; medium blue and cream; seven rows by seven rows of squares, each square approximately nine-inch square, alternating blue squares with cream squares; nine-inch wide cream border, blue binding, cream backing, blocks embroidered with names, date, flowers, hearts, other figures; from Indiana; straight-line, crisscross quilting overall, 8 stitches per inch; excellent assembly; good condition, minimal use, minimal washing, some aging stains in a few areas, small tear in binding; 82" × 82"; $850.

PATTERN SAMPLER: 1880s; white, reds, blues, browns, double pinks in prints and patterns; 15 different pattern blocks, including Jacob's Ladder, Tree of Life, Ohio Star, and Ocean Waves each in a predominant color and white; straight-line quilting overall, 4 stitches per inch; fair assembly, probably made by a child, patterns are interesting, but piecing is awkward; fair condition, tear in one place on backing, overall color fade, fabric deterioration, especially in browns; 37" × 45"; $595.

PATTERN SAMPLER: 1930s; multicolored solids and prints on white ground; 30 different pattern blocks, including Monkey Wrench, Bear's Paw, Dresden Plate, Mariner's Compass, and Basket; 12 blocks make center rectangle, with green print sashing around, rest of blocks are around outside with green sashing between and green border; minimal outline quilting, 4 stitches per inch; fair to good assembly, several blocks and sashing are misaligned; excellent condition; 66" × 82"; $575.

SAILBOAT QUILT: 1939; sea green, blue on white; five rows by six rows of pattern blocks, sea green sails and boat, blue ocean on white ground, set square with white blocks between, narrow sea green sashing; friendship or fund-raiser quilt, signed and dated in embroidery; outline and straight-line quilting overall, small and even stitches; excellent assembly; good condition, slight overall color fade, binding slightly worn; 72" × 88"; $800.

SAMPLER: 1930s; depression green, and multicolored prints and solids; 30 different pieced blocks, such as Drunkard's Path, Bear's Paw, Basket, Double-Nine Patch, Monkey Wrench; depression green sashing and border; straight and outline quilting overall, 4 stitches per inch; fair to good assembly, most points match, few edges uneven; good condition, minimal washing or use, some overall color fade; 66" × 82"; $575.

23 **Tops and Blocks**

A quilt that hasn't yet gotten its sandwich filling is, of course, a quilt top. We don't know why the maker never quilted it—maybe like one of the Authors, she loved to piece much more than to quilt—but the the unfinished top may leave a wonderful find for the collector.

There are definite advantages in buying a top. Since it was never quilted, a top was probably never used in any way, and was stored in some fairly safe place, so it will be in excellent condition. It may be such a wonderful pattern or have perfect colors that the owner held onto it instead of turning it into rags, so the collector may get a much more interesting quilt for less money. And you can see the assembly, the fabric, and the condition without having batting and backing in the way.

If you're a quilter, you'll have the pleasure of finishing an antique quilt by adding something of yourself. If you're not a quilter, there are plenty of individuals and shops that do lovely quilting for not too much cost. Either way you have the option of getting the amount and kind of quilting you want.

Or, if you just love the design and/or colors of a quilt top, you can leave it unfinished and hang it on the wall—a very contemporary form of decorating!

Most quilt dealers carry tops and will watch for them if you express interest. A dealer will almost always know where you can have a top quilted as well, and may be able to arrange this for you.

Unassembled blocks are also available from many dealers, and can be a wonderful find. They are generally of more interest to quilters, who enjoy assembling them and then doing the quilting, but they're also useful framed like a picture, or as little wall hangings. Look around, an unfinished treasure may be just around the corner.

61

61A

61 This unfinished top was folded to display both the front and back. It's a stunning visual quilt with the solid patches a deep, pure red which punches up the effect of the calico prints used.

61A The front of the quilt does little to inform us of the assembly techniques or their quality. From the front we see that the points match. From the back, in this close up, we see that some of the blocks were assembled with hand stitching and some were put together using a sewing machine. It suggests that this was a two generation quilt, that it was started by one quiltmaker and finished by another. The mystery is why this beautiful top was never quilted. For a fact, there will be at least one other quiltmaker to work on this top. Now that the top has been photographed and documented, the authors intend to complete it. Top from the authors' collection.

Tops

AT THE DEPOT/CRISSCROSS: 1900–10; red, white, blue; pattern blocks of several indigo with white and white with black calicoes in dots, stripes, plaids; five rows by six rows of pattern blocks with narrow red sashing between, wide red border; machine pieced, good assembly, most corners match; 70" × 80"; $195. *See illustrations #61 and #61A.*

BARN RAISING LOG CABIN: 1880s; lights are yellows and pinks in prints and florals, darks are dark red and dark blue prints; excellent assembly; excellent condition; 70" × 80"; $185.

BARRISTER'S BLOCK: 1920s; Turkey red and cream white; fair to good assembly, many points, some corners don't match; fair to good condition, water/age stains overall, small tear on one edge; 37" × 51"; $110.

BEAR'S PAW: dated 1851; fine cotton rust print and cream/natural solid; pattern blocks set straight with cream/natural sashing, set point/corners, and narrow border; from Florida; some color deterioration in rusts; 94" × 102"; $800.

BLAZING STAR/PRAIRIE STAR: 1860–80; large eight-point center star fabricated of 44 rows of diamonds in reds, wine, navy, white, on white background; from Kentucky; very good assembly; some staining in folds, some discolorations, few mildew stains; 65" × 80"; $650.

BRICK WALL/STREAK O' LIGHTNING: 1910–20; blacks, reds, blues, tans, creams, whites, grays in many prints; from Indiana; machine pieced, very good assembly, most edges even; excellent condition; 72" × 82"; $100.

BROKEN SASH VARIATION: late 1800s; cottons in prints, stripes, checks, and solids of deep reds, blues, navy, browns, with pink, tans, cream; navy sashing with tan check squares at the set points; navy border on sides, blue polka dot border on top and bottom; from Kentucky; both hand and machine pieced; some minor color loss and changes; 68" × 89"; $350.

BROKEN STAR: 1930s; yellows, pinks, multicolored bolds and pastels in prints and designs; excellent assembly; very good condition, needs washing for overall dustiness; 90" × 108"; $125.

CHIMNEY SWEEP: 1880s; primarily blues and reds; dark blue with tiny white and blue dots print, white with various color prints, many other color prints; three-patch pattern blocks are set on point with dark blue print blocks between; machine pieced, excellent assembly; excellent condition; 84" × 94"; $200.

CIRCULAR SAW: 1930s; rose red, rose pink, and cream white; two rose colors are slightly different shades; five rows by five rows of rose on white pattern blocks, set square with rose sashing between; from Texas; excellent assembly in difficult pattern; very good condition, few small spots; 72" × 76"; $125.

COLUMBIA STAR/TUMBLING BLOCKS VARIATION, POSTAGE STAMP: late 1800s; prints, calicoes, solids, plaids in reds, blues, and nearly every other color possible; three pale gray and white striped diamonds in tumbling block configuration between six-point stars; pointed edge created by star edges on both sides; from Kentucky; 66" × 84"; $700.

CRAZY QUILT: 1880s; multicolored dark and light silks and velvets, in 25 blocks joined five rows by five rows, with lots of multicolored and multipatterned embroidery on seams; narrow double border of plaid silk ribbon and black velvet; poor condition, lots of shattered and split silks, deteriorating velvets; 72" × 72"; $50.

CRAZY QUILT: 1888; multicolor in velvets, satins, silks; many inclusions, extensive embroidery of flowers, figures, animals, flags; extensive topstitching in dozens of colors; narrow black velvet sashing; signed and dated; some minor fabric fractures, otherwise excellent condition; 62" × 88"; $1,000.

CRAZY QUILT: 1890s; ribbons, velvets, satins, silk in burgundy, black, blue, brown, other darks; yellow herringbone and blanket-stitch embroidery on seams, looks like it was done as the pieces were added; very good assembly, seems balanced; fair to good condition, some areas of slight wear, many fabrics have shattered and disintegrated; 54" × 70"; $225.

CRAZY QUILT: 1900–10; silk and velvet fabrics in reds, browns, blacks, pink, burgundy, blues, greens, gold, purples and many others; detailed, extensive, multicolored embroidery stitches over pieces' seams; embroidered figures, flowers, leaves, many other items in blocks; from Ohio; excellent assembly and stitching; no backing or binding; some fabric deterioration, fractures; 58" × 58"; $4,000.

CRAZY QUILT: early 1900s; cottons, wools, silks in classic darks and lights, reds, blacks, blues; various styles of embroidery over seams, many embroidered figures, flowers, initials in the blocks; from Kentucky; some silks fractured, a few holes in other fabrics; 64" × 72"; $450.

CRAZY QUILT: late 1800s; all silks in turquoise blue, other blues, darks; 25 individualized crazy blocks joined together, herringbone embroidery stitches on pieces and block seams, in bright yellow, orange, pink; from California; good assembly, well pieced, even and creative embroidery; excellent condition; 65" × 65"; $750.

CRAZY QUILT: mid-1800s; wools of black, olive, dark red, tan; six rows by seven rows of pieced "crazy" blocks, on foundation fabric of black and white print; from Kentucky; simple blocks with five pieces or fewer, but lots of exquisite and varied topstitch embroidery on blocks and the seams between blocks, lots of colors of thread; excellent condition; 77" × 80"; $4,500.

DIAMOND IN THE SQUARE: 1890–1910; tan and gray on white shirting print, cream, white, various browns and tans, dark blue, red in prints, checks, plaids; pattern blocks set on point with plain blocks of tan and gray on white shirting print between; good assembly, most corners and points matched and even; fabric in good condition, but with many water spots and stains overall; 78" × 75"; $145.

DIAMONDS: 1930–40; cottons of reds, greens, blues, grays, many others; 22 straight horizontal rows of diamonds, each row of same fabric; from Kentucky; slightly uneven assembly; double bed size; $200.

DOUBLE IRISH CHAIN: 1880s; green on green print, rust with tiny cream and green print, on cream ground; green border on two sides; excellent assembly, nearly all corners match; good condition, some soiling and few small stains, some splotchy color fade; 88" × 100"; $325.

DOUBLE IRISH CHAIN: 1930s; white, rose/red chain centers, blue/violet chain sides; triple border, blue, rose, blue with small nine-patch of same colors in each corner; machine pieced, good assembly, except that squares are in the wrong color order in one section; good condition, few light spots; 76" × 86"; $160.

DOUBLE IRISH CHAIN: 1940; cottons of blue and natural white; double border, blue and natural white; set on point, making "chains" vertical and horizontal; from Ohio; excellent assembly, marked for quilting; small discoloration, may wash out; 79" × 92"; $300.

DOUBLE T: 1940s; red and white; pattern blocks set on point with red squares between, red border; excellent assembly, nearly all corners match, edges are flat; excellent condition; 54" × 54"; $125.

DOUBLE WEDDING RING: 1940s; white, multicolored period prints and florals; sides are scalloped, following the ring edges; very good assembly, machine pieced; very good condition, few stains; 62" × 84"; $300.

DOVE IN THE WINDOW: 1930s; yellow and white solids, blues in prints, stripes, solids, reds in solids, prints; five rows by four rows of pattern blocks, set straight with white diamonds around the red and blue doves, on plain yellow ground; from Texas; excellent assembly and color coordination in unusual block; very good condition, few tiny spots; 64" × 78"; $145.

EVENING STAR: mid-1800s; cottons in solids, plaids, checks, and stripes of reds, greens, tans, indigo; set on point with solid green blocks between, narrow green border on sides, double tan and green border on top and bottom; maker known, from Kentucky; excellent assembly; some age discoloration, few small holes, some seam separation; 64" × 78"; $700.

EVENING STAR: early 1900s; cottons in solids and prints of grays, reds, blues, and many others; lavender squares set between pattern blocks, narrow lavender border; from Pennsylvania; several stains and discolorations, some may wash out; 70" × 82"; $200.

FIVE CROSSES: 1850–70; cottons in prints, checks, plaids, solids, calico of reds, browns, navy, greens, many others; green sashing and narrow border, with Turkey red squares at set corners; from South Carolina; good assembly, most corners and points match in this complicated pattern; some discoloration and color loss/change, especially in browns; 74" × 77"; $650.

FLYFOOT: 1890s; prints, checks, plaids in reds, blues, solids of navy, gold, lavender, red; pink print sashing with tan calico squares at set corners; from Kentucky; hand and machine pieced; prominent water stain, may come out with cleaning; 70" × 88"; $200.

GRANDMOTHER'S FLOWER GARDEN, POSTAGE STAMP: 1850s; cottons in prints, dots, stripes of reds, rust, browns, some others; rust red paths between gardens; hundreds of one-inch hexagons, with paper backing/pattern intact; scalloped edges from gardens on sides; Florida; some seam separation, some frays and tears; 80" × 92"; $2,800.

HEXAGON CHARM: 1920s; multicolored, four inch hexagons, no two of same fabric; excellent condition, excellent assembly; few small stains in two areas; 80" × 84"; $175.

JACOB'S LADDER VARIATION: 1930s; very sturdy fabrics of purple, teal green, golden yellow solids; machine pieced, very good assembly, most corners match; fair condition, one two-inch hole, several other small holes, has been washed; 60" × 74"; $30.

LEMON STAR: 1880s; stars are four diamonds of red with white spots print, alternating with four diamonds of green with tiny yellow floral print, on white ground; dark pink on pink border on one side, six rows by seven rows of star blocks with dark pink on pink sashing between; from Pennsylvania; good assembly, some corners and points don't match; good condition, several small spots; 76" × 76"; $150.

LE MOYNE STAR: 1870s; tan, several blue prints; pattern blocks are blue stars on tan ground, set square with tan blocks between; excellent assembly; good condition, some of the fabrics are deteriorating in the print, several are stiff from age; 90" × 90"; $375.

LE MOYNE STAR: 1920s; green print, double pink, multicolored period prints, plaids, stripes, patterns, florals, checks; four rows by five rows of pattern blocks, with stars and ground of many colors and prints, etc., set square, with green sashing, and double pink squares at the set corners; machine pieced, fair to good assembly, many points are mismatched, some uneven edges; excellent condition; 61" × 76"; $285.

LE MOYNE STAR: 1920s; multicolored period prints, white; black featherstitch embroidery around the stars; excellent assembly; very good condition; 68" × 68"; $95.

MAGNOLIA (MAPLE) LEAF: 1890–1910; black with tiny leaf green geometric print, white with tiny black dots; five rows by six rows of pattern blocks, set on point with white blocks between; double border, narrow black with green, medium wide white; from Indiana; hand and machine pieced, excellent assembly; very good condition, few faint spots; 76" × 88"; $125.

MONKEY WRENCH: 1930s; solid yellow, red with tiny white and blue flower print; five rows by six rows of pattern block, narrow yellow border; fair to good assembly, many pattern blocks edges and corners misaligned; excellent condition; 80" × 95"; $90.

NEW CROSS AND CROWN VARIATION: 1890–10; shirtings of white with tiny blue stars, red with dot and squiggle print or white stripe, blue with tiny dot and line print; five rows by four rows of pattern blocks, set square, with white sashing between, and four-patch x-cross in set corners; hand and machine pieced, very good assembly, most points and corners match; very good condition, few tiny spots; 75" × 92"; $175.

NINE PATCH BARS: 1880s; reds, yellows, blues, browns in prints, patterns, dots, stripes; seven pattern blocks per bar, five bars with wide red sashing between, red border; hand and machine pieced; excellent condition; 70" × 78"; $225.

NINE-PATCH: 1890s; browns, tans, blues, creams, dark pink on pink in patterns, plaids, prints, checks, stripes; six rows by seven rows of pattern blocks, set square with tan and brown patterned sashing between, wide dark pink border; good assembly, most corners match; excellent condition; 73" × 84"; $175.

NINE-PATCH: 1900–10; dark pink on pink, black with tiny cream print, yellow with tiny red print, several pale striped shirtings, red with tiny cream dots print; five rows by six rows of pattern blocks with black sashing and yellow squares at the set corners; wide red border; from Pennsylvania; good assembly; unwashed, a few spots and water stains; 72" × 83"; $150.

OCEAN WAVES: 1930s; multicolored prints and solids "waves" blocks set around plain muslin; from Texas; fair to good assembly, many points, some corners don't match; good condition, one section has bleach or fade area; 72" × 86"; $150.

OLD SNOWFLAKE: 1930s; cottons in solids and prints of reds, greens, yellow, blues, many others; pink border and sashing with white and green hourglass squares in the set corners; from Maryland; some minor color loss and discoloration; somewhat misshapen, needs straightening; 80" × 88"; $200.

PICKLE DISH VARIATION OF DOUBLE WEDDING RING: 1930s; green, rusty/red, rose pink solids, several multicolored prints; plain rusty/red squares in ring corners; solid green centers in rings, narrow double border, green inner, rusty/red outer; good assembly, most corners match, although several ring edges are wavy; good condition, two areas repaired with same green fabric by appliqué; 68" × 84"; $160.

PINEAPPLE LOG CABIN: 1920–30; cottons and cotton feed sacks primarily of pastel blues, pinks, greens in prints as the darks, natural white sacking as the lights; five squares with darks actually dark red or blue; from Kentucky; good assembly; minor color loss, has been washed; 72" × 82"; $250.

PINWHEEL STAR: 1920s; medium blue solid, double pink print; three rows by four rows of pattern blocks, blue stars on pink ground, with blue sashing between, blue stars on pink in set corners; very wide pink border on two sides, very narrow pink border on other two sides; from Indiana; hand and machine pieced; fair to good assembly, some points and corners mismatched; good condition, few spots; 72" × 86"; $150.

RAILROAD CROSSING: 1930s; rose pink with pattern blocks in multicolored scrap bag fabrics, some feed bags; pattern blocks set square so "tracks" cross the quilt top diagonally, plain rose pink solid blocks alternate with pattern blocks; found in New Mexico; both hand and machine pieced, fair to good assembly, most corners match, but many "tracks" are misshapen; excellent condition, no color changes or fold lines; 72" × 86"; $110.

ROB PETER TO PAY PAUL: 1930s; medium blue and ivory; medium-wide blue border on one side; fair assembly, many corners and edges don't match; very good condition, few tiny spots; 68" × 78"; $125.

SEVEN SISTERS, POSTAGE STAMP: early 1900s; cottons of bright and pastel prints, solids, checks, plaids; bright red center star in each group, lavender background; from Kentucky; tiny pieces, excellent assembly; some discoloration; 66" × 84"; $900.

SHOO-FLY: late 1800s; cotton, two double pink prints and natural white; pattern blocks set with plain blocks between; from Pennsylvania; minor discoloration, may wash out, some seam separation, few small holes; 62" × 68"; $250.

SKYROCKET: 1930s; red, white, blue, purple print; five rows by five rows of pattern blocks, set square with purple print sashing between, colors work and balance well; fair assembly, many puckered piece edges, many points don't match; excellent condition; 72" × 72"; $200.

SLANTED DIAMONDS: 1900; cottons of creams, light and dark blues, grays, tans, pink, brown, many others in checks, stripes, dots, prints; blocks set square alternating with blocks of cream with small brown dots; from Vermont; fair assembly with some stretching of blocks, some corners unmatched; 80" × 82"; $195.

SNAIL'S TRAIL: 1950s; cottons and cotton blends in blues, greens, brown, few different whites; from Kentucky; few small holes, some discoloration; 76" × 86"; $200.

STARS AND STRIPES/MOUNTAIN STAR VARIATION: 1930s; solid yellow, green, multi-colored period prints; four rows by four rows of pattern blocks, yellow ground; stripes are very thin strips of various prints, outside stripe on each "wedge" solid green, medium-wide yellow border; foundation pieced, good assembly in difficult pattern, though many edges and stripes don't match; excellent condition; 72" × 72"; $175.

SUNSHINE AND SHADOWS LOG CABIN: late 1800s; cottons solids of brown and red darks, green and yellow lights; double border, red and brown; from Kentucky; good assembly; 76" × 86"; $350.

SWING IN THE CENTER: 1860s; cotton prints and checks in blues, grays, some black, some double pink; pattern squares set straight with solid gray squares between; from Kentucky; a few holes, some staining in folds, and age discoloration; 65" × 93"; $350.

TEXAS STAR: 1890s; dark blue with tiny white stars, white with tiny black dots, white; five rows by six rows of pattern blocks with white sashing between, white fabric has glue and paper labels attached, and manufacturer's name stenciled in one spot; fair assembly, hand and machine, sashing misaligned, many corners and edges don't match; fair condition, unwashed, one water stain in one section; 68" × 80"; $160.

THOUSANDS OF TRIANGLES, POSTAGE STAMP: 1880s; lights and darks of burgundy, grays, blues, greens, pink, black, many others in stripes, prints, dots, plaids, checks, solids; very good assembly in hand piecing; good condition, probably never washed; 82" × 86"; $200.

TRIP AROUND THE WORLD, POSTAGE STAMP: 1930–50; cottons in plaids, checks, some prints, primarily in blues, greens, grays, with some yellow, tans, pink, other colors; thousands of tiny squares; from Kentucky; very well assembled, nearly all corners match; overall soiling, needs cleaning, few small holes; 72" × 85"; $300.

TRIP AROUND THE WORLD: 1930s; sequential rows of diamonds, yellow, green, purple, lavender, teal, with five borders in same colors and order; rows start around three center diamonds, which makes whole top rectangular; excellent assembly; very good condition, one tiny spot on one edge; 82" × 102"; $185.

TRIPLE IRISH CHAIN: 1930s: center chain pink, yellow chain on each side of that, red chain on each side/outside of that, all solids, on white; hand and machine pieced, excellent assembly; very good condition, one tiny spot; 69" × 86"; $85.

TWISTED ROPE: 1930s; solid green, purple on white ground; one side unraveling, seams separating; very good assembly; very good condition; 54" × 70"; $75.

62 This is another sampling of quilt blocks available on the market. The strip of nine-patches on the left were found with three other strips never assembled. Blocks from the authors' collection.

WATERWHEEL: 1930s; cream, brown, tan, beige, burgundy solids, multicolored prints; 9 rows by 11 rows of pattern blocks, set on point, with plain cream solid blocks between, pattern blocks in each row are mostly the same color scheme; good assembly, most corners and points match; excellent condition; 64" × 82"; $110.

WEDDING RING: 1920s; cream white, rose pink, and yellow/orange solids, with black, dark green, and other darks in prints and plaids; rose pink sashing with yellow/orange squares at the set corners; pattern blocks are all print or plaid and cream white; machine pieced, excellent assembly; excellent condition, no soiling or stains; 64" × 82"; $125. *See illustration #62.*

Blocks

BOWTIE: 1910–20; 60 seven inch blocks in prints, stripes, checks, plaids in predominantly reds, blues, yellows; excellent assembly; excellent condition; $75.

CHECKERBOARD SQUARE POSTAGE STAMP: 1950s; bright solids of brown, purple, blues, reds, greens, pinks, yellows and prints, checks, florals of multicolored brights and pastels; 41 one-inch pieces, set on point, per block, with excellent color coordination in each block; excellent assembly; excellent condition; $95.

CRAZY QUILT SQUARE: 1890s; multi darks, black, blue, burgundy in silks and velvets; herringbone, zigzag, and rows of diamonds topstitching around each piece, silk fringe edging; good assembly, fair to good embroidery; excellent condition; 22" × 22"; $95.

NINE-PATCH CHECKERBOARD: 1890s; 42 identical 7½-inch blocks of pink and cream floral on dark brown, with solid cream/white; very good assembly, most points and corners match, was a top, was taken apart; good condition, some have a few spots; $90.

NINE-PATCH CHECKERBOARD: 1900–10; 30 9½-inch blocks of solids, prints, stripes, and checks primarily in blues, burgundy, grays, blacks; some hand pieced, some machine pieced; very good assembly, most points and corners match; good condition, some have a few spots; $50.

TWIN SISTERS/PINWHEEL: 1920s; 31 eight-inch blocks of solid pink, dark blue with tiny dot print shirting, white with tiny blue dot and line print shirting; was a top, has been taken apart; excellent assembly; excellent condition; $45.

24 Appliqué, Florals, Feathers, and Such

By definition, of course, quilts are pieces of fabric put together with other pieces of fabric to make a whole. In pieced quilting the pieces are generally attached side by side; in appliqué, one piece is stitched *onto* another. The first appliqués were large pieces of printed fabric, say of a tree and birds, that were cut out and stitched down to another, larger piece of fabric. This was the Broderie-Perse method, and it started with a large central medallion, possibly surrounded by smaller pieces of a printed pattern, appliquéd onto some bed-sized piece of fabric. After the pieces were stitched down, batting and backing were added, and the whole thing would be quilted. Handling large pieces made this method awkward, so in the early 1700s, the appliqué technique moved to smaller pieces, or blocks. *See illustration #63.*

Probably because the first appliqués started with botanical prints, the first free-form patterns also came from nature. The four basic patterns from which most appliqué evolved are the rose, wreath, leaf cluster and feathers; figures, shapes, and other subjects followed very quickly. Most women who were skilled enough to tackle an appliqué were probably very willing to change a known pattern to add something of themselves. The quilter who was preparing flower petals for an appliqué quilt might look at some of the pieces and think they looked more like butterflies than roses. So her quilt immediately evolved from "Rose of Sharon" to a free-form "Roses with Butterflies." Her neighbor, thinking (modestly, of course) that she was a better quilter and more creative, might pick up the idea and change it to "Roses with Honey Bees." So don't expect any two appliqué quilts, even if they are the same pattern, to look the same—they may, but don't expect it—since every quilter might add her own touch. Even two quilts with a fairly common and accepted pattern, say Ohio Rose, might have individual touches.

Because they required more time and fabric, and considerably more skill to create, an appliqué quilt was usually a "best" quilt. In Colonial America, and especially in the south, appliqué was considered a sign of affluence. In many cases, special fabric would be bought for such a special quilt.

63 Although there's no way to know for certain, this Flowering Vine appliqué appears to include all hand-dyed fabrics for the petals and leaves. Hand appliquéd, the quilt was quilted in 1996. An interesting addition is the vine stitching which was done by machine. Quilt from the authors' collection.

Many patterns were used in appliqué quilts, and sometimes several patterns were used on a single quilt to create an "album" quilt. The high point of the appliqué trend came in the late 1800s with the Baltimore Album quilts, which are some of the most costly and highly prized quilts ever made or sold. After that, the trend died out until the late 1920s, when it again became popular.

We were quite pleased to find over 150 appliqué quilts in the marketplace, since they have become more rare. Look carefully and you can still find a gem. Note that tops and blocks are included in the appropriate category.

The most common appliqué patterns are still the florals, not surprising since they came first and would have been most reproduced. As time passed, animals and birds, fruits and vegetables, and any number of other botanicals joined flowers and leaves. Most typically, appliqué was done on a white ground, using solid color fabrics, but sometimes print fabrics were used. The predominant colors were red and green, but others will be seen as well. Often, embroidered accents were added. A dedicated quilter's creativity knows no boundaries.

ART DECO FLOWERS IN POTS: 1920s; white, purple, green; pattern blocks have three flowers in a green "pot" on white ground, set on point with narrow green sashing, white squares at set corners; diamond and outline quilting overall, 9 stitches per inch; excellent appliqué, small and even stitches; very good condition, slight overall color fade from washing; 80" × 90"; $950.

BASKET WITH FLOWER GARLAND, PAIR: 1920s; solids of pink, rose, lavender, teal blue, gold, and green on white ground; central triangular gold basket with rose and pink roses, lavender and teal tulips, teal ribbon; around center is oval of green and gold ribbons, gold bows; roses, tulips with large rectangle on sides of the quilt, composed of same flowers and ribbons, gold binding; all shapes appliquéd on with white blanket-stitch embroidery; from Pennsylvania; straight-line, scalloped, and swirl quilting overall, very small and very even stitches; excellent assembly and appliqué; excellent condition; 78" × 86"; $1,875 for the pair.

BUNCH OF IRIS: 1920s; white, purple, lavender, green; large central oval of appliqué purple ribbon with bow around bunch of ten irises, purple and lavender, with green leaves and stems, all on white, white border with lavender swags and purple bows; grid quilting overall, 7–8 stitches per inch; good assembly and appliqué, although some areas of appliqué have rather uneven stitches; good condition, has been washed, some overall color fade; 76" × 84"; $1,000.

CARNATIONS: 1870s; white, red with tiny yellow hearts and dots, dark green on green; eight rows of seven carnations, identical individual red flowers with green stem and leaves, white border with another row of the same flowers all around the edge, white binding; from New York State; diamond grid quilting overall, pattern of hearts, moons, stars, leaves, others, very even, 11 stitches per inch; excellent assembly, tiny, nearly invisible appliqué stitches; very good condition, quilting lines remain, few tiny stains on backing; 82" × 94"; $2,400.

CAROLINA LILY: 1840s; white, red, green; eight pattern blocks, each with three red lilies, green leaves and stems, set on point, on white ground; very wide white border, with appliquéd lilies, Federal eagles, and small birds, narrow red border, red binding; from North Carolina; excellent outline, circular and medallion quilting, 11 stitches per inch; excellent assembly; good condition, slight overall fade; 78" × 88"; $4,350.

CAROLINA LILY: 1850s; ivory/white, solid green, red with tiny white flowers print, yellow tiny dots print; six by seven pattern blocks, three red lilies with green leaves and stems on ivory ground, set on point with ivory blocks between; wide ivory border with green vine and leaves, and red flowers with yellow centers, bunch of three red flowers with yellow in quilt's corners; from Pennsylvania; clamshells, crosses, other patterns quilted in set blocks, outline quilting in pattern blocks, outline and stipple in the border, around vines, small and even stitches; excellent assembly and appliqué; excellent condition, has been washed once; 84" × 94"; $1,685.

CAROLINA LILY: 1880s; white, solid red, green print; four rows by six rows of pattern blocks, each with traditional three lilies on green stem, with leaves, set on point, with white blocks between; triple border, red, white, green, green binding; from Texas; double outline quilting in pattern blocks, diamond grid in white blocks, rainbow on borders, 7 stitches per inch; excellent assembly and appliqué; very good condition, very slight overall age discoloration; 74" × 77"; $1,395.

CAROLINA LILY: 1930s; red, green on white; three rows by three rows of traditional pattern blocks, on white ground, set square, with white sashing between, all blocks oriented the same direction, double border, white then red, white binding; from Maryland; diagonal straight-line quilting overall, feather vine on sashing, chevrons on border, 8 stitches per inch; excellent assembly and appliqué; excellent condition; 83" × 83"; $695.

CAROLINA LILY: 1940s; red, green, on white; three rows by three rows of pattern blocks, on white ground, set square, with white sashing between, nine blocks oriented in four directions, without identifiable reason; white border, red binding; from Pennsylvania; square and dia-

64 The best guess is that this Pineapple Friendship appliqué quilt was made in Pennsylvania. It dates around 1850–60. The best element of this quilt is the appliquéd border, which sprouts vines, buds, flowers and berries from a vase centered on each edge of the quilt. A perfect example of the design skill of the period.

mond grid quilting in pattern blocks, feather vine and diagonal straight-line quilting on sashing and border, 8 stitches per inch; excellent assembly and appliqué; excellent condition; 87" × 87"; $890. *See illustration #64.*

CAT TAILS AND WATER LILIES: 1930s; pastel blue, pink, green, brown; very large central rectangle appliquéd with pink lilies on green pads, brown cattails with green stems and leaves, all on pastel blue ground; central block is surrounded by narrow pink border, then very wide pink border with appliquéd pink lilies on green pads, brown stems connecting the pads, pink binding; from Ohio; lots of close outline echo quilting overall, around the pads and cattails, creating the look of water ripples, small and even stitches; very good assembly and appliqué; excellent condition; 72" × 82"; $1,800.

COCK'S COMB AND VINES: 1850s; white, red, green, gold; pattern blocks have red eight-lobed flower with gold circle center, each flower has four green cock's combs around it, all on white ground; five rows by four rows of pattern blocks, set square with white sashing between, wide white border red binding, green vines on outside of border; from Central Ohio; outline and straight-line quilting overall, cable quilting in sashing and border, 9 stitches per inch; excellent assembly; excellent condition, unused and unwashed, pristine; 90" × 90"; $8,200.

COCK'S COMB WREATHS: 1920s; red, green, yellow on white; nine pattern blocks each with red and green wreath center, four green stems, going to eight red cock's comb flowers with yellow accents, and 12 red and yellow flower buds, all on white ground; wide white border with serpentine green vines, red and yellow flowers and buds, green stems, red binding; outline quilting around appliqués, extensive feather wreath stars, hearts, crossed, rings and other patterns in white areas and border, 11 stitches per inch; excellent appliqué, tiny, nearly invisible stitches; excellent condition; 80" × 80"; $1,250.

COCK'S COMB: 1930s; pure white with red, green, and yellow solids; nine large appliquéd blocks with four large plain white blocks between, and wide plain white border; pattern blocks of two red cock's combs, each with a yellow calyx and green stems and leaves; thin batting, white backing and scalloped edges with yellow binding; straight-line quilting overall, with leaflike patterns quilted in the plain white blocks at 8 stitches per inch; minimal washing, probably never used; 86" × 88"; $650.

COCK'S COMBS AND POTS: 1870s; teal green, red, golden yellow; nine large pattern blocks with tiny golden pot holding green stems with one large green leaf and two red cock's comb flowers, on white ground, with white blocks between; very narrow red and white sawtooth border, very wide white border; from Pennsylvania; tiny grid quilting on pattern blocks, long thin feathers overall, small and even stitches; excellent appliqué; very good condition, quilting lines remain, few small stains; 88" × 91"; $2,900.

COTTON BOLLS: 1860s; white, green, brown; four large pattern blocks, set square and close together, with four green stems radiating out from center of the block, each stem with three brown cotton bolls and small green leaves, on white ground; white border with green swags and brown bolls, brown binding, thin batting; outline and diamond grid quilting overall, small and even stitches; very good assembly, appliqué stitches are small and even, though visible; very good condition, significant color fade in brown overall; 86" × 86"; $2,200.

DAISIES: 1930s; off-white with solids of blue, purple, green, orange, others, multicolored period prints and florals; five rows by five rows of pattern blocks, set square, on off-white ground, each with eight-petal daisy-like flowers, four petals of solid color, four of print/floral, arranged so petals overlap and make a sort of airplane propeller look; each flower has green stem and two green leaves, off-white border and binding; from Pennsylvania; outline echo quilting on flowers, small flowers and vines in white areas around flowers, other patterns on border, very even stitches, 8 per inch; excellent appliqué, tiny, nearly invisible stitches; excellent condition; 87" × 87"; $750.

DOGWOOD BASKETS: 1926; pink, rose, green, and pale green solids on white; large square "wreath" in center of quilt of four green baskets, one in each corner and lots of four-petal pink dogwood flowers with green centers and green leaves; scalloped edges with pink and a few rose flowers with green leaves and stems that follow the scalloped edges, rose binding; kit quilt, signed and dated; diamond grid and straight-line overall, four-petal flowers scattered around the quilt, small and even stitches; very good appliqué; excellent condition; 82" × 84"; $1,285.

DOGWOOD BLOSSOMS: 1920s; white, pink, rose, green; pink and rose dogwood blossoms on white with green leaves; triple border, rose, white, pink, with prairie point edge; grid quilting overall, 6 stitches per inch; very good appliqué, small stitches, some are uneven; very good condition, minimal use, has been washed; 70" × 84"; $835.

DOGWOOD: 1930s; pinks, greens, brown, white on pastel blue; large central bouquet of brown dogwood branches, with pink and white flowers, green leaves, on pastel blue ground; very wide blue border with small clusters of pink and white dogwood flowers and green leaves, scalloped edges with pink binding; from Ohio; square grid quilting in central area,

215

straight-lines and dogwood flowers in border, small and even stitches; very good appliqué; very good condition, few stains; 79" × 87"; $1,450.

DOGWOOD: 1930s; white with pink, rose, green; pink and rose four-petal flowers with green stems and leaves in large circular central area, rose binding; from Ohio; outline and grid quilting overall, 8 stitches per inch; good assembly, most appliqué stitches are small and even; good condition, slight overall color fade from much washing; 74" × 88"; $735.

FERNS AND FLOWERS: 1860s; white, red, green; large ring of five-petal red flowers in center with green fern-like leaves around, swags of red flowers and ferns along edges of quilt; diagonal triple echo quilting overall, wreath and feather quilting in center, 8 stitches per inch; good condition, minimal use, few small spots in one area; 84" × 84"; $2,050.

FLORAL SWAGS AND WREATH: 1930s; pure white background with solid pastels of pink, pale blue, yellow, lavender, green; center swag forms wreath with pale blue, narrow bow; swags on four sides and bouquet in each corner, all with green vines, stems, and leaves, yellow and pink buds, and blue and lavender five-petal flowers with matching thread-embroidered centers; white backing, thin batting, pale blue binding; excellent assembly, perfectly executed appliqué; precise quilting in 12 stitches per inch; large center pattern of quilted lyre and butterflies, narrow crosshatch quilting overall; excellent, near-perfect condition with one tiny tear on one flower petal; 71" × 93"; $650.

FLORAL VINES: 1930s; Three "vines" of tulips, daffodils, hollyhocks in large center block, with very narrow lavender border, wide white border with scalloped edges, lavender binding; some chain and French knot embroidery on leaves and flowers, probably a kit quilt; curved and floral quilting on the border, straight-line quilting in center, 7–8 stitches per inch; excellent condition, very small appliqué stitches; excellent assembly, never used, minimal washing; 72" × 80"; $375.

FLOWER BASKETS: 1936; red, pink, lavender, bright blue, yellow, green, white, all solid colors; three rows by four rows of white blocks with appliqué five-and six-petal posies in blue and green baskets, with black handles on baskets; yellow sashing with white squares at set corners, very wide yellow border with wide, bright blue swags, pink flower buds and green ribbons; dated, from Nebraska; lots of crisscross grid and diamond quilting overall, feather chains and flower quilting in sashing and white squares, 8–9 stitches per inch; excellent assembly; excellent condition; 76" × 84"; $1,050.

FLOWERS AND BOW: 1930s; soft pastels, blue, yellow, green, lavender, pink, on cream; small, delicate flowers like periwinkles, tulips, buds with leaves and stems, arranged along sides of quilt in swags, one curved swag in center with blue bow; thin batting, wide blue border on three sides, triple (two wide blue, with narrow cream between) border on chin edge, all four edge corners rounded; ¾-inch diamond grid quilting overall, outline quilting around appliqués, 9 stitches per inch, tiny appliqué stitches; excellent assembly; excellent condition, unwashed, unused; 76" × 94"; $750.

FOUR BASKETS: 1930s; three shades of lavender on fourth, very pale lavender; four minimalist baskets with three posies, with small bits of embroidery, in corner of large central rectangle, surrounded by double border, two shades of lavender, surrounded by about

18-inch-wide very pale lavender border, with another one-inch-wide border outside all; appliqué and borders showcase exquisite and expert quilting: feather wreath in center, cable on inner borders, overlapping circles overall, 10 stitches per inch; excellent assembly; good condition, has been washed though some quilting lines remain, few small spots in one area; 75" × 85"; $450.

FULL BLOWN TULIP: 1860s; red, green, and red/orange solids; twelve pattern blocks set widely on white background; lots of wreath, straight-line, outline and flower shape quilting at 8 stitches per inch; green binding; 80" × 88"; $950.

GARDEN BOUQUET IN URNS: 1930s; white and pastel solids of tan, pink, yellow, mint green, blue; four rows of three tan urns, each urn with one flower, stem and leaves, and two birds appliquéd on white blocks; pattern blocks are set on point with plain white blocks between; narrow mint green border, then wide white border, and wide green border, with green squares in the corners; grid and diamond quilting overall, with birds, shells, cables, and flowers in plain blocks, 9 stitches per inch; colors have faded overall due to much washing, top binding worn, few small dark spots in one area; 62" × 80"; $400.

HOLLYHOCK FLORAL: 1930s; solids of pastel yellow, blue and green, rose, pink, lavender; white background, scalloped edge, four stalks of pink and rose hollyhocks with yellow centers in center of quilt, smaller flowers around sides; small knots and other embroidery in flower centers; from Vermont; outline quilting on flowers, diamond quilting elsewhere overall; small appliqué stitches, good assembly; good condition, some color bleed from washing; 74" × 90"; $500.

IRISES: 1940s; shades of pinks, yellows, lilacs, greens, all in solids, on white; kit quilt, large bunch of appliquéd irises in the center, smaller bunches of appliquéd irises in each corner, each bunch with full flowers and buds, few buds around sides of quilt, embroidered "veins" in petals of full flowers, all four sides scalloped; crisscross quilting in floral bunches, floral quilting elsewhere, 6 stitches per inch; excellent assembly, very small appliqué stitches; very good condition except for some yellowing in spots overall; 84" × 87"; $750.

LEAVES AND BERRIES: 1880s; red, green, white, golden tan, yellow; three rows by three rows of pattern blocks, each with small red center, four red and green comb-type flowers, eight green leaves, four green stems with red berries; wide white border with golden tan vines, and yellow grape clusters and leaves; from Ohio; extensive quilting, outline around appliqué pieces, tiny diamond grid quilting overall, triple echo diagonal line on border, tiny and even, 12 stitches per inch; superior appliqué, 14 stitches per inch, nearly invisible; excellent condition; 76" × 78"; $3,400.

LILIES WITH BLUEBELLS: 1930s; pink, rose, light and medium blue, green, gold on white; center rectangle with one lily and three bluebells, bunch of three lilies on each side of the quilt, all flowers have green leaves, embroidered stems; double row of bluebells go corner to corner across the quilt, very thin gold strip between these double rows and around center rectangle; straight-line quilting, 7 stitches per inch; excellent assembly and embroidery; excellent condition; 72" × 90"; $600.

LONG-STEM ROSES: 1860s; red and green on white background; nine medallions each with three red flowers on long thin green stems with small leaves, thin green vines with small leaves around border; signed with embroidered initials; excellent assembly with tiny appliqué stitches, diamond and straight-line quilting overall at 9 stitches per inch; 80" × 80"; $1,300.

MORNING GLORIES: 1900–10; two shades each of soft pastels of pink, green, blue, lavender, on white ground; large center wreath of flowers and flower buds, leaves, stems and vines, wide white border with green leaves and vines, all with coordinating color embroidery accents, yellow embroidered stamens on the flowers; from Pennsylvania; outline, sunburst and diamond grid quilting overall, feathers in border, small and very even stitches; excellent assembly and appliqué; excellent condition; 74" × 88"; $1,275.

OAK LEAF REEL: 1830s; white, gray-green on green print, tiny yellow flowers on rose pink print; three rows by four rows of pattern blocks of four green oak leaves, rose pink reels, on white ground; two sides and bottom have wide white border with additional green oak leaves; from New England; outline and diamond grid quilting overall, small stitches; very good assembly, small appliqué stitches, with neatly curved edges on pieces; good condition, has been washed and used, some color oxidation, especially in the green; 78" × 86"; $2,800.

OAK LEAVES AND ACORNS: 1850s; solids of brown, peach, faded green, cream; three rows by four rows of pattern blocks, set square, wide cream border; pattern blocks have four appliquéd oak leaves and eight acorns, each half brown and half peach, each perpendicular to a brown center square, acorns have green caps; from North Carolina; outline, straight-line, and various other patterns of quilting, 7 stitches per inch; excellent assembly and design; fair to good condition, overall discoloration, several areas with stains, some fabric deterioration; 77" × 87"; $1,600.

OAK LEAVES AND ACORNS: 1940s; white, green, gold, yellow; pattern blocks have four green leaves and four gold and yellow acorns around small yellow center circle, on white ground; kit quilt, white border, wavy edge, green binding; excellent outline quilting, with oak leaf and acorn quilting in the border, 10 stitches per inch; excellent assembly, tiny appliqué stitches; excellent condition; 80" × 92"; $1,200.

OAK LEAVES: 1850s; green, red on white; pattern blocks have green oak leaves around a red circle center on white ground, eight rows by nine rows of pattern blocks, wide white border, debris can be felt in very thin batting; minimal straight-line quilting overall, 7–8 stitches per inch; tiny, even appliqué stitches; fair to good condition, some loose appliqué stitches, some overall soiling, greens fading to khaki/tan; 107" × 107"; $1,125.

OAK LEAVES: 1930s; white with yellow; pattern blocks have four yellow oak leaves around a yellow print circle center, on white ground, six rows by seven rows of pattern blocks, yellow binding; straight-line quilting overall, 9 stitches per inch; excellent assembly; very good condition, has been washed but faint quilting lines remain; 72" × 82"; $635.

OHIO ROSE: 1870s; red, double pink, green print; 18 pattern blocks, on white ground, with plain white blocks between, each with a central pink and red rose, green stems, four red rosebuds; wide white border with elaborate swags and pink and red rosebuds and small roses, muslin binding and backing; from New York State; outline quilting overall, feather wreaths in white blocks, 10 stitches per inch; excellent assembly, tiny appliqué stitches; very good condition, some slight overall color fade and discoloration; 81" × 85"; $2,295.

OHIO ROSE: 1890s; white, red, blue, yellow, green; four rows by five rows of pattern blocks, blue and red flowers and yellow buds with green leaves on white ground, green embroidered stems; narrow white border, blue binding; excellent outline diagonal straight-line quilting in pattern blocks, feather leaf on border, 11 stitches per inch; very good assembly, tiny and even appliqué stitches; good condition, few stains, binding slightly worn; 67" × 80"; $1,250.

OHIO ROSE: 1920s; cream, pink, rose, green; 16 pattern blocks with rose and pink buds and roses on cream ground, wide cream border; excellent assembly and appliqué, tiny, almost invisible appliqué stitches; excellent condition; 82" × 100"; $450.

OHIO ROSE: 1930s; solids of green, two pinks on white; four rows by five rows of pattern blocks, set square, on white ground, white border with green vines and leaves, green binding; from Virginia; square grid quilting overall, 6 stitches per inch; excellent appliqué, small stitches; excellent condition; 85" × 105"; $995.

OHIO ROSE: 1930s; white, red, green; two rows by three rows of pattern blocks set on point, wide apart with white blocks between; red flowers and buds with green leaves and stems, on white ground, white border; circle and straight-line quilting overall, 10 stitches per inch; excellent assembly, tiny appliqué stitches; good condition, has been washed and used, few stains in one corner; 72" × 78"; $900.

OHIO ROSE: 1930s; white, two yellows, two greens; four rows by four rows of pattern blocks, yellow flowers and buds with green leaves on white ground, narrow white sashing and border, wavy edge, yellow binding; outline quilting in pattern blocks, cable on borders and sashing, 8 stitches per inch; very good assembly, even appliqué stitches; very good condition, slight overall fade, has been washed; 78" × 78"; $965.

OHIO ROSE: 1930s; yellow, tan, orange, green on white; three rows by four rows of pattern blocks, set square, each with yellow and orange roses with tan centers, green leaves and stems, yellow buds, on white ground; very wide white border with tan swags and yellow buds, narrow yellow border around all; from Indiana; outline quilting in pattern blocks, square grid and feather wreath quilting in white areas and border, 5 stitches per inch; very good assembly, small and even appliqué stitches; excellent condition; 72" × 92"; $650.

ORANGES AND BLOSSOMS: 1930s; white, orange, green, yellow; large center oval of orange oranges, white blossoms with yellow centers, green leaves and stems, on white ground; wide white border with green triangles appliquéd along the edges, green binding; quilting of leaves, trees, cables, 8 stitches per inch; very good workmanship, small appliqués stitches; excellent condition, unwashed, unused; 79" × 93"; $975.

PANSIES: 1930s; white, blues; three flowers in pattern block on white ground, blocks set square with plain blue blocks between, blue border; straight-line quilting in pattern blocks, grid quilting on border, pansies in blue blocks, 8–9 stitches per inch; excellent appliqués, small and even stitches, nearly invisible; very good condition, unwashed, slight overall age discoloration; 74" × 74"; $950.

PINEAPPLES: 1850s; white, green, red, double pink; four large central pattern blocks, set square; pattern blocks have green and red concentric eight-petal flowers in the center, with four red pineapples growing from this center, with eight green leaves, green crescents, circles, and other embellishments; very wide white border on all four sides, center of each side has red and green flowerpot, five red flowers with double pink accents, and two red buds on green stems in each pot; out from each pot, along the length of each side, twine vines and grape leaves with clusters of red grapes; from Pennsylvania; lots of outline and straight quilting, very small and even stitches; excellent assembly; very good condition, has been washed; 86" × 89"; $37,500.

PINK SUNFLOWERS: 1940s; white, solids of pink, green, yellow, brown; very large Ohio star pieced center block of pink on white, with appliqué five-petal flowers in center and four corners of the star; flowers have round yellow centers, thin brown stems and green leaves, all appliquéd on with black thread; wide pink border with white corner squares each with one small flower, stem, and leaf, wide white border all around, pink binding; kit quilt; diamond grid, feather wreath, and curved feather quilting overall, very small and even stitches; very good assembly and appliqué, stitches mostly even, deliberately visible; excellent condition; 74" × 76"; $1,400.

POMEGRANATE: late 1800s, backed and quilted mid-1900s; cottons, Turkey red, golden yellow, vegetable-dyed green, on white background; cotton blend backing; two rows of four pomegranates, one row of four, mirror image, simple vine with three small pomegranates on each side edge; from Kentucky; diamond hand quilting overall; fair assembly, some appliqué pieces slightly misshapen; some large yellow age/stained areas, colors fading in some areas; 64" × 78"; $1,450.

POSEY IN A POT: 1930s; white, solids of medium blue, pink, pastel yellow, pastel green; 28 pattern blocks set square, with plain blue blocks between; each pattern block has one rounded corner square pink flower with a yellow center, two large droopy green leaves on a green stem, all in a blue pot, on white ground, wide blue border; flowers quilted in blue blocks, swags on border, outline on pattern blocks, fairly large, not all even stitches; very good assembly; excellent condition; 70" × 76"; $900.

POSEY WREATHS: 1930s; pink, green, yellow, blue, white; pattern blocks have four pink posies with tiny yellow centers, green stems and leaves, each facing toward the center of the block, on white ground; pattern blocks are set on point with blue on white block most like one-quarter of a four-patch snowball block; white border with green vines and stems, pink flowers and buds; from Ohio; tiny square grid quilting in centers of blue and white blocks, curved echo quilting on blue corners of same blocks, outline quilting around appliqués, diamond grid on border, all very even, 8 stitches per inch; excellent assembly and appliqué, nearly invisible stitches; excellent condition; 79" × 93"; $1,650.

POTS OF FLOWERS: 1920s; purple, white, green, multicolored prints; pattern blocks have three print, hexagonal "posies" on solid green stems with two green leaves, in small print flowerpot, on white ground; five rows by six rows of pattern blocks, set on point with solid purple blocks between, wide purple border with scalloped edge, white binding; cable quilting on the border, feathered medallion quilting on the purple blocks, small even stitches; excellent assembly, tiny appliqué stitches; very good condition, minimal use, has been washed; 72" × 96"; $795.

PRINCESS FEATHER VARIATION: 1850s; solids of brown, green, gold on cream; nine large pattern blocks, with eight feathers of brown and green pieces or brown and lighter brown pieces, with a gold dot on the end of each feather, around a center of an eight-point star with a gold center dot; from North Carolina; outline and triple outline quilting in the feathers, various other designs elsewhere, 8 stitches per inch; excellent assembly; fair to good condition, stains and discoloration overall, some fabric loss in some colors, a few darker spots; 88" × 88"; $1,700.

PRINCESS FEATHER: 1860s; red, green, off-white; four large pattern blocks of eight green feathers around a red center, surrounded by very narrow green border, very wide white border with appliquéd green oak leaves, green binding; from Ohio; exquisite and extensive feather rope and feather wreath quilting in the large white areas, very close triple echo line and grid quilting overall, 10 stitches per inch; excellent appliqué, tiny, nearly invisible stitches; good condition, but red fabric feels fragile, green is stiff; 73" × 79"; $995.

PRINCESS FEATHER: 1870s; white, red, green; four large pattern blocks in center of quilt, each with alternating red and green curved feathers on white ground, with embroidered green star in center; wide white border on two sides with green swag and red flowers; outline and straight-line quilting overall, music lyres in quilting on the border, 7–8 stitches per inch; very good appliqué and assembly; good condition, has been washed, some fabric deterioration in red; 60" × 80"; $2,100.

PRINCESS FEATHER: 1880s; white, olive green that was probably a brighter green, rusty tan that was probably a rusty red; four large pattern squares, each with eight feathers, four tan, four green, with eight diamonds (four tan, four green) forming a star in the center; feathers and diamonds/stars very neatly and carefully machine appliquéd; both sides have narrow diamond border of tan and green, narrow green border, wide unfaded, different red border; top has narrow red border, no border on bottom, may have been cut off and re-hemmed; amateur-looking application of red border, may have been added at a later date; close, heavy contour line quilting around the feathers, straight-line on the feathers, grid quilting on the borders, all at 8 stitches per inch; good condition except for serious overall fading, few faint stains in some areas, some yellowing of the white, probably unwashed; 69" × 84"; $500.

PRINCESS FEATHER: 1910–20; Turkey red, teal green, off-white; four large pattern blocks each with traditional eight curved feathers, alternating red and teal, around round teal center, four small feathers in center of quilt, unadorned white border; from Pennsylvania; triple cable quilting on border, square grid quilting overall, veins quilted on feathers, outline quilting around feathers, 8 stitches per inch; excellent appliqué, tiny, nearly invisible stitches; excellent condition; 80" × 86"; $1,200. *See illustration #65.*

PRINCESS FEATHER: 1920s; red on cream/white; eight feather medallion with central pointed circle, two additional feathers in each corner of the quilt; from Pennsylvania; lots of excellent outline, grid, and feather quilting overall, 10 stitches per inch; excellent assembly and appliqué; excellent condition, has been washed; 72" × 88"; $1,400.

65

69 This Whig Rose Variation uses some Hawaiian stlye appliqué. An unusual find because the quilt is signed and dated: "M E Concierge Mar 18 1863" and came from New York State. Both the large and small medallions on the quilt contain the requisite eight roses or rosebuds. Pencil markings for the elaborate quilt design remain on the quilt so it's likely the quilt was never washed.

PRINCESS FEATHER: 1922; Turkey red on cream; one large medallion consisting of eight large princess feathers in red, in a fan shape around a red eight-point star with a small cream star in its center; eight additional feathers, two each in mirror image of each other, in each corner of the quilt; red border, probably added later by machine; signed and dated with location; from Pennsylvania; diamond grid quilting overall, 7 stitches per inch; some slight color loss, several very well done repairs, one small seam separation in border, has been washed, but faint quilting lines remain; 91" × 91"; $2,950.

PRINCESS FEATHER: 1930s; dark rose/pink on white; large central swirl of nine feathers around a small circle, small flowers on stems with leaves in each corner around the center pattern, all in rose on white ground; very wide rose border, rose binding; outline and diamond grid quilting overall, feather wreaths and vines in border; very small and even stitches; excellent assembly and appliqué; very good condition, very slight overall color fade; 80" × 80"; $585.

RED FLOWERS: 1880s; white, red, green; pattern blocks are white ground with red eight-lobed circular flowers at the centers, one green stem down from the flower, four green stems up from the flower, each with a red bud, four comblike leaves around each flower; three rows by three rows of pattern blocks, set straight; white border with thin green swags and three flower petals at the top of each swag, red binding; from Ohio; lots of straight-line and outline double echo quilting in the pattern blocks, 12 stitches per inch; excellent assembly, tiny appliqué stitches; good condition, some slight binding wear, some age discoloration on the back, one small spot; 62" × 76"; $800.

ROSE OF SHARON WREATHS: 1860s; white with red and green solids; three rows by five rows of pattern blocks, each with green leaf and stem wreath, four red roses and eight red buds on white ground, red binding; outline and diamond grid quilting overall, very small and even stitches; very good assembly, most of the appliqué stitches are even and well hidden; very good condition, has been washed; 74" × 86"; $1,700.

ROSE OF SHARON WREATHS: 1870s; white and solids of red, green, pink, yellow; three rows by three rows of pattern blocks, each with a green vine and leaves wreath, with four pink buds, eight red buds, four full roses, all on white ground; roses are eight-sided "circles" of pink, with inside circle of red, and center of yellow; triple sashing, red, white, red with nine patch red and white squares at set corners; narrow red border all around, narrow green border on two sides, white binding and backing; outline and straight-line echo quilting overall, medium large, somewhat uneven stitches; fair to good assembly, pieces are even, many appliqué stitches are large and uneven; good condition, some soiling on binding, some small spots in one area, minimal use; 78" × 84"; $1,775.

ROSE OF SHARON: 1850s; white, green, red; nine pattern blocks have red rose of Sharon in center, surrounded by four long green stems with thistlelike red flowers and four shorter green stems with red and green berries; very wide white border with green vines, stems, leaves, and red berries, four red roses in corners; excellent double-line echo quilting of hearts, straight-lines and other patterns overall, very small and even stitches; very good appliqué with small stitches and mostly smooth edges; excellent condition, never washed, never used; 90" × 90"; $2,900.

ROSE OF SHARON: 1860s; green, red, rose pink, yellow on white background fabric; nine medallions with red and rose pink circular centers, green cock's comb and vines, and red and rose pink flowers, with yellow centers; green leaves and curving vines around border, with red and yellow tulips; very good assembly, tiny appliqué stitches; diamond, feather, and outline quilting, large stitches, 7 per inch; some minor stains, probably from storage; 80" × 86"; $1,875.

ROSE OF SHARON: 1880s; red, green, cheddar on white; four large pattern squares set close together and square, with eight flat roses and four buds, red with cheddar centers, ragged leaves and thick stems of green, all on white ground; white border with red swags and green leaves; outline and clamshell quilting overall, 6 stitches per inch; very good assembly and good appliqué, stitches very even though visible; excellent condition; 87" × 87"; $2,200.

ROSE OF SHARON: 1884; white, red, green; white with large wreath of red roses with green leaves and stems, group of red roses with green leaves in four corners of quilt, double border, red then green, green binding; from Missouri, signed and dated; excellent heart, vine and wreath quilting; excellent appliqué; excellent condition, minimal use, faint quilting lines remain; 92" × 92"; $1,600.

ROSE OF SHARON: 1930s; three shades of pink, green, white; three rows by three rows of pattern blocks, each with traditional layered pink roses and four buds, green stems, on white ground; wide white border on three sides with dark pink swags and buds, white binding; from Ohio; outline quilting around appliqués, diamond grid overall, feather vine along swags, 10 stitches per inch; excellent appliqué, tiny, nearly invisible stitches; 73" × 83"; $895.

ROSE OF SHARON: 1938; pink, rose, yellow, dark green; nine pattern blocks, each with a pink and rose "fried egg" rose, with yellow center, green leaves and stem, on off-white ground, pink sashing between and around pattern blocks; triple border, white, narrow pink, white, pink binding; outline, fan and diamond grid quilting, 8 stitches per inch; excellent assembly and appliqué; excellent condition; 78" × 87"; $745.

ROSE OF SHARON: 1940s; white, rose pink, pale pink, dark green; nine pattern blocks, three rows by three rows, each with rose and pale pink petals, green leaves on white ground, rose pink sashing between and around, wide white border; outline, cable, floral, and diamond grid quilting, 3 stitches per inch; good assembly, some corners don't match, many appliqué stitches are large and evident; excellent condition; 84" × 88"; $300.

ROSE WREATHS: 1860s; solid red, green print, white; five rows by five rows of pattern blocks, each with four red roses and buds, green leaves on green vine wreath, all on white ground, wide white border with green swags and tassels with red accents, green binding; from Pennsylvania; diagonal-line echo quilting on border, sunburst echo from block centers, 8 stitches per inch; excellent assembly and appliqué, tiny, nearly invisible stitches; excellent condition; 82" × 82"; $2,150.

ROSE WREATHS: 1860s; red, green, golden yellow cotton solids, on cream background; 12 wreaths of green leaves, each with four red eight-petal flowers with golden yellow centers, three wreaths by four wreaths; flowerpots with stems and same flowers, and buds around outside edge of quilt; from New York State; excellent workmanship, near-perfect appliqué stitching; overall straight-line and crosshatch quilting; pristine condition, quilting lines remain, minor color loss; 79" × 82"; $37,500.

ROSE WREATHS: 1930s; red and green on white; two rows by three rows of pattern blocks, each with four red roses and four red buds, on a wreath of green stems with green leaves, set on point with white blocks between and around; double border, wide red, wide white, white binding and backing; outline quilting in pattern blocks, wreath and feather quilting between pattern blocks and on borders, mostly even stitches; good assembly, smooth piece edges; excellent condition; 73" × 95"; $475.

ROSEBUDS: 1860s; natural white with red and green solids; three rows by three rows of pattern blocks each with a red eight-lobed circular center, four green leaves, four red buds with green stems; wide white border with three green flowerpots along each edge, each pot with three red buds and green stems and leaves, small pot with one bud in each of the corners of the quilt; from Pennsylvania, initialed in all four corners; outline, curved, and straight-line quilting overall, small even stitches; excellent assembly and appliqué; excellent condition; 80" × 80"; $17,500.

STAR AND PLUME: 1860s; red, very dark green, cheddar, double pink on white; four pattern blocks with swirls of six crescents of red, green, pink with cheddar round-point star in center of the swirl and at each crescent end, on white ground; swags of same red, green, pink crescents with round-point cheddar stars around the sides of the quilt; clamshell and outline quilting overall, even stitches, 9 per inch; excellent assembly and appliqué; good condition, never washed, never used, quilting lines remain, colors remain true, few dark spots, overall age discoloration, two areas of damage on backing, none on front; 93" × 99"; $3,200.

SUNFLOWERS: 1920s; white, solids of yellow/orange, green, light brown; 22 sunflowers around outside of large white center area, flowers are yellow/orange, each with light brown center, green stems and three leaves; triple border, light brown, green, then yellow/orange; from New Hampshire; outline and leaf quilting overall, small and even stitches; very good appliqué, small stitches; excellent condition; 72" × 86"; $1,100.

TRIPLE TULIPS: 1880s; white with red/orange, orange and formerly green, now tan; three rows by four rows of pattern blocks, three five-petal tulips on one stem, on white ground; stems and outer two petals of the tulips are tan, but green appliqué thread indicates that they were green and have changed color, center petal is orange, two inner petals are red/orange; pattern blocks set on point, with white blocks between; from Pennsylvania; curved, outline, and star quilting overall, small even stitches; excellent assembly, small appliqué stitches; good condition, unwashed, staining in several areas; 68" × 84"; $695.

TULIP SWIRL: 1940s; pastels in blue, green, pink, peach, yellow on white; 16 tulips on eight stems with leaves swirl out from center like a pinwheel; wide green border, tulips were appliquéd after the straight-line/chevron machine quilting was done; very good appliqué; excellent condition; 22" × 22" doll quilt; $55.

TULIPS AND ROSES: 1860s; red, green, yellow on very pale blue calico background; nine medallions of four red tulips with yellow bases and green stems and leaves, and four medallions of red roses with green stems and leaves; medium-wide green border with red zigzag appliqué, very wide background fabric border with red appliquéd zigzags; from York County, Pennsylvania; excellent assembly and appliqué work, outline and patterned quilting at 7 stitches per inch; some minor stains on background fabric; 92" × 96"; $1,650.

TULIPS IN BASKETS: 1930s; white, red, green; pattern blocks have three red tulips in green "basket" with green stems and leaves, on white ground, 36 pattern blocks, set on point with white blocks between, red border; oval and cable quilting on border, wreath quilting in white blocks, 8 stitches per inch; excellent appliqué, tiny, nearly invisible stitches; very good condition, never used or washed, a few age stains in one area; 73" × 73"; $675.

TULIPS IN BLUE POTS: 1930s; rose, red, yellow, orange, green, blue on white; nine blue pots of six tulips, one red, two rose, two yellow, one orange with green leaves and stems; scalloped edge all around, with individual tulips, no pots around the edge, green binding; wreath, feather, and diamond quilting overall, 9 stitches per inch; excellent assembly; excellent condition; 78" × 80"; $800.

TULIPS: 1870s; red, yellow, teal green on white; bunches of three red and yellow tulips on green stems with green leaves in square green "pots," red and yellow tulip buds and greens swags around all four sides; red with tiny yellow print binding, white backing, thin batting; straight-line echo quilting overall, 8 stitches per inch; fair to good assembly, appliqué pieces not misshapen, but appliqué stitches clearly visible; good condition, few small tears in binding; 88" × 88"; $3,000.

TULIPS: 1870s; white with red and green; bunches of red tulips in central area, with green leaves and stems, single red tulips with green leaves and stems around edges; from New England; outline and grid quilting overall, 7 stitches per inch; good assembly, most appliqué stitches are small and even; good condition, slight color change/oxidation in some green areas; 78" × 98"; $1,200.

TULIPS: 1880s; white, yellow, green; large wreath of yellow tulips as central feature, with green leaves and stems; bunch of yellow tulips with green leaves and stems in each corner of quilt, yellow border; feathered wreath quilting overall, 8 stitches per inch; very good to excellent assembly, appliqué stitches are nearly invisible; poor to fair condition, very faded, very worn, much used, binding very worn; 78" × 90"; $600.

TULIPS: 1920s; pink, lavender, green, white; pair of twin-size quilts; pattern blocks are five pink and lavender tulips in green "pot" with green leaves on white ground, three rows by five rows of pattern blocks, set on point with lavender blocks between, double border, lavender and white; grid and outline quilting overall, 8–9 stitches per inch; excellent assembly and appliqué, small, even stitches, nearly invisible; very good condition, minimal use, has been washed; 50" × 80"; $1,500 for the pair.

TULIPS: 1920s; white, red, green; red tulips with green leaves and stems on white; circle and feather quilting overall; good assembly, most appliqué stitches small and even; good condition, unused and unwashed, several yellow stains in some areas; 72" × 76"; $600.

TULIPS: 1930–40; cottons of solid yellow, green, red, and black on natural white background; 20 blocks (five blocks by four blocks) with centers of four green leaves in turned-under appliqué, surrounded by four red, two black, and two yellow tulips in blanket stitched appliqué; from Kentucky; straight and outline quilting overall at 7 stitches per inch; minor discoloration and color loss; 68" × 88"; $2,000.

TULIPS: 1930s; red, dark pink, sea foam green on natural white; four large natural white blocks joined together to make center block, each of the four with three red and dark pink tulips, with green stems and leaves; center block surrounded by three narrow borders of green, dark pink, and red, then very wide natural white border appliquéd with green ribbons, with red and dark pink tulips in the corners; natural white binding and backing, thin batting; from Pennsylvania; excellent assembly and appliqué; grid quilting overall, small stitches; some age staining where folded, small brown stain on one leaf, few tiny spots elsewhere; 76" × 81"; $425.

WHIG ROSE VARIATION: 1840–60; typical red, green, some pink around center of each rose group, natural white background; each rose group with four roses and four buds, three groups by three groups; thin vines/stems with buds, flowers; appliqué vine, leaves, and roses create border on three sides; from Kentucky; excellent overall line and outline quilting; slight red bleed due to washing, fabric deterioration in green, frayed binding; 90" × 100"; $6,500.

WREATH OF FLOWERS: 1930s; white, yellow, pale yellow, green; large central wreath of green vines and leaves; 10 large yellow eight-petal, daisy-like flowers with pale yellow centers, on white ground; wide white border, pale yellow binding; outline and straight-line quilting overall, feather wreath quilting in center of flower wreath, 6 stitches per inch; very good appliqué; good condition, very slight overall color fade, few tiny tears, few loose appliqué stitches; 72" × 80"; $735.

25 Shapes and Figures

There are many figures and shapes to be found on appliqué quilts. Some were certainly created by ladies' magazines and some by creative quilters, who would find inspiration in everyday items or people they saw or read about. The most common figures are certainly Sunbonnet Sue and Overall Sam, which were probably inspired by farm children. The endearing little girl in the oversized hat became popular in the early 1900s, and really took off in the 1920s when kits and quilt magazines introduced all varieties of Sues to the world of quilters. Her popularity inspired a male counterpart, usually Overall Sam, but sometimes Overall Bill, an equally faceless figure whose straw hat and patch pocket overalls became common quilt patterns.

We've seen variations of these popular patterns that include southern belles, plantation mammies, and little Dutch girls, as well as the popular Scottie dog, all sorts of cats, birds, butterflies and other insects, teddy bears, and bunnies. A quilter could find an idea anywhere: lollipops, ice-cream cones, and candy canes from the sweets store; teapots, flat irons, and other household items; automobiles and other indications of advancing technology; musical instruments; organization emblems, political or military symbols. There were many chances for creativity.

ANIMALS: 1920s; various pastels and other solids; seven rows by seven rows of pattern blocks, set square with green sashing between, green border, white binding; pattern blocks are various animals, birds, insects with chain and buttonhole embroidery for appliqué; diamond grid quilting overall, large but very even stitches; very good assembly and appliqué; excellent condition, has been professionally washed; 72" × 72"; $1,875.

BUNNY: 1930s; white with bright pastels; appliquéd figures, mother and baby bunny, flowers; scalloped edge, blue binding; straight-line echo quilting overall, 6 stitches per inch; excellent assembly; excellent condition; 35" × 50"; $275.

BUTTERFLIES: 1930s; multicolored period prints on cream white; five rows by six rows of pattern blocks, each with a print butterfly, appliquéd with black chain stitch embroidery, on cream white ground, green binding and backing; from Virginia; uneven square grid quilting overall, 5 stitches per inch; uneven embroidery stitches, butterflies stretched and misshapen; very good condition, some slight overall discoloration; 72" × 80"; $550.

BUTTERFLIES: 1930s; multicolored period prints, white, solid golden yellow, green; six rows by seven rows of pattern blocks, each with print butterfly appliquéd on white ground by black chain stitch embroidery; blocks set on point, wide double border, green then golden yellow, golden yellow binding; from Virginia; heavy quilting in cables and grids on borders, flowers, and other patterns in pattern blocks, 9 stitches per inch; excellent assembly and appliqué; excellent condition; 78" × 80"; $695.

BUTTERFLIES: 1930s; navy blue, white, multicolored prints; 20 butterfly blocks with various prints for wings, embroidered antennae, set on point with navy blocks between, navy print border; straight-line quilting overall, 7–8 stitches per inch; very good appliqué, even stitches; excellent condition, unwashed, unused; 76" × 98"; $850.

BUTTERFLIES: 1930s; solids of red, green, blues, yellow, others, with tan, and various multicolored period prints and florals; 25 pattern blocks, each with a solid-colored butterfly, appliquéd with black herringbone embroidery; each pattern block has border of postage stamp squares of various prints and florals, is then set on point with zigzag tan sashing between, double border, gray print and tan, with tan binding; from Ohio; outline quilting in the pattern blocks, straight-line echo in the border and overall, large but even stitches; very good assembly, most points and corners match; excellent condition; 72" × 72"; $995.

BUTTERFLIES: 1930s; solids of green, white, pink, gold, purple, many others; prints of nearly every color possible; center rectangle of white with six appliquéd butterflies surrounded by wide green band, surrounded by white background band with 18 additional butterflies; wide green border; butterflies appliquéd with black overcast stitching; diamond quilting overall, 7 stitches per inch; two tiny repairs, very slight color fade overall; 66" × 76"; $400.

BUTTERFLY AND FLOWERS: 1930s; solids of pastels, blue, pink, green, yellow on white; one block with pink flowerpot, yellow and pink flowers with green stems and leaves, surrounded by yellow duck, blue bird, and yellow butterfly, on white ground; double border, yellow, then white, yellow binding; embroidered details, eyes, beaks, antennae, flower centers, etc.; from Pennsylvania; chevron quilting overall, 6 stitches per inch; good assembly, some appliqué pieces are misshapen; excellent condition; 24" × 32"; $295.

CIRCULAR MEDALLION WITH CHIMNEY SWEEP BLOCKS: 1860–80; red, green, double pink, brown and white print on white background; large center square with appliquéd circular wreath of green vines and red flowers, green vine with small red flowers around edge of center square; 12 chimney sweep pieced blocks in red and white on background of tiny brown on white print surround center square; border of double pink square diamonds, red binding; straight-line and grid quilting overall, with hearts, flowers, stars, leaves, and initials in various blocks and squares; has been washed, one small hole on front, some wear on binding, some light overall staining; 74" × 75"; $850.

HEARTS: 1930s; peach, green, other pastels in solids and prints; pattern block is four print fabric hearts appliquéd around small, solid-color center square, on a white ground with the corners of the block matching the center square solid fabric; colors carefully coordinated within each block; six rows by six rows of pattern blocks with peach sashing and wide peach scalloped border; appliquéd print fabric heart in each scallop of the border, thin batting, white backing, green binding; outline quilting in the pattern blocks, scalloped and heart quilting on the border, 7 stitches per inch; excellent assembly; very good condition, minimal washing; 84" × 84"; $650.

KITTENS IN BASKETS: 1930s; golden yellow, bright blue, white; three rows by four rows of pattern blocks, each with yellow kitten in blue basket, on white ground; yellow binding, embroidered accents, eyes, nose, mouth, in blue thread; from Pennsylvania; diamond grid quilting on baskets, clamshell echo in other areas, 8 stitches per inch; machine appliqué, neatly done; excellent condition; 32" × 50"; $550.

LITTLE BASKETS: 1930s; solid mint green and butter yellow, white; five rows by five rows of pattern blocks, each with simple basket with handle appliquéd to white ground, alternating colors, 12 green, 13 yellow baskets; pattern blocks set square, double border, yellow then white, scalloped edge with yellow binding; from Pennsylvania; double outline quilting on baskets, double zigzag on yellow border, quadruple cable on white border, various birds and flowers on white areas, 7 stitches per inch; good appliqué, some uneven piece edges, but very small stitches; excellent condition; 74" × 74"; $625.

LITTLE DUTCH GIRL: 1920s; rose, green, pink, purple, multicolored bright prints; variation of Sunbonnet Sue, figures look like that on cleanser box, multicolored embroidery around edges of girls; blocks with figures alternate with white blocks, pink border, green binding; straight-line quilting overall, 8–9 stitches per inch; excellent appliqué and assembly; excellent condition, minimal use; 80" × 84"; $950.

MAYPOLE: 1930s; white with pastels; kit quilt, large center area with intricate appliquéd baby animals, squirrel, dog, cat, birds, bunny with ribbons and flowers, around a detailed maypole; tiny tulips and vines around the scalloped edges, green binding; feather, diamond, and straight-line quilting overall, 7 stitches per inch; excellent assembly; excellent condition; 44" × 63"; $450.

MAYPOLE: 1930s; white with pastels; simple pattern of five appliquéd baby animals (lamb, cat, bear, rabbit, elephant) around maypole, with embroidered ribbons and flowers; machine quilted; excellent assembly; excellent condition; 30" × 42"; $195.

MEDALLIONS: 1890s; solids of cheddar yellow, maroon, teal green; medallions are scalloped-edge squares with crescents on all four sides, and open square in the center; three rows by three rows of pattern blocks, with cheddar medallions on maroon ground, with five-point teal green stars on the junction where the pattern blocks meet; beige quilting threads outline the medallions and radiate from the stars, tiny blue gingham check binding; backing is pieced "bars" pattern of the cheddar yellow and teal green fabrics, with two others; from Pennsylvania; outline and straight-line quilting, small stitches; very good assembly, small appliqué stitches; excellent condition; 48" × 48"; $650.

MERRY-GO-ROUND: 1930s; white with many colors in appliqué characters; large carousel in center with two horses and riders, and "Merry-Go-Round" embroidered on its roof, juggling clowns in two corners, monkey in the third, circus tent in the fourth; much detailed embroidery on and around figures, scalloped top and bottom edge, rounded corners, green binding; circular, shell, and straight-line quilting, 6 stitches per inch; excellent assembly of intricate pattern; excellent condition; 44" × 67"; $495.

OVERALL SAM: 1920s; blues, greens, grays, some others in solids and prints; pair of twin-size quilts; four rows by five rows of pattern blocks, black blanket-stitch embroidery on edges of figures, wide blue border; grid quilting overall, cable quilting on border, 7–8 stitches per inch; excellent embroidery and appliqué; good condition, some overall color fade, have been washed, few tiny spots on one quilt; 50" × 78" each; $1,200 for the pair.

PUSS IN BOOTS: 1930s; white, with five appliquéd yellow kittens, one in center, one in each corner, each with either a pink or pastel blue boot; scalloped edge with blue binding, "Puss In Boots" embroidered above and below the center kitten, blue ribbon in rectangle around center design; outline, diamond, and straight-line quilting, 6 stitches per inch, excellent assembly; very good condition, slight wear to binding; 35" × 50"; $295.

SNOWFLAKES: 1930s; blue six-sided snowflakes on cream ground, eight rows by eight rows of pattern blocks, triple border, cream, blue, cream; from Pennsylvania; outline and straight-line quilting, 9 stitches per inch; excellent assembly and appliqué, tiny, tight appliqué stitches, nearly invisible; fair to good condition, well washed, used, overall color fade, few water stains in one area; 90" × 90"; $1,125.

STRAWBERRY ICE-CREAM CONES: 1940s; pink, tan, white; pattern blocks are white with tan cone, pink "scoop," six rows by seven rows of pattern blocks, with sashing between and white squares at set corners, tan border and sashing; very good outline quilting overall; excellent assembly, small appliqué stitches; good condition, has been used and washed, slight overall color fade; 40" × 48"; $320.

SUNBONNET SUE: 1920s; pink, green, various coordinated solids and florals in red, green, lavender, yellows, blues; five rows by six rows of pattern blocks, Sue figures on ivory/white ground, black embroidery around Sues, arms, legs, on hats; green sashing between blocks, with pink squares at set corners, pink border with green squares in corners; outline quilting around Sues, cable quilting in sashing and border, small and even stitches; excellent assembly, appliqué and embroidery; excellent condition; 72" × 86"; $1,700.

SUNBONNET SUE: 1930; cottons in pastels, prints and solids; four rows of five Sue blocks, two rows face left, two rows face right; sashing of two purple outside, one center yellow stripe; purple and yellow nine-patch squares at set corners; border of three narrow stripes like sashing; from Kentucky; cross-hatch and outline quilting overall, 6 stitches per inch; minor discoloration on backing; 70" × 83"; $1,300.

SUNBONNET SUE: 1930s; yellow, off-white, solids and coordinated period prints; five rows by five rows of pattern blocks, set square, each on white ground, with triple yellow and white sashing between, nine-patch yellow and white squares at set corners, yellow binding; figures have matching solid-color hats, sleeves, and shoes, are appliqués with black overcast embroidery; from Illinois; outline and grid quilting overall, 7 stitches per inch; excellent assembly and embroidery, very small stitches; excellent condition, has been washed; 78" × 78"; $400.

SUNBONNET SUE: 1930s; yellow, white, solids and prints in purple, yellow, blues, some others; four rows by five rows of patterns blocks, white ground, each Sue with same solid-color feet, hands, hat with coordinating print dress; very narrow golden yellow sashing between pattern blocks, very wide lemon yellow border; outline quilting around Sues, diamond grid quilting in pattern blocks, shell quilting in border, 7 stitches per inch; excellent assembly and appliqué; excellent condition; 77" × 88"; $300.

SUNBONNET SUE: 1930s; pink, plain muslin, with prints and solids in many colors; Sues are appliquéd onto plain muslin squares, in four rows by five rows with pink sashing and border, and muslin squares at the set point corners; each Sue has a print dress with a coordinating solid-color bonnet, arms, and legs; diamond quilting in the corners and on the border, with square grid quilting overall at 8 stitches per inch; good assembly and appliqué; unwashed, near-perfect condition, with a few tiny spots in one area; 63" × 78"; $325.

SUNBONNET SUE: 1930s; plain muslin, red, blue, and many other colors in solids and prints; four columns of five Sues, center columns facing outer columns; Sues are appliquéd on plain muslin blocks and have solid-color bonnets, arms, and feet, print dresses, muslin "mitten" hands; tiny red on white print sashing, and border with solid medium blue squares at the set corners; good assembly, most corners match, fair to good appliqué, some unevenness in edges of figures; very good condition, but with several small spots and stains; 68" × 86"; $90.

SUNBONNET SUE: 1930s; solid medium blue, cream white, red, blue, lavender, pink, green, and many other dark and pastel colors in solids and prints; four columns of five Sues, center columns facing outer columns, outer columns face in; Sues are appliquéd on plain cream white blocks, with solid blue sashing and wide blue border; they have two legs in beige, with shoes in solid-color that matches bonnets, and arms, with coordinating print dresses; machine appliquéd, hand embroidered in dark thread around edges of bonnets, buttons on shoes, "cuffs" on sleeves, other areas; excellent condition, no soiling or stains; 74" × 92"; $150.

SUNBONNET SUE AND OVERALL SAM: 1930s; solid blue, pink print, white; four rows by five rows of pattern blocks, set square with blue sashing between, half Sues, half Sams, blue border; Sues have blue bonnets, pink print dresses, Sams have blue shorts, pink print shirts, white hats; all with black embroidery details, legs, shoes, hat bands, arms, etc.; outline quilting in pattern blocks, circle in sashing and border, 6 stitches per inch; fair to good appliqué, many misshapen pieces, large stitches; fair to good embroidery, stitches are even but are inconsistent block to block, creating some unusual legs, arms, etc.; very good condition, has been washed and used; 33" × 42"; $350.

TEDDY BEAR JACK-IN-THE-BOX: 1930s; pink, baby-blue, and white; appliquéd white teddy bear in jack-in-the-box appliquéd onto large, baby-blue rectangle with small scalloped edges, appliquéd onto white background; pink and blue baby rattles appliquéd in corners, small posies around edges; large scalloped edges; embroidered flower centers, teddy's eyes and mouth, and elsewhere; good assembly, well done, if fairly large, 5 stitches per inch straight-line, diamond, and outline quilting overall; very good condition 36" × 52"; $300.

TEDDY BEARS: 1930s; white, pink, eight different pastel prints; two rows by four rows of pattern blocks, set square with triple sashing and border between and around, pink, white, pink, and pink and white nine-patch squares at set corners; wide white border, appliqué pink sawtooth binding; each bear is different print, appliquéd with black blanket-stitch embroidery; from Pennsylvania; cable and diamond grid quilting overall, small and even stitches; excellent assembly and embroidery/appliqué; excellent condition; 33" × 54"; $695.

TURKEY TRACKS/WANDERING FOOT: 1830s; white, aqua-blue with tiny black dots, red with white and black leaves and lines; four red and aqua-blue "feet" around diamond center, on white ground, four rows by five rows of pattern blocks, set square with white sashing between, wide white border on three sides, with aqua-blue leaves and vines; outline quilting on pattern blocks, diagonal line quilting overall, small and even stitches; excellent assembly; very good to excellent condition, probably washed once; 82" × 82"; $3,900.

WANDERING FOOT VARIATION: 1860s; red and green on white background; 12 medallions each with four red and green "feet" around a green diamond center, green vine and leaves with red and green "feet" around the border, green binding; lots of echo, straight-line, and outline quilting overall at 8 stitches per inch; good condition; 70" × 86"; $1,150.

26 Dresden Plate

The Dresden Plate is a crossover pattern that starts with piecework and advances to appliqué. The wedge-shaped pieces that make up the plate are joined together as in piecework, then appliquéd around the outside edge of the plate to the traditionally white ground fabric. Sometimes the inside of the plate is appliquéd as well, but usually a separate circle is added and appliquéd, holding the inside of the plate down. Variations abound, and names may change to some version of fans, or suns, or whatever struck the quilter's fancy. The plate edges may be straight, pointed, or curved, depending on how the wedge-shaped pieces are cut. Stars, diamonds, or other shapes may be added in the center. Black or white embroidery thread in a blanket stitch or herringbone design might be used in place of appliqué stitches to anchor the plate.

Dresden Plate quilts were most popular between 1925 and the early 1950s and, traditionally, were made from a quilter's scrap bag. They were also very popular as precut kit quilts, so there were so many made that they are hardly a rarity. Yet many collectors love this pattern, and if you are one of them, you should be able to find one that is unique enough to triumph over its abundant kin.

DRESDEN PLATE: 1920s; all wools in solids of black, dark green, burgundy, plaids and solids of grays, green, blue, cream; full plate in center, four half plates on sides, four quarter plates in corners, all on black ground; plates have pointed edges, large centers where ground shows through; excellent featherstitch embroidery in yellow thread appliqués plate pieces to ground; green border, wide burgundy border, quilted with red thread; from Pennsylvania; diamond grid quilting overall, diagonal straight-line on green border, chevron on burgundy border, very small and very even stitches; excellent assembly; excellent condition; 66" × 68"; $695. *See illustration #66.*

DRESDEN PLATE: 1920–30; classic pattern in bright and pastel prints, cream centers in each plate and around each plate, pink and blue sashing and border; five plates across by six plates down, 7½-inch diameter plates, with much space around each, narrow sashing of two blue

66

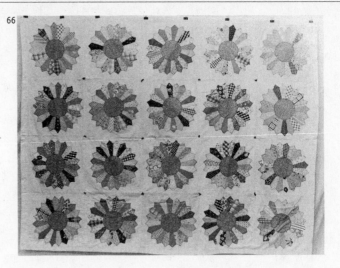

66 A tied coverlet with no quilting, this 1920s Dresden Plate shows neat centers, all of the same fabric, and pointed plate edges, a nice variation on the traditional curved edges. Quilt courtesy of the Dean Family.

strips with one pink strip between, pink and blue nine-patch at sashing points; from Kentucky; overall line quilting; very good assembly, straight seams, tiny appliqué stitches; excellent condition, unused; 72" × 88"; $1,150.

DRESDEN PLATE: 1920s; ivory white with solid pastels of blue, green, lavender; five rows by six rows of plates on white ground, white centers, curved edges follow the plates' sides; outline and sunrays quilting overall, small, mostly even stitches; excellent assembly; excellent condition; $475.

DRESDEN PLATE: 1930s; bright green and pale green, scrap bag fabrics in multicolor and patterns; machine pieced "plates" with pointed edges, hand appliquéd onto pale green background blocks; wide bright green sashing and pale green "ice-cream cone" border and edging; well assembled, very good appliqué; some small areas of staining; 82" × 82"; $195.

DRESDEN PLATE: 1930s; multicolored prints, stripes, florals, checks on cheddar yellow; five rows by six rows of plates with curved edges, wide areas of yellow between, yellow binding, and yellow centers; pieced cones border, lavender backing, thin batting; outline quilting on plates, grid and leaves overall, 7 stitches per inch; very good assembly, nearly all corners and edges match, small appliqué stitches; fair to good condition, colors holding true, few small spots in some areas, some fading on back along fold lines; 74" × 88"; $350.

DRESDEN PLATE: 1930s; multicolored prints, stripes, florals, checks, plaids on purple background, with golden yellow plate centers; cone border, alternate multicolored and purple cones, making curved edges; five rows by four rows of curved edge plates; from Missouri; excellent assembly; excellent condition; 78" × 94"; $175.

DRESDEN PLATE: 1930s; pink, white, multicolored pastels and brights in florals, prints, stripes, plaids, checks; five rows by four rows of plates, with pink four-point stars in plate centers and between plates, plates have curved edges; wide pink borders and prairie point edging;

all appliqué (star edges, plate centers and edges) have contrasting color overcast embroidery stitches; leaves, flowers, chains, diamonds, other patterns of quilting overall, 8 stitches per inch; excellent assembly; very good condition, with just minor color loss in pink border; 76" × 90"; $425.

DRESDEN PLATE: 1930s; pink, white, multicolored period prints, designs, florals, checks; four rows by four rows of pattern blocks, each plate with pink center, four pink segments, other segments multicolored, pointed plate edges, triple border, pink, white, pink; from Pennsylvania; square grid quilting in plate centers, outline quilting on plate segments, other patterns between plates, diamond chains on borders, 10 stitches per inch; excellent assembly and appliqué, nearly invisible stitches; excellent condition; 84" × 84"; $775.

DRESDEN PLATE: 1930s; solid green, cream, and pink, multicolored period prints and patterns; unique and stylized variation of the pattern, every plate has four green segments with pointed edges, arranged in "star" fashion, and three different print segments, with rounded edges, each in duplicate order after the green segment; four rows by four rows of pattern blocks on muslin cream ground, with triple sashing (green, pink, green) between pattern rows, with pink and green squares at set corners; centers of plates are also pink and green; cone border with pink, cream, green cones, sequentially excellent assembly; very good condition, few light stains in one area; 84" × 88"; $140.

DRESDEN PLATE: 1930s; white, blue, grays, pinks, multicolored period prints and patterns; plates have pointed edges, very small centers, quilt has scalloped edges that follow plate sides; outline quilting overall, 5 stitches per inch; fair assembly, many appliqué stitches uneven, large, awkward; fair to good condition, some overall color fade, very worn binding; 72" × 80"; $380.

DRESDEN PLATE: 1930s; white, blues, greens, darks in multiple period prints and patterns; plates on white ground, have scalloped edges, edge of quilt follows scalloped edges of the plates; outline quilting overall, 8 stitches per inch; fair condition, overall color fade, some mildew stains, backing was torn, has been repaired; 70" × 72"; $450. *See illustration #67.*

DRESDEN PLATE: 1930–40; multicolored cottons in prints, stripes, calicoes, checks, plaids; three plate squares by four plate squares with bright pink sashing between and golden yellow squares at the set corners; double border, one golden yellow, one pink; from Indiana; diamond quilting on borders and sashing; well assembled; quilting lines remain; 68" × 88"; $450.

DRESDEN PLATE: 1930s; cottons in bright rose pink and white, with plate pieces of prints, plaids, checks, stripes, solids in nearly every color imaginable; plates appliquéd onto plain white blocks, set checkerboard style with plain rose pink blocks; multicolored ice-cream cone border, each plate has golden yellow center, half curved edges to each plate piece; outline quilting in plate pieces, large feathered wreath and floral quilting in plain rose pink blocks, 8 stitches per inch; very good assembly, pieces well matched; very good condition, minimal use and washing; 72" × 90"; $600.

DRESDEN PLATE: 1930s; lavender, yellow, white, green, black, red, multicolored period prints; plates appliquéd on white ground using black thread and buttonhole stitch around outside and inside of each; also, yellow circles appliquéd same way in center of each plate, not

67

67 A closer look at the Dresden Plate quilt reveals black topstitching, a machine applied binding, and all of the wonderful printed fabrics from the maker's scrap bag. Quilt courtesy of the Dean Family.

filling center (looks like fried eggs!); five rows by six rows of pattern blocks, with lavender sashing between, with yellow squares at set corners, yellow border; good assembly, most corners match and edges are fairly even; very good condition, few small, pale spots; 74" × 86"; $140.

DRESDEN PLATE: 1930s; white, solid pink, multicolored period prints and florals; four rows by four rows of pattern blocks, set square with pink sashing; plates have pointed edges, pink centers, wide pink border, outside cone border of pink and white cones, white binding; from Ohio; outline and zigzag quilting in pattern blocks, overlapping ovals in border and sashing, small and even stitches; very good appliqué and assembly; excellent condition; 80" × 85"; $1,400.

27 Hawaiian-Style and Reverse Appliqué

Before the missionaries arrived in Hawaii in 1820, native woman were already creating colorful bed coverings. The addition of quilting gave them another means of expressing their art. The first design made in the Hawaiian style is attributed to a native woman who saw the shadow of a breadfruit tree on a white sheet she had left out in the sun to bleach. She liked the pattern so much that she cut it out of a piece of red cloth and appliquéd it to the white sheet, exactly where the shadow had fallen.

The designs for these quilts are distinctly individual. To create the design a quilter would take a piece of paper as large as she wanted the final design to be. The paper would be folded into eight sections—half, then quarters, then eighths—and the design cut out. The trick with this method is to cut along the correct fold to make a desirable design; cutting the wrong way on the wrong fold makes the whole pattern fall apart. Try it! It isn't that easy, especially when the design becomes as intricate and elaborate as many of the quilt patterns became.

The designs were primarily inspired by the natural things found on the islands, such as the lush foliage, flowers, birds and fruits. The quilter who stole another woman's design was required to beg forgiveness for her crime.

Traditionally, Hawaiian quilts are made in one color—usually red, although green and blue are sometimes seen—with a white ground. Once the pattern is created and the fabric cut, the color and the ground fabrics are put together and appliquéd. Hawaiian appliqué is actually a form of reverse appliqué. In appliqué, after a piece of fabric is cut in the desired shape, its edges are folded under, and it is appliquéd to the ground, so the ground shows around the piece. In reverse appliqué, the piece that is cut out leaves a hole, and the edges of that hole are folded over and appliquéd to the ground. So the ground showing through actually creates the design. This is much more difficult than traditional appliqué, requiring precise cutting and stitching. With Hawaiian appliqué the process is even harder, because the quilter is working with a bed-size piece of fabric.

Authentic Hawaiian appliqué quilts are very valuable and very rare. Traditionally they were made as gifts for very special occasions, were highly prized by the owner, and so were passed down in families, never to be sold. The few that we have seen in our travels were not for sale. Reverse appliqué quilts of any style are also rare, for only the most proficient quilter attempted them. If you come across either, you'll have a unique prize.

FOUR MEDALLIONS: 1927; Turkey red on cream background; four large medallions in the Hawaiian style, each of a large "x" with two mirror image hearts on each arm of the "x"; wide red sashing between and around the medallions; small pinwheel squares in the sashing points, cream border; from Pennsylvania; signed and dated, with location; extensive outline, cross-hatch, and echo quilting overall, 7 stitches per inch; very good assembly, small appliqué stitches; some minor color loss, slight discolorations in small area, has been washed, has been repaired in several spots, repairs done very well; 73" × 74"; $2,950.

HEARTS AND FLOWERS: 1890s; red on white; large center block of red hearts arranged to look like arrows, and flowers, on white ground, reminiscent of Hawaiian-style appliqué, central block is surrounded by twelve other blocks, also appliquéd in same style, red on white, with narrow red sashing between and around each block, very wide white border, red binding; from Pennsylvania; extensive and exquisite quilting of scrolls with diamond grid centers, other patterns in the border, tiny diamond grid in the center block, outline and scrolling in the other blocks, even stitches, 7 per inch; excellent assembly and appliqué; excellent condition; 70" × 82"; $1,700.

28 Political, Patriotic and Commemorative

Quiltmakers have always used their art to record history and make political comments. Throughout American history, printed cloth has depicted historic leaders, buildings, and events, and that cloth was often included in quilts. Like pieced quilt blocks, appliqué patterns were created to commemorate events and represent viewpoints. Quilts were made to celebrate and remember the nation's centennial, the 1933 Chicago World's Fair, and even the Nixon resignation. More recently, quilts have been important historic documentation of the battle against AIDS and the horror of the September 11 terrorist attacks.

One of the most popular appliqué patterns is the Whig Rose, a variation of the Rose of Sharon pattern. The Whigs were active from the late 1820s to the 1850s, but the pattern is still being quilted today. Although all but one of the Whig Roses we found were made during the years that the Whig Party was in favor, there is no way to tell if the maker was a proponent of that group or if she just liked the pattern.

With their ability to reproduce just about any shape, appliqué quilters have incorporated many popular figures into their patriotic quilt patterns. For example, eagles showed up in quilts around 1807 and have always been tied to times of intense patriotism. Their popularity rose during the War of 1812, again in 1846 during the Mexican War, and once again during the Civil War.

Political, patriotic, and commemorative appliqué quilts are even rarer than the same in piece-work; most of them are in the hands of private collectors or museums. If you're looking for one of these rare gems, tell every quilt dealer you meet because these quilts, when they surface, usually go right into the hands of collectors, bypassing the quilt shop showroom. Save up your money, too, since they'll certainly be expensive.

AMERICAN EAGLE: 1880–1920; bright Turkey red, green, and golden yellow cottons; wide green border, geometric central medallion, four large red eagles around this center, golden yellow shield over each eagle's breast, spread wings of green; from Pennsylvania; intricate feathered circle and cross-hatch quilting overall; few faint stains, quilting lines remain; 88" × 88"; $8,450.

REMEMBER THE *MAINE*: 1890s; blue and white with red embroidery; twenty-one blue and white appliquéd schoolhouse blocks in blue on white background alternate with twenty-one white blocks embroidered with the names and outlined faces of the first twenty U.S. presidents; twenty-first/center block has embroidered "Remember the *Maine*" and ship; straight-line and crisscross quilting overall; some small fabric damage; 70" × 82"; $4,500.

STARS: 1940s: three red and three blue diamonds pieced into six-point stars appliquéd onto a white background; three rows by five rows of star blocks, with white blocks between; center star block replaced by appliquéd red, white, and blue shield with spread-winged eagle in khaki brown/green; not quilted or backed, but edges bound; bordered with swagged "bunting" of red and white pieced stripes, fastened at junctions with white stars on blue shields; from New York State; 90" × 108"; $1,250.

WHIG ROSE VARIATION: 1817; white, green, red, gold, double pink; five large pattern blocks, set on point with triangular blocks on sides and corners to make sides straight; pattern blocks have red, yellow, pink concentric circle centers with four cock's comb-type leaves, eight red flowers with touch of double pink, eight green flowers and leaves growing from the center circles; side triangles have three flowers with stems and leaves, corner triangles have one each, all flowers are lightly stuffed; narrow red with pieced white diamonds sashing between the pattern blocks and as a border; from Pennsylvania; signed and dated, maker and history known; outline and grid quilting overall, very small and even stitches; very good condition, few tiny spots; 84" × 84"; $59,500.

WHIG ROSE VARIATION: 1855; white, red, pink, green, yellow; four pattern blocks on each corner of central pattern block, on white ground; pattern blocks have eight small roses with pink center, green leaves and stems surround large center rose of red and pink with yellow center; very wide white border with twining vines, large leaves, small red roses with pink centers; initialed and dated; outline and echo diamond grid quilting overall, feather wreaths in large white areas, very small and even stitches; excellent assembly; very good condition, very slight color fade in one area; 86" × 86"; $1,225.

WHIG ROSE VARIATION: 1863; natural white, solids of red and green; three rows by four rows of pattern blocks, pattern blocks have red circle center with thick green leaves and stems growing from center, eight carnation-type flowers and eight buds; wide white border with green vines and leaves all around, with thick green stems and leaves, flowers and buds; from New York State, signed and dated; outline, straight-line, and grid quilting overall, very small, even stitches; excellent, tiny appliqué stitches, well executed pattern; very good condition, faint quilting lines remain, few areas of discoloration; 80" × 96"; $32,500.

WHIG ROSE: 1860s; red, green, yellow on white background; four large medallions with red and yellow circular centers, green cock's comb, red and yellow flowers and buds, red and yellow vines between blocks and around borders; diamond and echo straight-line quilting overall; green has faded or changed color and is slightly different in one medallion, binding has been replaced; some other places where color has faded; 70" × 72"; $1,295.

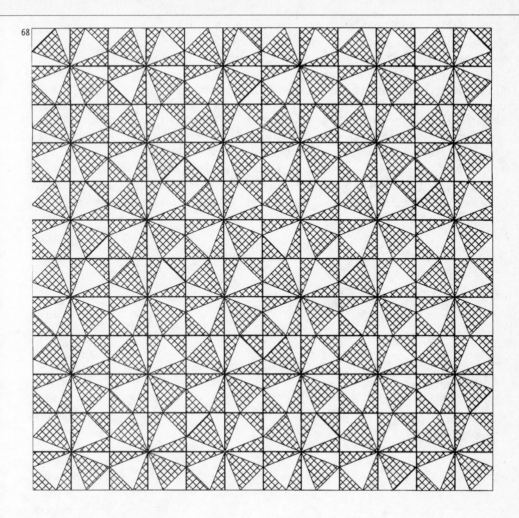

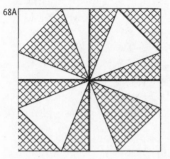

68 & 68A Fooling the Eye. While the full quilt of the Connecticut Quilt Block (also known as Shoeman's Puzzle) appears to be interlocking and overlapping circles, there isn't a curved piece in the entire quilt! The individual block shows the straight edged triangles that comprise the basic block. Such optical illusion quilts are some of the most intriguing to be found.

WHIG ROSE: 1840–50; red, green, gold on natural; nine (three rows of three) Whig rose squares, with red/gold/green rose centers, with four red flowers with gold centers, four green rooster combs, and four white buds around each center rose; green stems and leaves with red roses across top and bottom of quilt; from Kentucky; double-row cross-hatch quilting, 8 stitches per inch; some fabric loss/discoloration; 76" × 94"; $8,950.

WHIG ROSE: 1930s; red, cheddar, green, on white; four large pattern blocks, each with central red and cheddar wreath, four fern-like leaves, four stems with four cheddar rosebuds and four red rosebuds, all on white ground; additional red and cheddar wreath in exact center of quilt, red border, green binding; from Texas; outline quilting around appliqués, diamond grid quilting overall, with swags on border, even stitches, 6 per inch; excellent appliqué, tiny, nearly invisible stitches; excellent condition; 76" × 80"; $1,075. *See illustrations #68 and #68A.*

29 Embroidered Quilts

In the 1880s, the artist Kate Greenaway created a trend by depicting pictures specifically for children in her unique and innocent style. Quilt experts feel that this was the inspiration for the first embroidered quilts, which showed children, animals, circus characters, and others in simple scenes and activities. Usually the embroidery was done in a chain stitch, using red thread on a white ground fabric, often on individual blocks, which were then joined together to make a crib or child's quilt. These embroidered crib quilts were very popular until the mid-1920s.

Of course, during that time, every quilter who made one of these quilts added or changed something, and soon there were full-size quilts with embroidered flowers, quilts with other color threads, embroidered quilts with appliqué accents, friendship quilts with embroidered signature wheels, and pieced blocks with embroidered nursery rhyme characters in their centers.

Since embroidered quilts represent a fairly specific time period, more of their history and origins is known, making them very desirable collectibles. Their uniqueness is quite attractive, too. *See illustration #69.*

ALPHABET: 1930s; pink on white; twenty-six alphabet squares, each with small flowers, birds, or butterflies, four corner blocks with just flowers, herringbone embroidery on block seams, white backing, no batting, tied with pink thread in each block corner; very good assembly and embroidery, neat and even stitches; very good condition, few stains in one area; 35" × 50"; $500.

BABY ANIMALS: 1930s; pink and white, multicolored embroidery; six pattern blocks with embroidered baby animals (squirrel, cat, mouse, frog, bear, rabbit), set with six plain solid pink blocks, very wide pink border, pink backing and binding; from Ohio; straight-line quilting overall, 9 stitches per inch; excellent assembly and embroidery; excellent condition; 27" × 38"; $195.

69 This classic 1910 coverlet is called Dreams of the Forest and features red embroidery on white muslin squares. This is a quilt top with the edges finished so it can be used for a bed cover. Quilt courtesy of the Atwater family.

BIBLE SCENES: 1900–1910s; red on white; twenty-four pattern blocks with various Bible scenes, with red sashing between, red binding and border; minimal straight-line quilting, 4 stitches per inch; very good embroidery; good condition, binding has small repair; 55" × 66"; $290.

CIRCUS ANIMALS: 1890s; fourteen redwork embroidered blocks of various circus animals, with red sashing between, around a center block of a circus tent and elephant, red border, red binding, no batting, no quilting; very good embroidery; good condition, some overall age discoloration, one faded area, few tiny spots; 47" × 57"; $375.

EMBROIDERED BABY ANIMALS: 1930s; pink and white; six white blocks embroidered with baby mice and rabbits in children's clothing alternate with six plain pink blocks, very wide pink border and pink backing; from Ohio; excellent embroidery and assembly, straight-line quilting with 9 stitches per inch; 27" × 38"; $195.

EMBROIDERED FRIENDSHIP TOP: 1930; thirty-five white blocks, five by seven, embroidered with names, places in Canada and Oklahoma, dated; all styles and skills of embroidery, one block says "Happy Birthday," other embroidery of flowers, other shapes; good condition, one small tear at one edge; 56" × 80"; $145.

FEATHER WREATHS: 1920s; white with blue, and blue embroidery; nine pattern blocks are actually blue, churn dash nine-patch with very large, white centers in which are embroidered, in blue thread, delicate wreaths of flowers; narrow sashing and border of blue, with white squares at the set corners, white binding; from Pennsylvania; diagonal straight-line quilting overall, 6 stitches per inch; very good assembly and embroidery; excellent condition; 86" × 86"; $895.

FLORALS: 1920s; white, with dark blue embroidery; twenty-eight pattern blocks with chain stitched embroidered flowers in bunches and wreaths, with vines, leaves, and stems, very wide white border; excellent embroidery and quilting in cable, wreath, and straight-line, 11 stitches per inch, tiny and even; excellent condition; 70" × 78"; $450.

FLOWERS IN BASKETS: 1930s; rose pink on white; thirty pattern blocks, most with flower baskets, some others with doves, other flowers, pink sashing and border; grid quilting in the pattern blocks, cable and leaf quilting in the sashing and border, 7–8 stitches per inch; excellent assembly and embroidery, small, even stitches; very good condition, unused, few tiny stains; 76" × 78"; $775.

FLOWERS IN EMBROIDERY AND APPLIQUÉ: 1930s; multicolored embroidery on white, green; nine pattern blocks, each with a different flower motif, rose, nasturtium, tulip, posy, etc., on white ground, set square with green sashing between, green border and binding; each pattern flower is appliquéd in appropriate pastels, with the embroidery as an accent and creating the stems and leaves; from Ohio; diamond grid quilting on the pattern blocks, double cable on the sashing and border, even stitches, 8 per inch; very good assembly, appliqué and embroidery; excellent condition; 68" × 74"; $685.

FLOWERS: 1920s; red on white; various flowers embroidered in red on white ground, red border and binding; grid quilting overall, cable quilting on the border, 7–8 stitches per inch; excellent embroidery and assembly; good condition, a few discolorations in small area, unused and unwashed, quilting lines remain; 76" × 80"; $625.

FLOWERS: 1930s; golden tan and white, multicolored embroidery; twelve pattern blocks of various flowers in pots, bunches or wreaths, with stems and leaves, with tan sashing between, tan binding and border; straight-line and cable quilting overall, 8 stitches per inch; good assembly, very well done embroidery; very good condition, some slight overall color fade; 66" × 86"; $200.

FLOWERS: 1930s; multicolored embroidery, various types of flowers; twenty pattern blocks with plain white blocks between; feathered ring quilting in white blocks, 8 stitches per inch; excellent embroidery, small even stitches; very god condition, minimal use, few tiny stains; 77" × 77"; $425.

FLOWERS: 1930s; polished cotton, medium yellow, alternating with cream blocks, approx. 8½"-square, seven blocks by nine blocks; various primary-color embroidery threads; from Kentucky; heart and line quilting, 8 quilting stitches per inch; good assembly, most corners match; excellent condition, some quilting lines visible, some slight fading, age discoloration; 60" × 78"; $800.

LAUREL LEAF WREATHS AND FLOWERS: 1940s; gold and brown cross-stitch embroidery on white; large white central rectangle with eight brown and gold cross-stitch wreaths and fifteen sunflowers, very wide white border with half wreaths arranged to make swags, with additional sunflowers; feather wreath quilting around cross-stitch wreaths, sunflowers inside cross-stitch wreaths and sunflowers, diagonal-line quilting overall, feather vines on border, 7 stitches per inch; excellent cross-stitch embroidery, even and correctly spaced; excellent condition; 64" × 92"; $295.

MONTHS: early 1900s; natural cotton background with 49 squares (seven by seven) of embroidered months, figures, flowers, butterflies, animals, others in multicolored threads; narrow, solid blue border with wide white border, embroidered with vines and grapes; Wisconsin Amish; overall patterned quilting; some minor stains and discoloration, has been washed; 76" × 78"; $4,950.

MORNING GLORY VINES: 1930s; pink, white; green embroidery of vines and leaves, purple, pink, blue flowers with coordinating appliqué fabric petals; three rows of morning glory vines encircle the center rectangle, white ground; quadruple border, pink, white, pink, white, pink binding; from Pennsylvania; diamond grid quilting overall, 8 stitches per inch; excellent appliqué, nearly invisible stitches, excellent embroidery, neat and even; excellent condition; 75" × 87"; $500.

MORNING GLORY WREATHS: 1930s; white, green, bright blue, rose, lavender; thirteen pattern blocks, on white ground, set on point with white half blocks along sides, each pattern block has green embroidered wreath with three leaves, six flowers, two each of blue, lavender, rose; each flower with coordinated fabric appliqué petals with embroidery details, yellow knot centers, white border, white prairie point edging; from Pennsylvania; cable quilting on border, chevrons on white half blocks, flowers in center of wreaths, 6 stitches per inch; very good appliqué and embroidery, even stitches; excellent condition; 70" × 80"; $425.

MOTHER GOOSE: early 1900s; red on white; twenty pattern blocks with various Mother Goose stories, with red sashing between, red binding and border; diagonal straight-line quilting overall, 8–9 stitches per inch; even embroidery stitches, well executed; good condition, minimal use and washing; 50" × 63"; $300.

PENNY SQUARES REDWORK: dated 1894, 1897, 1903; cottons of bright red and natural white; plain, solid red squares alternate with white squares, embroidered with red figures, symbols, animals, flowers, plants, medallions, crockery, and initials; from Missouri; square cross-hatch quilting overall, large stitches, 5 stitches per inch; minor discolorations, a few tiny holes; 76" × 88"; $3,375.

REDWORK CRIB QUILT: 1901; red embroidery on white; figures of stork, flowers, birds, bunnies, girl and boy, horseshoes with butterflies and flowers in each corner, ducks, other shapes, white binding, white backing; initialed and dated; curved-line quilting overall, even stitches, good embroidery; good condition, some overall discoloration, some stains, has been washed many times; 36" × 32"; $625.

REDWORK: 1897; natural white with red embroidery; 80 blocks, each with a different picture, horseshoe, spiderweb, bucket, shoes, flowers, teapot, etc.; signed and dated; tiny stitches quilted in cross-hatch pattern; yellowing/discoloration indicate storage folded, one half yellowed and along fold lines; 64" × 80"; $6,500.

REDWORK: 1930s; red and red embroidery on cream/white; ten rows by twelve rows of pattern blocks, each surrounded by its own narrow border, making a double border/sashing where blocks join, single red border around the whole quilt, red binding; pattern blocks depict various household items, flowers, animals, people, buildings, boats, letters; no batting, summer spread; from Maryland; tied, no quilting; fair to good assembly, some edges and corners mismatched, embroidery stitching makes some items look rather unusual; excellent condition; 64" × 74"; $1,350.

REDWORK: 1930s; red and white, red embroidery; twenty-five pattern blocks are actually red on white churn dash nine patch with very large centers in which are embroidered, with red thread on white, botanicals, birds, animals, flowers, other items; wide red sashing between square-set pattern blocks, red binding, red backing; cable and diamond grid quilting on sashing, diamond grid on pattern blocks, 8 stitches per inch; very good assembly, most corners match, excellent embroidery; very good condition, very slight overall color fade; 76" × 76"; $950.

STORYBOOK: 1900–1910; red embroidery on white ground; ten pattern blocks of various storybook characters (Puss in Boots, Little Red Riding Hood, similar) with plain white block between; tied, no quilting; excellent embroidery, even stitches; good condition, one small stain; 72" × 82"; $475.

30 Trapunto

Trapunto is a form of Italian quilting that dates back to the fourteenth century. The word comes from *trapugere*, 'to embroider,' which is derived from the Latin *trans-*, meaning 'through,' and *pungere*, meaning 'to prick.' That pretty much describes trapunto.

In this time-consuming and involved process, two layers of cloth are stitched together using a design that has identifiable items such as leaves, flowers, ropes, grapes, vines, and/or fruits. Once the overall design is complete, the identifiable areas are singled out. A tiny slit is made in the backing fabric, say behind an apple, and pieces of batting are stuffed in until the apple, on the front fabric, is three-dimensional and defined. When the quiltmaker was satisfied, and liked the look of the apple, she would slipstitch the slit closed. If she were making vines or stems, she could use a cording, pulling it through the channel, instead of the batting, and get the same effect. After all of the desired areas were stuffed, a third layer of fabric would be added on the back to hide the slits and cording holes. Elaborate quilting would then be added, which would not only hold the three layers together but also add to the overall look.

If the quilter could find a loosely woven backing, it might not be necessary to slit the fabric at all. If the fabric threads could be pushed aside, the batting could be stuffed in, the threads coaxed back into place when the stuffing was finished, and the need for a third layer eliminated.

Trapunto is typically made on a whole cloth, although occasionally blocks are made. It is sometimes confused with whitework, and there is some overlap. Though it is traditionally done on white, it can, in fact, be done on any type or color of fabric; the word refers to the stuffing process, not the quilt color. Whitework is a whole cloth, and its unique feature is the quilting. Trapunto may, and usually does, have extensive quilting but that is not what makes it Trapunto.

The popularity of this style started around 1800 and dropped off dramatically after the Civil War. Some historians attribute this to the availability of inexpensive and plentiful cotton and cotton thread during that time. Trapunto on an antique quilt is one clue that the quilt was made before 1865.

BASKET TRAPUNTO: 1700s; whole-cloth natural cotton, four-poster cutout style; large center medallion of basket with roses, other flowers, and leaves; vines, grapes, leaves, twisted rope designs around center; sides that hang down around bed post covered with vines, leaves, grapes, other elaborate designs; wider than long; from Massachusetts or Connecticut; quilted between trapunto patterns with echo quilting so close as to look stippled; edges slightly frayed in some spots, some age discoloration, few tiny holes in various spots; 107" × 95"; $7,000.

GRAPES AND LEAVES: 1830s; large central wreath of grape vines and leaves, with bunches of grapes, vines, and leaves running along all sides of the quilt; outline, straight-line, and cable quilting, 8 stitches per inch; good workmanship; good condition, some wear along binding, few tiny stains in one area; 82" × 84"; $7,950.

LEAVES AND GRAPES: 1860s; extremely detailed bunches of grapes, vines, leaves in large central medallion with leaves and vines all around; from Wisconsin; small and even outline in close lines overall, 8 stitches per inch; excellent workmanship; excellent condition; 78" × 80"; $12,800.

MEDALLION TRAPUNTO: mid-1800s; whitework, whole-cloth cotton with large circular center medallion, with intricate vine and leaf designs, lyres, and cornucopias, quilted patterns, diamonds, triangles, fish scales, and cross-hatch overall quilting; from Indiana, history known; fine quilt stitches, 9–11 per inch; some stains and discolorations, one small tear on back; 82" × 92"; $1,850.

ROSE WREATH: 1850s; large center wreath with roses, feather, leaves, and vines; lots of stipple and line quilting overall, 10 stitches per inch; excellent workmanship; excellent condition; 78" × 100"; $5,775.

31 Whole-Cloth Quilts

Whole-cloth quilts were the very first quilts, two whole pieces of cloth with batting between. Regardless of when you consider that quilting got started, even back to the ancient Persians, there is no doubt that when a more modern quilter got hold of the original quilt format, it rapidly became a way to show off exquisite quilting. The assembly didn't matter, the colors didn't matter, but the quilting certainly did. Impressive quilting on a whole-cloth quilt was the mark of a superior quilter. By the time a girl made her thirteenth quilt, usually her bridal quilt, she would feel confident enough in her abilities to do an elaborate whole-cloth. Many of such quilts were never used but were handed down as heirlooms from one generation to the next. This is one reason why many of the whole-cloth quilts to be found in good condition are whitework bridal quilts. Look hard; you still won't find many.

BRODERIE PERSE WITH APPLIQUÉ BIRDS: 1800–1810; cream/white background with large center diamond of nature print, with wild roses, vines, berries in pale and subtle burgundy, fuchsia/pink, sea green, brown, tan, same fabric makes binding and backing; around center piece are cutouts of various birds and butterflies in the same colors; from New England; minimal outline quilting around appliqués, straight-line in other areas; good assembly and appliqué, but has had some restoration done; good condition, some overall color fade, some overall soiling that has not washed out; 33" × 35"; $2,600.

CHEATER'S CLOTH: 1880s; printed patchwork, eight-point stars, four-patch, other block patterns, primarily in reds, grays, some blues; reversible, backing is assembled in very wide bars, red with tiny white flowers print and dark green with light green flowers print; from Pennsylvania; diamond grid and triple cable quilting overall, small and even stitches; excellent, unused condition; 86" × 94"; $775.

CHINTZ WHOLE-CLOTH: 1840s; one-piece nature print of formal style birds, trees, leaves, flowers in shaded browns, blues, greens, beige on tan background; echo diamond grid quilting overall, very small and even stitches; excellent condition, glaze on chintz remains; 87" × 99"; $1,495.

CHINTZ: early 1800s; red, blue, gray on cream/white chintz print; made of four panels joined together; large amateurish quilting stitches; original glaze remains on chintz, some minor wear on edges; 88" × 92"; $1,250.

FLORAL CHINTZ: 1930s; beige with blue flowers; large center with grid quilting, clamshell quilting along sides, 9–10 stitches per inch; fair condition, few tears on backing, some areas of color loss, overall soiling and discoloration; 100" × 100"; $325.

WHITE-ON-WHITE: 1900–1910; probably brides quilt; peacock in center with flower, leaf, and vine quilting all around, grid quilting around that, flower and leaf quilting along edges, in scallops; scalloped edge; exquisite and extensive quilting, excellent condition, unwashed, unused, carefully stored, quilting lines remain; 80" × 82"; $1,000.

WHITE-ON-WHITE: 1910–1920; one piece of pure white cloth, thin batting; feather quilting in large central area with feather and straight-line all around, 8 stitches per inch; good condition, minimal use, few tiny spots in one area; 44" × 48"; $550.

WHITE-ON-WHITE: 1920s; large central six-point star with oak leaves, vines, feathers, wreaths; from Ohio; excellent quilting, 10 stitches per inch; excellent condition; 74" × 74"; $1,200.

WHITE WORK: 1900–1910; large rectangular center medallion with flowers, concentric circles, leaves, scalloped circles, feathered wreath; very wide white border with grapes and leaves on vines, many other smaller motifs in various areas on the quilt; from Pennsylvania; fill-ins with diamond grid quilting, so almost the whole top has some sort of quilting, 8 stitches per inch; excellent condition, has been washed; 77" × 81"; $770.

WHITE WORK: early 1900s; large central pattern with three fleur-de-lis, surrounded by lots of grid quilting, cable quilting along borders, uniform and even stitches, 7 per inch; fair to good condition, some overall soiling, few small stains; 68" × 78"; $350.

32 Uniques and Unusuals

All of our "Other" quilts are unique, but this last group is the most unusual. It can be argued that these are not even quilts, since most don't have quilting, some have strange stuffing or none at all, and some even have deliberate holes!

The Yo-Yo quilt is made of little circles of fabric, gathered on one side, and joined with a bunch of like circles to make a "quilt" that is certainly full of holes! Even the addition of a fabric backing isn't going to provide much warmth, but it certainly is decorative. *See illustration #70.*

Also decorative, and without much utility, Puff Quilts have one factor that we generally don't like in a quilt: puckered piece sides! Of course, they are not really puckered but are considered gathered, so the puff has lots of room inside and therefore is usually stuffed to excess.

The Cigar or Tobacco Silk Quilt is another unusual type. In the late 1800s and early 1900s, tobacco companies would include imprinted silk ribbons or flags with their products, or give the items away at fairs and other events as an embellishment or for advertising purposes. Since the ribbons were silk and usually came in brilliant colors, creative folks were soon joining them together to make decorative items, just as they did with fabric strips to make quilts. Of course, the ribbons were typically small and narrow (the flags were larger), so it would take far too many to make an entire quilt; thus they usually ended up as squares, pillow covers, or such. They are highly collectible, and there are still some out there.

CIGAR SILKS BLOCK: 1890s; alternating gold and cream silks, two cigar brands; good assembly; good condition; 16" × 16"; $195.

CIGAR SILKS BLOCK: 1890s; golds, creams, dark blue, light blue, dark green, pink; assembled in a sort of log cabin arrangement of a square in a square; along the edges of the silk strips, center square has black featherstitch embroidery that goes through the backing, holds quilt block together; white with tiny print backing; good assembly and embroidery; poor to fair

70 This typical Yo-Yo Quilt has peach
sashing and backing which peeks
through the spaces between the
yo-yo's. The decorative quilt was
made in the 1940s. Quilt courtesy
of Joan Halla.

71 A close-up of one yo-yo shows how
fabric circles are gathered and
fastened, then stitched together to
form this non-utilitarian but
whimsical and decorative quilt
top. Quilt courtesy of Joan Halla.

72A

72

72 Tricky Blocks. The Sister's Choice block is deceiving at first glance. Looking at the entire quilt, one's first impression is that the block is a four-patch with white sashing between the pattern blocks. It is, in fact, a nine-patch with a small center square.

condition, slight color bleed, water staining on the back, three strips are missing, probably shattered; 17" × 17"; $95.

CIGAR SILKS TOP: 1890s; bright green, dark green, red, rust orange, cream, white, yellow cigar silks assembled into a central block, surrounded by additional rows of silks; sewn onto a solid blue/green silk backing; "top," no quilting; 21" × 21"; $300.

PUFFS: 1900–1910; browns, blues, other darks of cottons and wools, in solids, prints, and stripes; fifteen rows by fifteen rows of puffs, lightly stuffed, embroidered accents on each puff, ruffled edging; good assembly, puffs consistent size, neatly assembled on foundation fabric; good condition, some tiny holes on several wools, some light stains on several cottons; 50" × 50"; $160.

TOBACCO SILKS TOP: 1920s; deep reds, golds, others; large ribbon flags from several tobacco companies; from New Jersey; some embroidery around flags; good assembly; good condition; 70" × 83"; $2,950.

YO-YO'S: 1930s: multicolored prints and patterns; thousands of quarter-sized yo-yos, very well made, nice assembly with pleasing color arrangement; 70" × 94"; $295. *See illustration #71.*

YO-YO'S: 1930s; solid blue and white, many multicolored fabrics; multicolored blocks of five yo-yos by five yo-yos, with one row of white yo-yos around the block and one row of solid blue yo-yos around that, form "pavement blocks" reminiscent of square Grandmother's Flower Garden blocks; excellent assembly of very well made and even yo-yos; 70" × 90"; $400.

YO-YO'S: 1930s; purple, multicolored period prints; yo-yos assembled into eight-inch blocks with purple "tube" sashing between, purple border; excellent assembly; very good condition, some very slight overall color fade; 84" × 108"; $500. *See illustration #72.*

33 Amish

Amish quilts are among the most prized of antique quilts. The fascination lies in their use of pure colors: magentas, blues, greens, reds, and purples. Also, the Amish quiltmakers used black as a color, a practice unique to these quilts—with the marked exception of the crazy quilts of the Victorian era. Both the design and color choices of Amish quilters grew directly from their religious beliefs.

The followers of Jacob Amman, originally associated with the Mennonite religion, migrated away from religious persecution and settled in the Pennsylvania Dutch Colony in the early 1720s. Their migration to the New World was initiated by an invitation from William Penn. Later they, like many other new Americans, migrated West. Now the largest population of Amish people exists in Holmes County, Ohio. Lancaster, Pennsylvania, the earliest settlement, and northern Indiana also boast large Amish populations. Today Amish communities exist in 21 states.

The basis of Amish quilt design comes from their belief that life should be simple, that people should be humble, and that they should avoid anything that draws attention outward—such as printed fabrics for their clothing—instead of inward to their faith. *The Ordnung*, the written doctrine of the Amish religion, expresses rules for all Amish members to follow. Individual church district guidelines are created by each district's leadership. In most districts, printed pattern fabrics are considered too worldly, too outward to be used in Amish homes and clothing. A few districts even ban the use of the colors white and yellow. *See illustration #73.*

Like all quiltmakers, the Amish used fabric left over from other home needlework to create their beautiful quilts. For the Amish, wasting anything was not just frivolous, it was irresponsible. Because their lifestyle and religion prohibited adornment of either their bodies or their homes, plain colored fabrics were all they bought. When we think of the Amish, we think of plain, black fabrics, but they used bright, clear colors for their clothing and household furnishings. It is these colors, combined with the same basic black, that make the Amish quilts

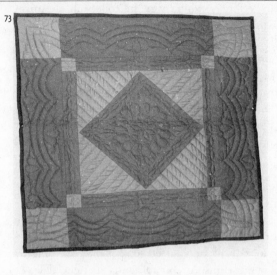

73 A traditional Diamond in a Square quilt shows the intricate quilting design typical of Amish quilts. The colors in this wall hanging are also typical using purple, green and red in primary tones. Quilt from the authors' collection.

so visually startling. Amish quilts were made in three predominant styles. One is reminiscent of the old English-style medallion quilts. These incorporated a central diamond bordered by strips and triangles of alternating black and colored fabric.

Strip and Bar quilts are also common. Another distinctly Amish design is the Trip Around the World, or Sunshine and Shadows quilt. Gradations and varieties of colors radiate in diamond-like strips out from a central square. Although this pattern looks difficult to piece, these quilts were made from prearranged grids showing where each color should be placed in a strip. Then the strips were sewed together to form the radiating diamond illusion.

The Amish had a distinctive way of combining colors in their quilts. Colors that seem inappropriate together when we are told about them, create wonderful movement and appeal when placed in close proximity in the Amish quilt. The combinations of magenta with blue, or red with purple, actually work exceptionally well in the hands of the expert Amish quiltmaker.

Amish quilting also separates itself from other traditional American quilts in its quantity. While the quilt patterns are strictly geometric and the colors bold, quilting designs are elaborate, with many curves, vines, and continuous line-quilting. And, because of restrictions against using the color white, Amish quiltmakers stitched with black thread. Quality quilting stitches were even more noticeable when stitched in black!

Amish quilts first became collectible in the late 1960s during a handcraft movement spurred on by the upcoming Bicentennial. In the watershed exhibit of antique quilts held at the Whitney Museum in 1971, one Amish quilt was displayed. Its unique design and color coordination along with the excellence of its quilting showed a contemporary flavor suited to the public's demand for both traditional craftsmanship and popular bold design. The collecting boom began, and Amish antique quilts, as well as contemporary ones, are still in high demand.

Perhaps the most noticeable outcome of the Whitney exhibit was the collection of Amish quilts put together by Doug Tompkins, the founder of Esprit de Corps. He collected Amish quilts based only on their visual appeal. He did not concentrate solely on antiques. A new Amish quilt would make it into the collection, as long as it was visually stimulating. The Esprit headquarters in San Francisco displayed the collection with the offices open to public viewing. Today, the collection can be seen by appointment only and has evolved into a collection of all types of quilts from the most elaborate appliqués to the most utilitarian wools. The original collection is still assumed to be the best assembly of Amish quilts in the world. Esprit de Corps remains unique in the business world as the only company with its own quilt curator.

Because antique Amish quilts are so valuable, fakes have appeared on the market. They're difficult to spot. Unlike scrap bag quilts, in which we can find colors and prints that indicate a specific time period in fabric manufacture, Amish quilts of natural fibers were made into the 1940s. Similar fabric in the same bright colors can be bought today, aged, then assembled into a brand-new Amish quilt with an antique look. Educate yourself to spot the real thing by viewing as many authentic quilts as you can at museums. A reputable and experienced dealer should be able to spot a fake Amish quilt.

If you decide to specialize your collecting in Amish antique quilts, be prepared for much competition. They continue in popularity today, and the prices reflect it.

CHIMNEY SWEEP: 1903; black and medium blue; four by five rows of pattern blocks, blue on black, set on point with plain black blocks between; machine pieced, black quilting thread, narrow blue border, wide black border, blue binding, muslin backing; Ohio Amish, dated and initialed in the quilting; echo line quilting in pattern blocks, floral feathers in plain blocks, cable quilting on borders, 7 stitches per inch; excellent assembly; fair condition, overall and uneven fade in blue, black has held fairly well, few minor spots, one repair, few tears in binding; 66" × 78"; $2,250.

CHURN DASH: early 1900s; cotton and wool solids in black, blue, teal, gold, dark red; four rows by five rows of pattern blocks, on blue ground, set on point with black blocks between, double border, blue then black; Ohio Amish; minimal quilting, chevron quilting in border; good assembly, most corners match, edges even; fair to good condition, areas of discoloration, some overall color fade, binding worn; 66" × 78"; $1,300.

DOUBLE NINE-PATCH: 1900–1910; solids of greens, lavender, teal, blues, red, rose, fuchsia; wools and cottons; four rows by four rows of pattern blocks, set on point, with dark green blocks between; narrow lavender border with green corners, wide fuchsia border with green corners; Pennsylvania Amish; elaborate quilting, floral in green blocks, cable in narrow border, flower wreaths in wide border, bows in border corner blocks, crisscross in pattern blocks, small and even stitches; excellent assembly; very good condition, some slight overall color fade; 84" × 84"; $11,995.

DOUBLE NINE-PATCH: early 1900s; wools and cottons of pinks, greens, blues, reds, many others; five multicolored nine-patch blocks in corners with four pink/fuchsia blocks on sides make double nine-patch squares; four squares by four squares, set on point with olive green solid squares between; narrow lavender border with small green squares in corners, wide pink/fuchsia border also with large green squares in corners; purple backing; Pennsylvania Amish; very precise flower design quilting in olive green squares, twisted rope and flower quilting in borders, cross-hatch quilting in pattern squares; very good condition, some minor color loss; 84" × 84"; $12,000.

DOUBLE NINE-PATCH POSTAGE STAMP DOLL QUILT: 1950s; burgundy, red, medium blue, dark blue, cream, white; five pattern blocks of two colors each, four plain black blocks between; triple border, black border, medium blue, wide black, medium blue binding; Kentucky Amish; crisscross straight-line quilting overall, small, even stitches; excellent assembly, all corners match; good condition, overall color loss/fade from washing; 22" × 22"; $200.

NINE-PATCH: late 1800s; cottons, wools, silks in blues, greens, reds, many others, with white; six squares by seven nine-patch squares, set on point with white squares between, and red half squares between and around sides; very wide white border; Amish; tiny 12 stitches per inch basket, flower, and straight-line quilting; severe overall staining, soiling, discoloration, much deterioration of silk backing, some fabric deterioration on front; 71" × 78"; $3,000.

ROMAN STRIPE VARIATION: 1930–50; cottons in black, purple, blue solids, narrow blue border, wide black border, purple edging; Pennsylvania Amish; outline and twisted rope quilting; few tears, some discoloration; 52" × 80"; $499.

SAWTOOTH STAR VARIATION: early 1900s; black and burgundy; only the eight points of each star are burgundy, rest of the block is black, three rows by five rows of pattern blocks, set on point with plain black blocks between; burgundy border, then very wide black border, burgundy binding, brown backing; Pennsylvania Amish; crisscross straight-line quilting overall, small, even stitches; excellent assembly, all corners/points match; fair condition, binding frayed in one area, black very faded unevenly overall, burgundy faded more evenly overall; 50" × 70"; $1,850.

TRIP AROUND THE WORLD LOG CABIN: 1930s; all solids in red, blues, burgundy, pink, purple, lavender, grays, black; 1½-inch squares in wools, cotton, rayon, wool crepe; very wide dark blue border with purple corner blocks; Pennsylvania Amish; crisscross quilting in the squares, excellent and extensive rose and vine quilting on the border, 10 stitches per inch; excellent assembly; fair to good condition, two tiny moth holes, a few separated seams, some color bleed on backing; 79" × 79"; $1,850.

TRIP AROUND THE WORLD LOG CABIN: 1930s; all solids in red, blues, burgundy, pink, purple, lavender, grays, black; wools, cotton, rayon; very wide fuchsia border with purple corner blocks, blue binding, gray wool backing; Pennsylvania Amish; crisscross quilting in the squares, excellent and extensive floral and vine quilting with bows on the border, 7 stitches per inch; excellent assembly; good to excellent condition, no moth holes, wear, or fading, few tiny spots in one area; 79" × 79"; $2,500.

TRIP AROUND THE WORLD: 1940s; deep burgundy, two shades of purple, green, blue, red; top is wool crepe, backing is cotton; very wide deep burgundy border and corner blocks; from Lancaster, Pennsylvania, Amish; crisscross line quilting in pattern squares, florals, and clamshell quilting on border; excellent assembly; excellent condition; 82" × 88"; $950.

74

74 This beautiful Lily variation was made in Iowa in the 1880s of fabric scraps that included apron ties and shirt tails. With white sashing and border, the quilt is a balanced delight. Quilt courtesy of the Zimmer Family.

TRIP AROUND THE WORLD: early 1900s; blues, red, burgundy, pink, yellow, greens, lavender, purple, black backing, wide purple border, narrow lavender binding; Pennsylvania Amish; tiny stitch flower wreath and crosshatch quilting; some discoloration, minor color loss, a few seam separations; 89" × 92"; $12,000.

WILD GOOSE CHASE: early 1900s; black and brown solids, with some green; cotton and wool, "geese" rows go corner to corner in nine parallel rows, with alternating black and brown squares in the junctions of each row, medium wide black border surrounded by very wide black border; Ohio Amish; excellent quilting and workmanship; good condition, but needs cleaning, some discoloration, some color loss in black especially; 69" × 69"; $450. *See illustration #74.*

34 African-American Quilts

We wrote a book similar to this about twelve years ago, and at that time we predicted that African-American improvisational quilts would soon be the hot collectible in the market. Our prediction did not materialize. We found only four listings for African-American-made quilts for sale, and one dealer told us she had never had so much as one request for a slave-made or African-American-made antique quilt. But we are encouraged again to go out on a limb and repeat our prediction, though slightly amended. We still feel that African-American quilts, most notably those made by slaves, and improvisational quilts will continue to draw the attention of scholars and researchers and then, ultimately, collectors.

The research for this chapter provided us with the most interesting, intriguing, and captivating reading about quilts and quiltmakers available. The study of African-American quilt design provides the opportunity for a focus on the evolutionary aspect of quilting that is not as easily available in traditional American quilt design. The link between African-American quilt design and the art of African cultures is not easy to prove, but research continues in this field that is both fascinating and necessary to completing the lore and facts of quiltmaking available to us. *The Quilters* by Patricia Cooper and Norma Bradley Buferd, revealed to us how predominantly white American traditional quiltmakers create and feel about their quilts, while *Afro-American Folk Art and Crafts*, edited by William Ferris, revealed the innate design sense and sensibilities of the African-American improvisational quiltmaker. Both books profile quiltmakers whose stories warmed and awed us.

The earliest African-American quilts known today are the two pictorial Bible quilts made by Harriet Powers in 1886 and 1898. The first quilt, now owned by the Smithsonian Institution, was shown by Powers at the Cotton Fair of 1886 in Athens, Georgia. A white woman, Jennie Smith, saw the quilt and wanted to buy it. Powers refused. Four years later, after falling on hard times and needing money, she offered it to Smith, who bought it. Through Smith, Powers received a commission from women in Atlanta to create a second quilt, now owned by the Museum of Fine Arts in Boston. Both quilts illustrate Powers's own artistic and creative intent in the selection of scenes. Powers is considered the mother of African-American quiltmaking, and efforts are under way to petition the U.S. Postal Service to issue a stamp with her image. (See our Sources and Resources section for information on how to join the petition.)

African-American quiltmakers did, and do, work in traditional American quilt formats. The African-American improvisational quilt, on the other hand, is a type of quilt that is as different, in visual impact, from the traditional pieced and appliqué quilts that we see most often, as a Picasso is from a Rembrandt.

Several recent events confirm for us that the desirability of the improvisational antique African-American-made quilts will rise.

The first of these events was the 1999 publication of *Hidden in Plain View* by historians and authors Jacqueline L. Tobin and Raymond G. Dobard. The book is the result of a chance encounter Tobin had with Ozella McDaniel Williams, a quiltmaker who sold quilts in the Old Market Building of Charleston, South Carolina. Williams shared the oral history passed down to her by her ancestors with Tobin about how quilts were used as guides, signals, and instructions for slaves moving along the Underground Railroad. Tobin was so intrigued, she embarked on a five-year research journey to find support for the code Williams revealed to her. Tobin invited the help of Raymond G. Dobard, Ph.D., as co-author, and together they produced *Hidden in Plain View*.

The book is both an amazing personal story and a fascinating study of the impact of quilts on American history. The book received some heavy criticism from historians who said that some of the quilt patterns mentioned were not documented to be in use during the time line of the slave migration to freedom along the Underground Railroad. Other questions were raised: Where did the fabric, thread, and time come from with which the slaves made these "map" quilts? How did the slaves have access to the geographic information required to stitch the 'map' into the quilts? Why would anyone spend the time and creative energy on a quilt just to hang it out in weather and sun, sure to hasten its deterioration? Where was the written proof to support the theories presented?

Dobard wrote, in the chapter "Stitching Ideas into Patterns: Methodology in the Writing of Hidden in Plain View," "Since the field of African-American quilt history is relatively new . . . (we) acknowledge that ideas and theories might not always be conclusively proven as much as presented for serious consideration."

It bothers us not a whit that *Hidden in Plain View* raises more questions than it answers. In fact, we find it exhilarating! We see the book and its critics as spurring on research into African-American antique quilts that will encourage those who own them to bring them to light and share their stories. It's just the type of mystery that a collector enjoys. We're hoping the controversy over this book, and the book itself, will result in increased awareness of this category of antique quilts and make them collectible.

Another event sparking interest in African-American quilts occurred in November 2002 through March 2003, when the Whitney Museum became part of a touring exhibit of Gee's Bend, Alabama quilts. Gee's Bend, a historically black community, and historically economically challenged as well, exists on a U-shaped peninsula hemmed in on three sides by the

Alabama River. Its quilters have kept alive the tradition of scrap bag quilts and African-American improvisational design. Sixty quilts were featured in the exhibit at the same museum that, in 1971, initiated the movement of viewing quilts as art by launching an exhibit that hung quilts on walls and started the collecting boom that continues today.

The improvisational design of the quilts of Gee's Bend and other African-American quiltmakers has been misunderstood in the past. At one time, African-American improvisational quilts were thought to be the work of novice quilters and that the result was simply poor workmanship. Dealers and collectors were used to the standards of uniform pieces, harmonious color balance, and an overall, precisely pieced pattern. African-American improvisational quilts at first looked jarring with their use of vibrant primary colors (which certainly didn't match a traditional living room or bedroom) and the irregularity of the piecing with sashings of several colors or printed fabrics that didn't line up in the neat, precise rows we're accustomed to in traditional geometric quilts. Instead, people learned that the irregular piecing is what gives the African-American improvisational quilt one of its many layers of movement.

Another design difference between African-American-style quilts and traditional American patchwork is the use of color. Bright, contrasting colors are used close together to heighten not only the impact of each individual color but their combination as well. The quilts themselves show purple and green, purple with yellow, red and white, orange with green, and black and pink as frequently used combinations. Instead of making the color combinations uniform throughout the quilt, as is the tendency in scrap bag traditional quilts, African-American improvisational quilts use color to move the eye toward what the maker considers the important parts of the quilt. The color placement adds multiple layers of movement within the quilt top. Viewed as a whole, the quilt sports an almost kaleidoscopic array of color. The placement of a color in one part of the quilt that is used nowhere else concentrates the eye on that particular section and reveals the pattern design used there and only there. Traditional-style quilts have a uniform pattern of color placement, but African-American improvisational quiltmakers arrange color to draw us back to the quilt to discover something new within it every time we look at it.

Luckily for us, scholars and quilt historians went to work debunking the myth of sloppy workmanship. Improvisational quilts are now viewed with educated artistic sensibilities and recognized as design innovation.

"The results, not incidentally, turn out to be some of the most miraculous works of modern art America has produced," wrote Michael Kimmelman of the *New York Times,* reviewing *The Quilts of Gee's Bend* exhibit at the Whitney Museum. He notes, "This may be the last moment to record and celebrate what is one of the country's most idiosyncratic and vivid living art traditions."

The national attention given the exhibit will also further the cause of bringing African-American antique quilts to the attention of collectors.

The third and most recent event to occur in pushing us out once again on the trend-predicting limb is the publication of *Black Threads: An African-American Quilting Sourcebook* by Kyra Hicks. Hicks, whose quilts have appeared in over thirty group exhibitions at such venues as the American Craft Museum in New York, the Renwick Gallery in Washington, D.C., and the Wadsworth Atheneum Museum in Hartford, Connecticut, actually began the book, albeit unknowingly, over a decade ago. Her passion for quilting and quilt history began with a trip to the *Stitching Memories: African-American Story Quilts* exhibit held at the Taft Museum in Cincinnati, Ohio, in 1991. She made her first quilt soon after and also started collecting books, articles, patterns, quilts, and oral histories on African-American quilting. The result, a decade later, is *Black Threads*.

"My primary goal in compiling this book is to document the range of ways African-American quiltmaking has been interpreted: in cloth, in art and in written and spoken words," Hicks wrote in her introduction. "The book includes references to famous Black quilters as well as casual quilters across America." *Black Threads* includes a wealth of information, ranging from the estimated number of quilters per household and the estimated number of Black quilters per household in the United States, to references to African-American quilting in poetry. Hicks includes an almost 100-page bibliography featuring books, articles, exhibition catalogues, dissertations, speeches, videos, fiction, and curricula material. She lists nine pages of African-American quilting organizations and over 90 museums that own 585 African-American antique quilts, and she presents an African-American quilting and needle arts timeline from 1800 through 2000. In *Black Threads*, Kyra Hicks has given the quilt collector the information needed to study and appreciate African-American antique quilts.

As is true for any category of quilt, be it feedsack, Amish, Baltimore Album, or African-American, the astute collector is well advised to study the category in depth in order to make sound purchases. Some quilts that look improvisational just might be the work of the novice quilter. But don't pass by a quilt because its rows are not perfectly aligned or each of its blocks are not precisely the same dimensions. Study the information we've suggested above to determine if what's regarded as sloppy workmanship by one dealer or collector just might be an excellent example of African-American improvisational antique quilting to the collector in the know—you!

It's impossible to tell, no matter how closely you inspect a quilt, its maker's race, gender, age, political preferences, creed, or religion. Remember the importance of provenance previously discussed and insist on knowing the history of the quilt you're considering.

Yes, we still consider African-American antique quilts as the collectible of the future. As scholars, both professional and amateur, and historians reveal the history of these quilts, more of them should become available. As appreciation for this style of quilt increases and their value rises, the forgotten and hoarded store of these quilts will be uncovered and placed on the market. At the very least, more of their stories will appear, more of their owners will have them appraised and share them with researchers and museums, and we'll know more about them. The knowledgeable collector, and those collecting to preserve and increase our store of knowledge of women and their work, will recognize the historic importance of these quilts and the mystique of their makers.

So, once again, we're predicting that as consciousness of these quilts rises, so will their value to collectors.

BABY BLOCKS AND STARS: 1930s; white, pink with tiny black dots, black with tiny white lines; from New Jersey, African-American, maker known; outline quilting overall, 6 stitches per inch; excellent assembly, points match, piece edges are smooth; very good condition, has been washed, minimal use, one binding edge slightly worn; 70" × 80"; $625.

CATS: 1930s; electric blue cats on white ground, red border and binding, red sashing with forest green squares at set junctions; cats appliquéd, black chain topstitching accents, collars, feet, eyes; probably African-American, partial history known; outline quilting around cats, clamshell in sashing and border, uneven stitches, 5 per inch; very good appliqué, nearly invisible stitches, good embroidery accents; excellent condition, unused and unwashed; 72" × 78"; $3,200.

NINE-PATCH: 1830s; browns, tan, cream, cheddar, reds; all homespun woolen fabrics, madder-dyed reds, pattern blocks of five dark squares and four light squares, brown wool backing, thin batting, probably blanket; from South Carolina, probably slave-made per family history, signed on back same as regional slave-made pottery; outline and straight-line quilting overall, 6 stitches per inch; very good assembly and design, nearly all corners and junctions match; fair to good condition, some overall wear, front and back, some overall color fade, few moth and other holes; 72" × 78"; $4,100.

NINE-PATCH: 1890s; Turkey red and white; five rows by six rows of pattern blocks, each with five red squares and four white, red binding, printed flower seed sacks backing; from Missouri, African-American, family known; grid quilting overall, 6–7 stitches per inch; good assembly, most corners match, piece edges flat; good condition, has been used and washed, some overall color loss, slight wear to binding; 62" × 82"; $625.

SOURCES

Since this is a book about collecting quilts, you might think we need only list quilt dealers in a section about resources. We have done just that, but we also believe it to be very important that you have places to find *information*. While museums will not have quilts for sale, they will have access to all sorts of quilt-related information. The Internet is also a wonderful place for help and information; just remember that, like anywhere, there is bad information to be found on the World Wide Web, just as there is good.

Quilt and Antiques Dealers

There are sources of antiques in just about any place across the country; just look in the yellow pages under "Quilts" and/or "Antiques." Someone who deals primarily in antique quilts will be your best source and resource, of course, but don't overlook smaller, less-specialized antiques shops. They may or may not have the same inventory or knowledge as the specialist, but we found many of them to be very well informed and to stock some wonderful quilts.

An Internet search will yield even more quilt sources, but be aware of the limitations therein. A query for "antique quilts" on three major search engines brought four or five large quilt dealers. But we never found "stellarubinantiques.com" until we set up a search for "Carolina Lily." Missing Ms. Rubin would have been a loss, since she has not only great quilts but also lots of knowledge.

You may be a little anxious about buying a quilt on the Internet, since all you can see are pictures, you can't hold, smell, and feel the actual quilt. Check the site carefully for its policies, and call to ask questions about how it deals with returns. Most of the sites have a 24- or 48-hour return policy that allows you to look at a quilt for that length of time and return it if you don't want it, usually for the cost of shipping and insurance. Since that is not always an inexpensive proposition, you may want to stick with local dealers, at least to start.

It may be better to start with experienced local dealers anyway, and to develop a relationship with one or two. That way, even if you find a prize in a little out-of-the-way antiques or Americana shop, you will have someone to help evaluate your find.

The quilts we listed in the previous chapters came from all sorts of sources across the country. As you might expect, we found more specialized dealers in large cities than in small towns. You may be amazed, as we were, at how many sources you can find just by talking to other dealers and collectors.

The people we have listed below are some of those we dealt with in collecting both the quilts and the information we share in this guide, and we list them because we found them to be knowledgeable and willing to help. You may, of course, find them otherwise, and certainly our experience is no guarantee, but they are a good place to start. Note that some have retail locations, and some are accessible only on the Internet or by telephone. Decide how you feel most comfortable and go from there.

American Quilts
P.O. Drawer 200
Upton, KY 42784-0200
270-531-1619
1-877-531-1619
Frank Geeslin
americanquilts.com

Antique Heirloom Quilts
4016 Willow Oak Road
Raleigh, NC 27604
antiqueheirloomquilts.com

Black Mountain Antiques
100 Sutton Avenue
Black Mountain, NC 28711
Aly Goodwin

Bonnie J. Cook, Inc.
P.O. Box 134
East Greenbush, NY 12061
518-477-7272
bonniejcook.com

Calico Country: Antique Quilts and
Country Furnishings
92 Washington Street
Marblehead, MA
617-631-3607
Lynne Wynne

Creekside Antiques Collective
241 Sir Francis Drake Boulevard
San Anselmo, CA 94960
415-457-1266

Ginnie Christie Quilts
38996 NE Scravel Hill Road
Albany, OR 97321
503-327-1473

Grandma's Quilts
296 North 10th Road
Palmyra, NE 68418-9790
402-780-5773
1-800-284-8574
Gloria Hall
grandmasquilts.com

Laura Fisher Antique Quilts and
Americana
Gallery # 57
1050 Second Avenue at 55th Street
New York, NY
212-838-2596

Log Cabin Quilts
quiltsquilts.com
Marie Miller Antique Quilts
1489 Route 30
Dorset, VT 05251
802-867-5969

Oh, Suzanna
18 South Broadway
Lebanon, OH 45036
513-932-8246
Joan Townsend

Regent Street Antique Corner
153 Regent Street
Saratoga Springs, NY 12866
518-584-0107

The Quilt Gallery
107 North Second Street
P.O. Box 458
Cissna Park, IL 60924
John and Suzanne Bruns
thequiltgallery.com

Rocky Mountain Quilts and Restoration
130 York Street
York, ME 03909
207-363-6800
1-800-762-5940
Betsey Telford
rockymountainquilts.com

Sharon's Antiques/Vintage Fabrics
610-756-6048
Sharon Stark
rickrack.com

Stella Rubin Antique Quilts
12300 Glen Road
Potomac, MD 20854
301-948-4187
stellarubinantiques.com

Susan Parrish Antiques
390 Bleecker Street
New York, NY 10014
212-645-5020

Undercover Quilts
1411 First Avenue, Suite 106
Seattle, WA 98101
106-622-6382
1-800-469-6511
undercoverquilts.com

Woodin Wheel Antiques
515 "B" Avenue
Kalona, IA 52247
319-656-2240
Marilyn Woodin

Museums, Societies, and Historical Associations

Many museums that feature American historical items or Americana also have some quilts as part of their collection. Some others have or host temporary displays featuring quilts. Some are dedicated primarily to quilts. While museums are not, of course, a place to buy quilts, they are among the best places to increase your knowledge. If a museum deals in any sort of textiles, it may have on staff a textile conservator who can be of great help to you. Dedicated quilt museums have huge amounts of information about quilts and may have newsletters or other printed material that will be most helpful to the collector. Quilt guilds can also be a source of help in education. Check around in your area and start forming relationships.

The following museums are dedicated completely to quilts or have large quilt collections that they often display.

American Quilter's Society Quilt Museum
215 Jefferson Street
Paducah, KY 42011
270-442-8856

The New England Quilt Museum
18 Shattuck
Lowell, MA 01852
978-452-4207

Esprit, USA
Vista Del Grande
San Carlos, CA 94070
650-596-6557

The Rocky Mountain Quilt Museum
1111 Washington Street
Golden, CO 80401
303-277-0377

American Folk Art Museum
45 West 53rd Street
New York, NY
212-265-1040

The following museums have small to moderate numbers of quilts in their collections and sponsor quilt displays. The Cooper-Hewitt Museum and the Smithsonian offer help on textile care and conservation.

Arizona Historical Society
949 East Street
Tucson, AZ 85719
520-628-5774

The Cooper-Hewitt Museum
2 East 91st Street
New York, NY 10010
212-849-8400

The Art Institute of Chicago
111 South Michigan Avenue
Chicago, IL 60603
312-443-3600

The Denver Art Museum
Fourteenth and Bannock
Denver, CO 80202
720-865-5001

The Atlanta Historical Society
130 West Paces Ferry Road, NW
Atlanta, GA 30305
404-233-1715

The Detroit Institute of the Arts
5200 Woodward Avenue
Detroit, MI 48202
313-833-7900

Cape Ann Historical Society
27 Pleasant Street
Gloucester, MA 01930
978-283-0455

Hennepin County Historical Society
Museum
2303 Third Avenue South
Minneapolis, MN 55404
612-870-1329

Connecticut Historical Society
One Elizabeth Street
Hartford, CT 06105
869-236-5621

The Henry Ford Museum and
Greenfield Village
20900 Oakwood Boulevard
Dearborn, MI 48121
313-271-1620

The Louisiana State Museum
751 Chartres Street
New Orleans, LA 70176
504-568-6968

The Lyman Allyn Museum
625 Williams Street
New London, CT 06320
860-443-2545

The Mattatuck Historical Society Museum
144 West Main Street
Waterbury, CT 06702
203-735-0381

The Milwaukee Public Museum
800 West Wells Street
Milwaukee, WI 53233
414-278-2720

The Mount Vernon Ladies Association
Mount Vernon, VA 22121
703-780-2000

Museum of American Textile History
491 Dutton
Lowell, MA 01854
978-441-0400

The Museum of Fine Arts
465 Huntington Street
Boston, MA 02115
617-267-9300

The National Museum of American
History of the Smithsonian Institution
Fourteenth and Constitution Avenue,
Northwest
Washington, DC 20560
202-357-1300

The Oakland Museum
1000 Oak Street
Oakland, CA 94612

Old Sturbridge Village
Route 20
Sturbridge, MA 01566
508-347-3362

The Shelburne Museum
Route 7
Shelburne, VT 05482
802-985-3346

The Torrington Historical Society, Inc.
192 Main Street
Torrington, CT 06790
830-482-8260

The Wadsworth Athenaeum
600 Main Street
Hartford, CT 06105
869-236-5621

The Witte Museum
3801 Broadway
San Antonio, TX 78209
210-357-1900

Care, Storage, Repair, Cleaning, and Vintage Fabrics

Just a few years ago the dedicated quilt collector had to go to a conservation materials supplier to get acid-free paper and other such items for the storage of prize quilts. Now these things can be bought in your local craft store. Still, you may want advice along with your paper, so you may want to look into a shop that is more specialized.

Most quilt dealers can help with this by either selling the items themselves or by knowing the best place to get them. They also may be textile restorers or may be able to put you in touch with restorers or those who deal in antique and vintage fabrics. And, of course, the yellow pages and the Internet are good places to start.

Grandma's Quilts
296 North 10th Street
Palmyra, NE 68418
1-800-284-8574
grandmasquilts.com

K & K Quilts/Quilt Restoration Society
Box 23, Route 23
Hillsdale, NY 12529
518-325-4502

M. Finkel and Daughter
936 Pine Street
Philadelphia, PA 19107
215-627-7797

Sharon's Antiques and Vintage Fabrics
610-756-6048
rickrack.com

University Products, Inc.
P.O. Box 101
Holyoke, MA 01041
413-532-3372

Other

Of course there are other services that we want to mention and that you need to know about.

Appraisal Associations:

Professional Association of Appraisers—Quilted Textiles
www.quiltappraisers.org

American Society of Appraisers
www.appraisers.org

Finding Lost or Stolen Quilts on the Internet
Lost Quilts Come Home Page
www.lostquilt.com

GLOSSARY

Allover set: when a one-patch pattern is used for an entire quilt.

Aniline dyes: synthetic dyes created using coal tar.

Appliqué: the process of sewing a piece of cloth to a ground fabric.

Asymmetrical: also called split blocks; optical effect changes when the blocks are turned.

Autograph quilt: a quilt in which each block is signed by a friend usually with a poem, picture, or Bible verse.

Batting: the middle of the quilt sandwich; usually cotton, wool, or polyester.

Bees: gatherings of quiltmakers to stitch finished tops; at first families were involved, later only quiltmakers.

Binding: fabric used to finish the raw, outside edges of the quilt sandwich.

Bleeding: color loss from washing.

Block: the units of a quilt that, when assembled, or set, form the quilt top; either appliqué or pieced.

Border: the fabric frame added around the outside of the patchwork top. Can be plain strips of fabric, pieced, or appliqué.

Bridal quilt: the thirteenth in a Colonial girl's baker's dozen of quilts she took with her in marriage; not started until she was betrothed.

Broadcloth: so named because it was woven wider than other fabrics, anywhere from 54" to 63".

Broderie-Perse: the method of cutting large-scale designs out of fabric and appliquéing them to whole-cloth tops.

Buyer's premium: the charge an auction house adds to the highest bid for an item. This fee pays the house's expenses and leaves the entire bid amount to go to the seller.

Calender: a process using heat and rollers to glaze wool.

Calico: a cotton valued for its bright colors and small to medium-sized prints of figures, florals, and geometrics.

Challis: a soft wool or wool and cotton cloth in plain, printed, or figured and unglazed twill weave.

Chambray: a gingham-type fabric, plain weave, often with a colored warp and a white weft.

Cheater cloth: fabric printed with patchwork designs that look like completed blocks.

Cherryderrys: a fabric with silk warp and cotton weft from the 1750s.

Color balance: the effect of colors placed next to each other, across from each other, or in patterns that are most pleasing to the eye.

Colorfastness: when a dye doesn't bleed, or fade, when it's washed.

Color loss: when fabrics fade or change color from washing, inferior dyes, exposure to light, crocking.

Comforter: three layers—a fabric top, usually whole-cloth, sometimes pieced, a batting, and a backing held together by knots tied with thread or yarn.

Commemorative quilts: made to record a special event in history.

Compactness: how tightly a fabric is woven; the more threads per square inch, the more compact the weave.

Copper cylinder: used when a design is cut into copper, but instead of being pressed on a fabric, the fabric is rolled under the cylinder to print it.

Copperplate printing: designs are cut into copperplates, which are then inked and pressed onto fabric.

Crocking: when a fabric loses color from its surface. Check for crocking by rubbing a white cloth or paper over the fabric.

Dozens: refers to the practice of selling a cheap wool in lengths of about twelve yards.

Four-Square: a quilt whose top is composed of four large blocks; thought to be the precursor of blockstyle.

Friendship quilts or blocks: quilts of blocks made by more than one quiltmaker, or, if made by one quiltmaker, given to memorialize a friendship.

Geometric: refers to the use of squares, triangles, diamonds, and other straight-lined shapes; usually refers to pieced quilts, especially those with optical illusion effects.

Glaze: an additive to make fabric stiffer and appear shiny.

Grogrinetts: a worsted with watermarks.

Ground: the fabric that smaller pieces of cloth are appliquéd to.

Homespun: cloth handwoven from homegrown wool, cotton, or flax by Colonial and pioneer households.

Linsey-Woolsey: a fabric made using two threads, one from wool and one from linen.

Loft: the puffiness on a quilt top from the batting beneath.

Madder browns: a term used to describe the reddish, deep browns used in quilts in the middle 1800s.

Medallion style: used with Broderie-Perse, this refers to a large intricate design filling the center of a quilt top.

Microwaving: a method of artificially aging fabric.

Mordant: an agent used to fix dyes in fabric.

Multigenerational quilt: any quilt worked on by quiltmakers of different generations.

Muslin: a fine cotton fabric first made in India.

Nine-Patch: the most frequently used division in geometric pieced blocks. Refers to the basic block being broken into three rows of three squares, each making nine segments that could be further divided.

One-Patch: when the same single shape, such as hexagons, tumblers, or triangles is used to create an entire quilt top.

Patchwork: the process of assembling smaller pieces of cloth together to make a quilt top.

Percale: a fine white cloth; used as a ground in India for painted chintz.

Picker: a person who locates quilts to sell to dealers.

Piecing: when patchwork is done by seaming two smaller pieces of cloth together instead of sewing them to a ground fabric.

Plain weave: where each warp and weft thread runs over and under each other in an even pattern.

Presentation quilt: a quilt made in any style and given to a respected member of the community, usually a minister or his wife.

Preview: the time offered before an auction at which one can closely inspect the offered merchandise.

Quilt: a sandwich of three layers—a top, usually of patchwork but sometimes whole-cloth; a batting; and a backing fabric.

Quilt dealer: one who specializes in finding, buying, and selling antique quilts.

Quilt frame: four long boards with clamps used to hold the quilt sandwich tight while stitching.

Quilt kits: packaged, precut, pre-designed quilt materials and directions.

Quilt shop: usually offers materials and patterns to make quilts; may also sell new quilts on consignment.

Quilting: the stitching that holds the quilt sandwich together.

Redwork: red thread embroidered quilt on a white background fabric typically depicting children or flowers. Many designs came from children's coloring books.

Resist: an agent to keep cloth from taking a dye.

Reverse appliqué: the method of placing two fabrics together, cutting out the top fabric so the back fabric shows through and then turning under and stitching down the raw edges.

Sampler quilt: composed of blocks of different patterns; used to learn quilting techniques.

Sashings: fabric strips that frame the blocks in the quilt top.

Satin weave: where each weft yarn passes over several warps and "floats," producing a surface sheen.

Scrap bag: the accumulation of pieces of fabric saved from other needlework or other quilts that are too small to use for clothing but too big to be thrown out.

Set: the way the blocks are assembled in the top. Straight set puts the blocks in horizontal and vertical rows. Blocks set on point appear as diamond shapes in a quilt top.

Signature quilt: usually a fund-raiser, people paid to have their names embroidered on a quilt top.

Staple: the fibers, of animal or vegetable origin, used to make thread.

Stipple quilting: when tiny stitches are sewed in close rows to create a higher loft in unquilted areas.

Stuff: a general term for worsted cloth; includes merino, shalloons, lastings, tammers, calimancoes, moreens, camblets, and plaids.

Symmetrical blocks: geometric pieced patterns that always form the same design no matter how they're assembled.

Tea dyeing: an artificial method of aging fabric; sometimes used to make new fabrics blend in with old, sometimes used to make a new quilt appear as an antique. Hard on the fabrics.

Tendering: when fabric wears out. Many times caused by the harsh mordant and resist chemicals used to fix dyes.

Tied and tying: holding the three layers of the fabric sandwich together with knotted thread or yarn.

Trapunto: sometimes called stuffed quilting, developed in Italy; used in whitework, in which two pieces of cloth are stitched together and stuffing is inserted in the unquilted areas.

Twill weave: like the satin weave, but the fibers that "float" don't all pass over the same warp threads, producing diagonal lines across the surface of the fabric.

Velvet: a pile fabric made of silk, wool, or cotton fibers.

Warp: the lengthwise threads in a fabric.

Weft: the fabric threads that run side to side.

Whitework: the design of these quilts is solely from the quilting pattern; usually done with whole-cloth, although newer quilts may use plain colored fabric.

Whole-cloth: quilts in which the tops are not patchwork but a single piece of fabric.

Woodblock printing: a method in which patterns are added to cloth by using woodblocks cut into designs. Either dye or mordants were pressed onto the cloth.

Worsted: a lightweight cloth made from long-staple, combed yarn.

BIBLIOGRAPHY

Books

Adrosko, Rita J. *Natural Dyes and Home Dying.* New York: Dover Publications, Inc., 1971.

Affleck, Diane L. Fagan. *Just New from the Mills.* North Andover, MA: Museum of American Textile History, 1987.

Benberry, Cuesta. *Always There: The African-American Presence in American Quilts.* Louisville: The Kentucky Quilt Project, Inc., 1992.

Better Homes and Gardens. *Friendship Quilting.* Des Moines, IA: Meredith Corp., 1990.

Beyer, Jinny. *Patchwork Patterns.* McLean, VA: EPM Publications, Inc., 1979.

Bishop, Robert, and Carter Houck. *All Flags Flying: American Patriotic Quilts as Expressions of Liberty.* New York: E. P. Dutton in association with the Museum of American Folk Art, 1986.

Bogdonoff, Nancy D. *Handwoven Textiles of Early New England.* Harrisburg, PA: Stackpole Books, 1975.

Bowman, Doris M. *The Smithsonian Treasury. American Quilts.* Washington, D.C.: Smithsonian Institution, 1991.

Brackman, Barbara. *Clues in the Calico: A Guide to Identifying and Dating Antique Quilts.* McLean, VA: EPM Publications, Inc., 1987.

Brackman, Barbara. *Encyclopedia of Appliqué: An Illustrated, Numerical Index to Traditional and Modern Patterns.* McLean, VA: EPM Publications, Inc., 1993.

Brackman, Barbara. *Encyclopedia of Pieced Quilt Patterns.* Paducah, KY: American Quilter's Society, 1993.

Burnham, Dorothy K. *Warp & Weft: A Dictionary of Textile Terms.* New York: Charles Scribner's Sons, 1980.

Cooper, Patricia, and Norma Bradley Buferd. *The Quilters.* New York: Doubleday & Co., 1977.

Dee, Anne Patterson. *Quilter's Sourcebook.* Lombard, IL: Wallace-Homestead Book Co., 1987.

Fennelly, Catherine. *Textiles in New England, 1790–1840.* Sturbridge, MA: Old Sturbridge Village, 1961.

Ferris, William. *Afro-American Folk Art and Crafts.* Boston: G. K. Hall & Co., 1983.

Finley, Ruth E. *Old Patchwork Quilts and the Women Who Made Them.* Newton Centre, MA: Charles T. Branford Co., 1929, 1957, 1970.

Fisher, Laura. *Quilts of Illusion.* Pittstown, NJ: The Main Street Press, 1988.

Florence, Cathy Gaines. *Collecting Quilts: Investments in America's Heritage.* Paducah, KY: American Quilter's Society, 1985.

Fons, Marianne. *Fine Feathers: A Quilter's Guide to Customizing Traditional Feather Quilting Designs.* Lafayette, CA: C & T Publishing, 1988.

Freeman, Roland A. *A Communion of Spirits: African-American Quilters, Preservers, and Their Stories.* Nashville, TN: Rutledge Hill Press, 1996.

Hardingham, Martin. *The Fabric Catalog.* New York: Pocket Books, 1978.

Hechtinger, Adelaide. *American Quilts, Quilting, and Patchwork.* Harrisburg, PA: Stackpole Books, 1974.

Hicks, Kyra E. *Black Threads: An African-American Quilting Sourcebook.* Jefferson, NC: McFarland & Company, Inc., 2003.

Hoffman, Victoria. *Quilts: A Window to the Past.* North Andover, MA: Museum of American Textile History, 1991.

Holstein, Jonathan. *The Pieced Quilt: An American Design Tradition.* New York: Galahad Books, 1973.

Ickis, Marguerite. *The Standard Book of Quilt Making and Collecting.* New York: Dover Publications, Inc., 1949.

Kentucky Quilt Project. *Kentucky Quilts: 1800–1900.* Louisville, KY: The Kentucky Quilt Project, 1982.

Khin, Yvonne. *The Collector's Dictionary of Quilt Names and Patterns.* Washington, DC: Acropolis Books, 1980.

Kile, Michael. "On The Road," in *The Quilt Digest,* 76–85. San Francisco: The Quilt Digest Press, 1986.

Laury, Jean Ray, and the California Heritage Quilt Project. *Ho for California! Pioneer Women and Their Quilts.* New York: E.P. Dutton, 1990.

Leman, Bonnie, and Judy Martin. *Log Cabin Quilts.* Denver, CO: Moon Over the Mountain Publishing Co., 1980.

Leon, Eli. *Who'd Thought It: Improvisation in African-American Quiltmaking.* San Francisco: San Francisco Craft and Folk Art Museum, 1987.

Lipsett, Linda Otto. *Remember Me: Women and Their Friendship Quilts.* San Francisco: The Quilt Digest Press, 1985.

Lithgow, Marilyn. Photographs by Peter Kiar. *Quiltmaking and Quiltmakers.* New York: Funk & Wagnalls, 1974.

Lyons, Mary E. *Stitching Stars: The Story Quilts of Harriet Powers.* New York: Charles Scribner's Sons, 1993.

Montgomery, Florence M. *Textiles in America 1650–1870.* New York: W. W. Norton & Co., 1984.

Museum of Fine Arts, Boston. *A Pattern Book, Based on Appliqué Quilts by Mrs. Harriet Powers, American, 19th Century.* Boston: Museum of Fine Arts, 1973.

Peto, Florence. *Historic Quilts.* New York: The American Historical Co., 1939.

Pfeffer, Susanna. *Quilt Masterpieces.* New York: Hugh Lauter Levin Associates, Inc., distributed by MacMillan Publishing Co., 1988.

Pottinger, David. *Quilts from the Indiana Amish: A Regional Collection.* New York: E. P. Dutton in association with the Museum of American Folk Art, 1983.

Puentes, Nancy O'Bryant. *First Aid for Family Quilts.* Wheatridge, CO: Moon Over the Mountain Publishing Co., 1986.

Rubin, Stella. *Miller's Treasure or Not? How to Compare & Value American Quilts.* London: Octopus Publishing Group, Ltd., 2001.

Selsam, Millicent E. Photographs by Jerome Wexler. *Cotton.* New York: William Morrow and Company, 1982.

Spencer, Audrey. *Spinning and Weaving at Upper Canada Village.* Toronto: The Ryerson Press, 1964.

Tobin, Jacqueline L., and Raymond G. Dobard, PhD. *Hidden in Plain View: A Secret Story of Quilts and the Underground Railroad.* New York: Anchor Books, 1999.

Trestain, Eileen Jahnke. *Dating Fabrics: A Color Guide 1800–1960.* Paducah, KY: American Quilter's Society, 1998.

Wahlman, Maude Southwell. *Signs and Symbols: African Images in African-American Quilts.* New York: Studio Books, 1993.

Webster, Marie D. *Quilts: Their Story and How to Make Them.* New York: Doubleday, Page, and Company, 1915.

Weigle, Palmy. *Ancient Dyes for Modern Weavers.* New York: Watson-Guptill Publications, 1974.

Articles

American Craft. "Homage to the Quilt." Exhibition at the American Craft Museum, *American Craft,* December 1987–January 1988, 42–48.

Antiques and Collecting. "Susan McCord's Quilts: A Farmwife's Legacy." *Antiques and Collectibles,* April 1989, 37–38.

Brackman, Barbara. "Patterns from Oregon and the Oregon Trail." *Quilter's Newsletter Magazine,* April 1991, 22–26. "Crescendo of Quilts." *Americana,* May–June 1990, 35–39.

Braunstein, Jack. "Dixie McBride's Rags to Riches Stories." *Traditional Quiltworks,* no. 14, 5–8.

Brown, Linda J. "Guide to Buying a Quilt." *Good Housekeeping,* October 1988, 227.

Brown, Patricia Leigh. "From the Bottomlands, Soulful Stitches." *New York Times,* November 21, 2002, House & Home, F1.

Callahan, Nancy. "Hard Times for Freedom Quilters." *The Christian Century,* 22 Mar. 1989, 317–318.

Carter, Catherine. "Stars—The Most Favored of Patterns." *Traditional Quiltworks,* no. 3, 34–35.

Cozart, Dorothy. "A Century of Fundraising Quilts 1860-1960." *Uncovering—Research Papers of the American Quilt Study Group,* 5 1984, 41–54.

Donegan, Frank. "Quiet Time for Quilts." *Americana,* December 1988, 64–66.

Fox, Sandi. "Comments From the Quilt." *Modern Maturity,* August–September 1990, 58–63.

Freeman, Roland. "Quilts: From the Mississippi Heartland." *American Visions,* June 1986, 28–32.

Gately, Rosemary Connolly. "Crazy Quilts in the Collection of the Maryland Historical Society." *The Magazine Antiques*, September 1988, 558–573.

Gleason, Jeanne. "Sue Rodgers: Quilter, Teacher, Trapunto Maestro." *Traditional Quiltworks*, no. 13, 5–7.

Gordon, Meryl. "Bold Appeal of 20th-Century Quilts." *Architectural Digest*, June 1990, 48–60.

Gutcheon, Jeffrey. "Not for Shopkeepers Only. The Dyestuffs." *Quilter's Newsletter Magazine*, April 1991, 58, 70.

Halpin, Linda. "Hanging Quilts." *Traditional Quiltworks*, no. 13, 65–66.

Hargrave, Harriet. "Quiltsense. Care of Today's Quilts." *Traditional Quiltworks*, no. 3, 47–48.

Harrington, Gail. "Lancaster Color." *Trailer Life*, March 1987, 76–77.

Harriss, Joseph. "The Newest Quilt Fad Seems to Be Going Like Crazy." *Smithsonian*, May 1987, 114–124.

Houck, Carter. "A View of the 1920s and 1930." *Quilt Craft*, Spring 1991, 6–9.

Jones, Lila Lee. "Something Old. . . Something New." *Quilt Craft*, Summer 1991, 56–59.

Keck, Viola. "The Sunbonnet Alphabet Quilt." *Quilt World*, October/November 1991, 17.

Kimmelman, Michael. "Jazzy Geometry, Cool Quilters." *New York Times*, November 29, 2002, Weekend Fine Arts & Leisure section, E33.

Lipshultz, Sandra Lawall. "Blanket Approval." *Minneapolis-St. Paul Magazine*, February 1987, 15–17, 54.

Marshall, Diane P. "Sewing Traditions in Lancaster County." *Travel-Holiday*, July 1988, 85–88.

McBride, Dixie. "Repair and Restoration of Old Quilts." *Traditional Quiltworks*, no. 14, 9–10.

Mori, Joyce. "How Quilters Can Help Their Local Historical Society." *Quilt World*, December 1991/January 1992, 30, 37.

Morris, Pat. "Quilters' Queries & Quotes." *Quilt World*, December 1991/January 1992, 28–29.

Nadelstern, Paula. "Citiquilts: A Show of Diversity." *Quilters Newsletter Magazine*, April 1991, 35–39.

"Notes and Comment." Talk of the Town. *New Yorker*, 5 October 1987, 31–32.

People Weekly. "A Summit Gift from Nancy to Raisa." *People Weekly*, 20 June 1988, 51.

Quilt Craft. "A Century of Progress." *Quilt Craft*, Spring 1991, 28–31.

Quilt Craft. "Designing With Scrap." *Quilt Craft*, Summer 1991, 20–23.

Rubin, Cynthia E. "Amish Needlework: Tradition and Change." *Early American Life*, June 1988, 30–33, 74.

Ruskin, Cindy. "Taking up Needles and Thread to Honor the Dead Helps AIDS Survivors Patch up Their Lives." *People Weekly*, 12 October 1987, 42–49.

Satterfield, Archie. "Hawaii's Prized Quilts." *Travel Holiday,* January 1987, 12–13.

Simons, Scott. "Quilts as a New Art Form." *Quilt World*, October/November 1991, 24–25.

INDEX

Italicized page numbers indicate illustrations.

A

African-American quilts, 73, 108, 261–265
Afro-American Folk Art and Crafts (Ferris), 261
Album quilts, 24, 26, 29, 55, 199–200
American Quilts, Quilting, and Patchwork (Hechtinger), 23, 59
Amish quilts, 64, 69, 108, 256–260, *257, 260*
Appliqué quilts, 55–56, 72–73, 211–242, *212, 214, 222*
    Broderie-Perse, 20–21, 55, 211
    commemorative, 28, 239
    Dresden Plate, 233–236, *234, 236*
    Hawaiian, 237–238
    reverse, 55, 237–238
    stitches, 56, 72–73
    Sunbonnet Sue, 30, 41, 227
    techniques, 55–56
    see also Embroidered quilts; Pieced quilts; Puff quilts; Trapunto quilts; Whole-cloth quilts; Yo-yo quilts
Appraisal, 101–105
    sources for help in, 272
The Art Quilt (McMorris and Kile), 29, 31, 106
Auctions, 14–17
Autograph quilts, 24

B

Backings, 60–61
Baltimore Album quilts, 3, 29, 107, 108, 199
Barn Raising quilt, 79, 169
    pattern, *171*
Basic Quilt Block Assembly pattern, *134*
Basket quilt, 75, 180–185
Batting, 57, 58–59, 64
Bindings, 67–68, 88
Black Threads: An African-American Quilting Sourcebook (Hicks), 107, 263–264

Block-style quilting, 23–24, 55–56, 73–75, *74*
    see also Quilt blocks
Bombazine silk fabric, 38
Borders, 56, 60, 80
Bridal quilts, 21–22, 24, 25
Broderie-Perse style quilts, 20–21, 55, 211

C

Calico fabric, 39
Cambric fabric, 41
Caring for quilts, 94–95
    sources for help in, 271–272
    see also Cleaning quilts
Cathedral Window quilt, 57
Charm quilts, *53,* 54, 79–80, 116
Cheater fabrics, 30, 54
Chintz fabric, 39, 41–42, 53
Cigar silk quilts, 252
Civil War quilting, 28
Cleaning quilts, 64, 91, 95–98
    professionally, 64, 91, 96
    sources for cleaners, 271–272
    testing for colorfastness, 92, 96
Clues in the Calico (Brackman), 12, 21, 26, 37, 44, 54–55, 59, 105
Collecting Quilts (Florence), 98
Collecting quilts, how to start, 7–19
    auctions, 14–17
    dating quilts, 12–13, 35–62
    family quilts, 7–10
    quilt dealers, 11–12, 14, 104, 267–269
    quilt documentation form (sample), 9
    quilt pickers, 10–11
    specializing in specific types, 10
    trends in, 106–110
Colorfastness, testing for, 92, 96
Colors, 42–51, *43*
    balance of, *48,* 79–80

black, 50
blue, 45
brown, 47
green, 47–49
loss of, *see* Fading
purple, 50–51
red, 46–47
white, 45
yellow, 49–50
Comforter, 57
Commemorative quilts, 2, 28, 31, 186–187, 239–242
Condition, quilt, 63–70, 109
    creasing, 70, 98–99
    fabric deterioration, 65–68, *66,* 75
    fading, *43, 44,* 68–70, *69*
    repairs, 67–68, *68*
    stains, 64–65, *65*
    washed and unwashed quilts, 63–65
Connecticut Quilt Block pattern, *241*
Cotton fabric, 39, 41–42
Courthouse Steps Log Cabin quilt, 169
    pattern, *172*
Crazy quilts, 3, 22–23, *23,* 29, 55, 67, 108, 159–162, *160, 162,* 186
Creasing, 70, 98–99
Cretonne fabric, 41
Crib quilts, 108–109
Crosses and Losses pattern, *134*
Cutter quilts, 65–67, 84, 88–89
Cutter's Red Book of Ready Reference, 29

D

Dating fabric: *See* Fabric
Dating Fabrics: A Color Guide 1800–1960 (Trestain), 51
Dating quilts, 12–13, 35–62
    by backing, 60–61
    by border, 56, 60
    by color, 42–51, *43*
    by design, 61–62
    by fabric, 38–42
    by maker, 35, *36, 37*

HOUSE OF COLLECTIBLES
COMPLETE TITLE LIST

THE OFFICIAL PRICE GUIDES TO

American Arts and Crafts, 3rd ed.	0-609-80989-X	$21.95	David Rago
American Patriotic Memorabilia	0-609-81014-6	$16.95	Michael Polak
America's State Quarters	0-609-80770-6	$6.99	David L. Ganz
Collecting Books, 4th ed.	0-609-80769-2	$18.00	Marie Tedford
Collecting Clocks	0-609-80973-3	$19.95	Frederick W. Korz
Collector Knives, 14th ed.	1-4000-4834-6	$17.95	C. Houston Price
Collector Plates	0-676-60154-5	$19.95	Harry L. Rinker
Costume Jewelry, 3rd ed.	0-609-80668-8	$17.95	Harrice Simmons Miller
Dinnerware of the 20th Century	0-676-60085-9	$29.95	Harry L. Rinker
Flea Market Prices, 2nd ed.	1-4000-4889-3	$14.95	Harry L. Rinker
Glassware, 3rd ed.	0-676-60188-X	$17.00	Mark Pickvet
Hake's Character Toys, 4th ed.	0-609-80822-2	$35.00	Ted Hake
Hislop's International Guide to Fine Art	0-609-80874-5	$20.00	Duncan Hislop
Military Collectibles, 7th ed.	1-4000-4941-5	$20.00	Richard Austin
Mint Errors, 6th ed.	0-609-80855-9	$15.00	Alan Herbert
Movie Autographs and Memorabilia	1-4000-4731-5	$20.00	Daniel Cohen
Native American Art	0-609-80966-0	$24.00	Dawn E. Reno
Overstreet Comic Book Companion, 8th ed.	0-375-72065-0	$7.99	Robert M. Overstreet
Overstreet Comic Book Grading	0-609-81052-9	$24.00	Robert M. Overstreet
Overstreet Comic Book Price Guide, 33rd ed.	1-4000-4668-8	$25.00	Robert M. Overstreet
Overstreet Indian Arrowheads Price Guide, 8th ed.	0-609-81053-7	$26.00	Robert M. Overstreet
Pottery and Porcelain	0-87637-893-9	$18.00	Harvey Duke
Quilts, 2nd ed.	1-4000-4797-8	$16.00	Aleshire/Barach
Records, 16th ed.	0-609-80908-3	$25.95	Jerry Osborne

THE OFFICIAL GUIDES TO

Coin Grading and Counterfeit Detection	0-375-72050-2	$19.95	P. C. G. S.
How to Make Money in Coins Right Now	0-609-80746-3	$14.95	Scott A. Travers
The Official Directory to U.S. Flea Markets	0-609-80922-9	$14.00	Kitty Werner
The One-Minute Coin Expert, 4th ed.	0-609-80747-1	$7.99	Scott A. Travers
The Official Stamp Collector's Bible	0-609-80884-2	$22.00	Stephen Datz

THE OFFICIAL BECKETT SPORTS CARDS PRICE GUIDES TO

Baseball Cards 2004, 24th ed.	0-375-72055-3	$7.99	Dr. James Beckett
Basketball Cards 2004, 13th ed.	1-4000-4863-X	$7.99	Dr. James Beckett
Football Cards 2004, 23rd ed.	1-4000-4864-8	$7.99	Dr. James Beckett

THE OFFICIAL BLACKBOOK PRICE GUIDES TO

U.S. Coins, 42nd ed.	1-4000-4805-2	$7.99	Marc & Tom Hudgeons
U.S. Paper Money, 36th ed.	1-4000-4806-0	$6.99	Marc & Tom Hudgeons
U.S. Postage Stamps, 26th ed.	1-4000-4807-9	$8.99	Marc & Tom Hudgeons
World Coins, 7th ed.	1-4000-4808-7	$7.99	Marc & Tom Hudgeons

AVAILABLE AT BOOKSTORES EVERYWHERE!